HEIDE CHRISTIANSEN

Charming MALLORCA

teNeues

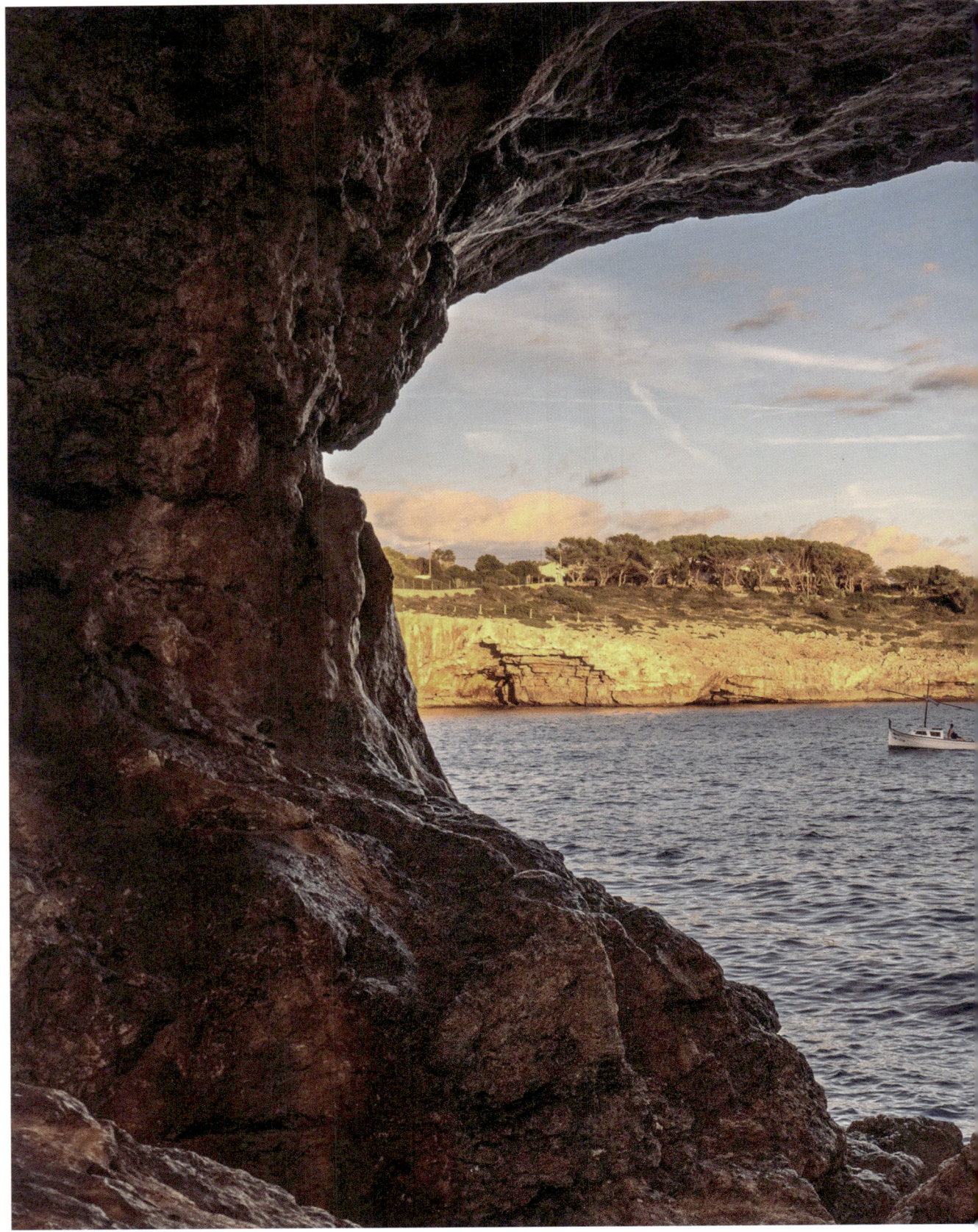

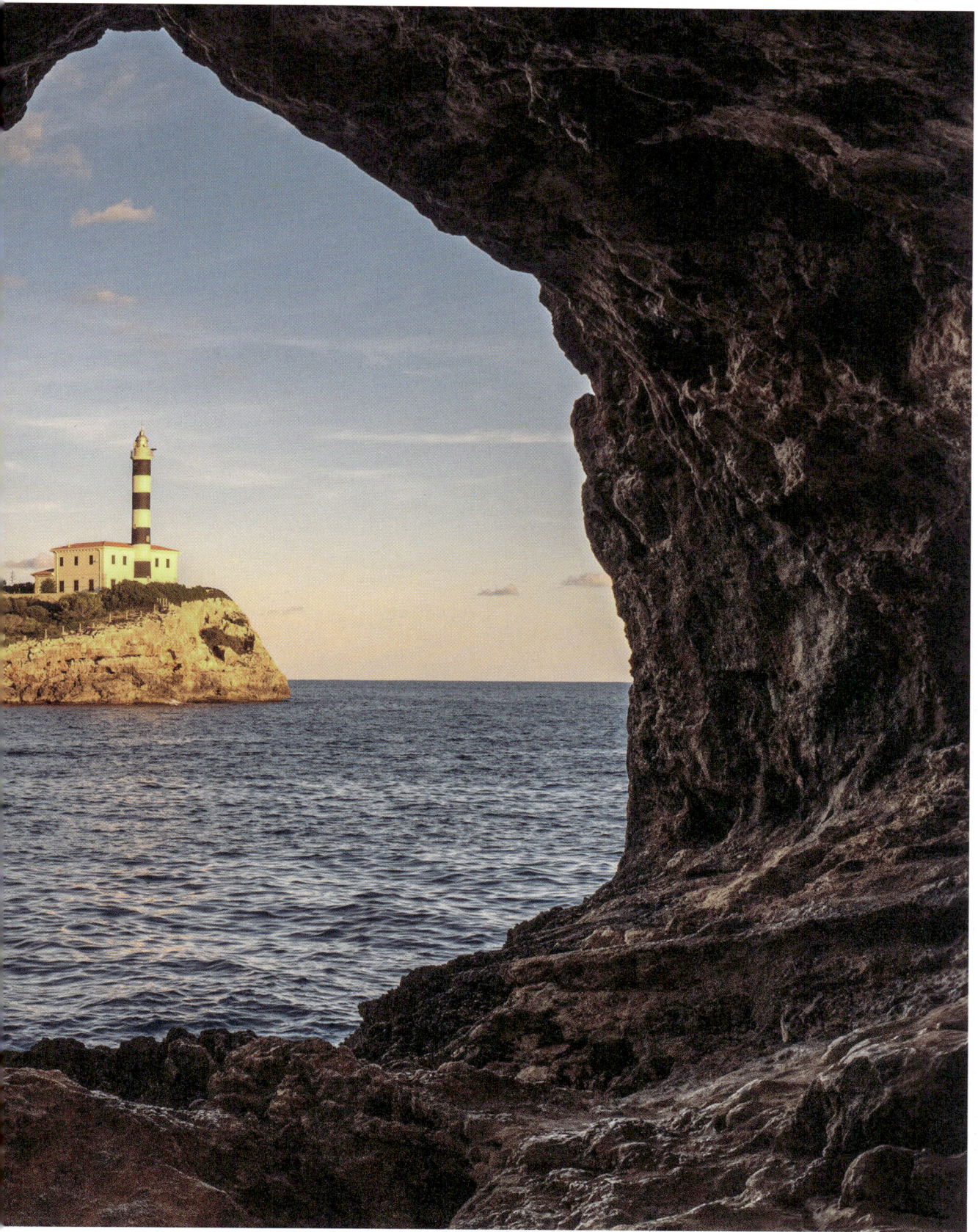

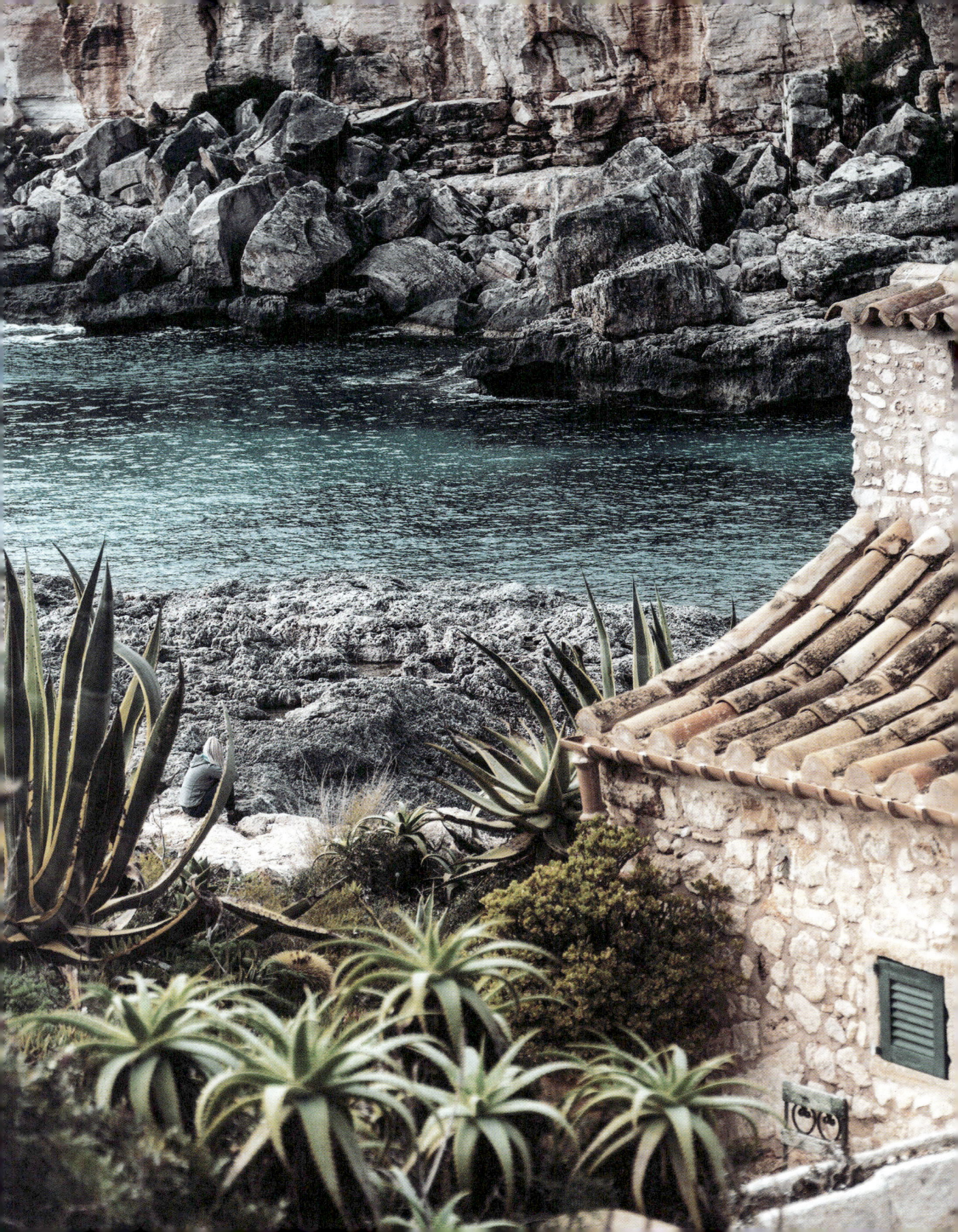

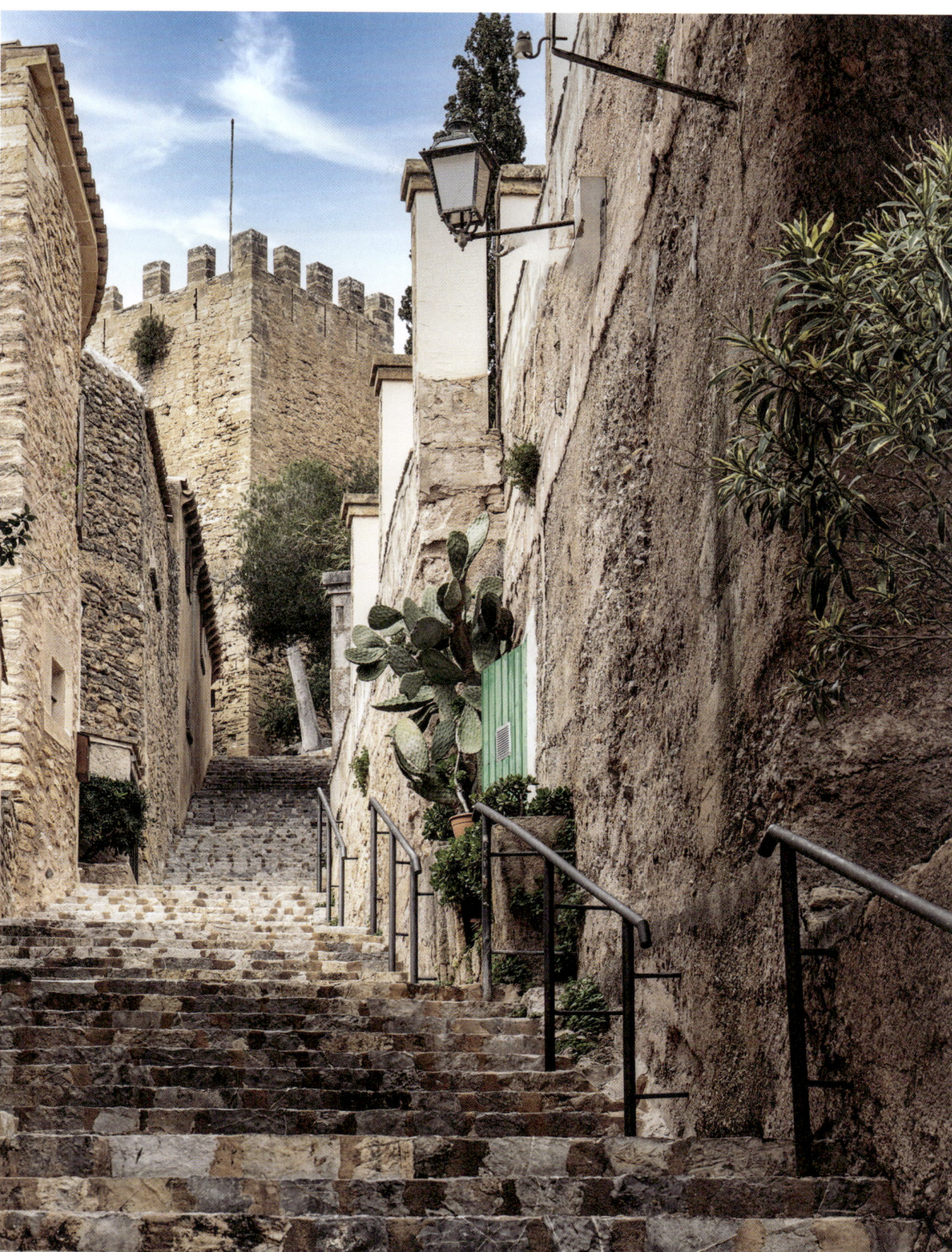

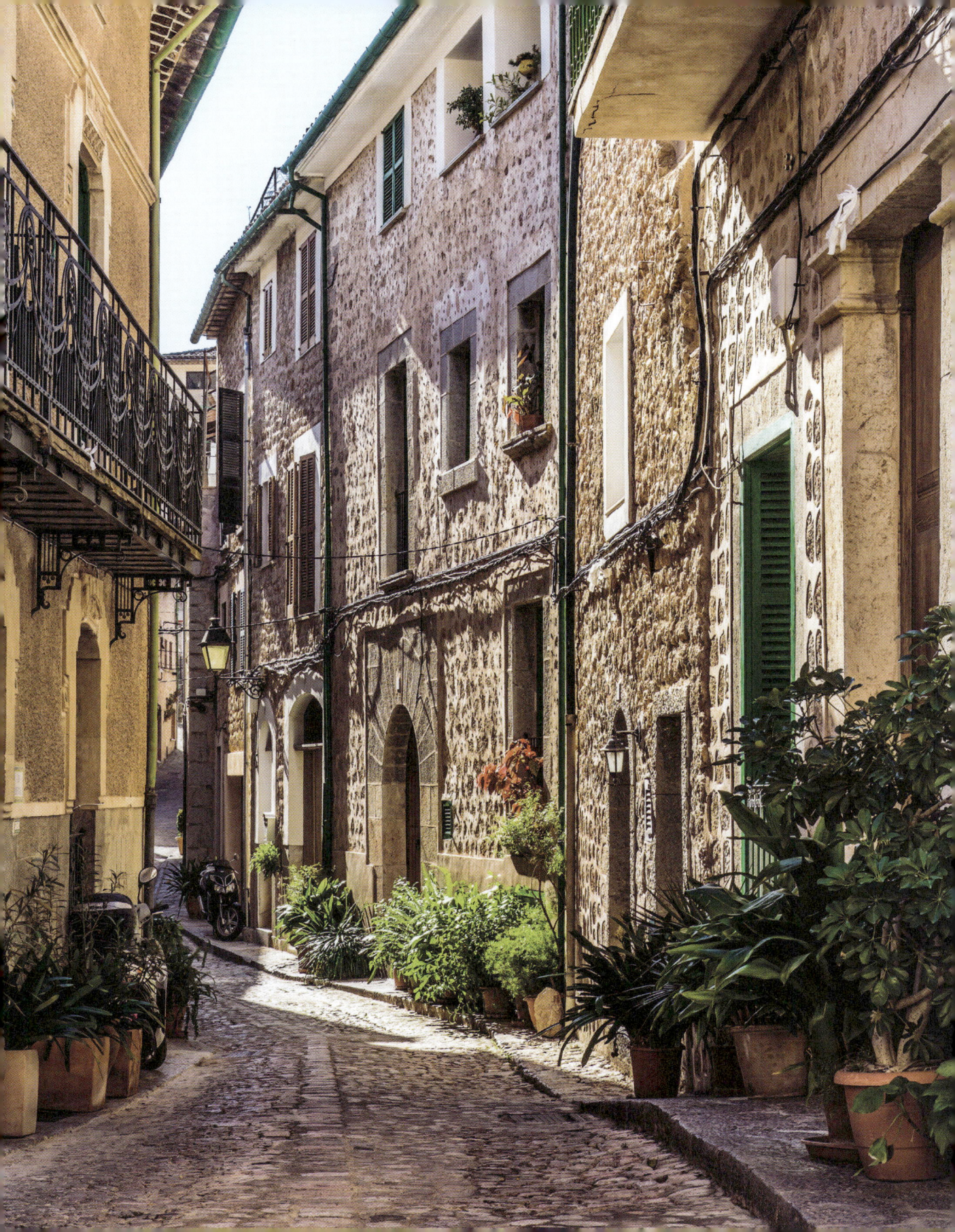

ꟻOREWORD

For more than twenty years now, Mallorca has been a refuge for me. I firmly believe the island possesses some kind of superpower: It stops my mind from racing. Upon arriving on Mallorca I immediately step into the moment, into the immediacy of the here and now, curious and ready for whatever the world has in store for me, for new experiences both large and small. Mallorca has never let me down in this, never failed to deliver. Even after all these years and several extended stays, with every visit I discover something new: a small cove, a quiet café away from the crowds, a bench with a sea view, a colorful stained-glass window in the cathedral in Palma I had simply walked past for years, a store run by inspiring people who have lived fascinating lives. This book is an invitation to explore special places that mean very much to me and that have touched me in some way; places whose message to me is that this is where I belong. My favorite among many examples is the fishing port in Portocolom during the blue hour. One's sense of familiarity with any given place on Mallorca can be overturned in an instant of realization. More recently I have also gained a new appreciation for the neighboring islands of Ibiza and Menorca, and I realized this book had to give them their due, which it does in the latter chapters. In a nutshell: Don't believe everything you may have heard. Luxury yachts, mega-clubs, a monotonous paradise packed with retirees? Definitely not. None of the Balearic Islands will suffer such labels. Each island has its own soul—to get the more subtle angles, you just need to look past the spectacle. May this book bring you pleasure and inspire you to discover and rediscover wonderful places.

Heide Christiansen takes us on a tour of Mallorca and the other Balearic Islands and shows us many of their hidden wonders in stories told through the photographic medium. Journalist Katja Klementz, who has known the islands since childhood and has family roots there, brings Heide's visual narratives to life with her words.

PAGE 2/3: *The lighthouse of Portocolom on the eastern shore of Mallorca.*

PAGE 4: *Mallorca's heavily indented coastline is always good for a surprise. Shown here is the cove at Cala s'Almunia near Santanyí.*

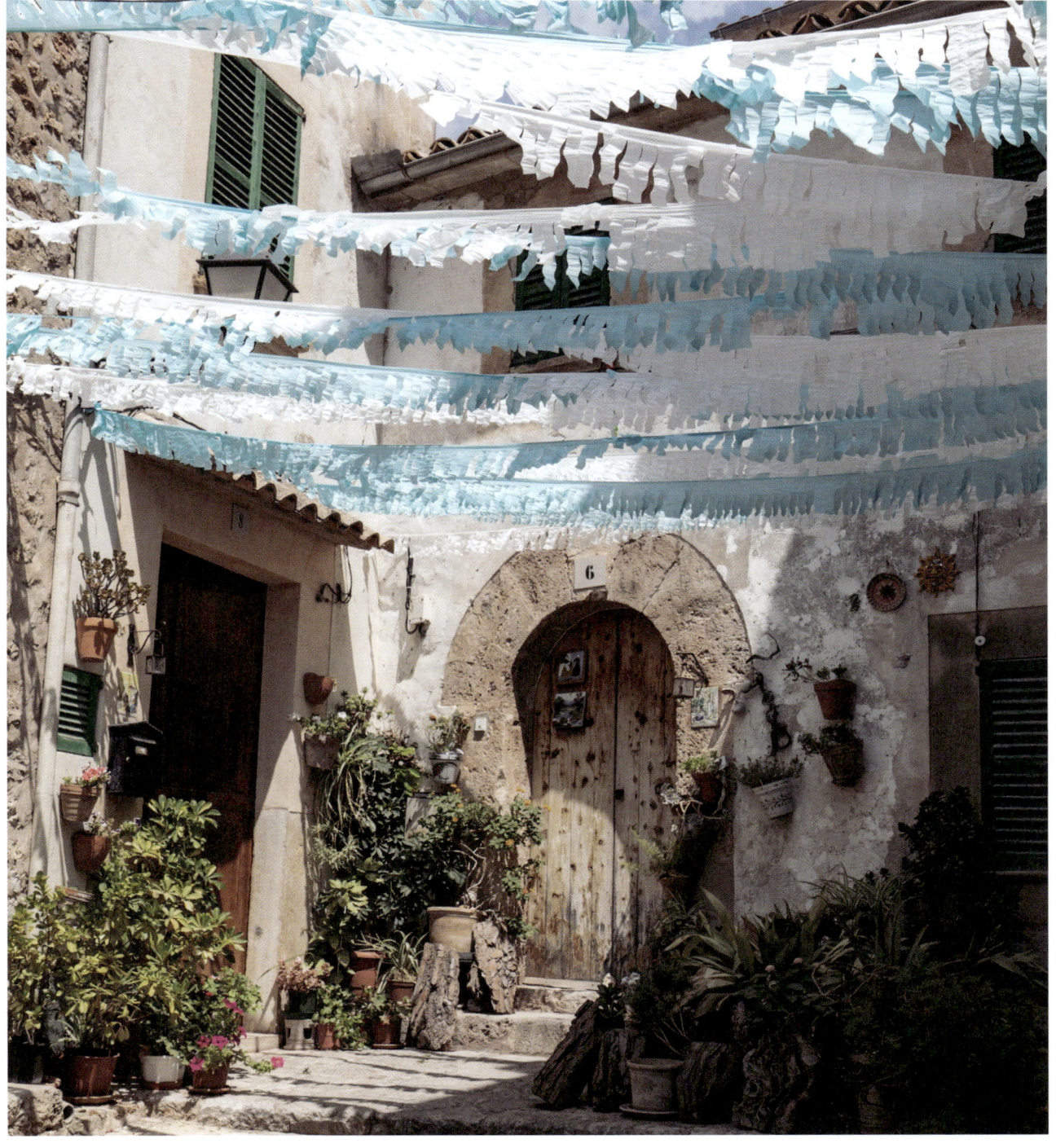

ABOVE: *Plenty of romance in the narrow streets of one of the most striking places on Mallorca:*
The village of Valldemossa in the Serra de Tramuntana.

PAGE 5: *Evocative of an earlier time: The historic old town of Capdepera on the eastern shore, with its distinctive castle.*

PAGE 7: *The old town of Felanitx, a tranquil village in a rural section of Mallorca's southeastern shore, is known*
for the color of the stone used in its buildings.

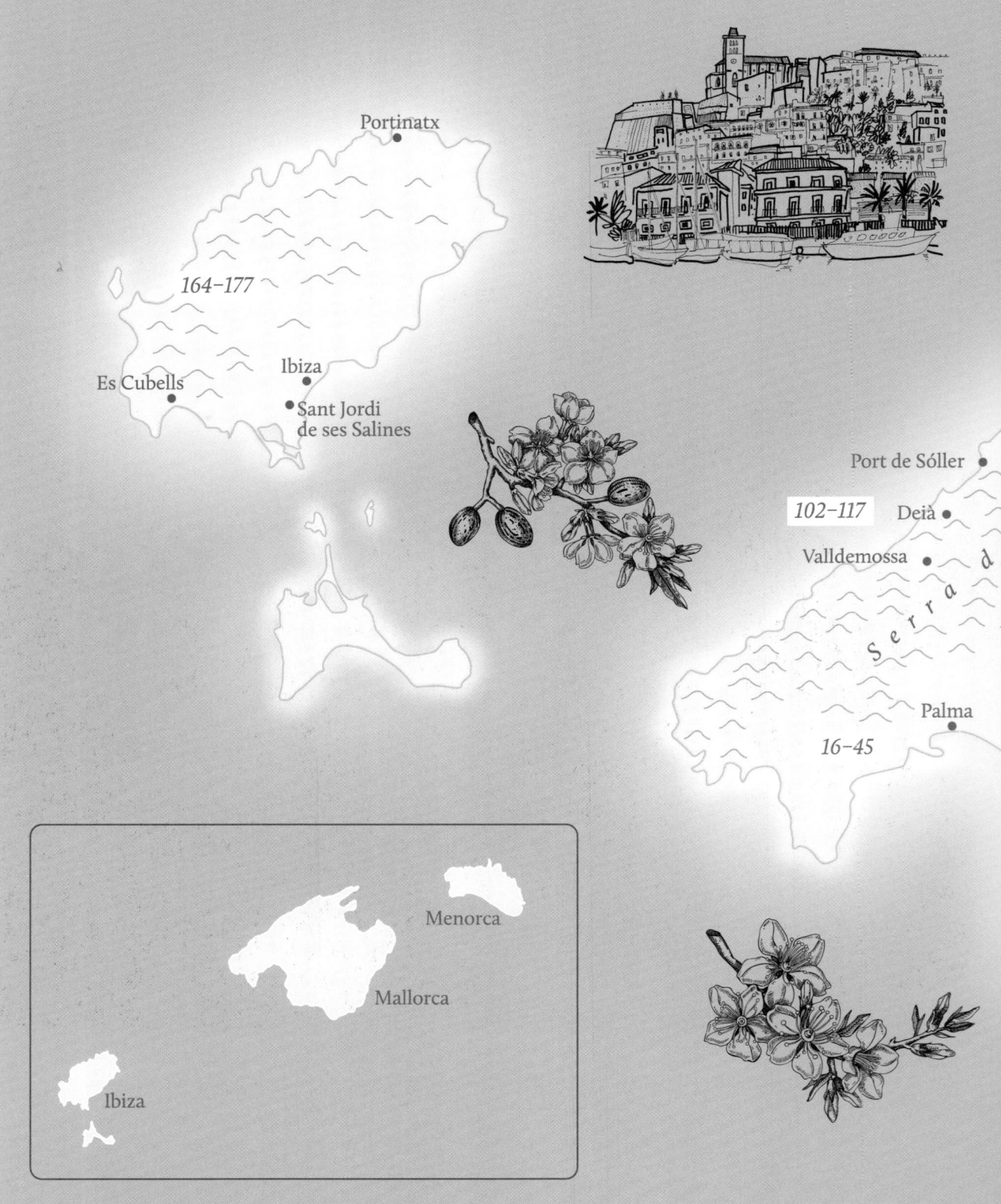

Portinatx

164–177

Es Cubells

Ibiza

Sant Jordi
de ses Salines

Port de Sóller

102–117   Deià

Valldemossa

Serra de

Palma

16–45

Menorca

Mallorca

Ibiza

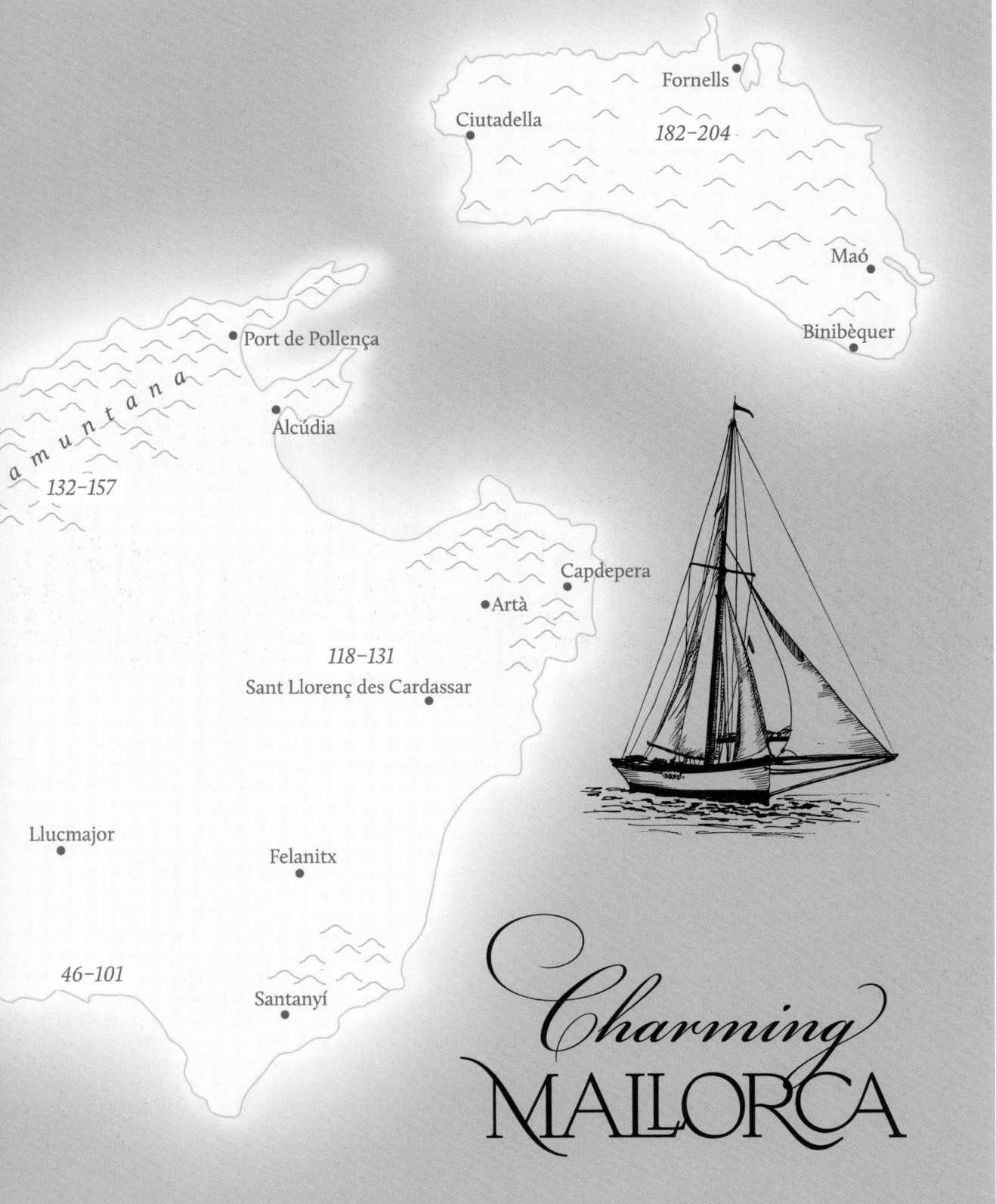

Fornells

Ciutadella

182–204

Maó

Binibèquer

Port de Pollença

a m u n t a n a

Alcúdia

132–157

Capdepera

Artà

118–131

Sant Llorenç des Cardassar

Llucmajor

Felanitx

46–101

Santanyí

Charming

MALLORCA

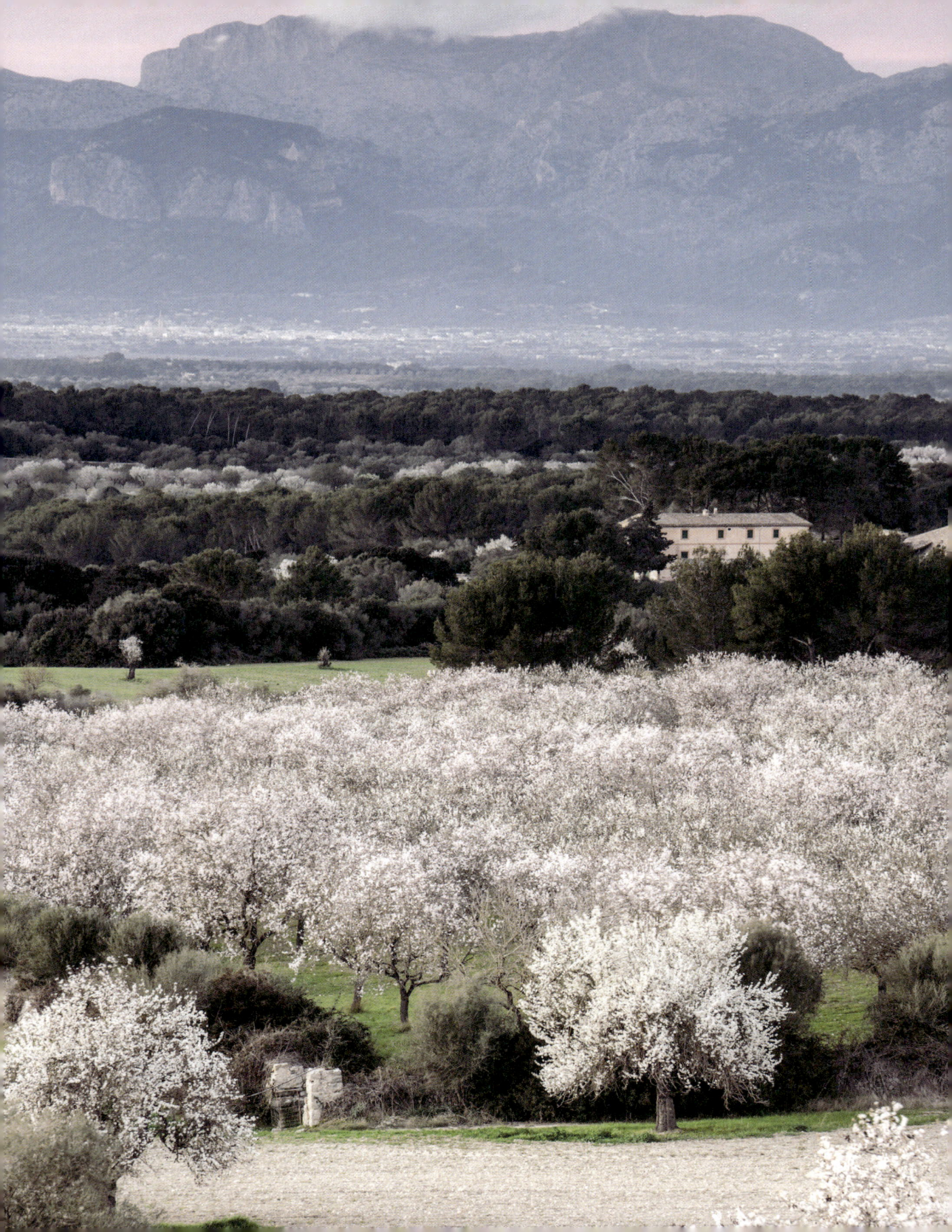

ALMOND BLOSSOMS

HOW BEAUTIFUL CAN WINTER BE? IN SOUTHEASTERN MALLORCA, THE FIRST BLOSSOMS APPEAR AS EARLY AS JANUARY

The year on the Balearic island begins with a striking display of color. Delicate pink and white blossoms form broad swaths across the landscape, set against green meadows and yellow clover. Mallorca's almond blossoms trace back to a more somber chapter of its history. A phylloxera outbreak at the end of the nineteenth century nearly brought viticulture to a halt. Many winegrowers were forced to look for alternatives and turned to almond cultivation. Almond trees reached the island as early as the tenth century, introduced by the Moors from the East. Today, Mallorca is home to around seven million of them. The drive from Palma toward Palmanyola and Bunyola passes through valleys at the foot of the Tramuntana range, where extensive almond groves line the route. Paired with a stop in the small village of Orient, it makes an ideal winter outing. One highlight of the season is the Firó de la Flor d'Ametler almond blossom festival. It takes place on the first weekend in February on the grounds of a historic finca in Son Servera and includes folk dancing, almond-based products, and background on the almond harvest tradition. The almond itself also takes center stage. Thanks to the island's climate and soil, it develops a pronounced aroma and a flavor that leans sweet rather than bitter. Sometimes it is enough to find a quiet lookout during blossom season and take in the rows of almond trees and the low hum of bees—a simple way to mark the start of the year.

LEFT: *Blooming almond orchards at the Aubenya estate near Algaida, with the Tramuntana mountains in the background.*

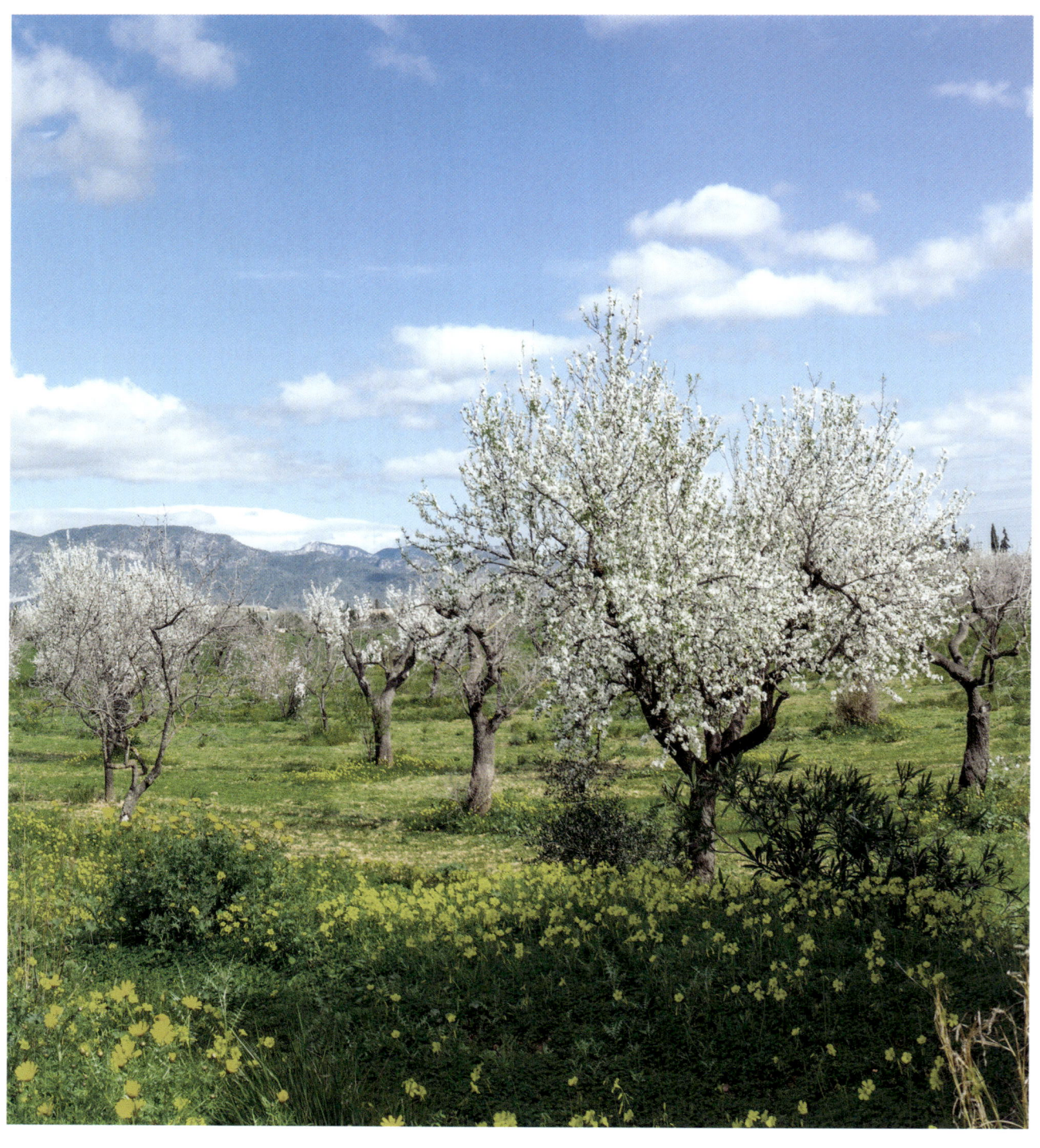

ABOVE AND RIGHT: *Nature's spectacle of delicate almond blossoms emerging from gnarled, wind-shaped trees form a visual parallel to multifaceted Mallorca—raw in places, quiet in others.*

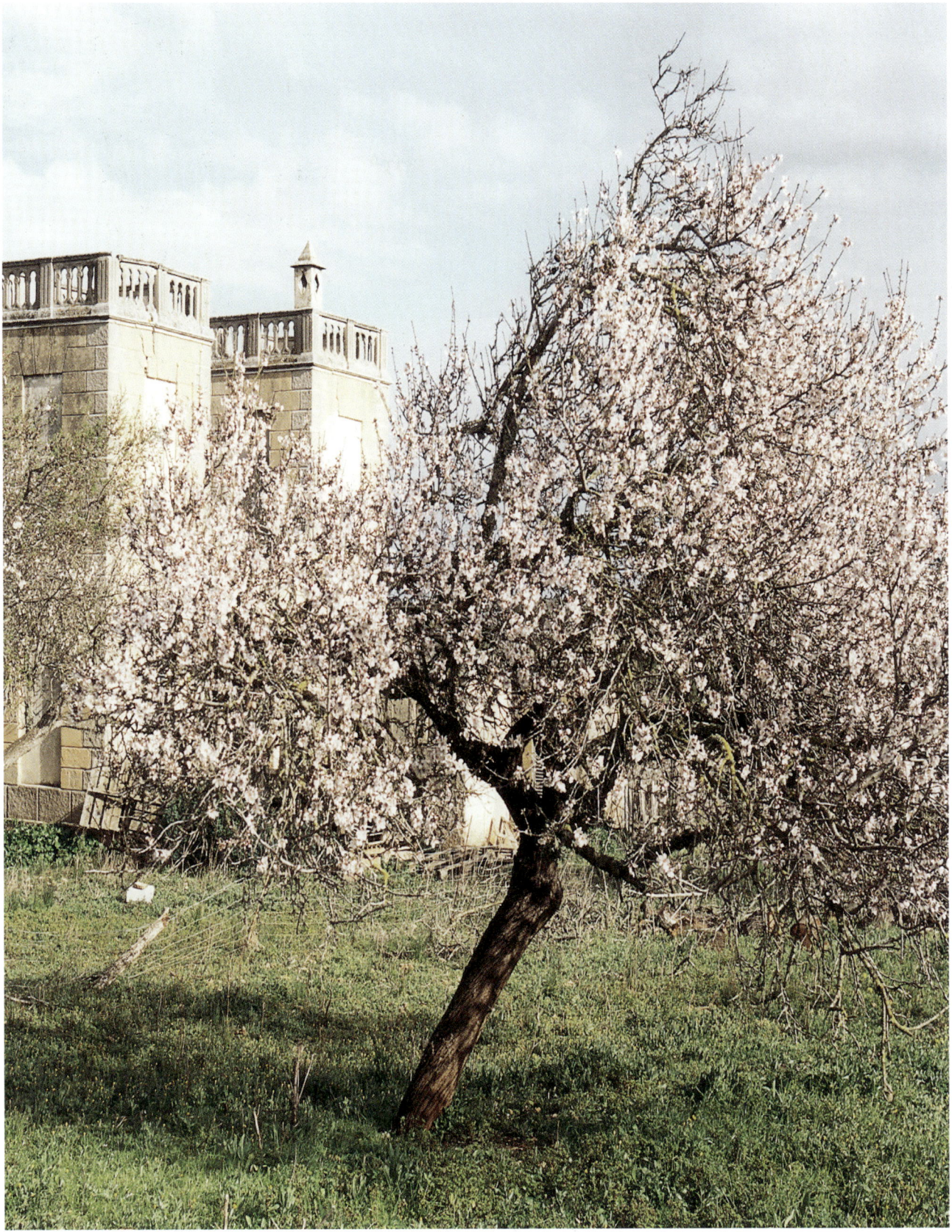

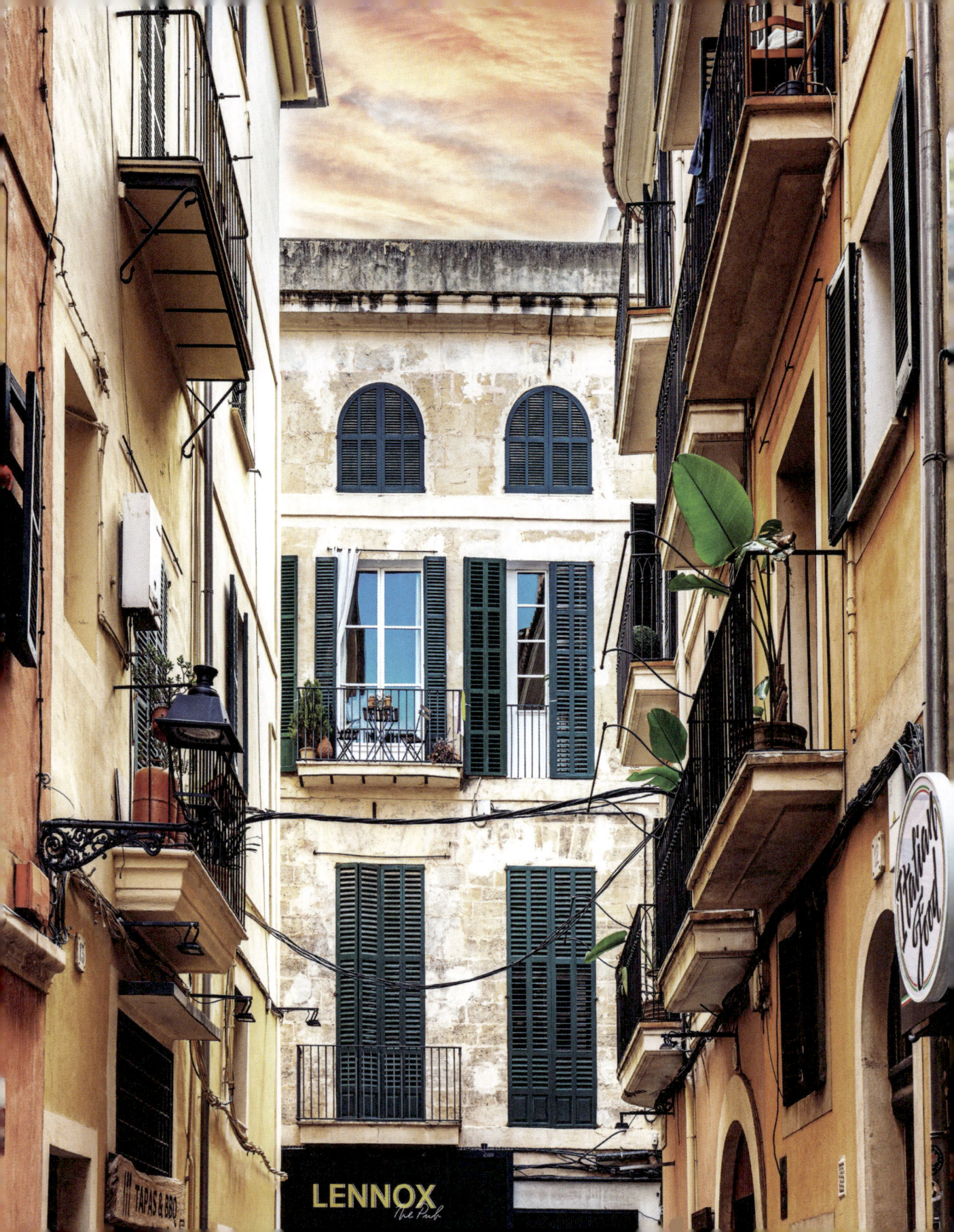

℘ALMA

COSMOPOLITAN, COLORFUL, AND OPEN. FOR THOUSANDS OF YEARS, DIFFERENT CULTURES HAVE CONVERGED IN THE ISLAND'S CAPITAL

Palma does not require a carefully planned itinerary. Time is enough. Something appears on nearly every corner: ceramic details on Art Nouveau façades around the Plaça Major; historic town palaces built from Santanyí sandstone; Gothic churches; Arab baths; narrow, sometimes teeming old-town streets with nostalgic shops and contemporary bars. A slow drift works best here. A brief chat with a *turrón* vendor. *Sobrasada* from the butcher. Time spent in a haberdashery with intricate wooden paneling. In front of the cast-concrete walls of the Es Baluard museum, modern architectural shadows fall alongside the historic city ramparts. Palma has been shaped by successive cultures for centuries. Founded by the Romans in 123 BC, later settled by the Moors, their traces remain visible throughout the city. With Jaume I and the Aragonese, Christianity returned to the island in 1229. The cathedral rose soon after, and Palma developed into a maritime center. Perhaps this layered history explains the city's distinctive rhythm. Nowhere is it more evident than above the harbor, in the former fishing district of Santa Catalina, today a bohemian neighborhood of artists, restaurants, and bars. The Mercat Santa Catalina brings together an international mix: local fishmongers beside sushi counters, fresh pasta next to traditional spice stalls, Spanish home cooks alongside Michelin-starred chefs provisioning charter yachts. Mallorca in a nutshell.

LEFT: *Palma's old town features numerous hidden gems, among them the narrow alleyway Carrer de la Mar, located near the cathedral.*

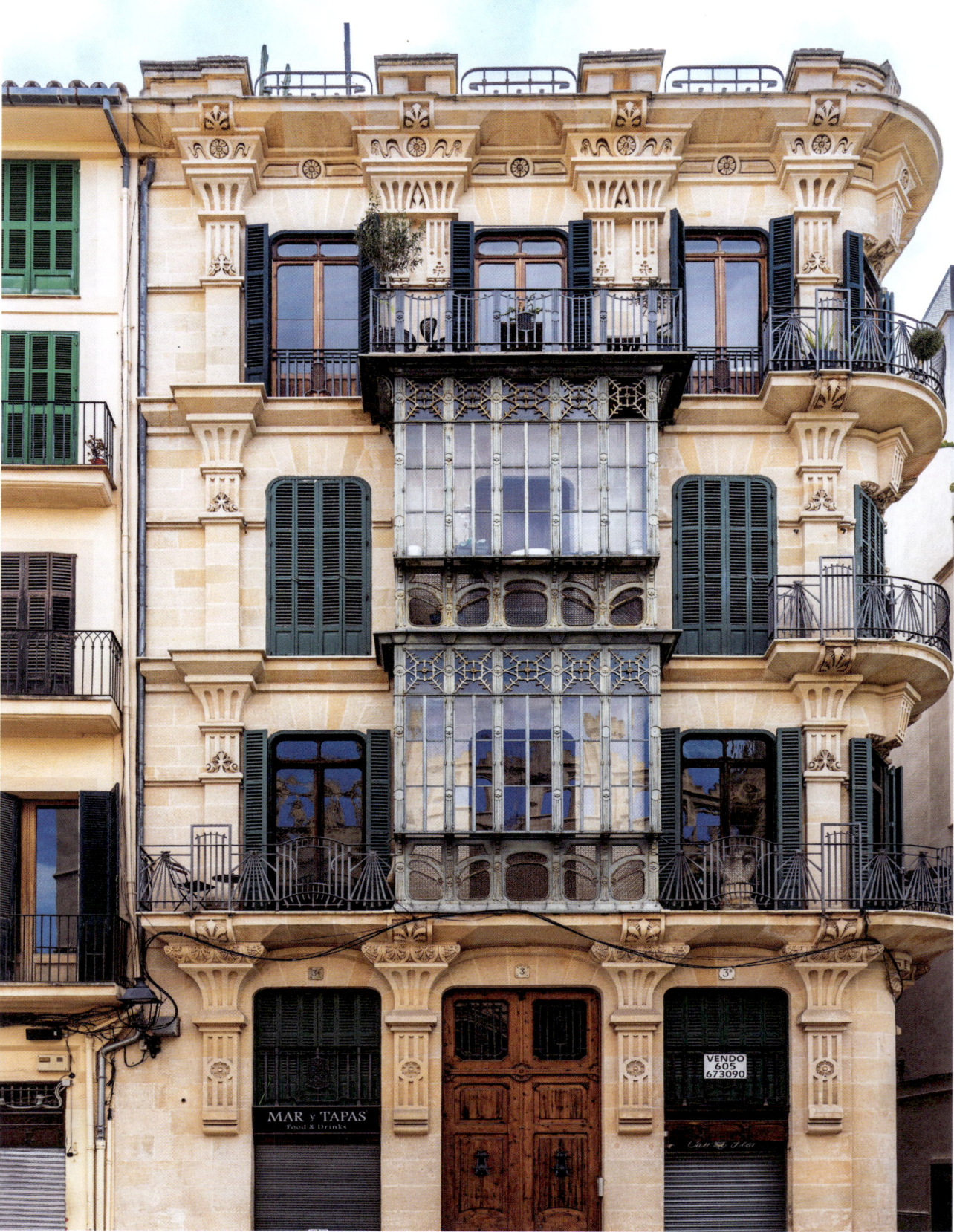

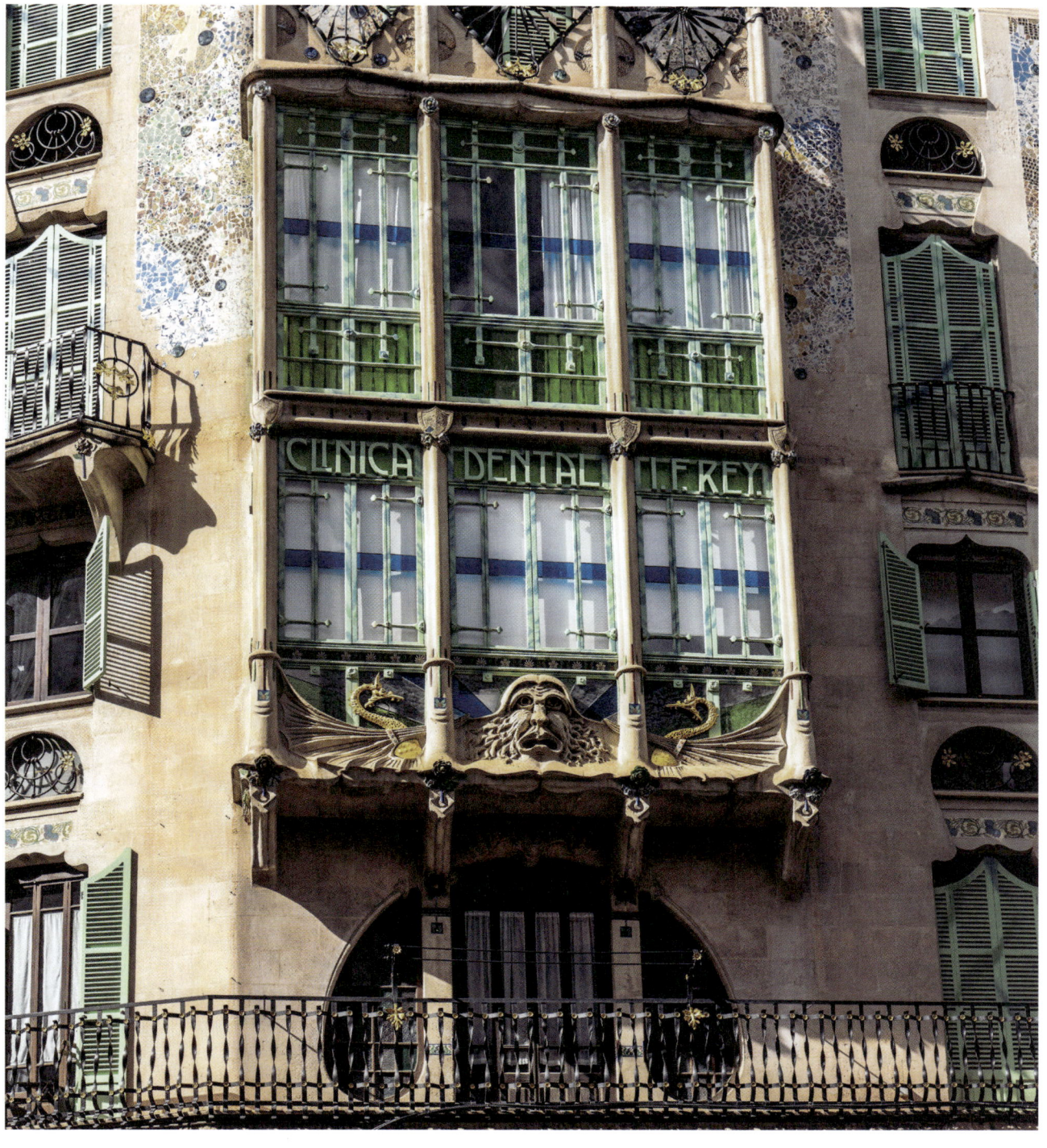

ABOVE: *Gaudí-influenced Art Nouveau architecture: the ornate façade of the 1909 building Can Forteza Rey.*

LEFT: *Modernisme, the Spanish Art Nouveau style, is found in the architecture of many residential and commercial buildings in Palma.*

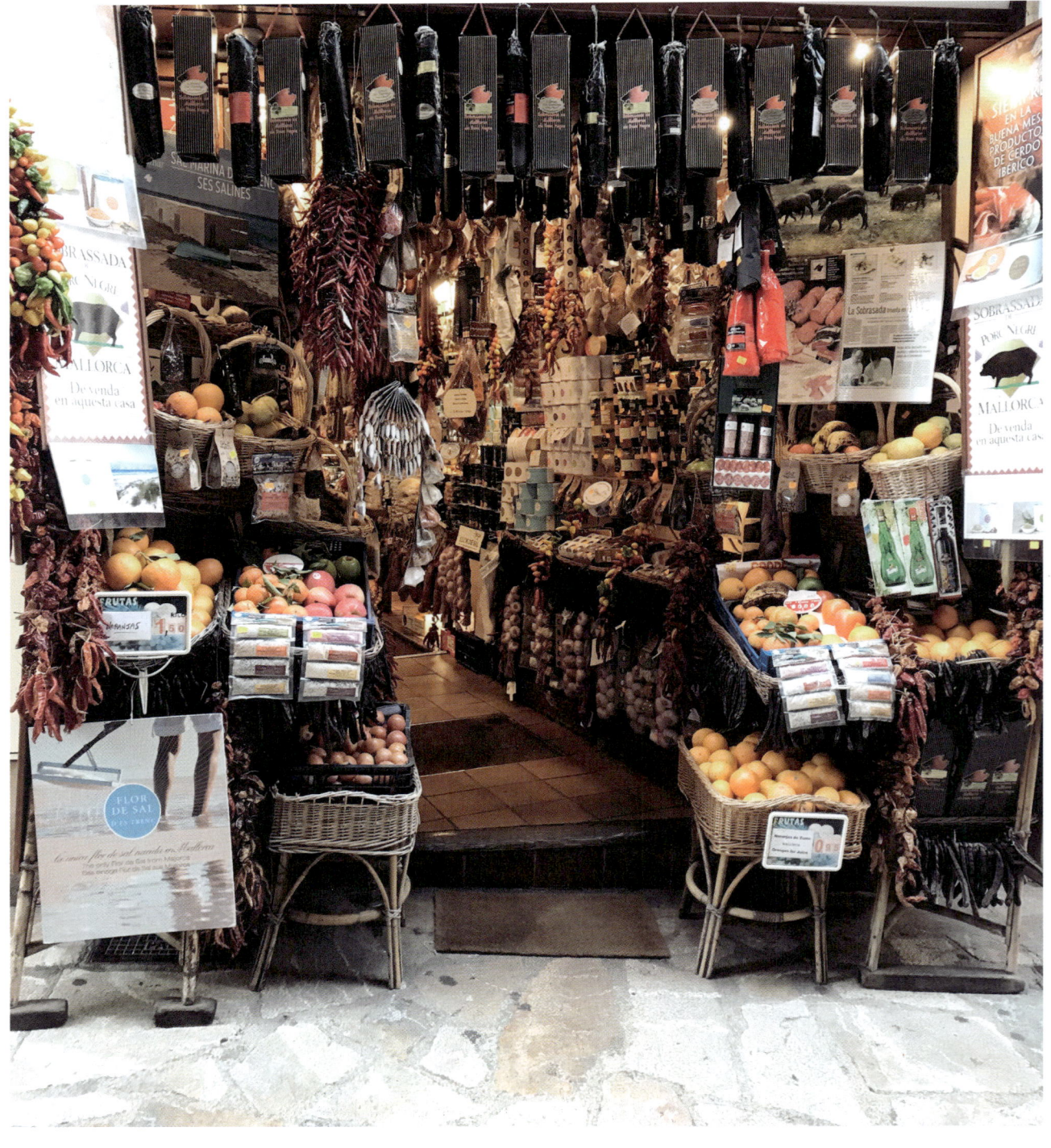

ABOVE: *Mallorcan delicacies at Colmado Santo Domingo:* sobrasada, *sea salt from Es Trenc, and regional specialties.*

RIGHT: *Probably the world's most beautiful bakery: traditional Mallorcan pastries are hand-crafted with love at Fornet de la Soca on Plaça de Weyler 9.*

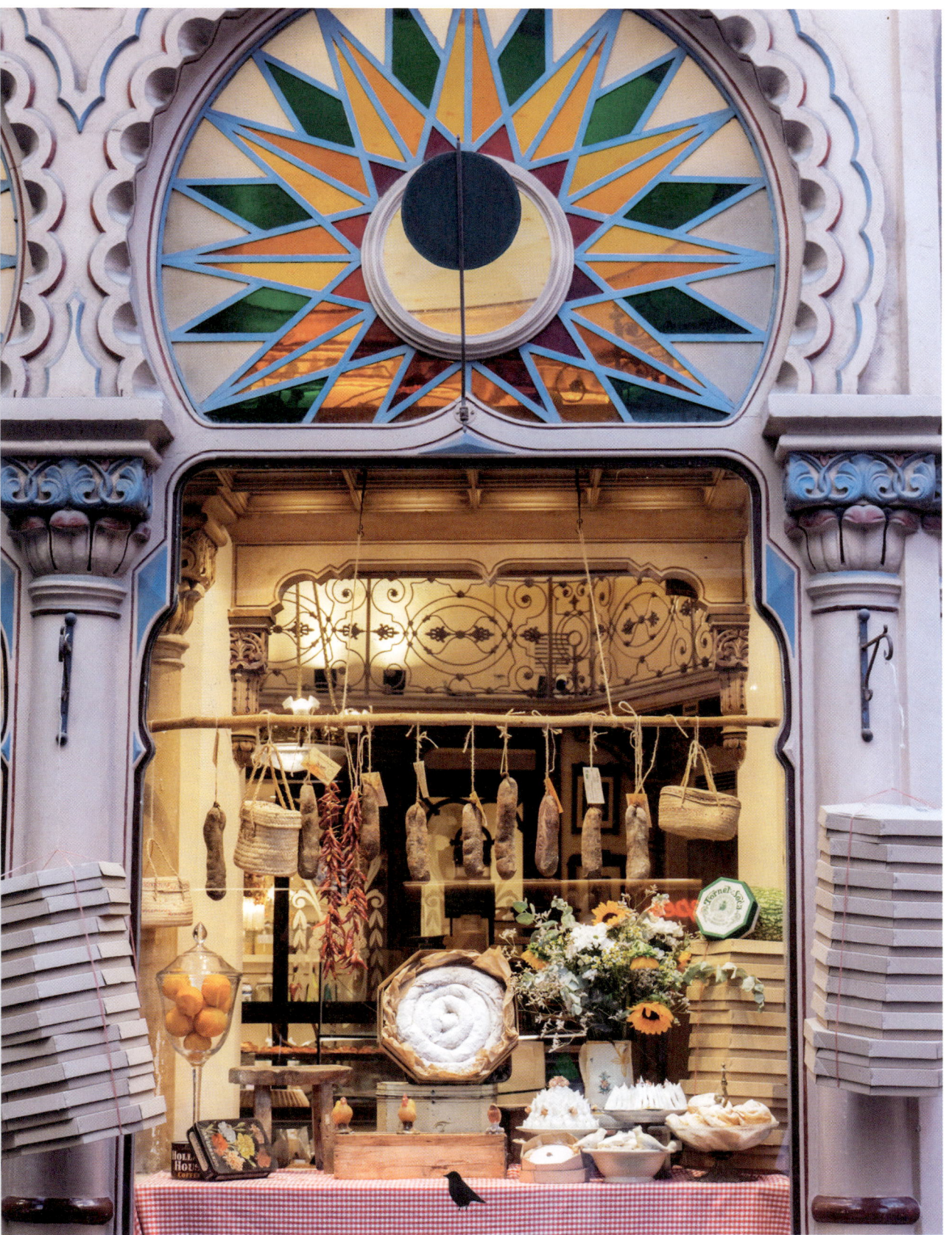

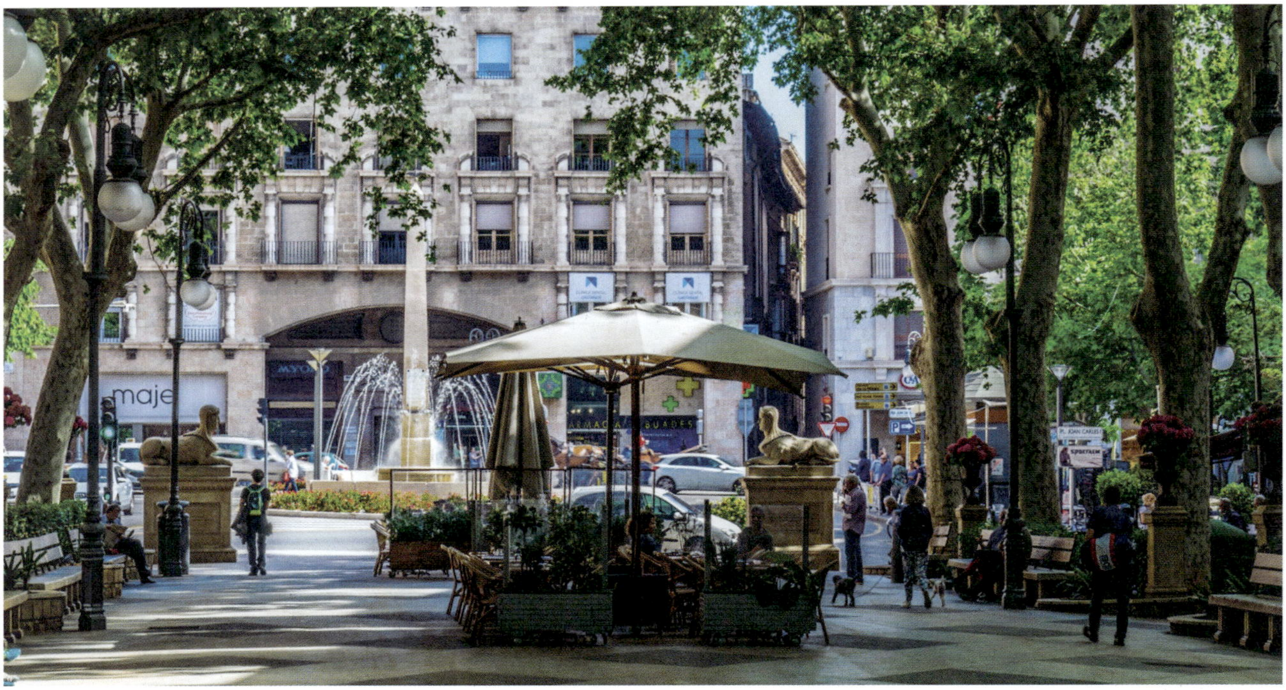

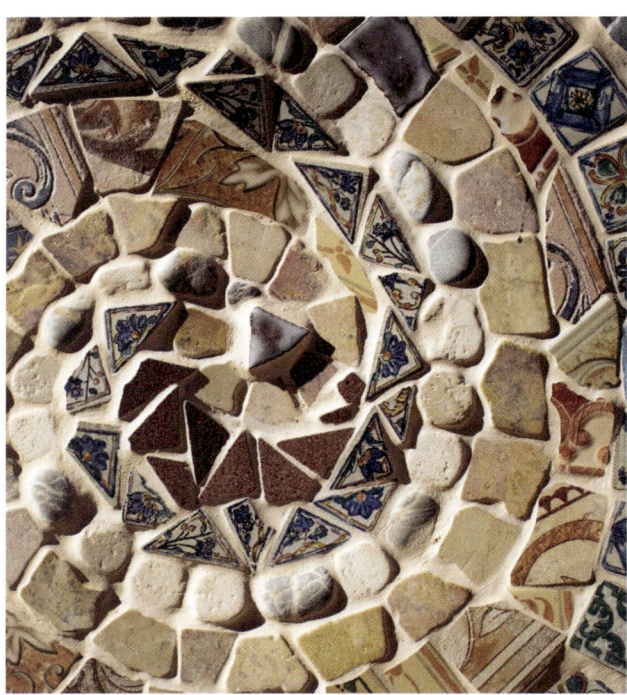

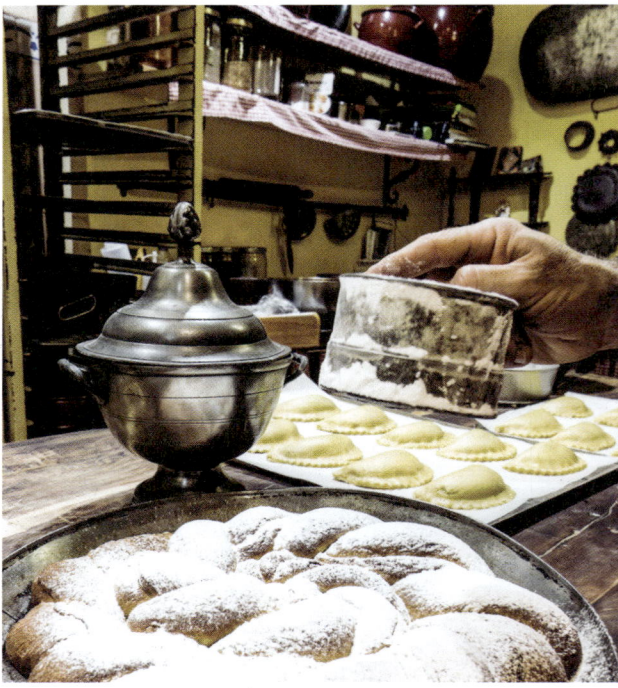

ABOVE: *"Nice" is an understatement at Passeig del Born. Shops, cafés, bars, and decorated Art Nouveau façades surround the square.*

RIGHT: *Small shops line a dense network of narrow streets and winding alleys near Carrer de Sant Domingo.*

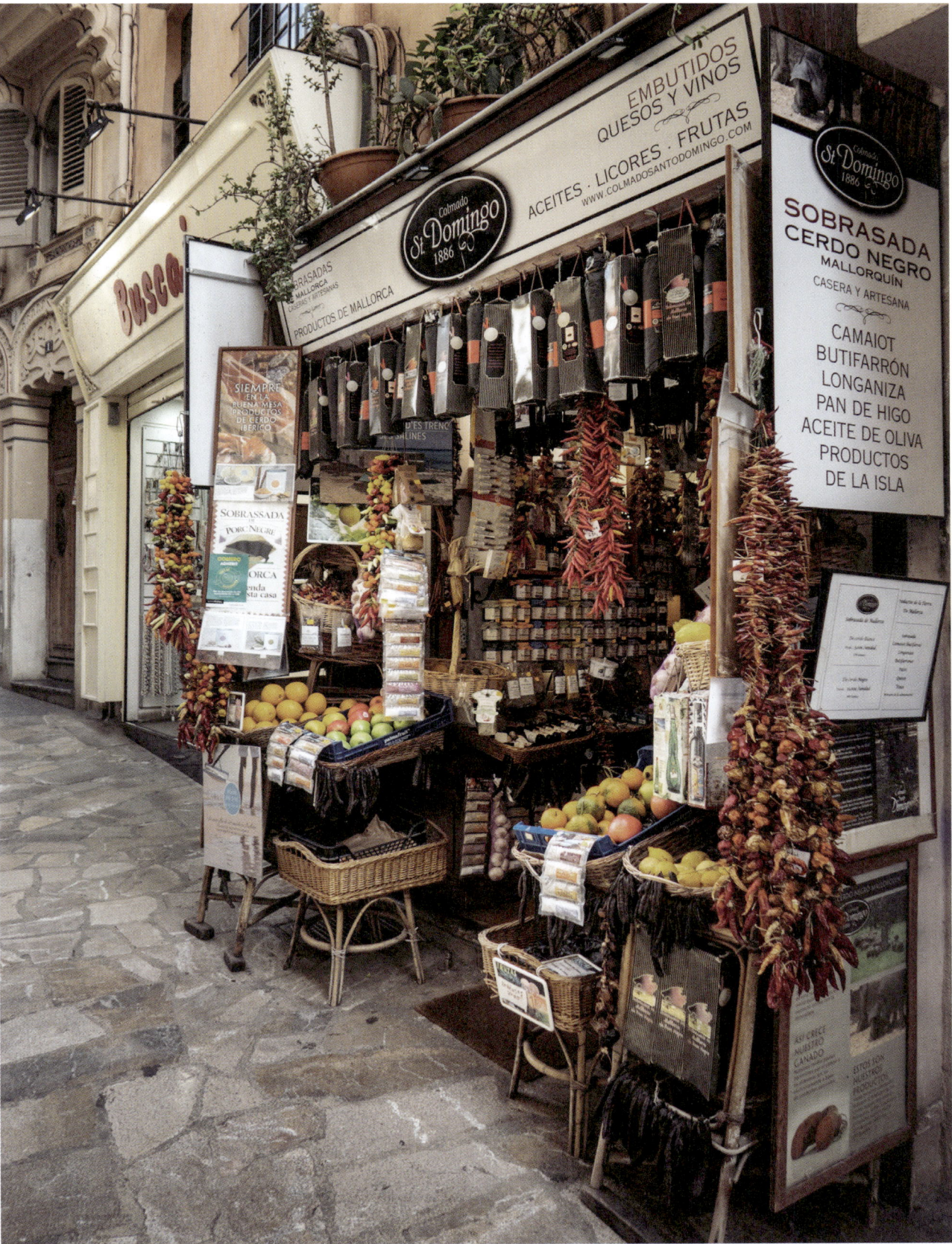

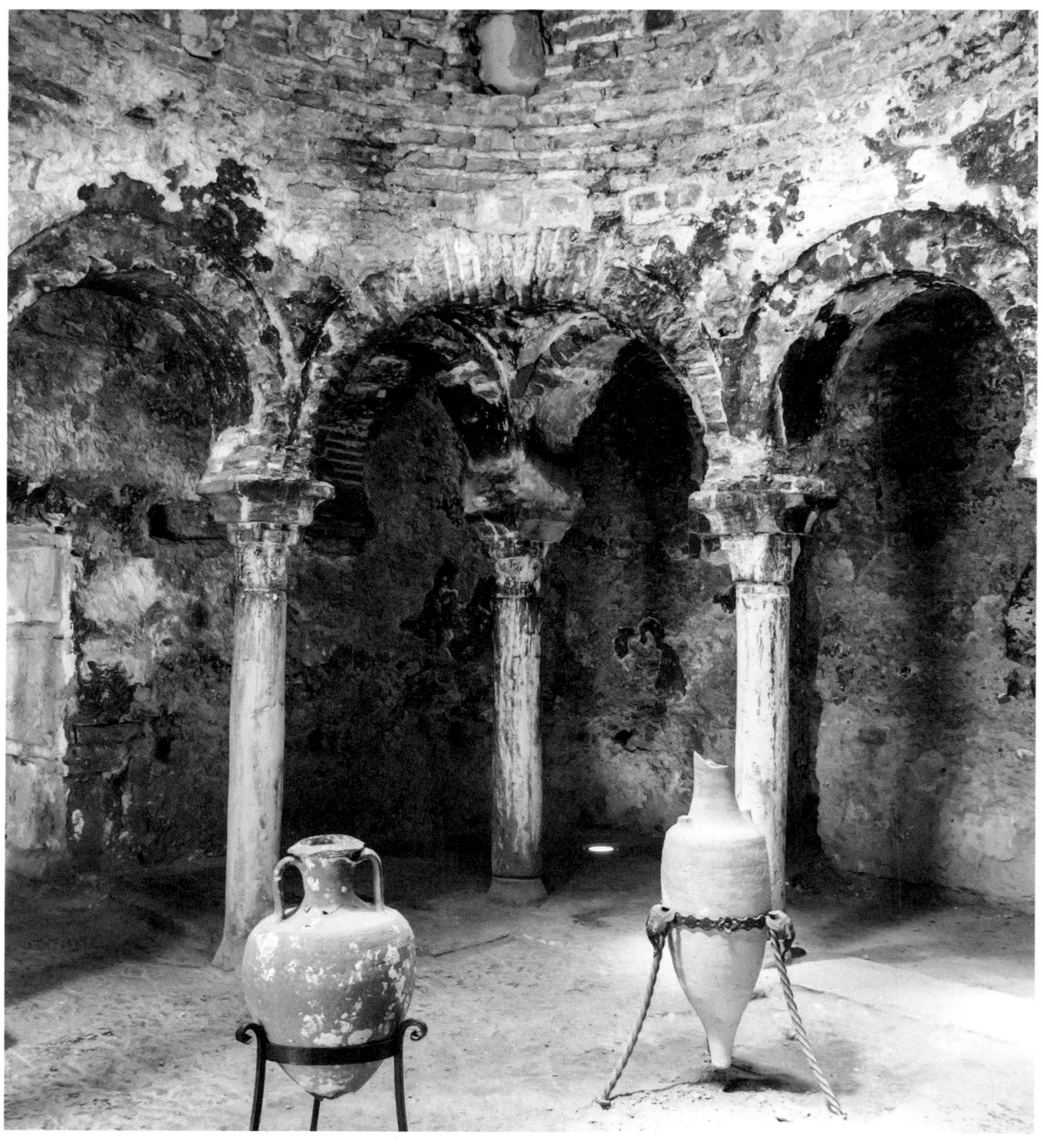

ABOVE: *Moorish architectural heritage: the eleventh-century Arab baths of Banys Arabs in the gardens of Can Fontirroig.*

RIGHT: *Gaudí-style organic forms and delicate ornamental façades are the essence of Spanish Modernisme. At his father's request, jeweler Lluís Forteza Rey designed this façade for the family home.*

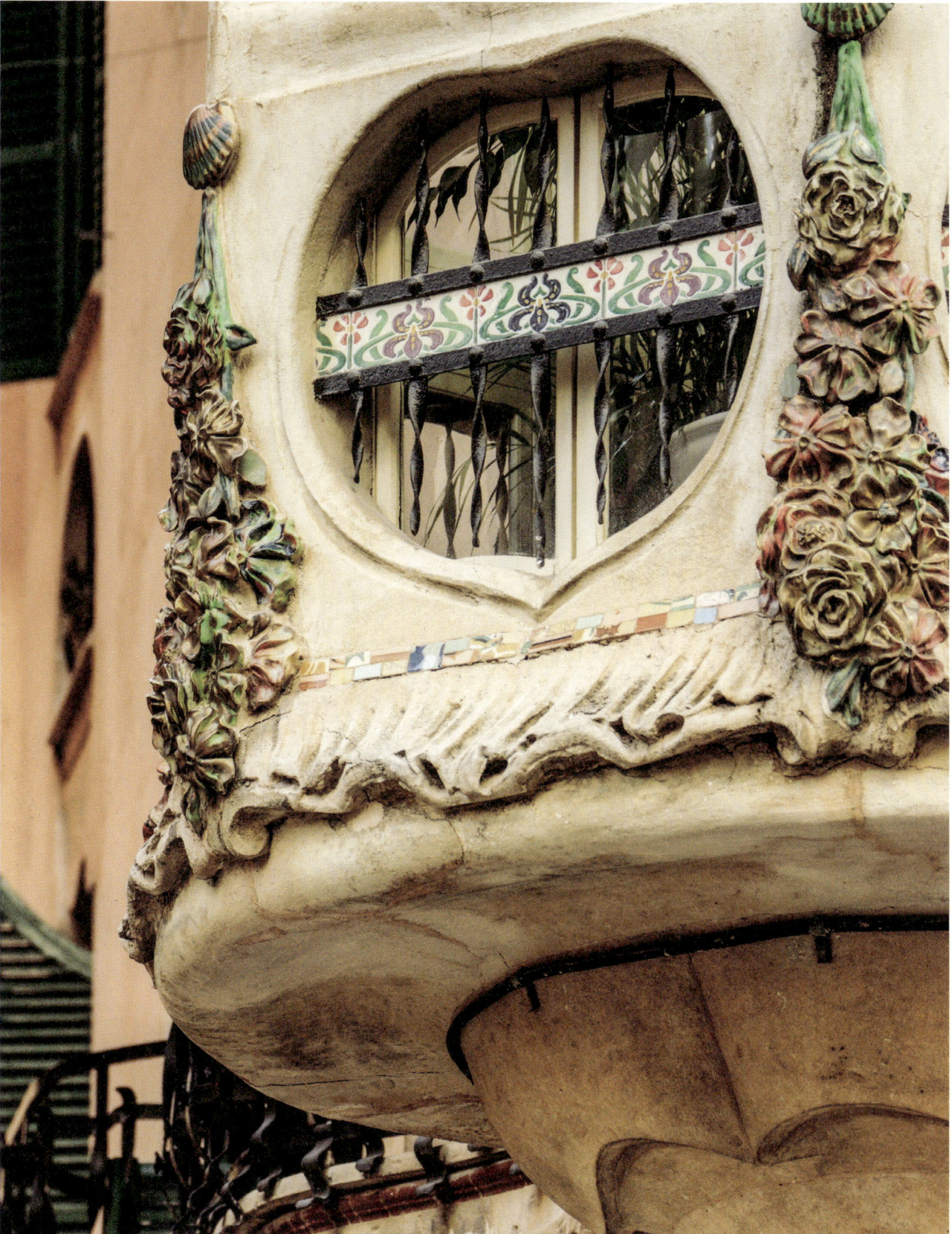

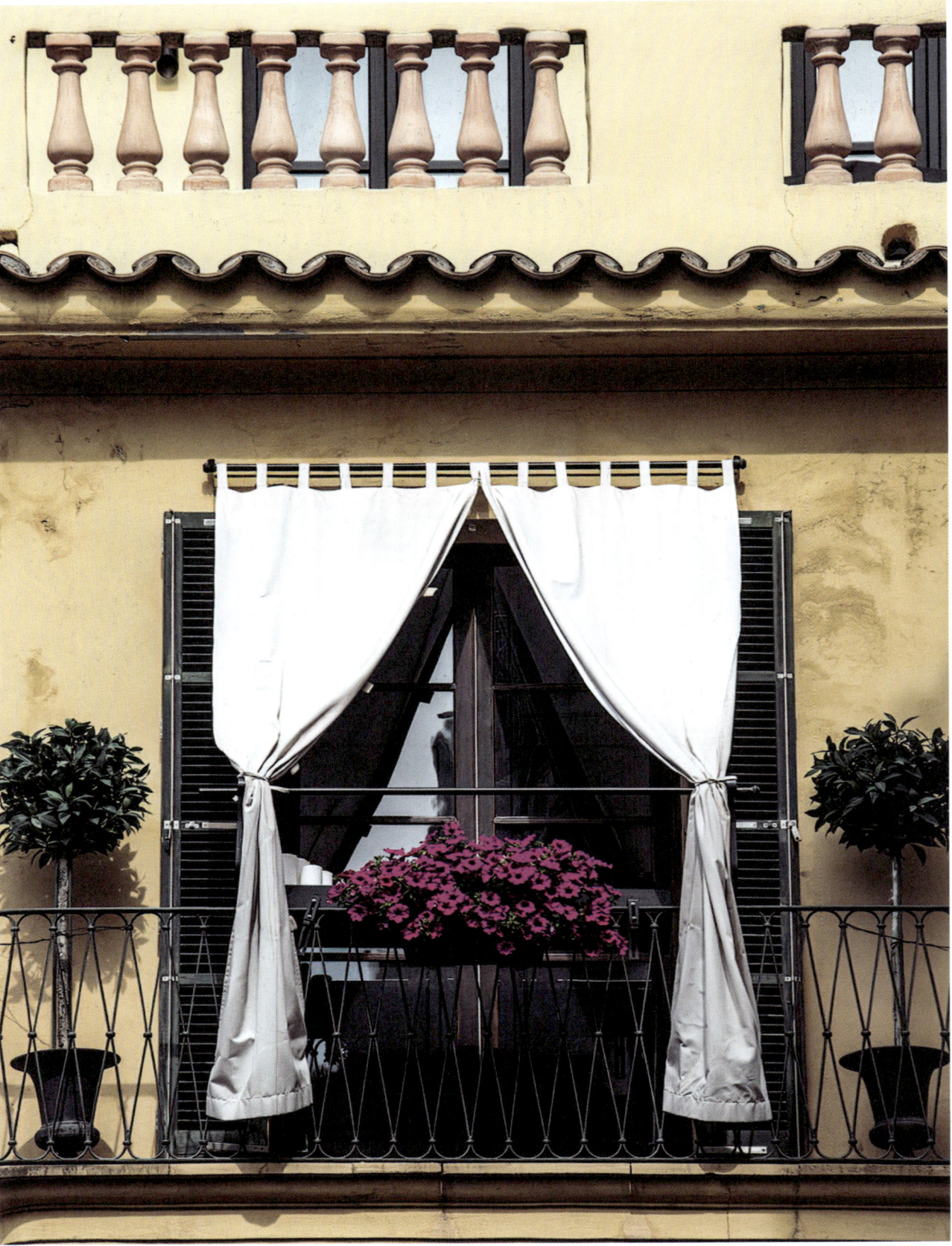

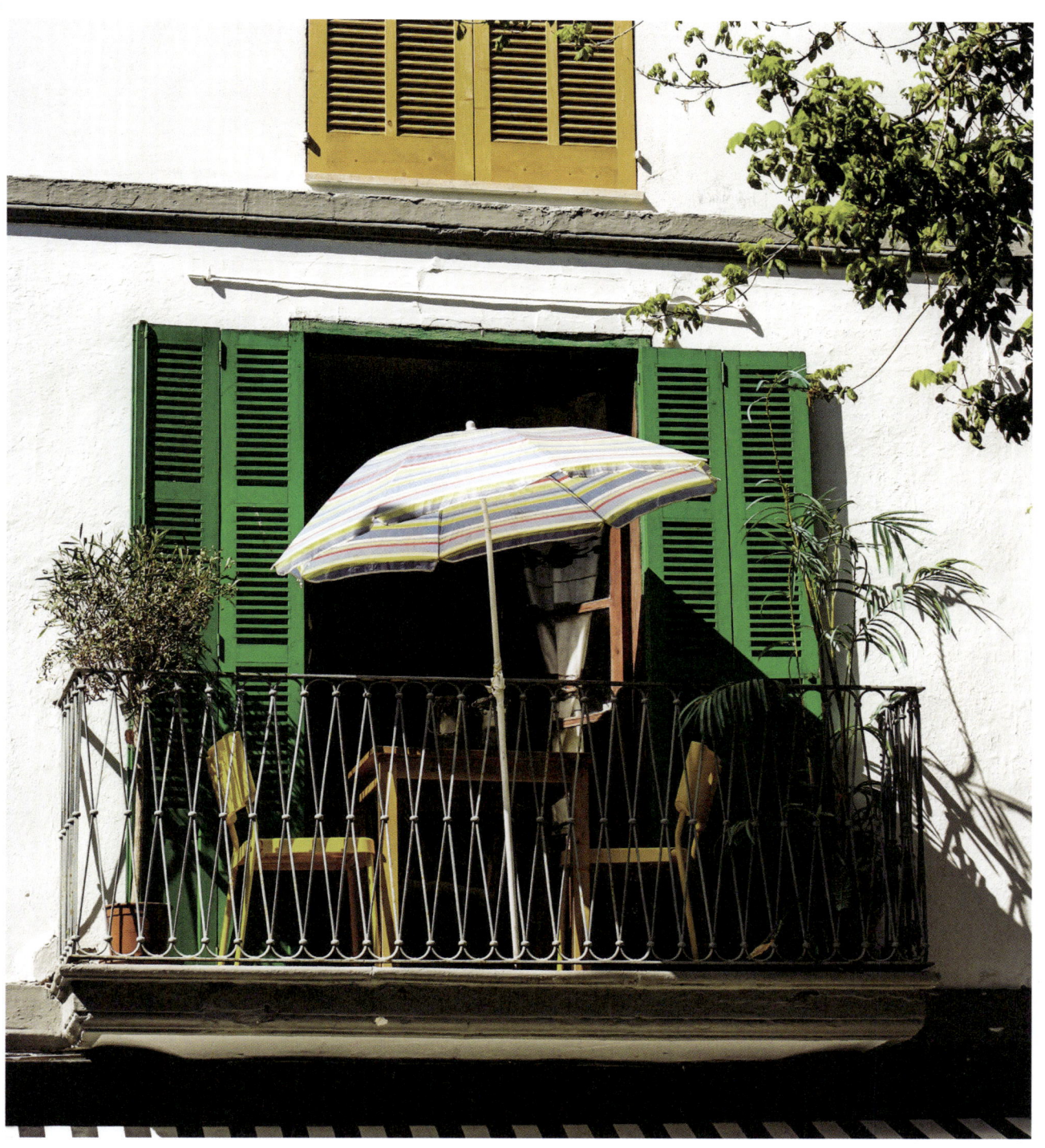

ABOVE AND LEFT: *Slender balconies draw upward gazes above Palma's colorful old town streets. Flowered railings, shaded seating—details that make life in Palma so colorful.*

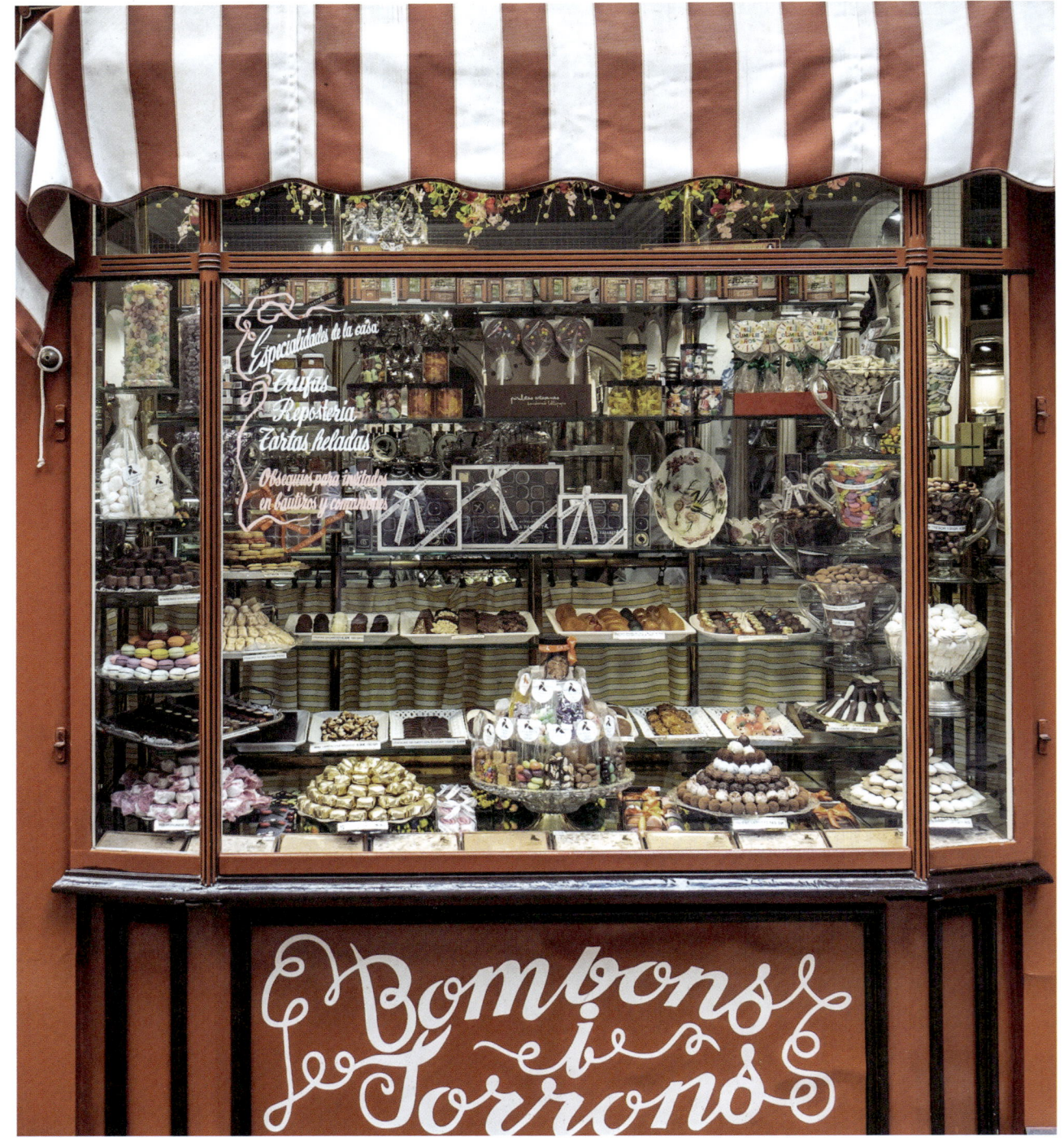

ABOVE: *Mallorca's sweet traditions: nougat, caramel, chocolate, and confections at La Pajarita on Carrer Sant Nicolau. The best (and sweetest) spot for artisanal chocolates and bonbons.*

RIGHT: *The sometimes-quiet streets of Palma's old town, where long walks down narrow lanes offer distinct characters in every season.*

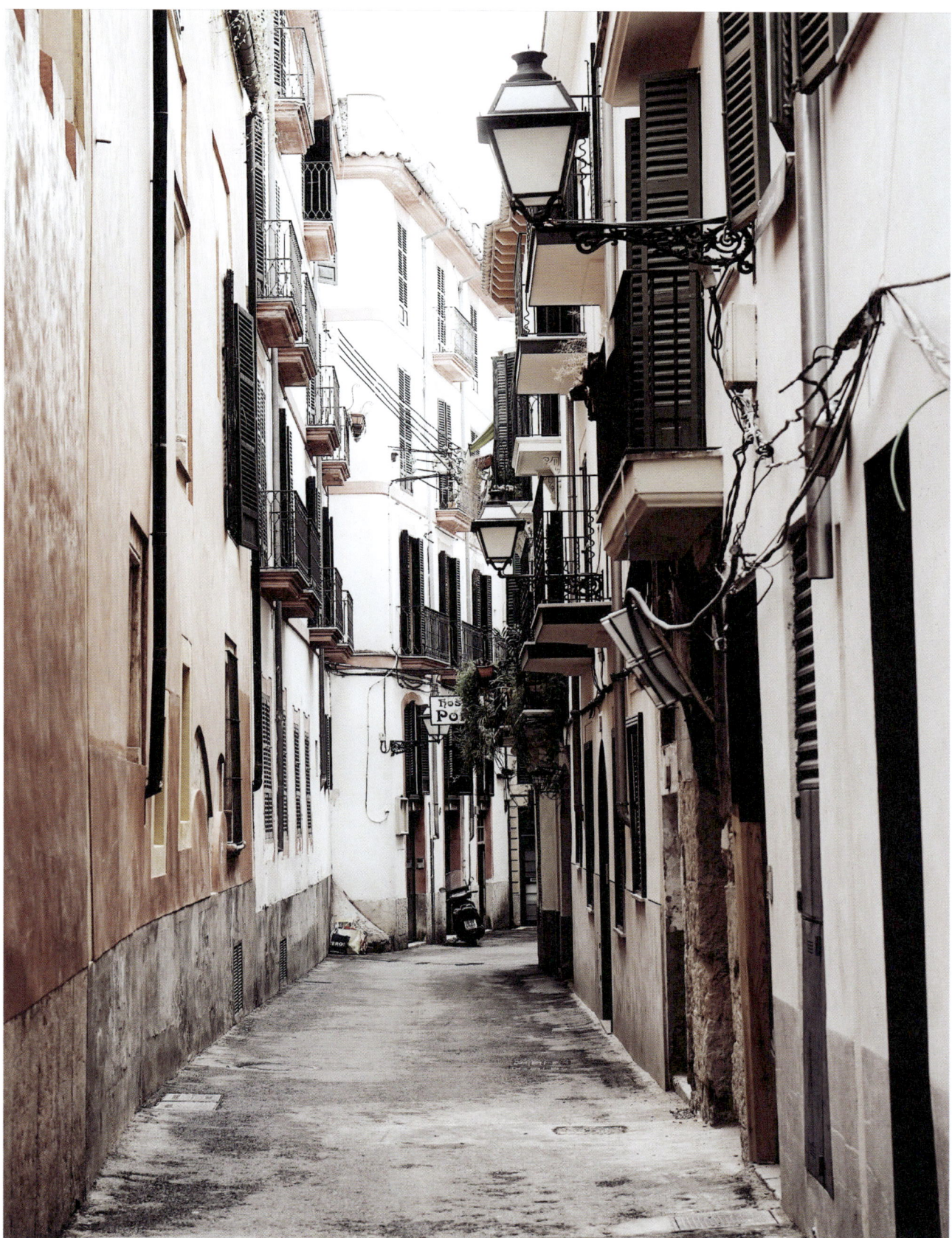

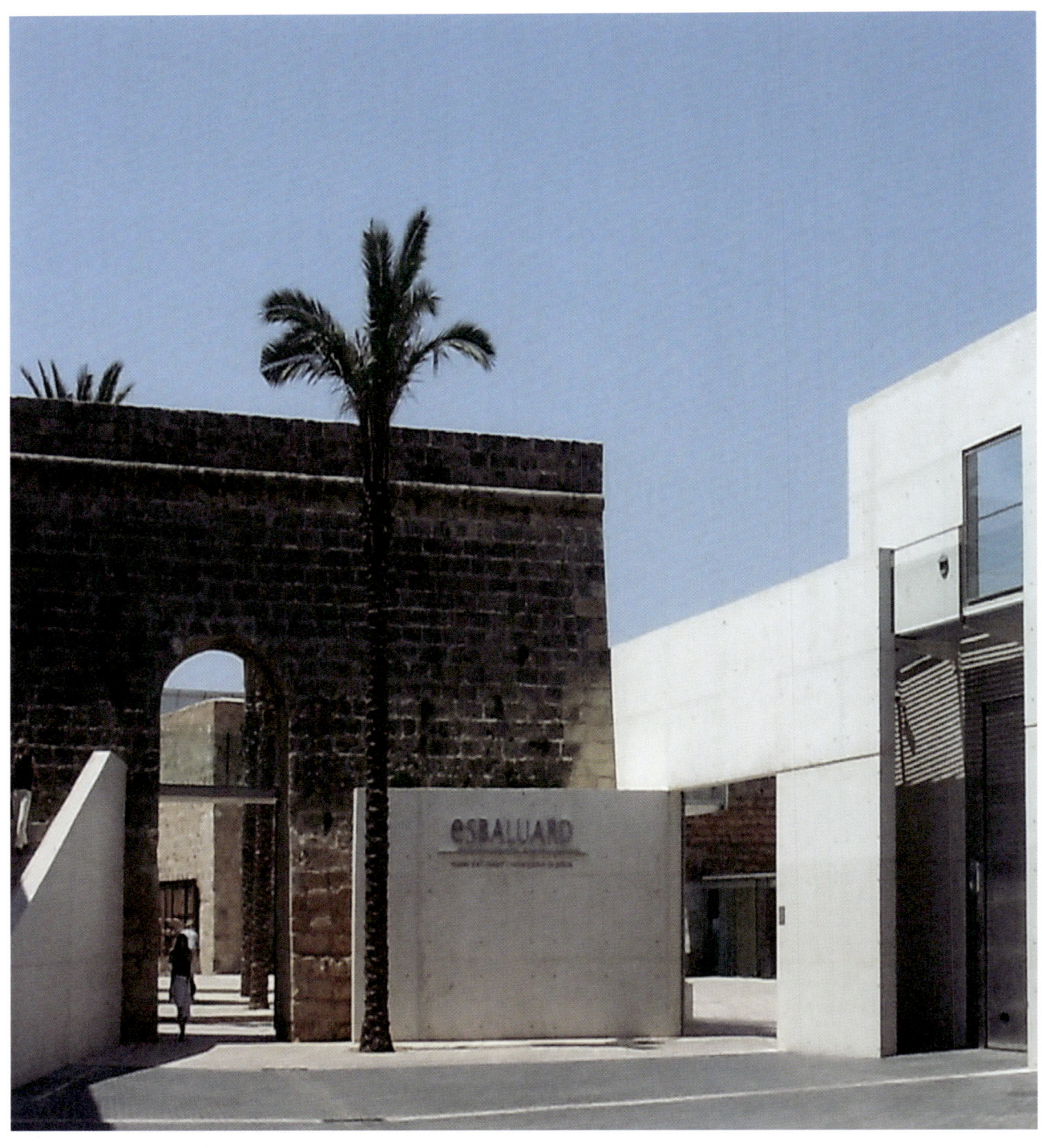

ABOVE AND RIGHT: *Contemporary concrete architecture against historic fortifications: the Es Baluard Museum of Contemporary Art seamlessly combines old and new across multiple levels. It houses paintings, sculptures, and one of Spain's major modern art collections, with works by Joaquín Sorolla—often described as a painter of light—as well as Marina Abramović, Pablo Picasso, and Joan Miró.*

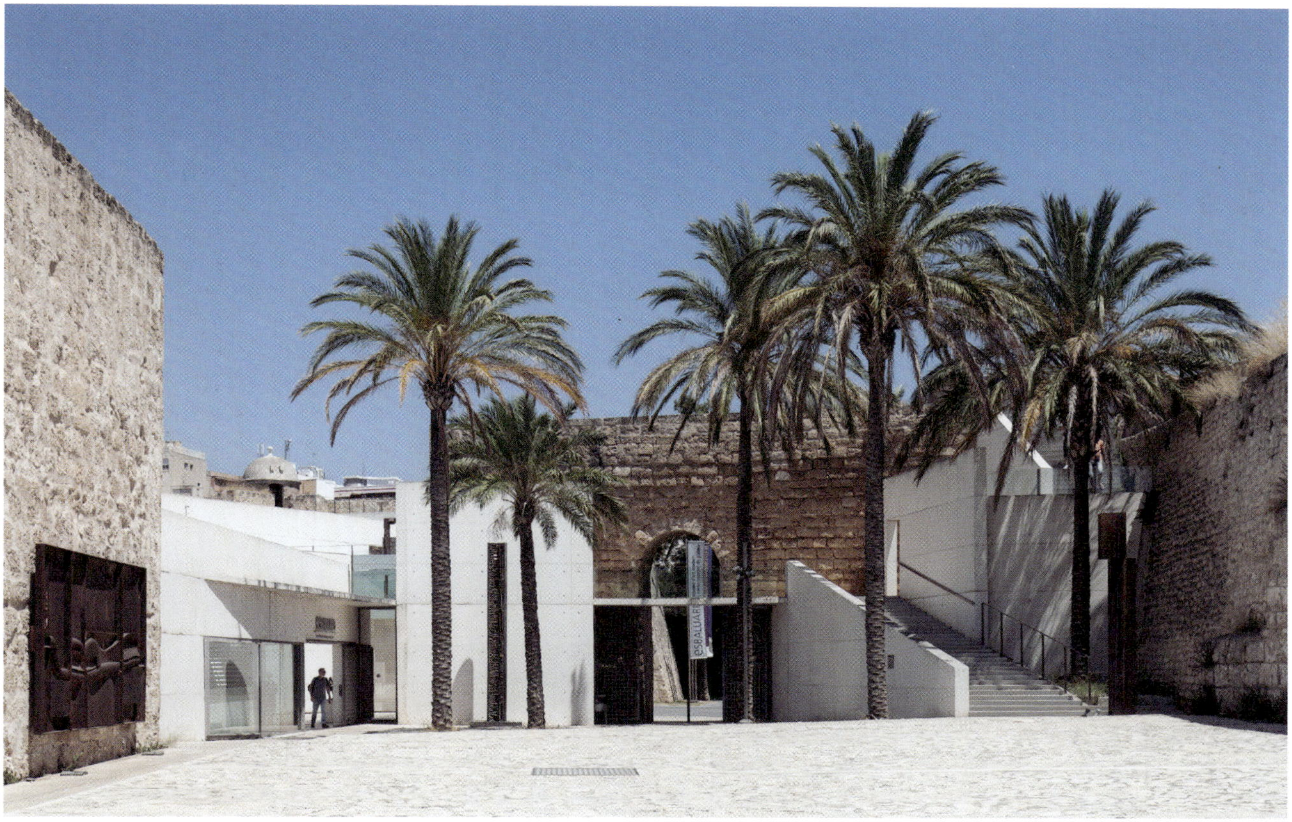

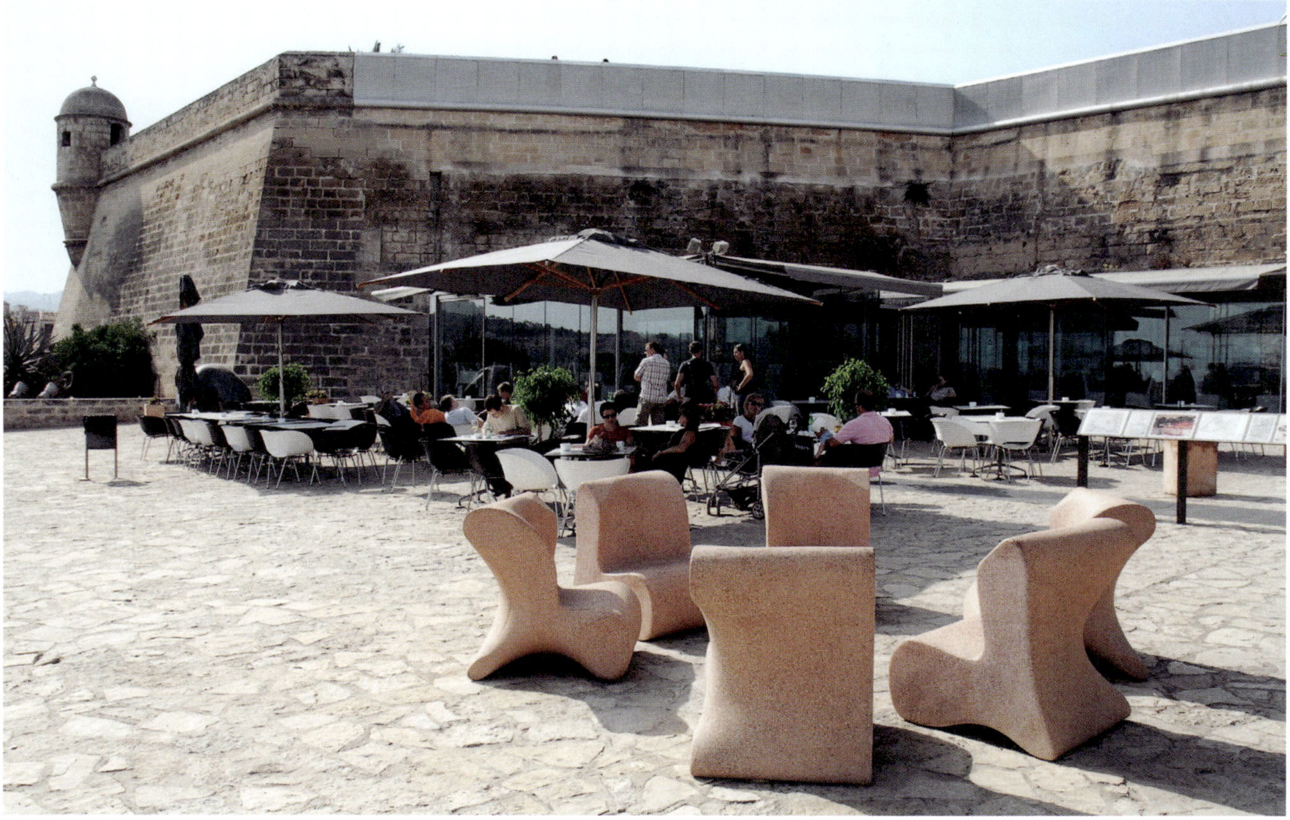

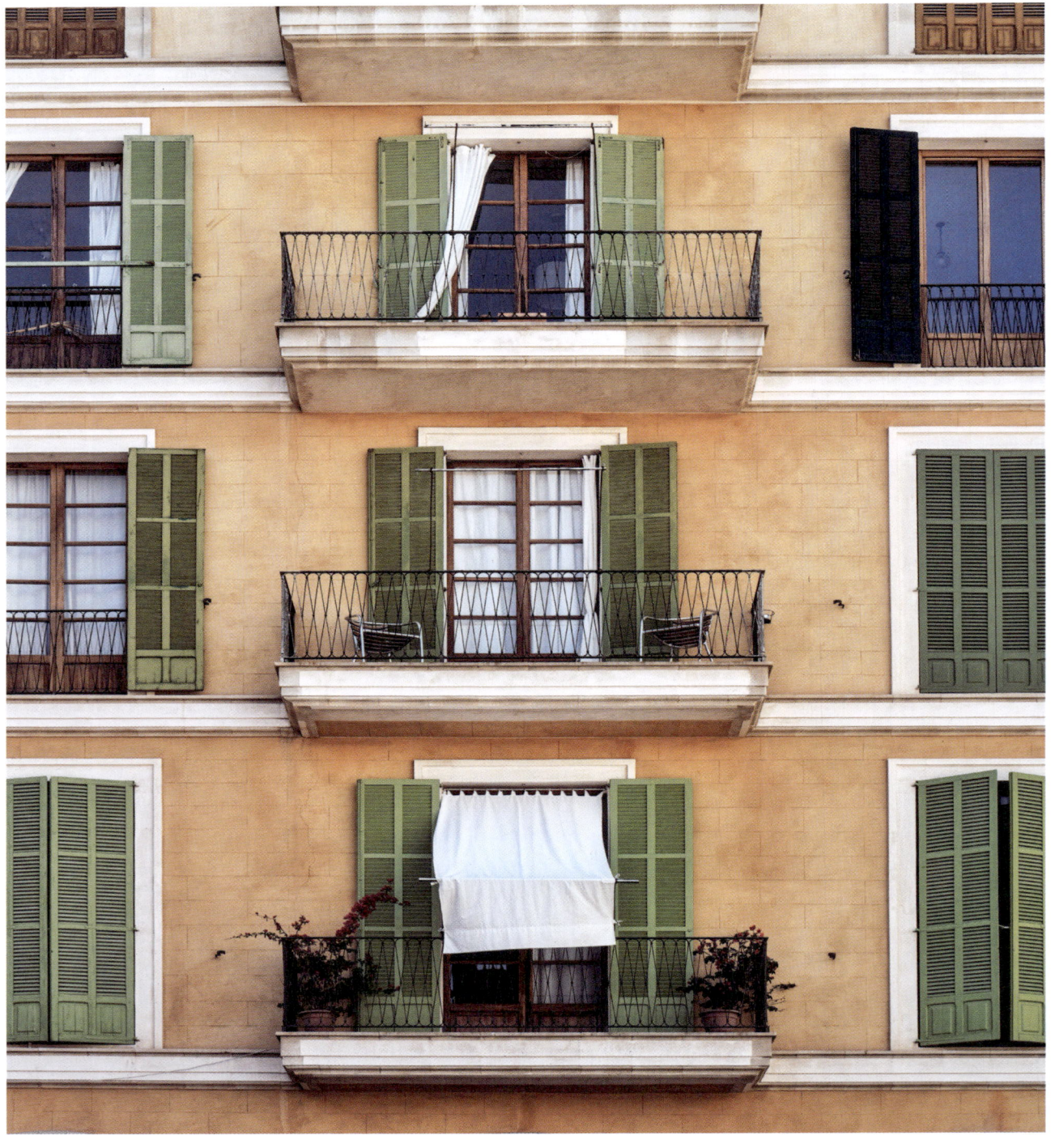

ABOVE: *Terracotta façades, small balconies, and green shutters adorn the iconic colonnaded buildings enclosing the wonderfully vibrant Plaça Major.*

RIGHT: *Unique and renowned for its neo-Mudéjar architecture, with rounded arches, ornate façades, and a tower, Can Corbella, on Palma's pedestrian zone, reflects Moorish stylistic elements fashionable in the nineteenth century.*

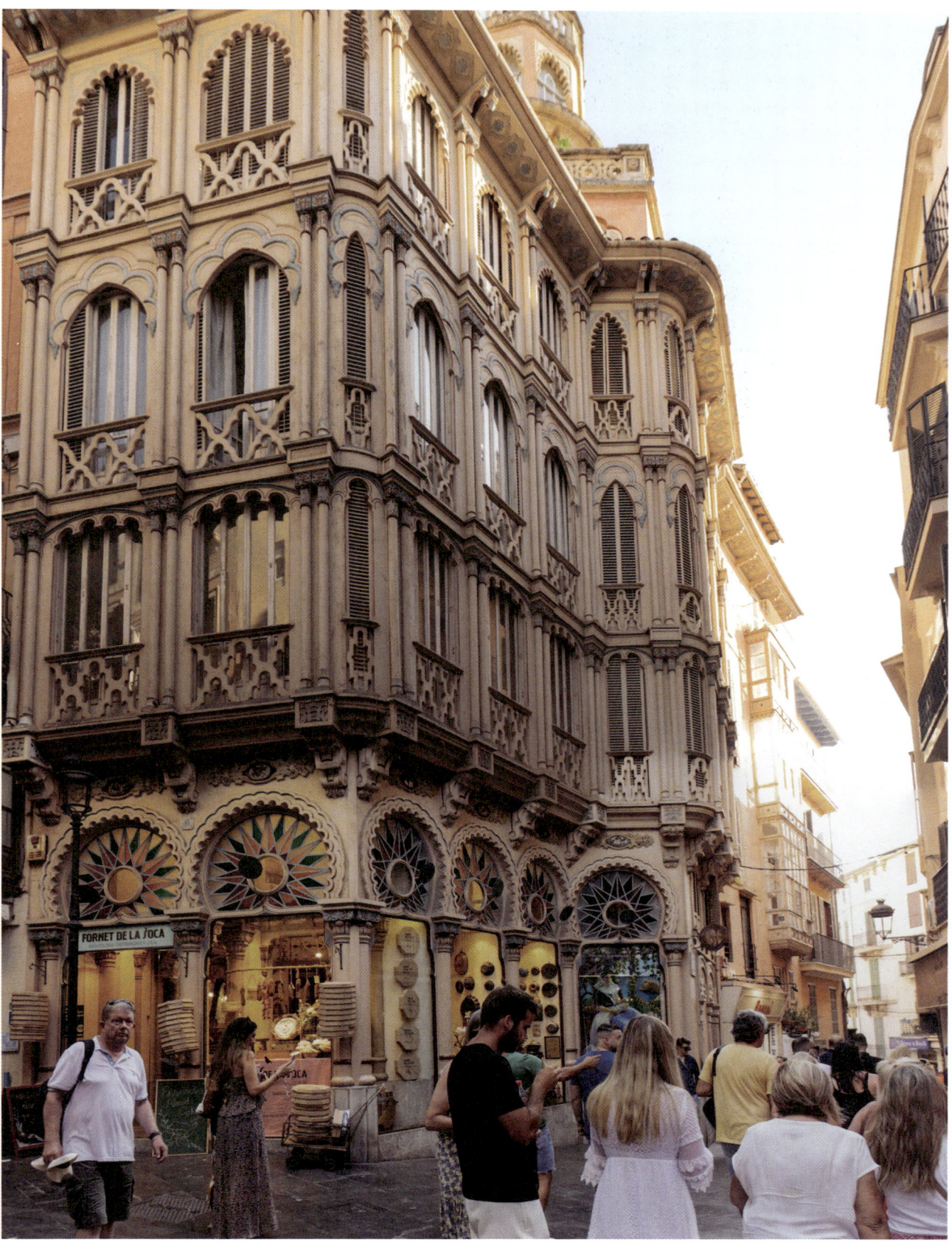

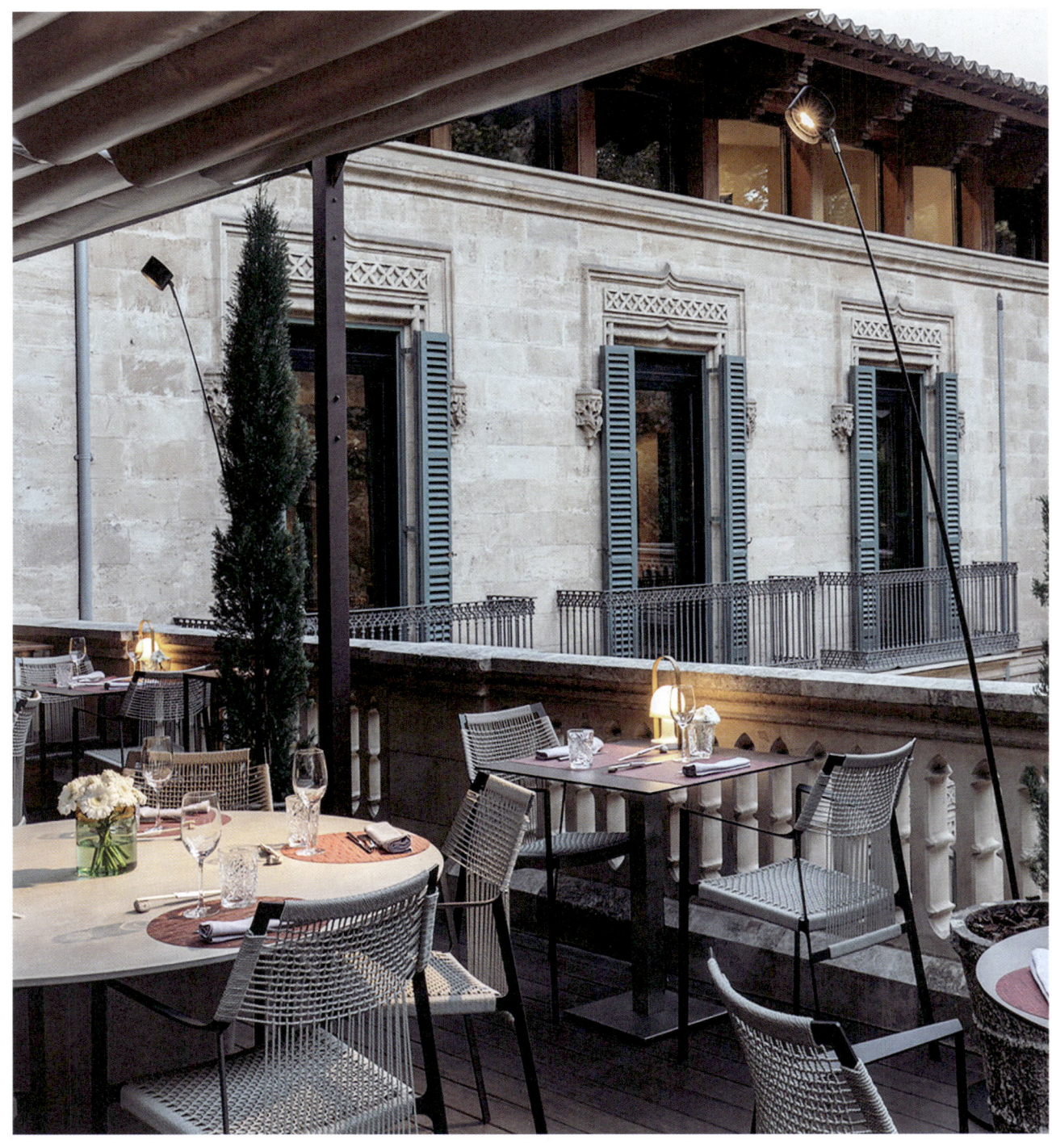

ABOVE AND RIGHT: *Among Palma's most beautiful places is the Passeig del Born. From the terrace of De Tokio a Lima, a view from above opens across the tree-lined square. The fusion restaurant is part of the stylish boutique hotel Can Alomar, located within a breathtaking seventeenth-century palace restored in the neo-Gothic style.*

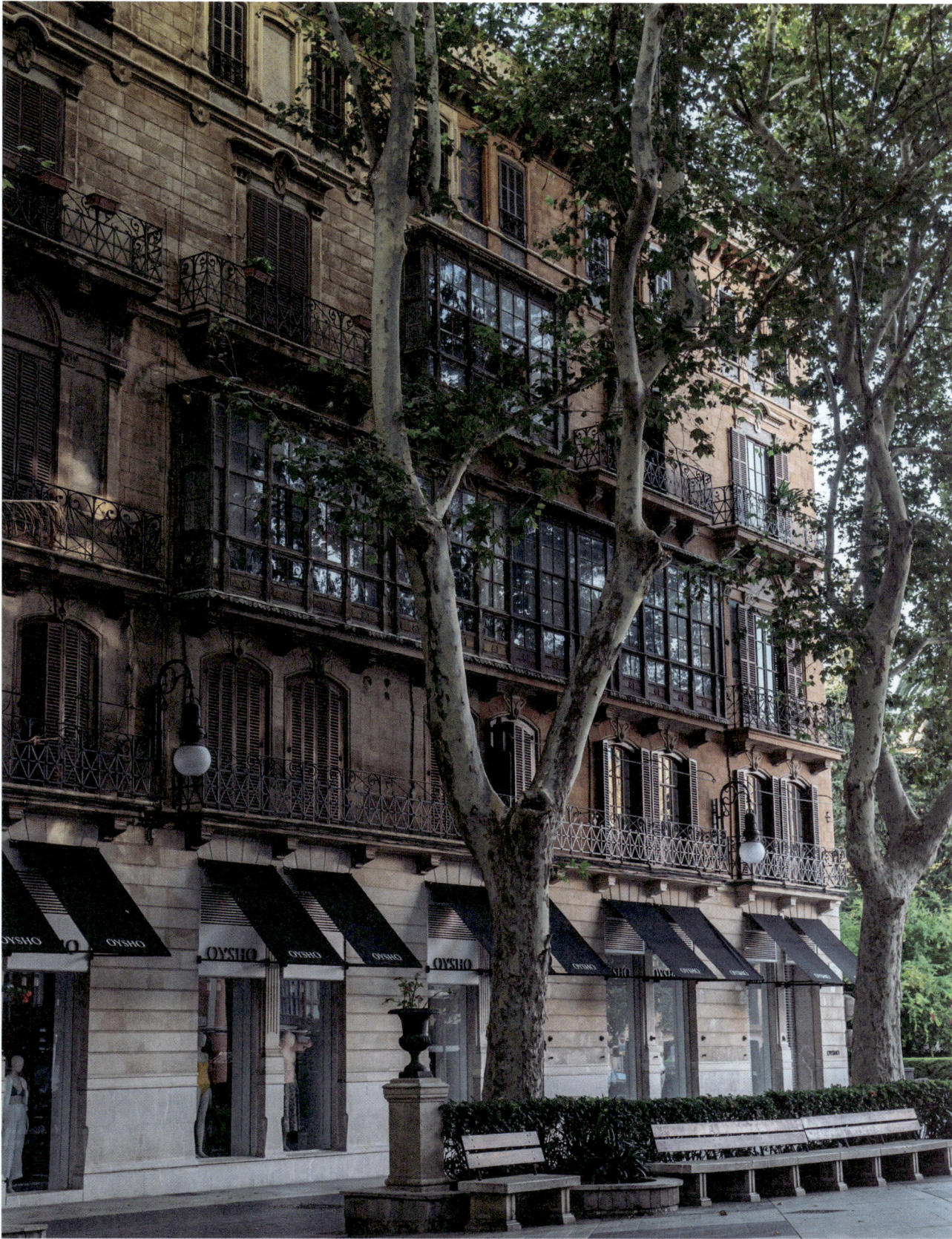

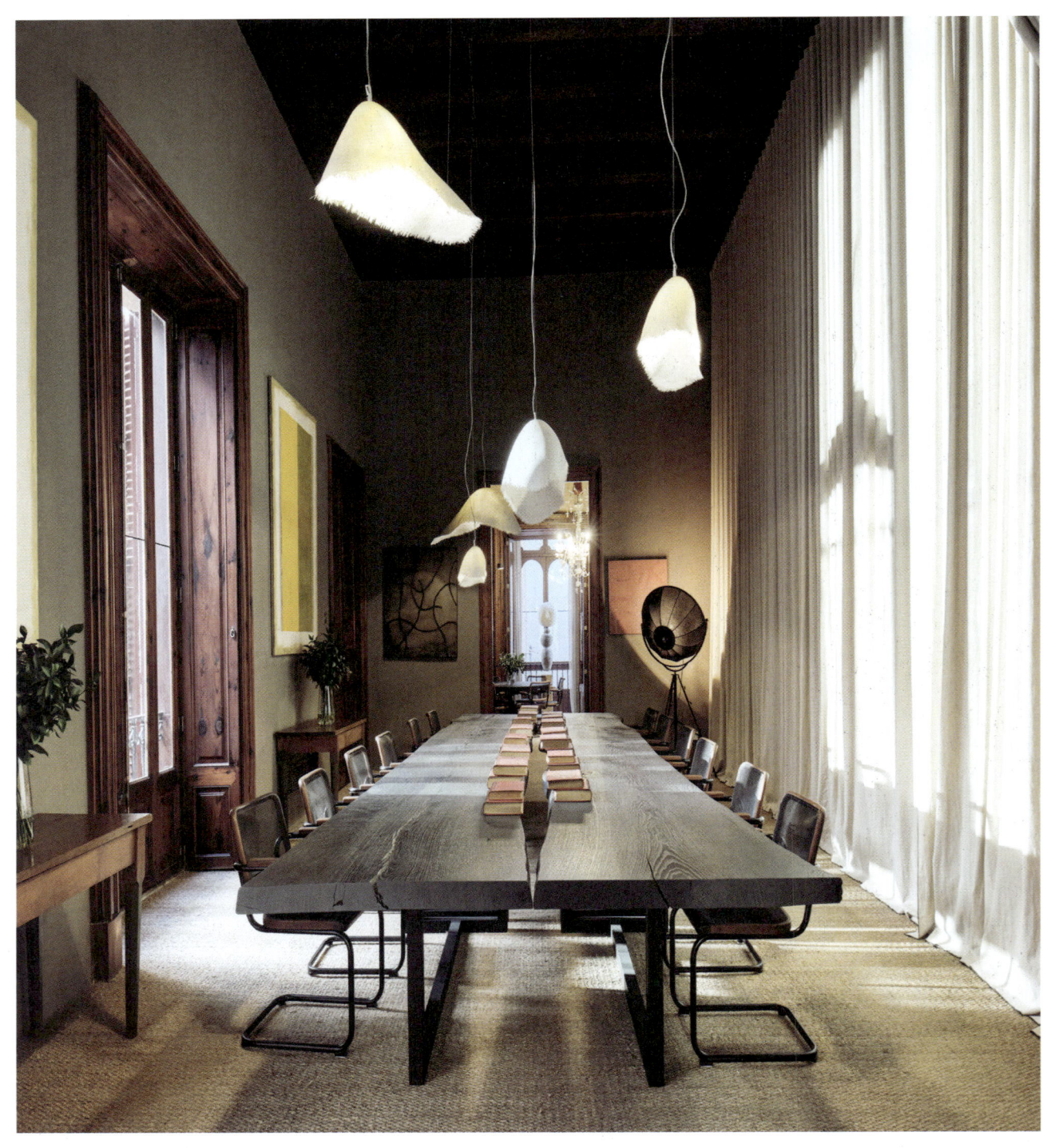

ABOVE AND RIGHT: *Buildings with soaring ceilings, floor-to-ceiling windows, and courtyard patios open to the sky:
this is the typical architecture of Palma's old town. The historic palacio on the narrow Carrer de Sant Francesc houses
the 14-room Hotel Can Cera, furnished largely with pieces from local workshops and studios.*

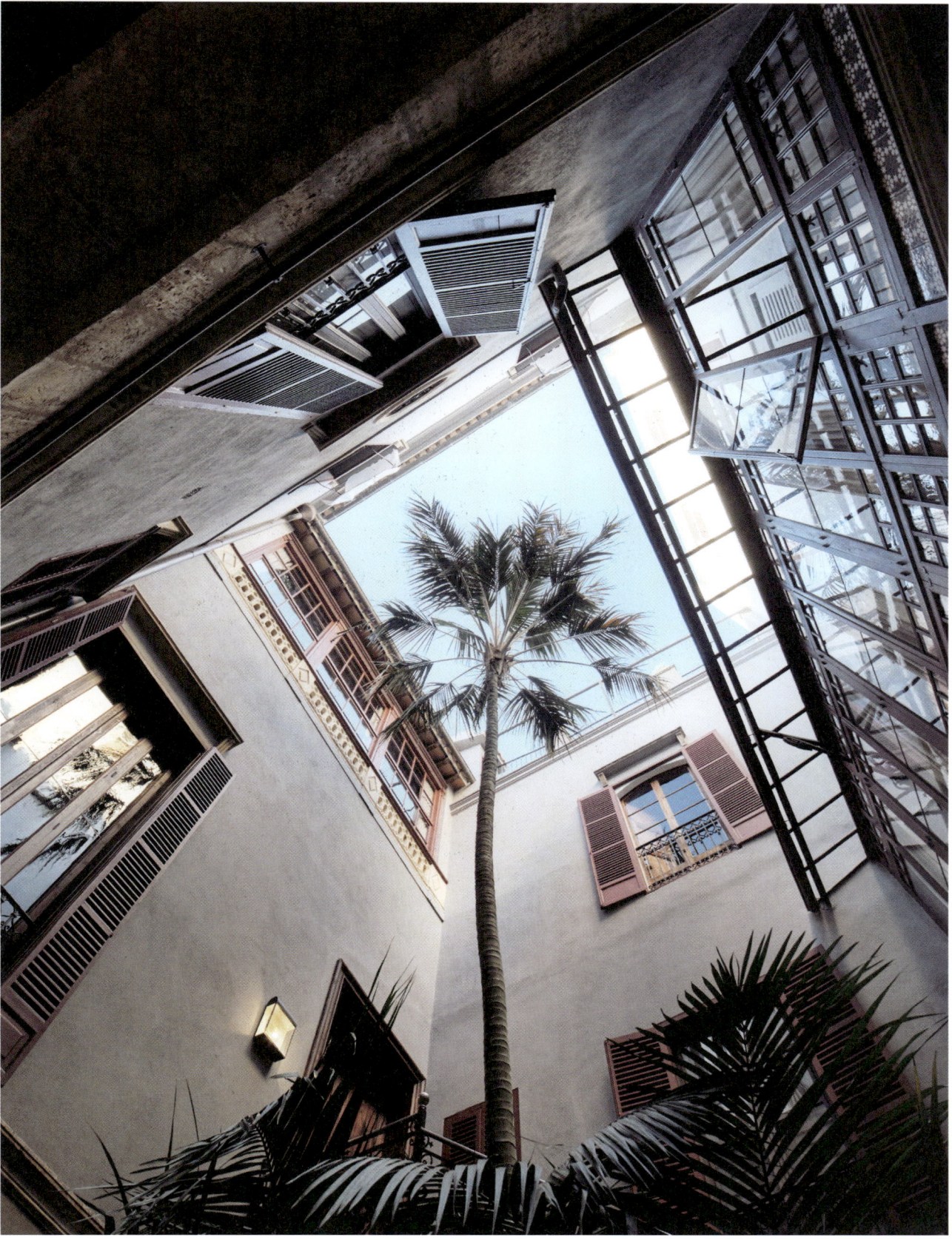

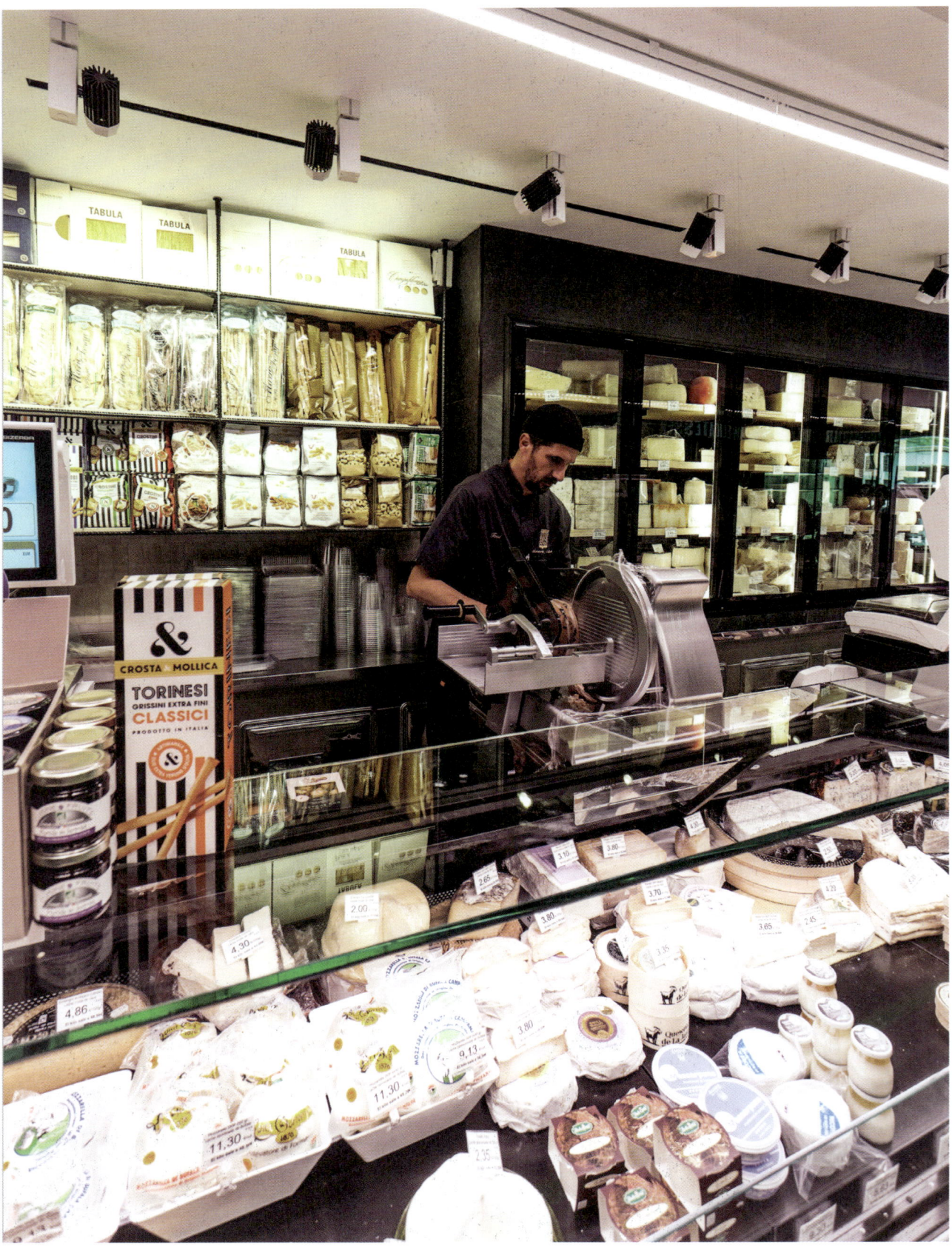

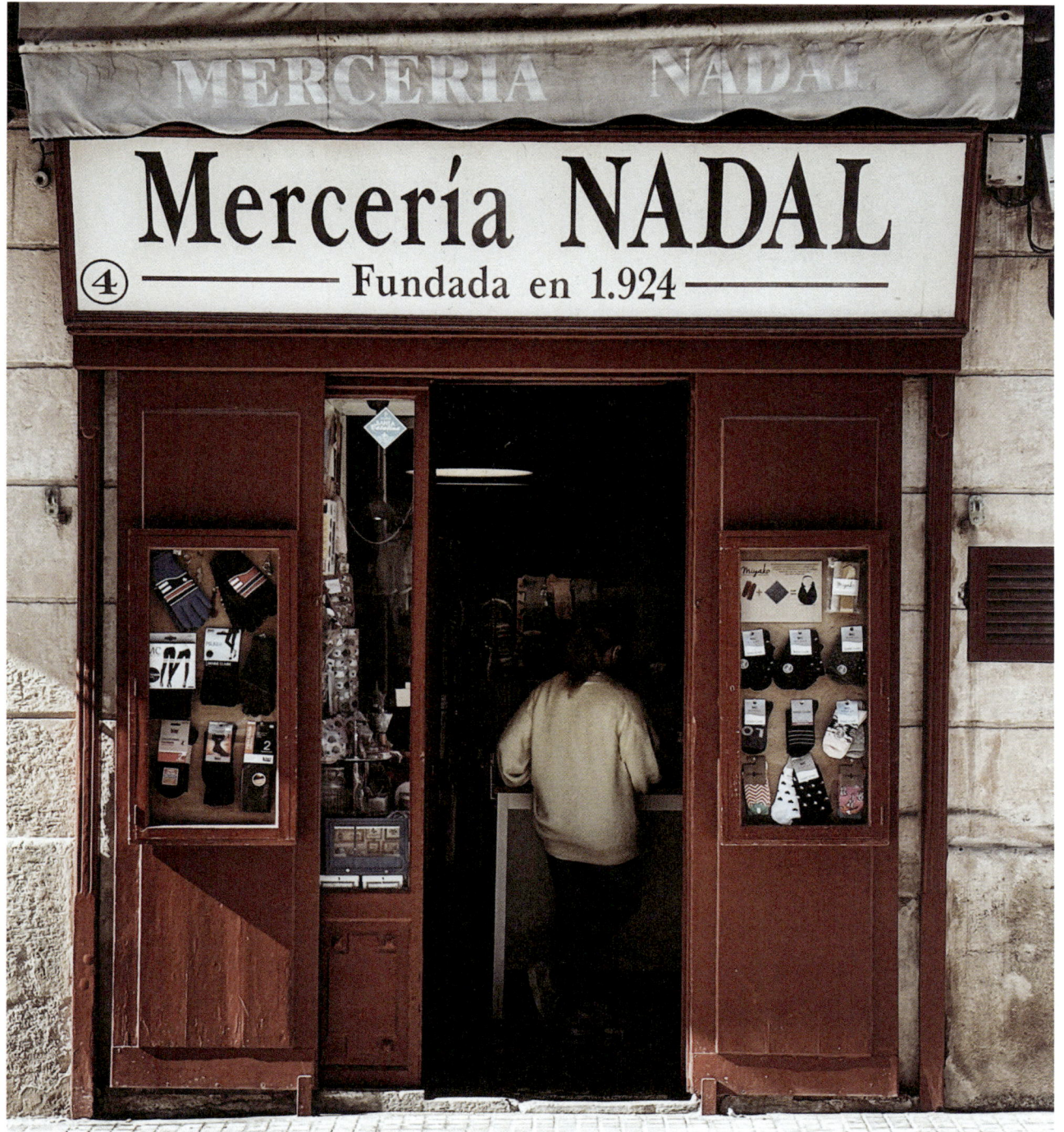

ABOVE AND LEFT: *The former fishing district of Santa Catalina, where local shops sit alongside bars and popular restaurants, neighborhood exchanges, and everyday commerce. Hear the latest local dish over a tasty local dish.*

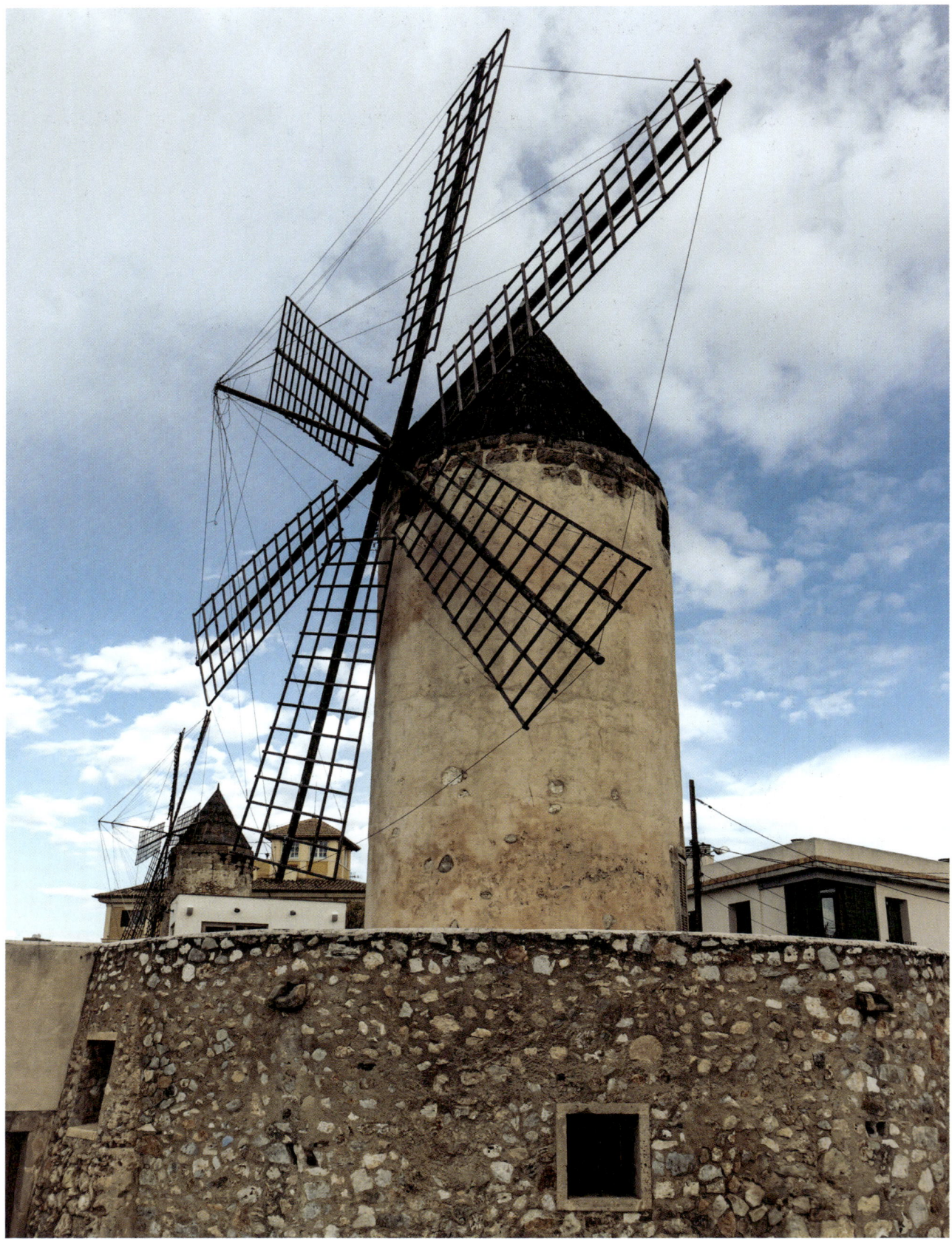

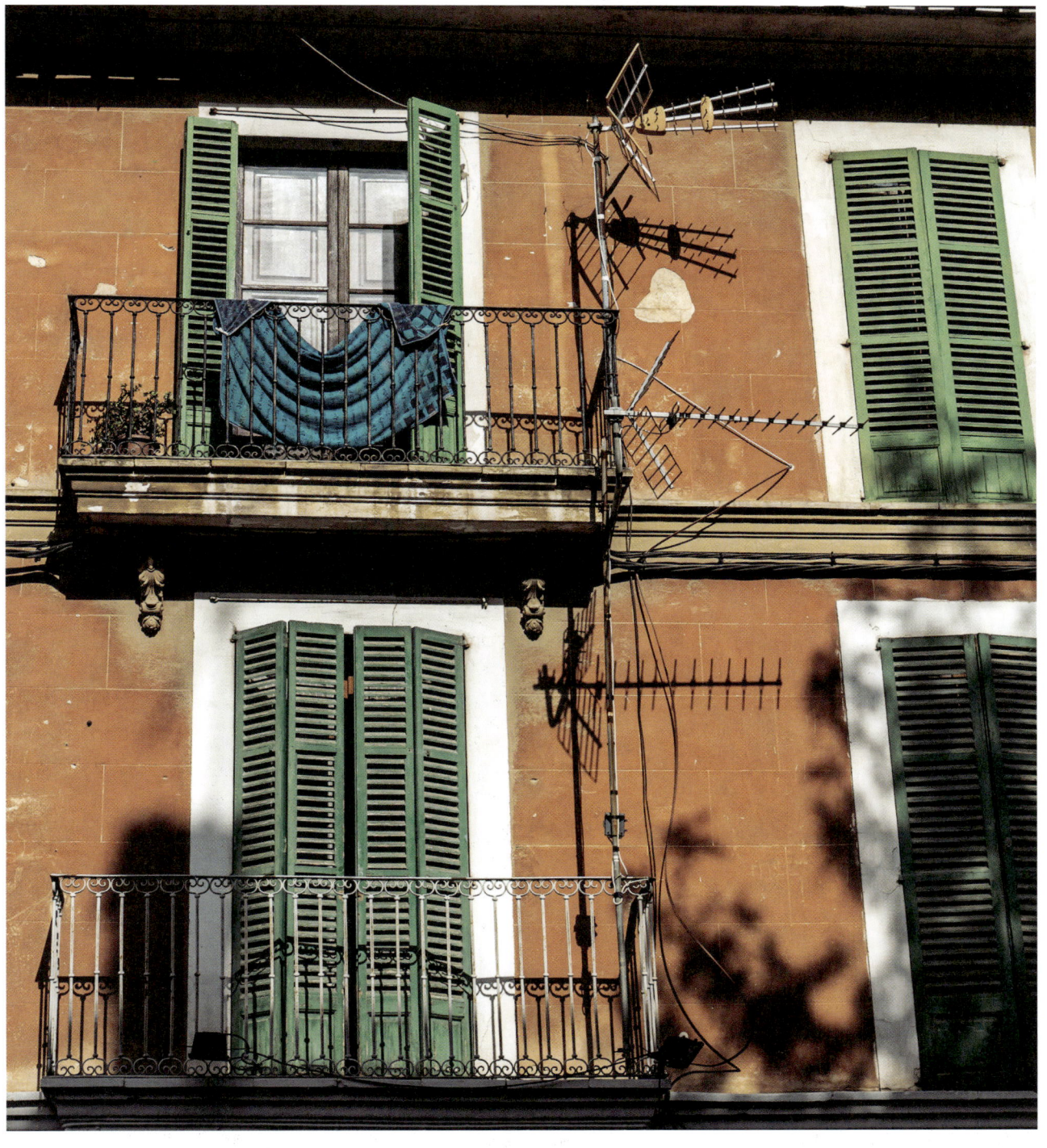

ABOVE: *A room with a view: typical residential building in Santa Catalina, the lively artists' quarter above Palma's harbor.*

LEFT: *Bordering Santa Catalina is the mill district of El Jonquet, with its idyllic houses, narrow lanes, and what used to be wind-powered mills for grain.*

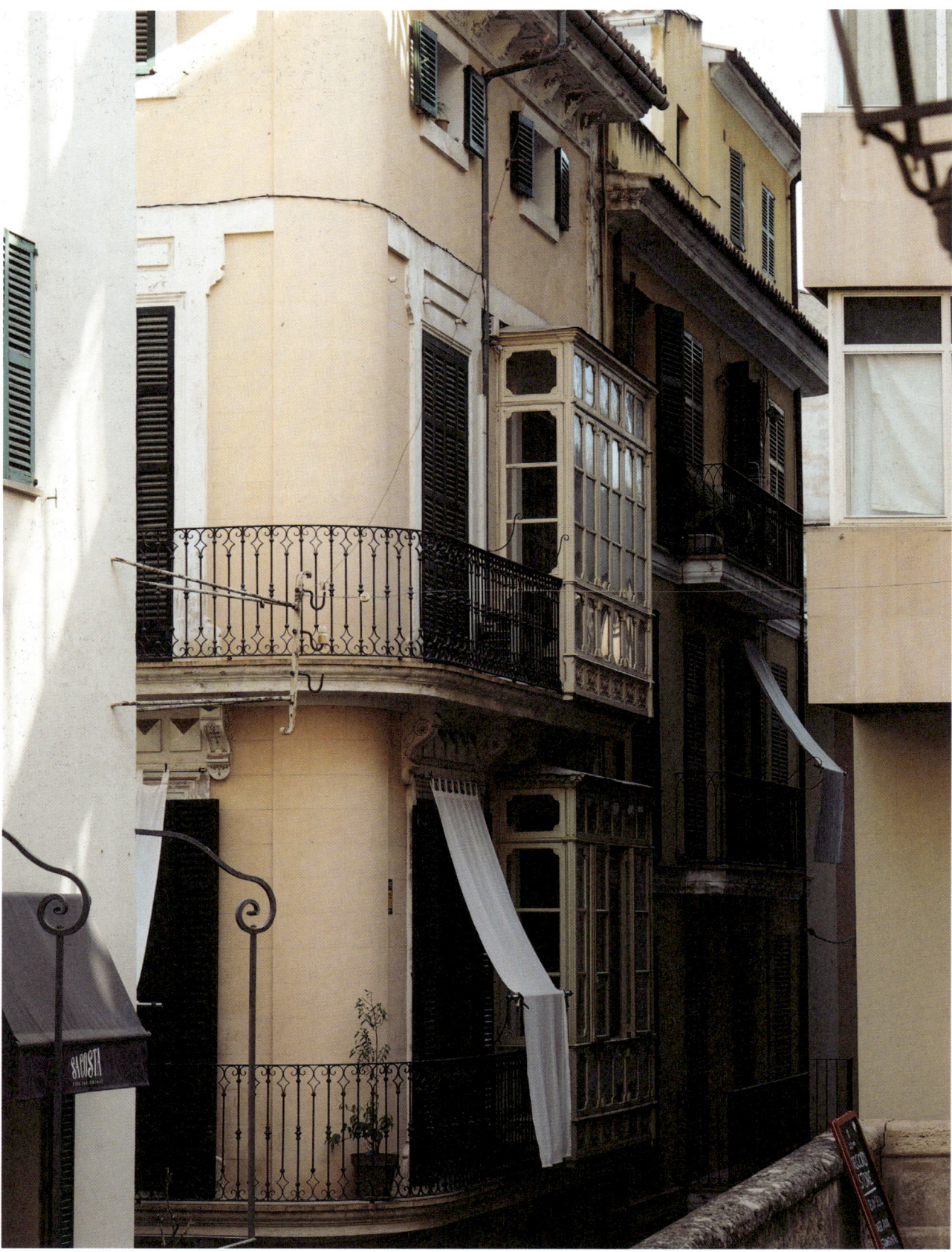

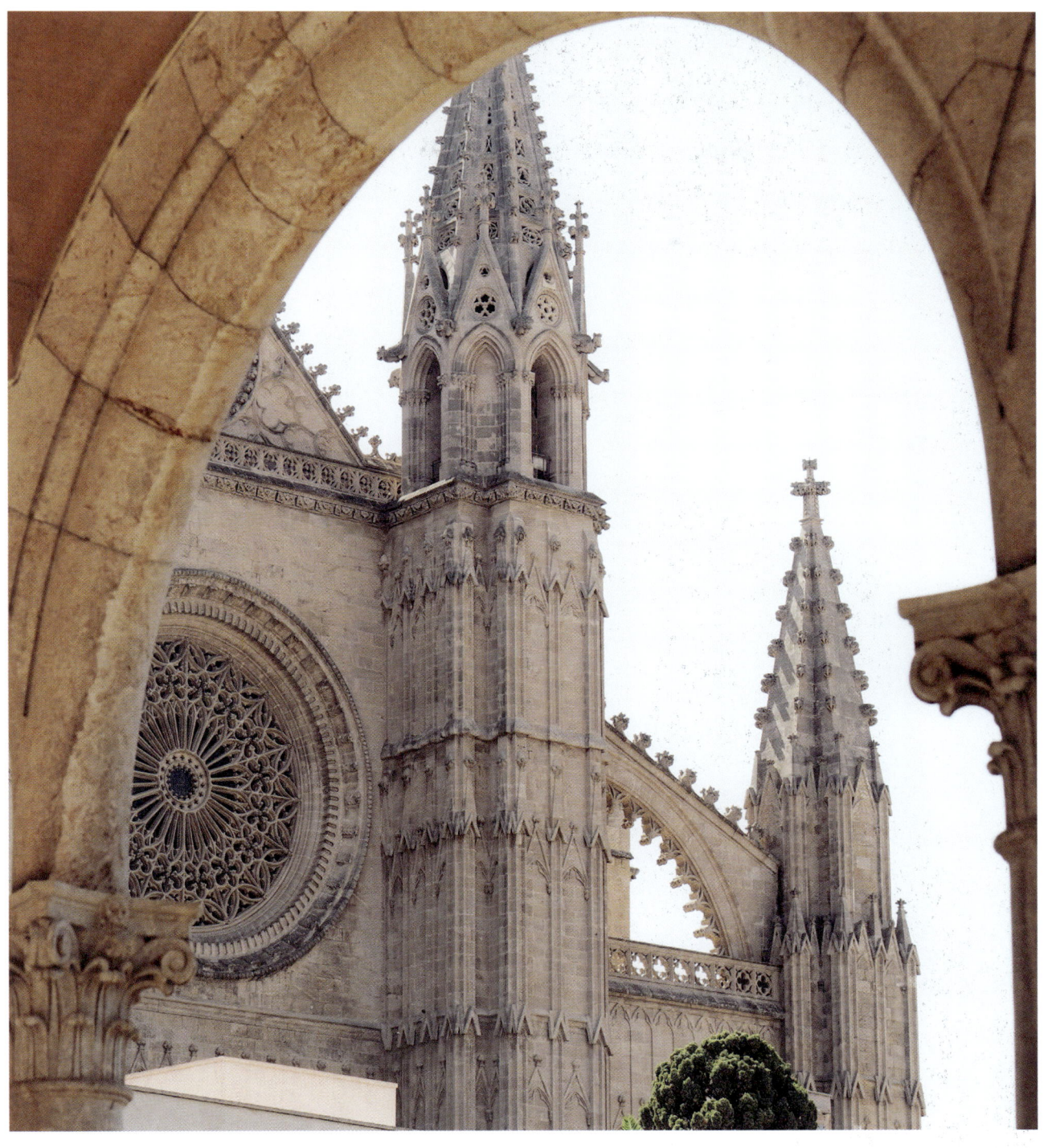

ABOVE AND LEFT: La Seu, *the Cathedral of Santa María de Mallorca, was built on the foundations of an old Muslim fortress as a symbol of the victory of the Crown of Aragón. This impressive Gothic structure is often described as a palace of light, its vast stained-glass windows flooding the interior with color. The rear of the cathedral is flanked by Palma's characteristically narrow streets.*

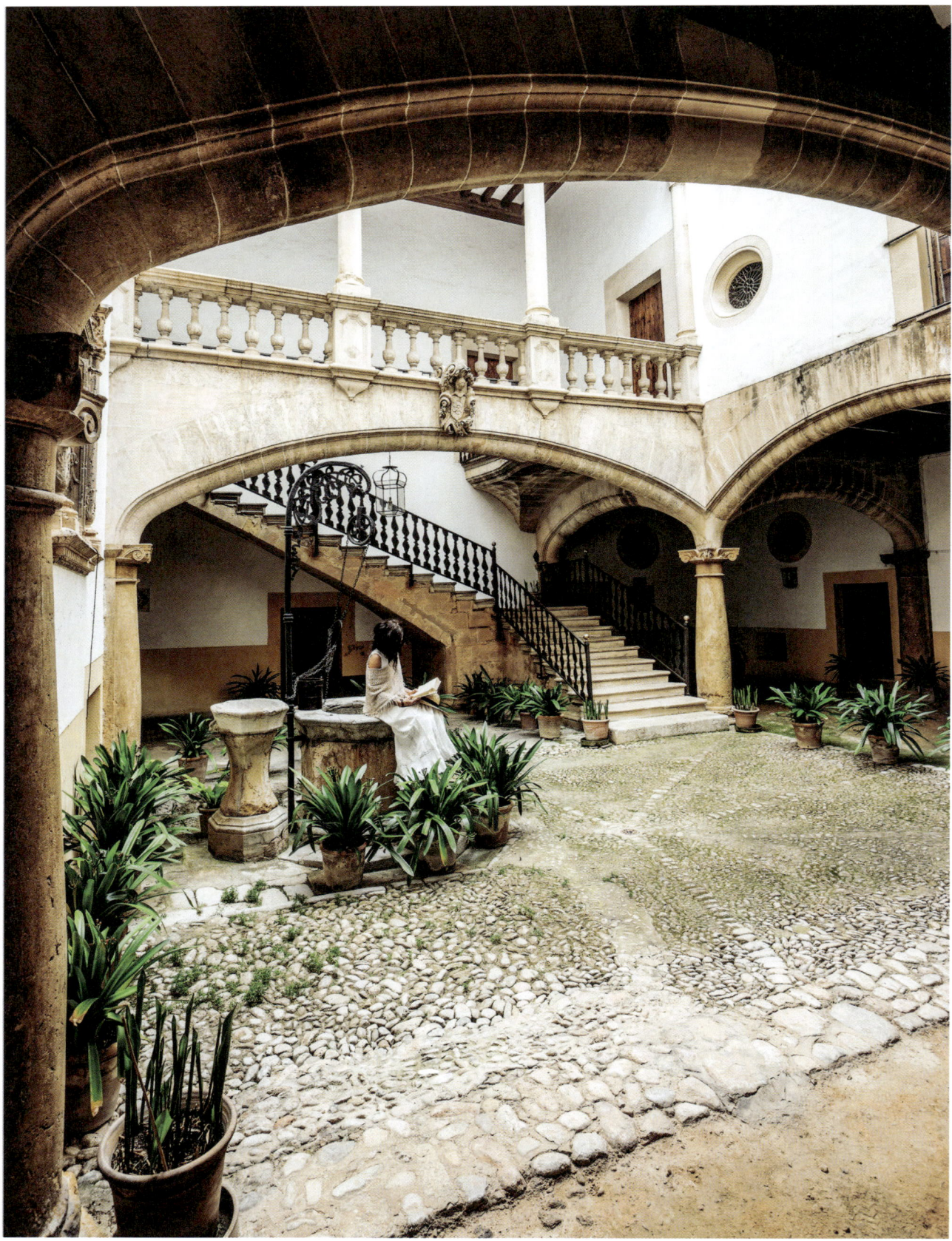

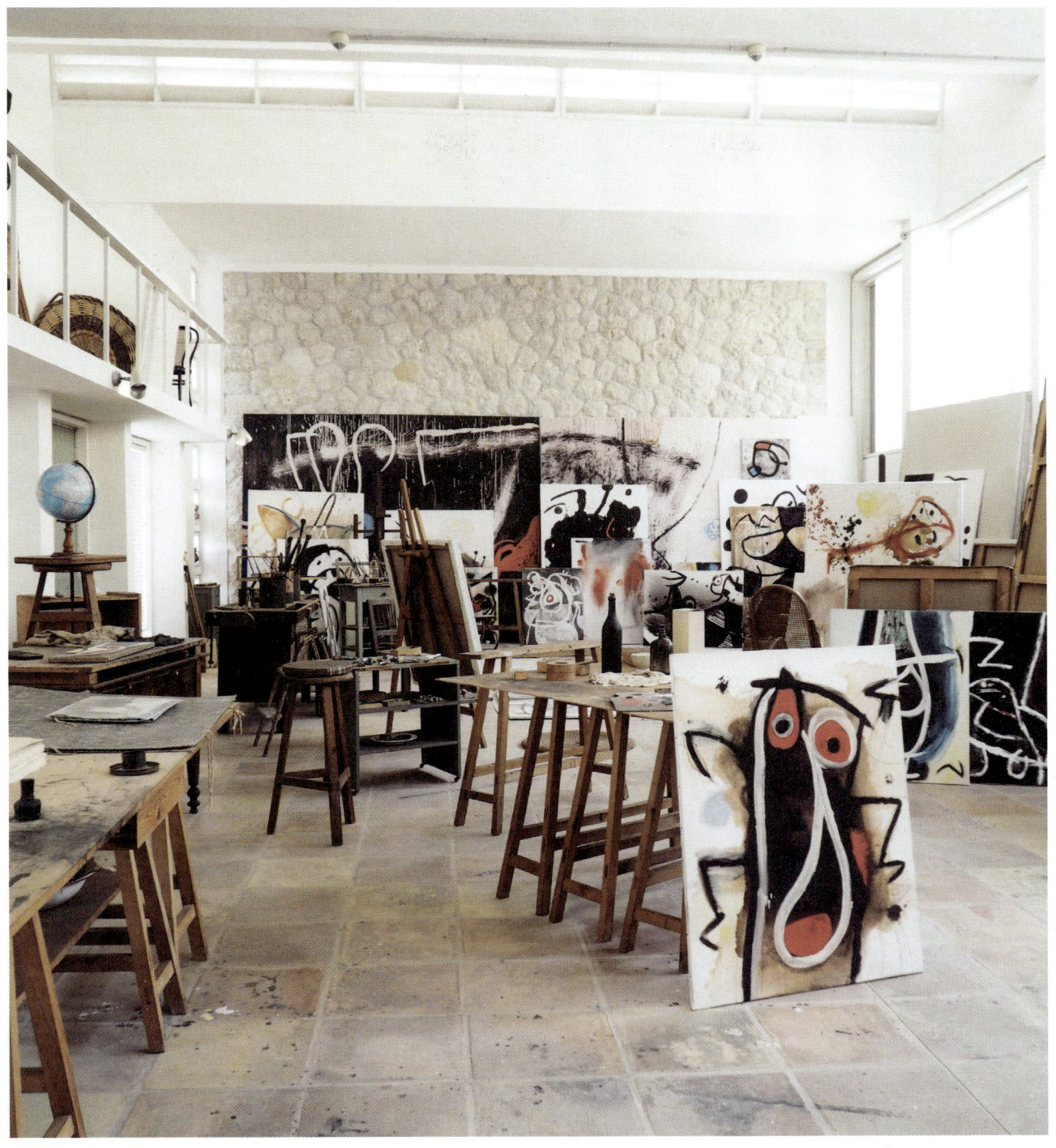

ABOVE: *Creative chaos at the studio of Joan Miró, who moved from mainland Spain to Mallorca in the 1950s. Former workshops and studios and numerous works from the artist's years in Mallorca can be viewed at the Fundació Pilar i Joan Miró in Cala Major.*

LEFT: *The picturesque inner courtyard of Can Oleza, a historic city palace in Palma with Roman foundations.*

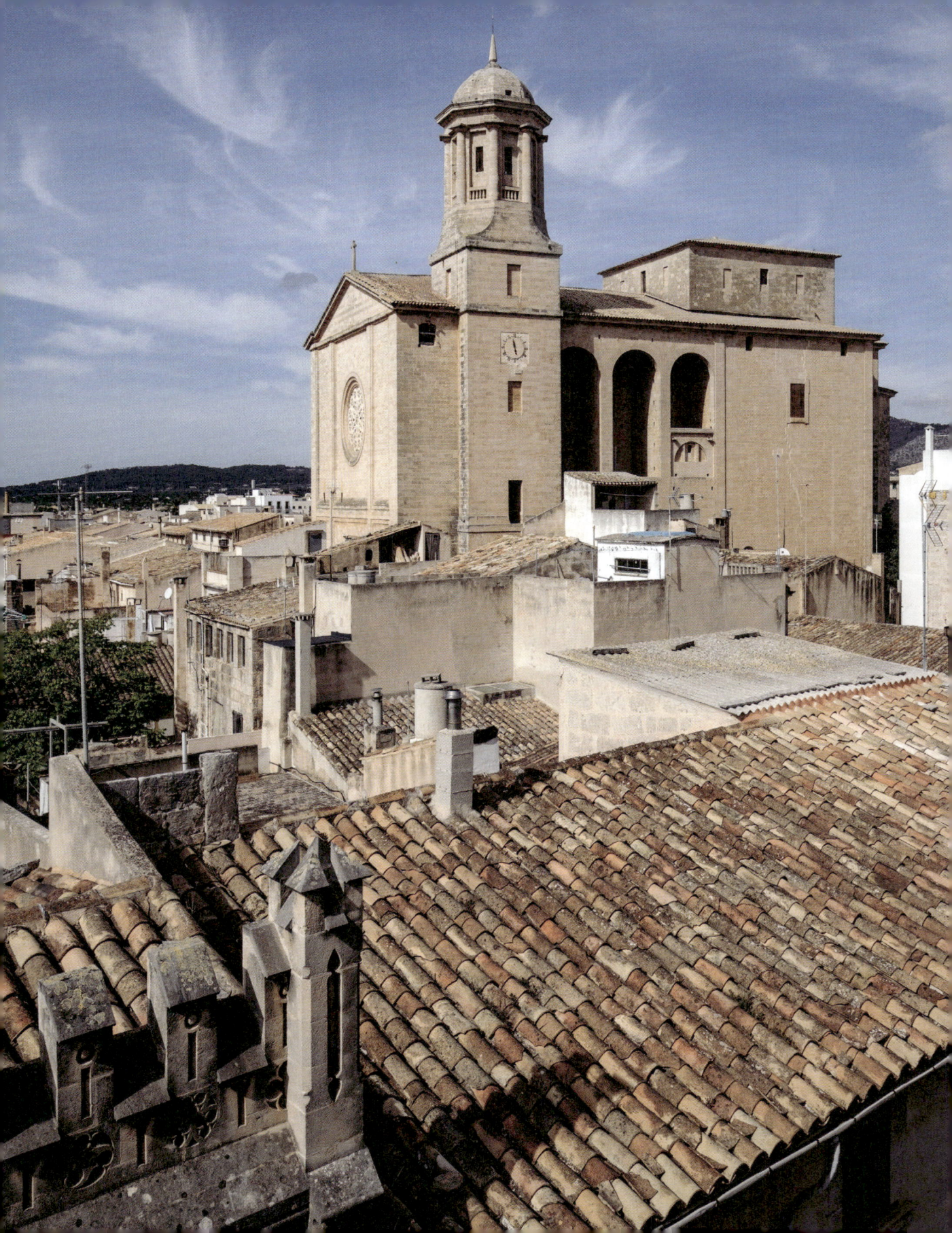

THE SOUTH

FISHING VILLAGES, FORMER PIRATE HIDEOUTS, AND SMALL TOWNS WITH LAYERED HISTORIES

When Mallorcans refer to the south, they usually mean everything from west to east that lies below the Bay of Palma. That includes the widely overlooked rural town of Llucmajor. Despite its size, it rarely appears on standard tourist itineraries. The surrounding countryside adds to its appeal. Almond and apricot groves, low hills, and open terrain lend themselves well to hiking and cycling. Llucmajor carries visible traces of the past. Local history here has shaped both the island and the people who live on it. The same applies to places such as Sant Elm, once a pirate refuge at the island's southwestern tip, or the fishing village of Portocolom in the southeast. Its broad, sheltered bay offers reliable protection from swell, regardless of wind direction, which explains its popularity with sailors. Felanitx follows a similar pattern. The historic town can be explored entirely on foot and turns into a lively flea market and weekly market every Sunday. These are places that invite longer stays. The idea of settling in quietly takes hold. And then there is Santanyí, whose houses and narrow streets possess an appeal that is hard to resist. Historic buildings and traditional crafts have been handled with a deep sense of respect. Old trades continue in updated forms, without being stripped of their character. The south has many sides. Away from large resorts, it offers a sense of calm—to enjoy yourself, to gather your strength, and perhaps even to stay.

LEFT: *The tall tower of the Church of Sant Miquel above Llucmajor, a visible landmark in a town often overlooked by visitors—all the more reason to go.*

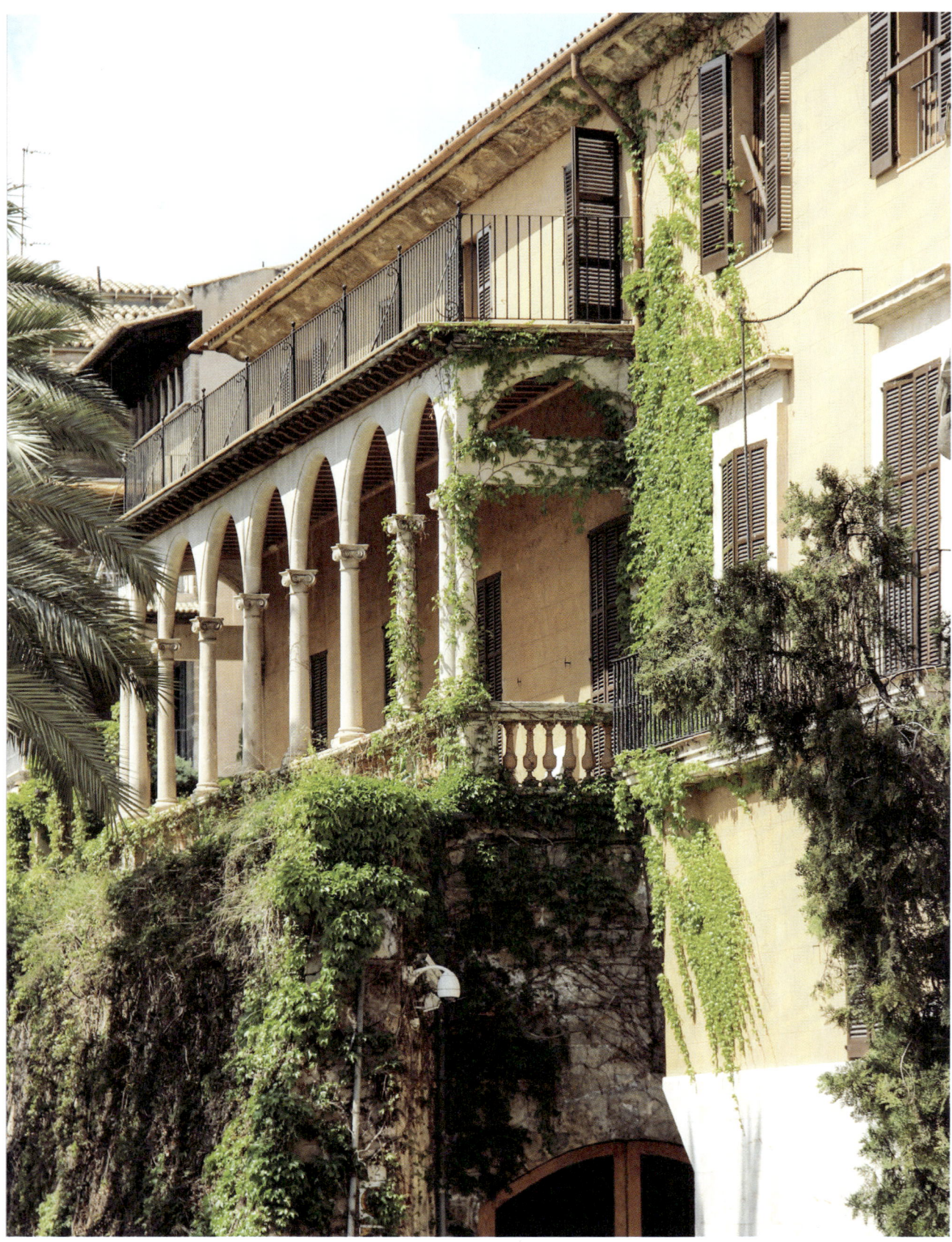

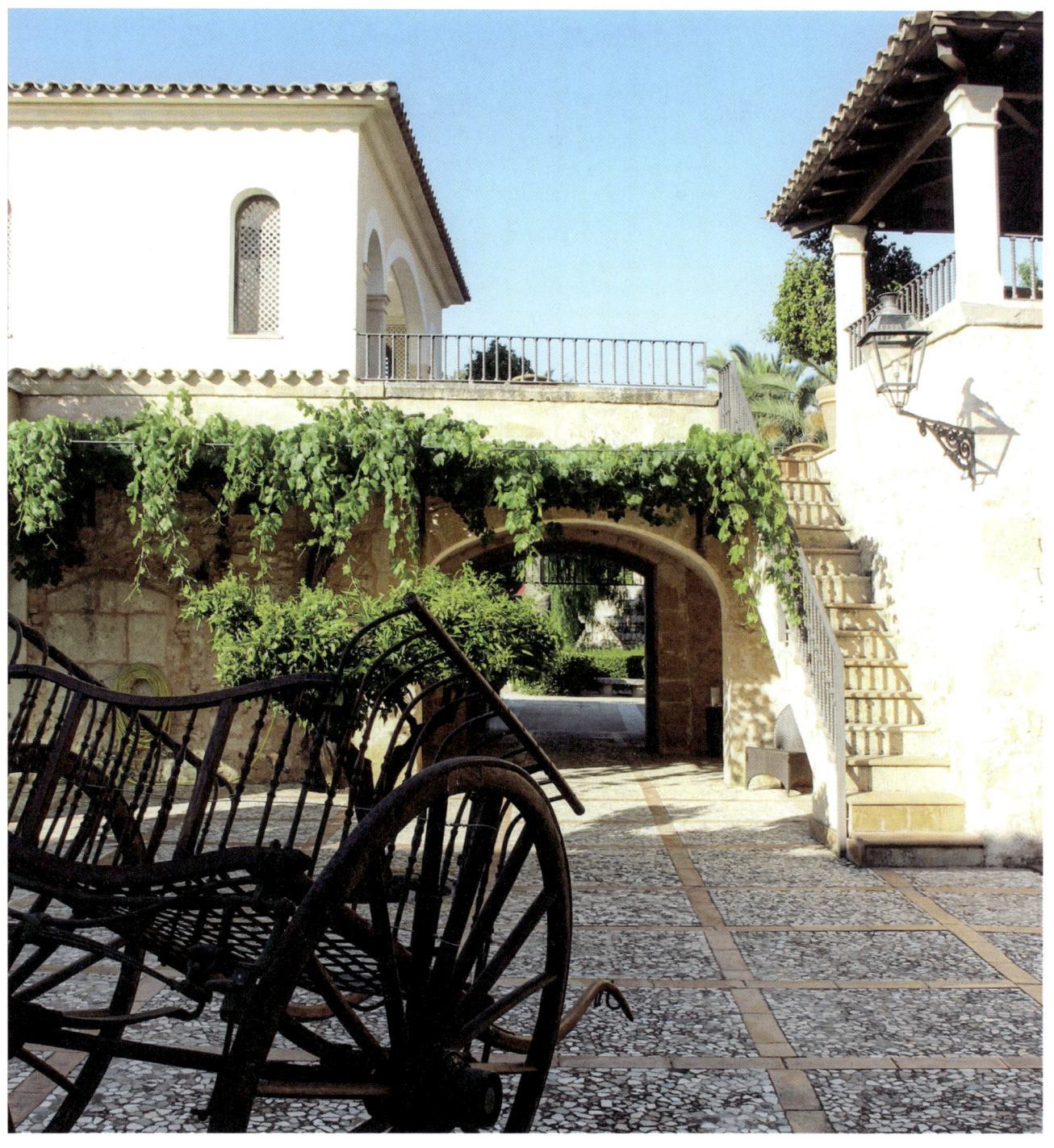

ABOVE: *Tasteful country-house charm at the Son Julia estate in Llucmajor, a fifteenth-century property converted into a boutique hotel.*

LEFT: *Typical Mallorcan street architecture in Llucmajor, with round arches, stone walls, and dense greenery.*

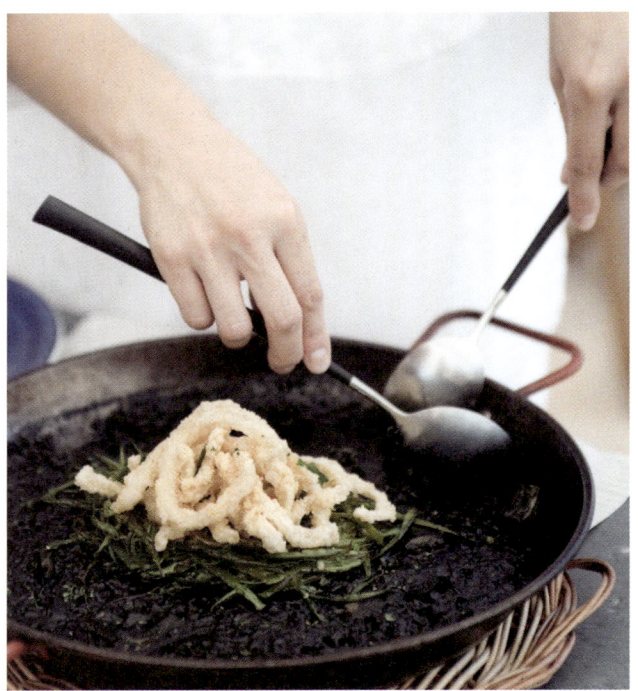

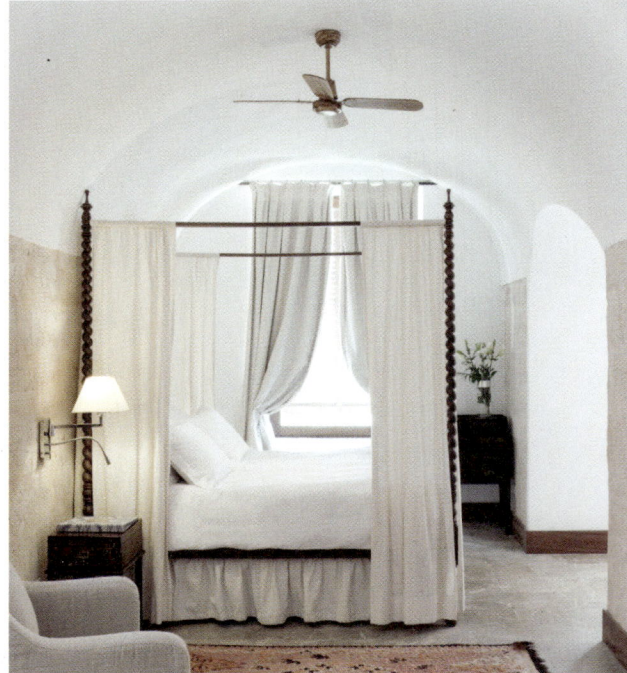

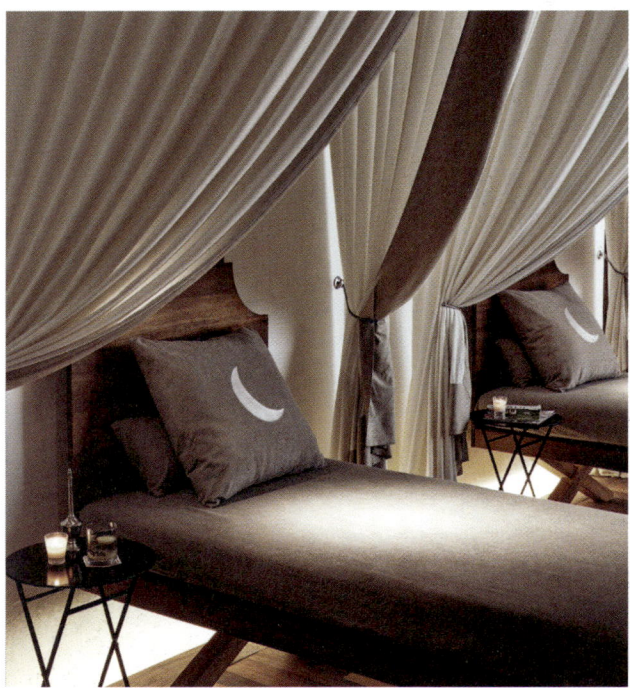

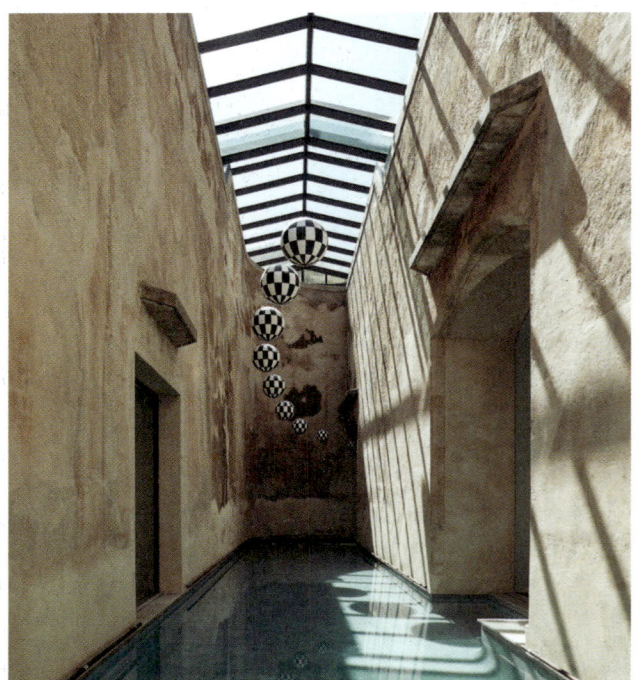

ABOVE AND RIGHT: *In the heart of the protected landscape of Cap Enderrocat, a nineteenth-century military complex carved into the rock has been transformed into a truly exceptional retreat. Today, the partly subterranean fortress is home to the Hotel Cap Rocat, with spa and restaurants, and a clear commitment to nature conservation and soft tourism.*

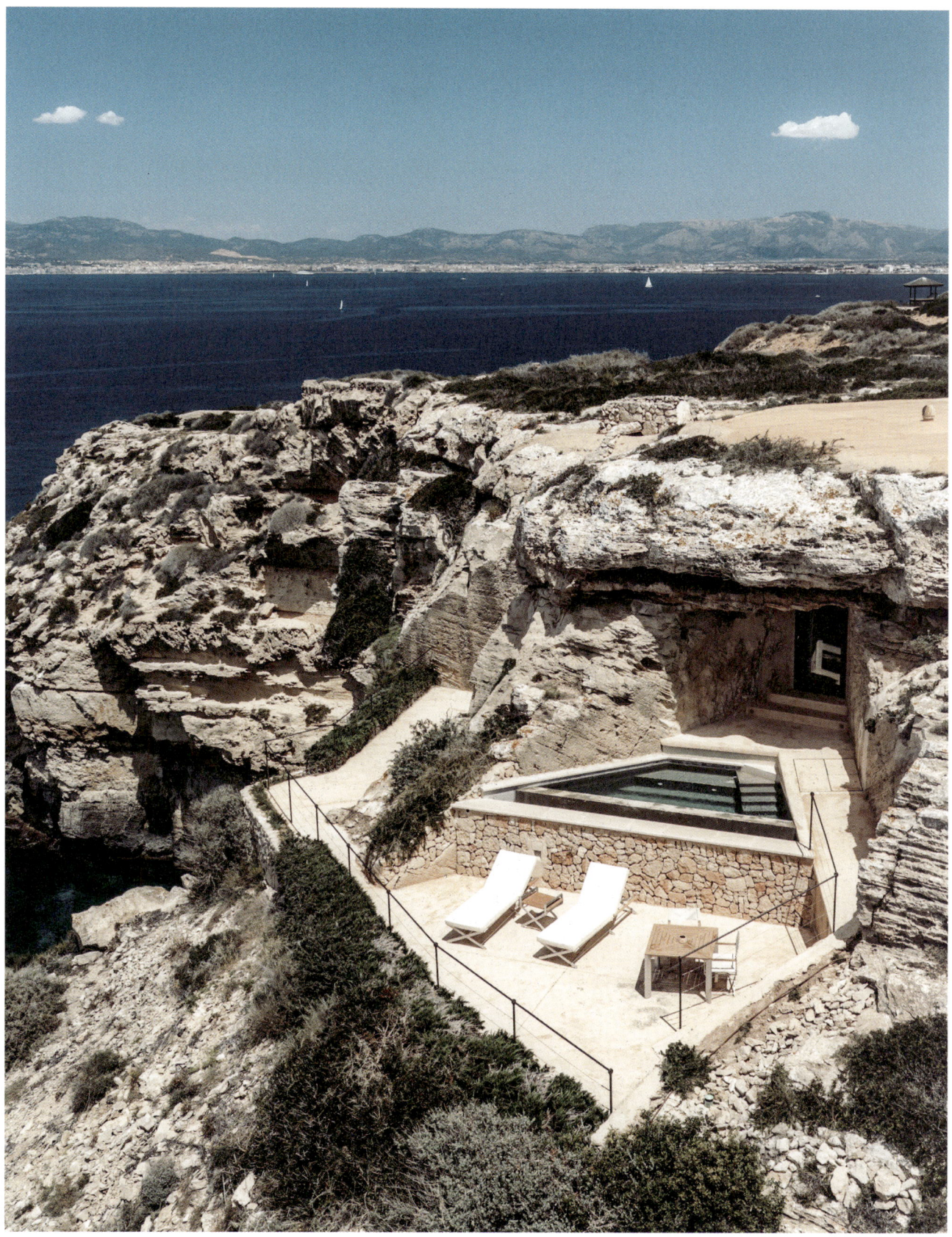

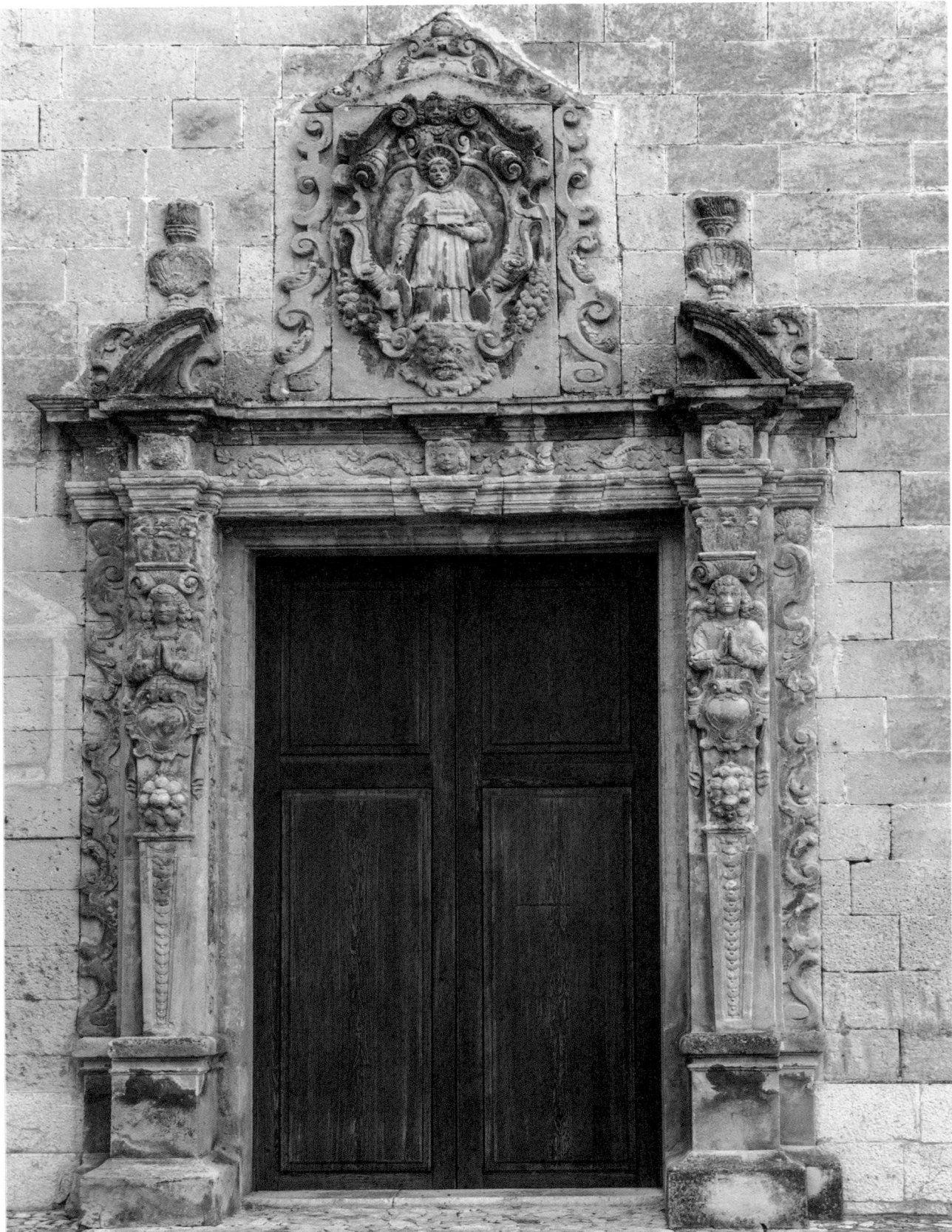

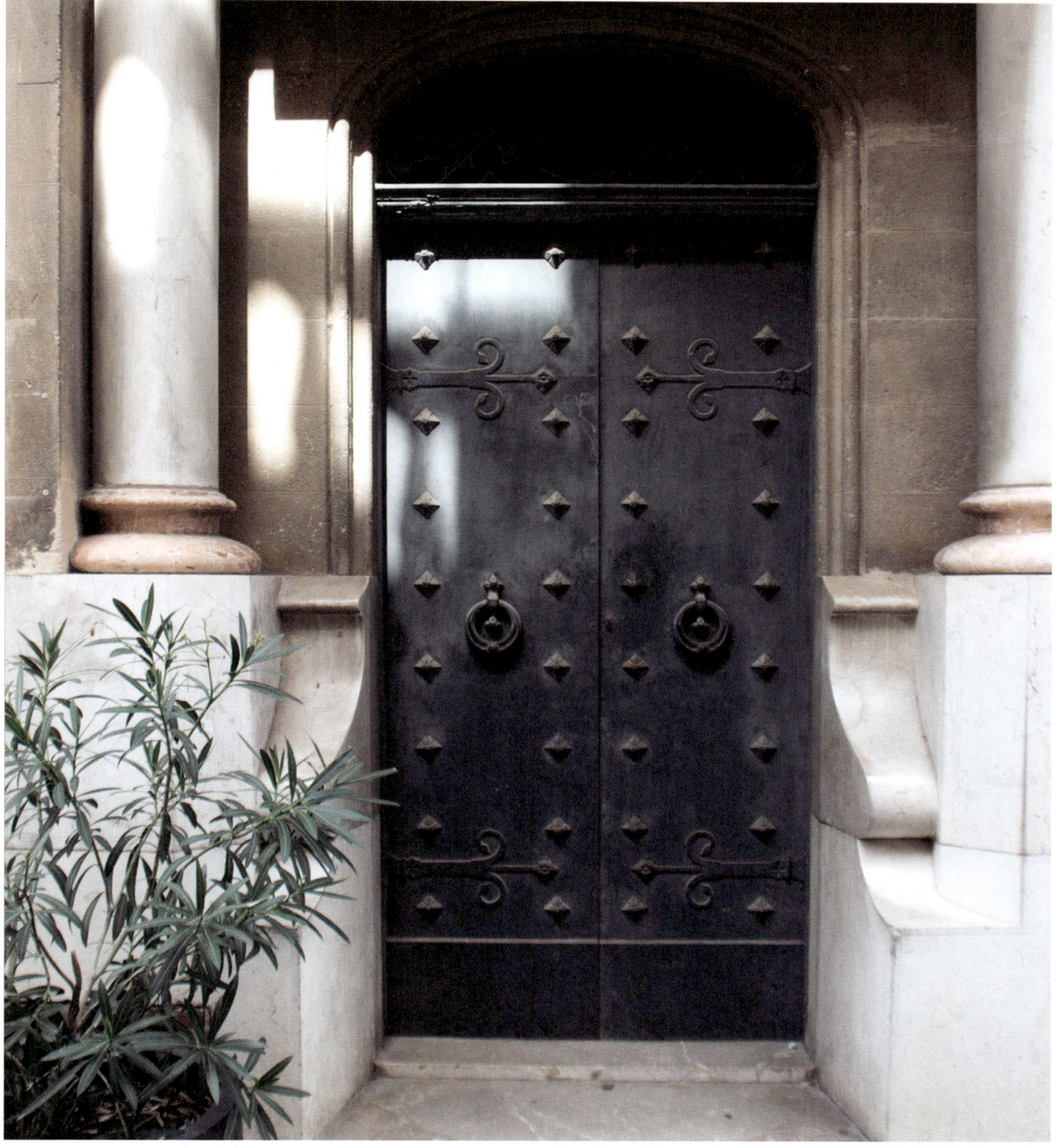

ABOVE: *Who might live behind this heavy iron door? A historic entrance in Llucmajor, with a heavy iron door framed by marble columns.*

LEFT: *The imposing main portal of the Sant Bonaventura monastery in Llucmajor. Inhabited by Franciscan monks in the seventeenth and eighteenth centuries, it later served a variety of purposes and is now open to visitors, who find quiet interiors and notable murals.*

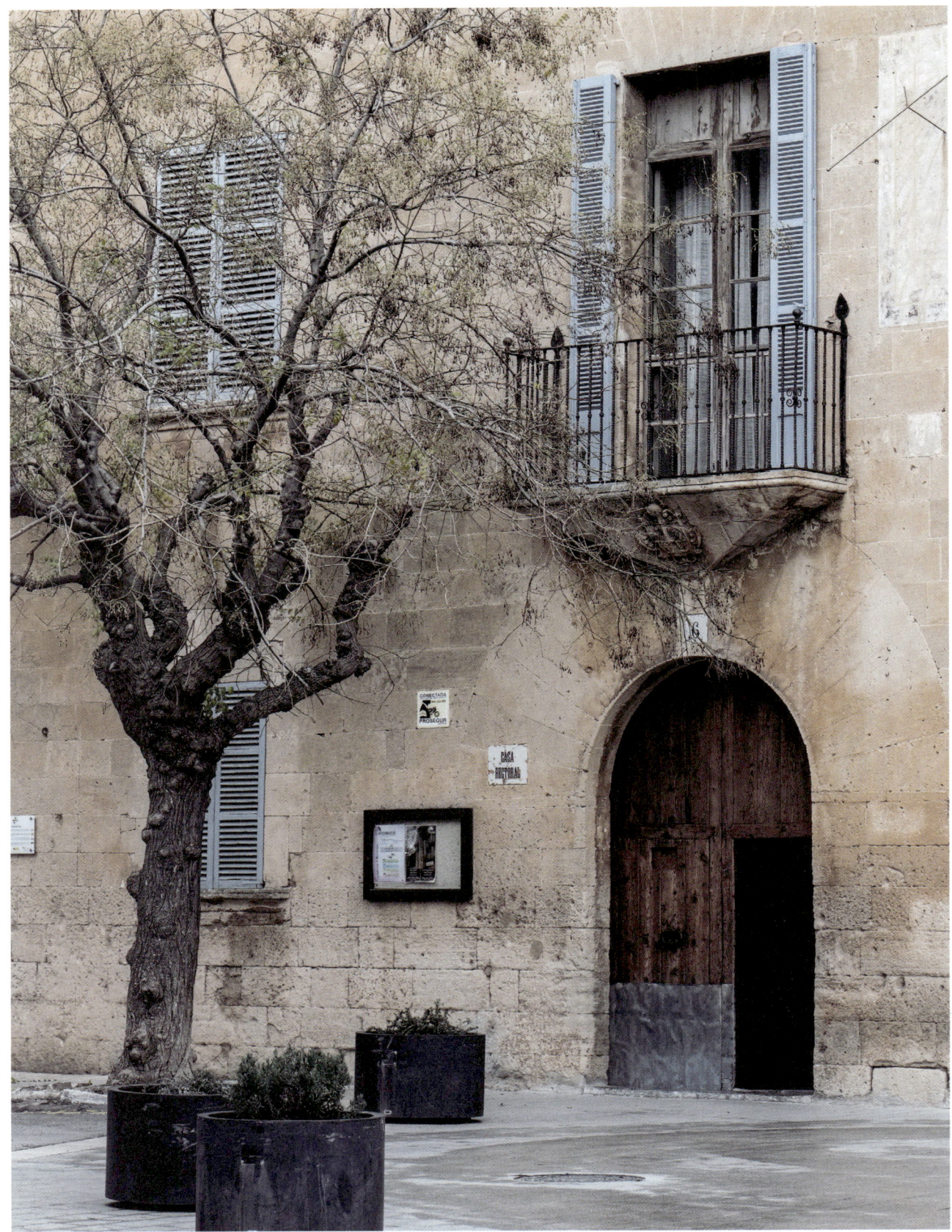

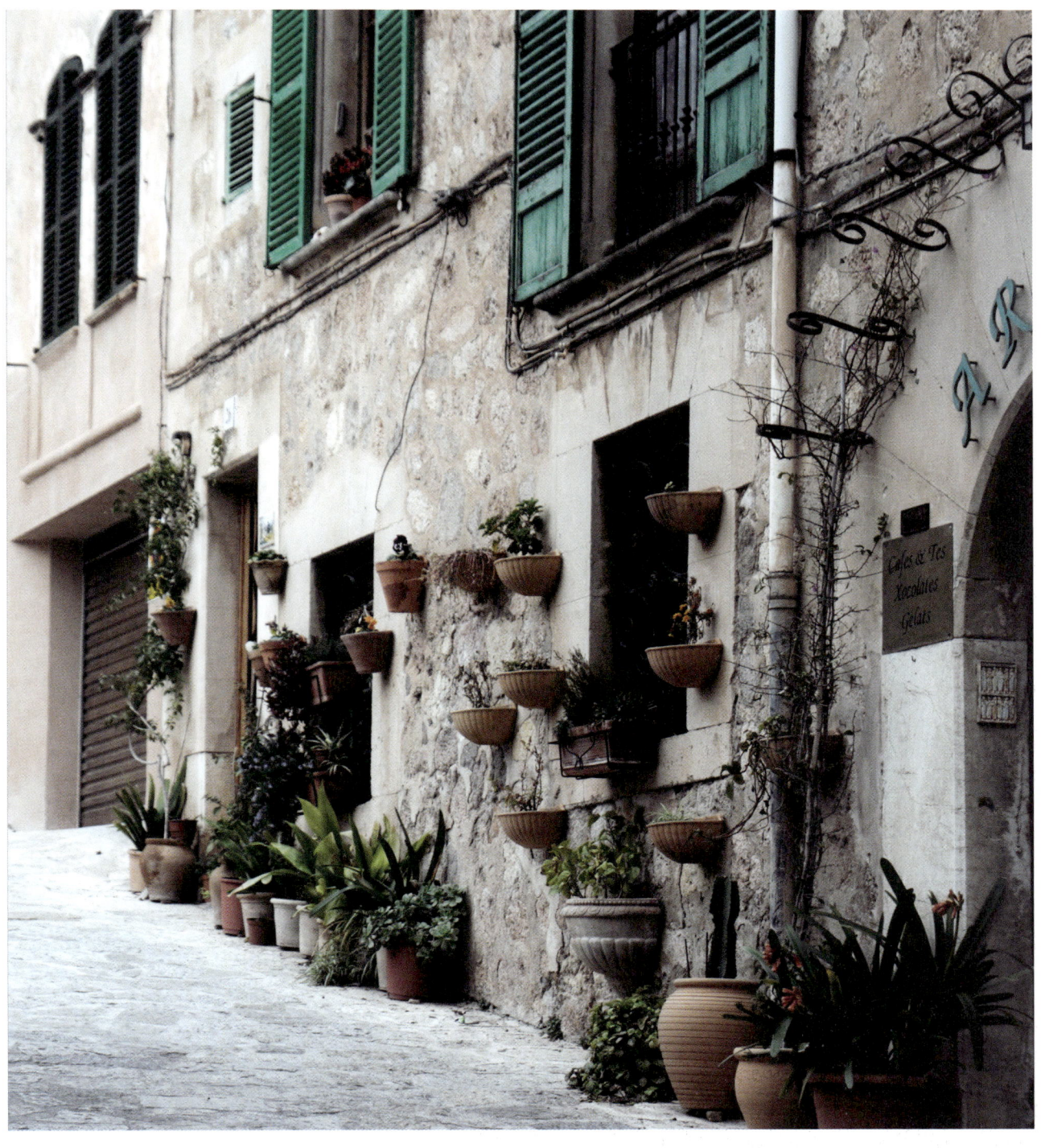

ABOVE: *Insider tip: a walk through Llucmajor's old town, with flower-lined streets reminiscent of decorated alleyways of Andalusia.*

LEFT: *The eighteenth-century sandstone rectory beside the Church of Sant Miquel in Llucmajor, featuring a carved coat-of-arms portal.*

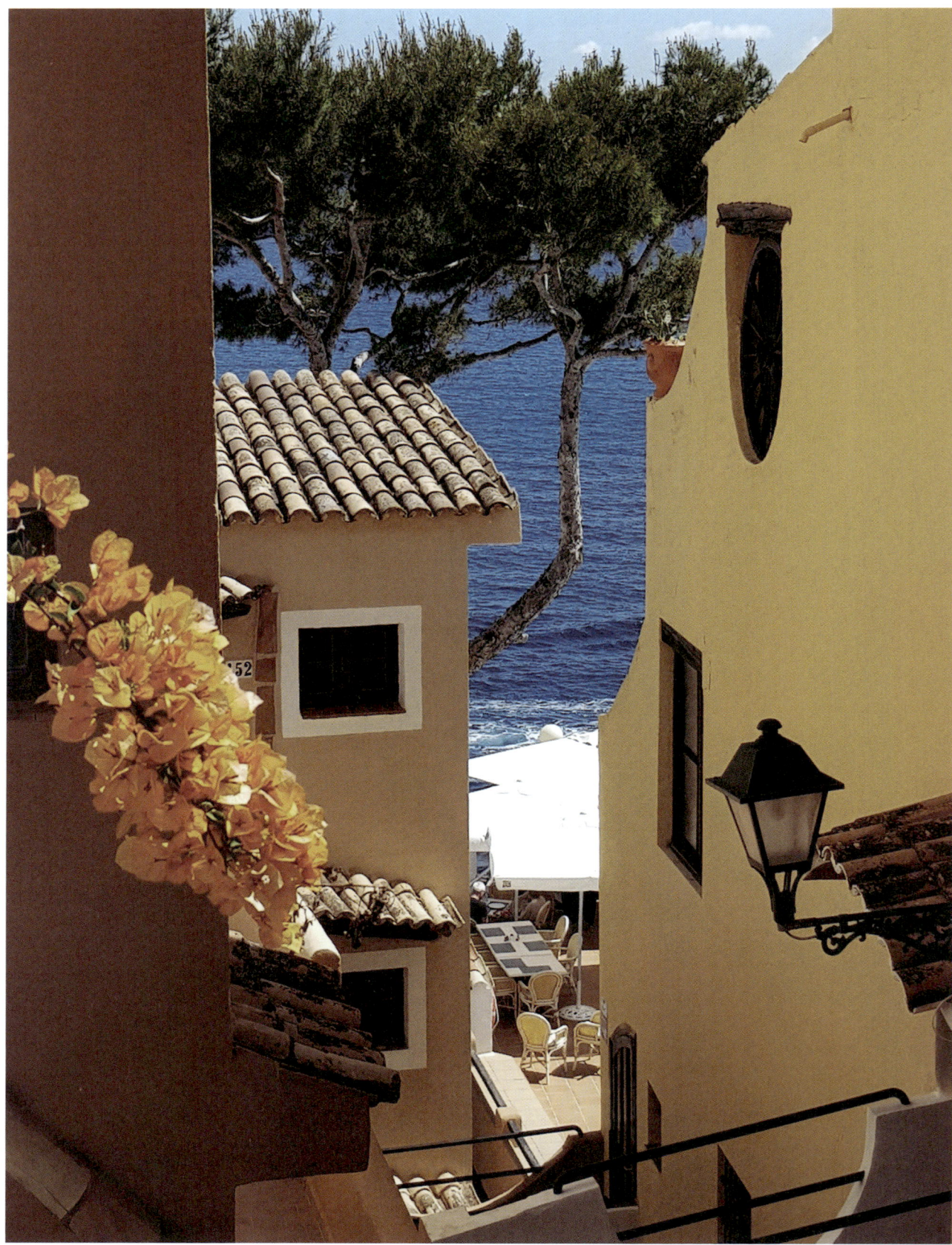

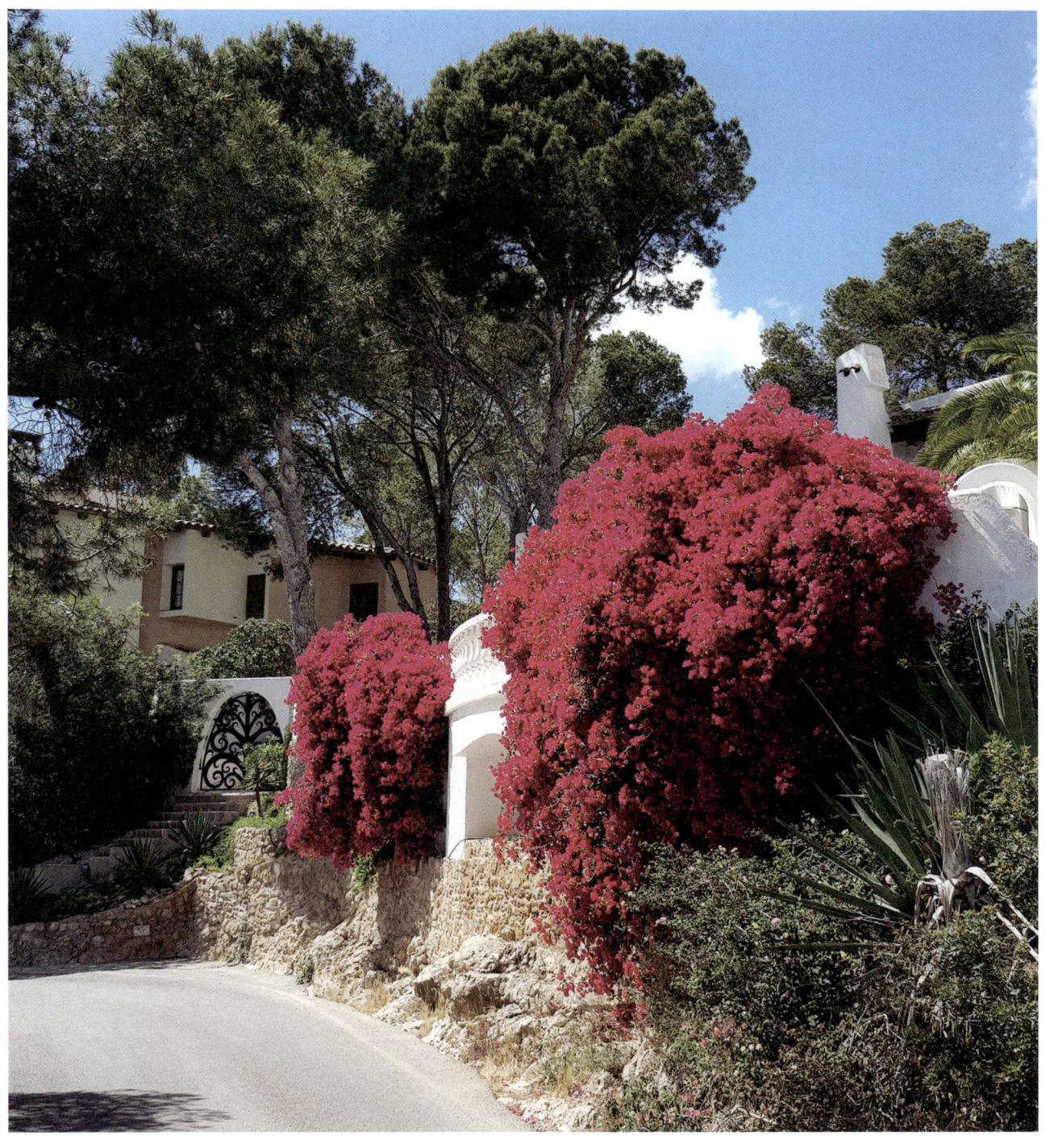

ABOVE: *Everything is aglow: bougainvillea in full bloom, with vivid pink and red tones made possible several times a year by the Mallorcan climate.*

LEFT: *Rare orange bougainvillea in a narrow lane in Cala Fornells, with views toward the sea.*

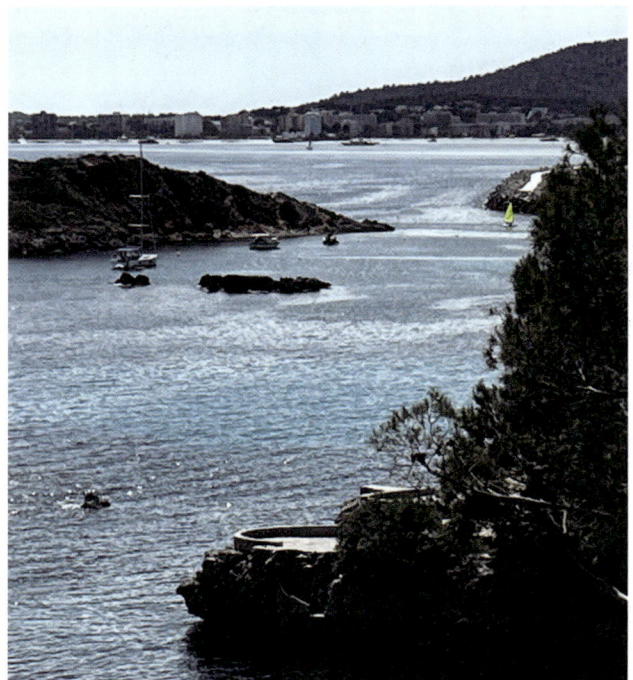
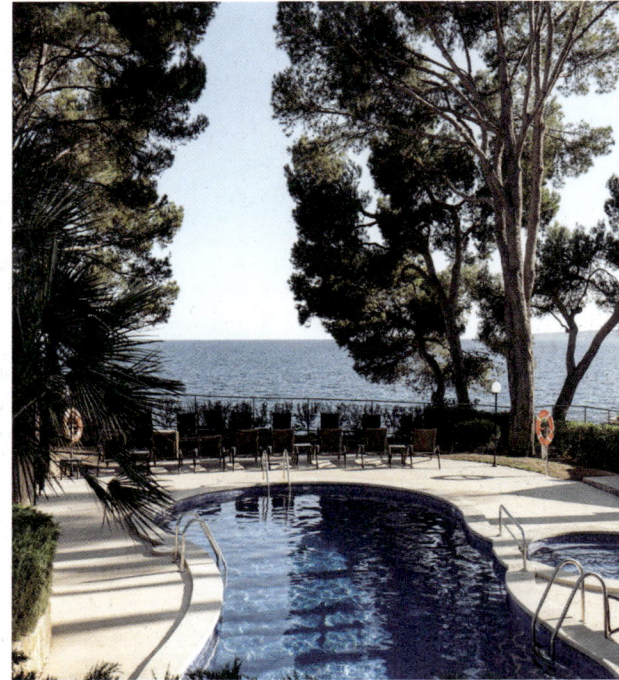
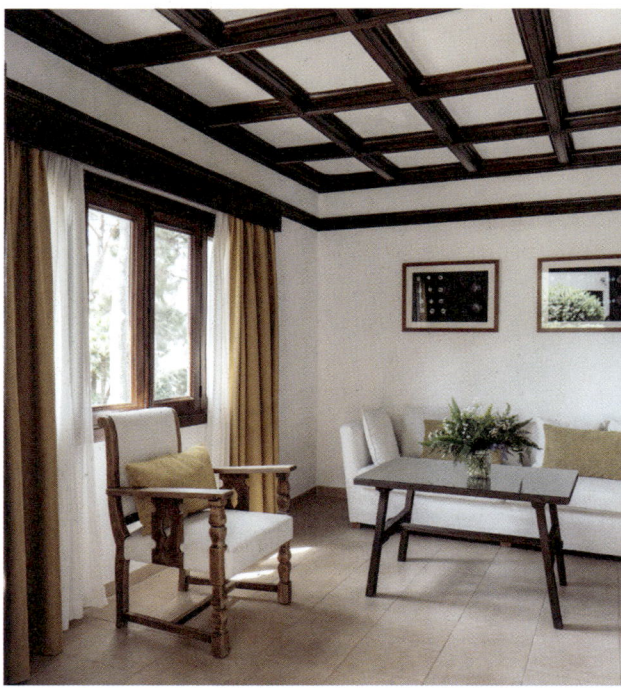
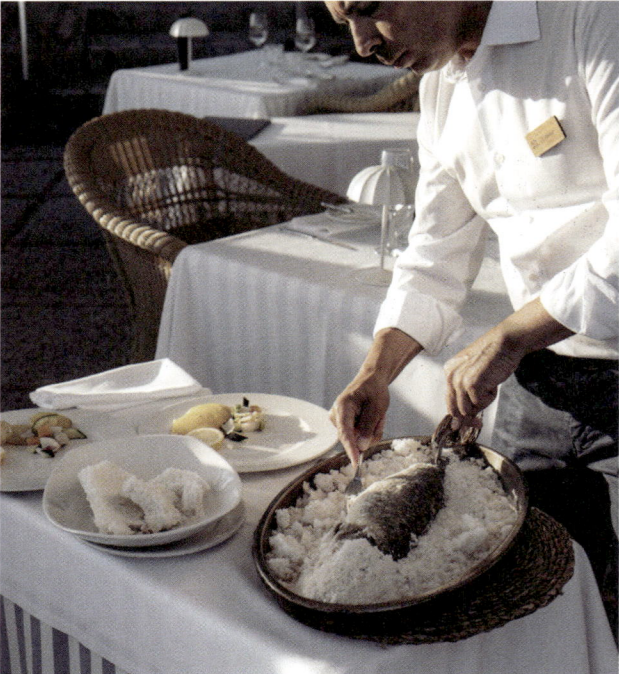

ABOVE AND RIGHT: *A sublime idea: savoring sea bass baked in a salt crust during the blue hour.*
The Las Terrazas de Bendinat restaurant in Portals Nous is one of Mallorca's most beautiful places and part of the
long-established Hotel Bendinat, built on a rocky outcrop directly above the water.

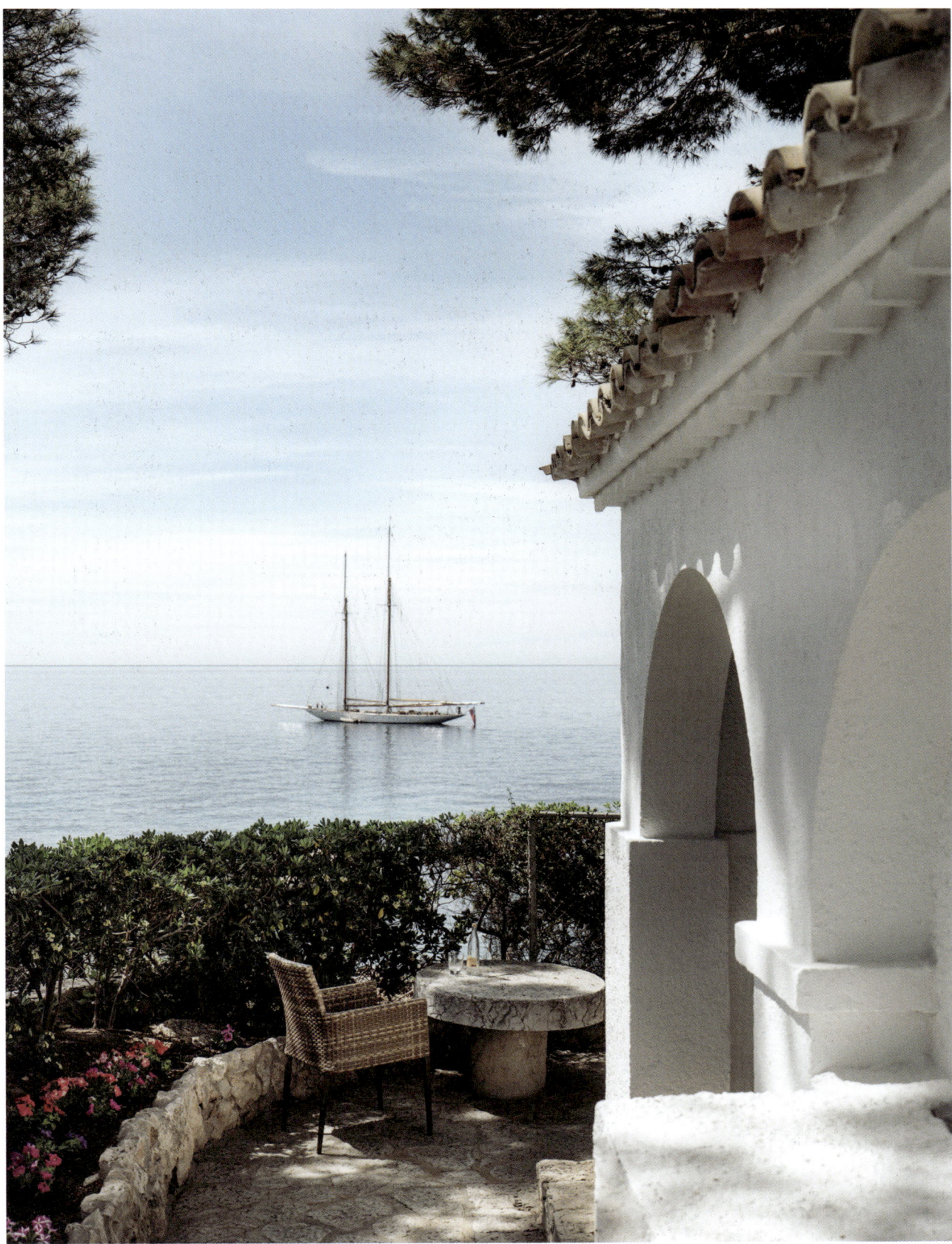

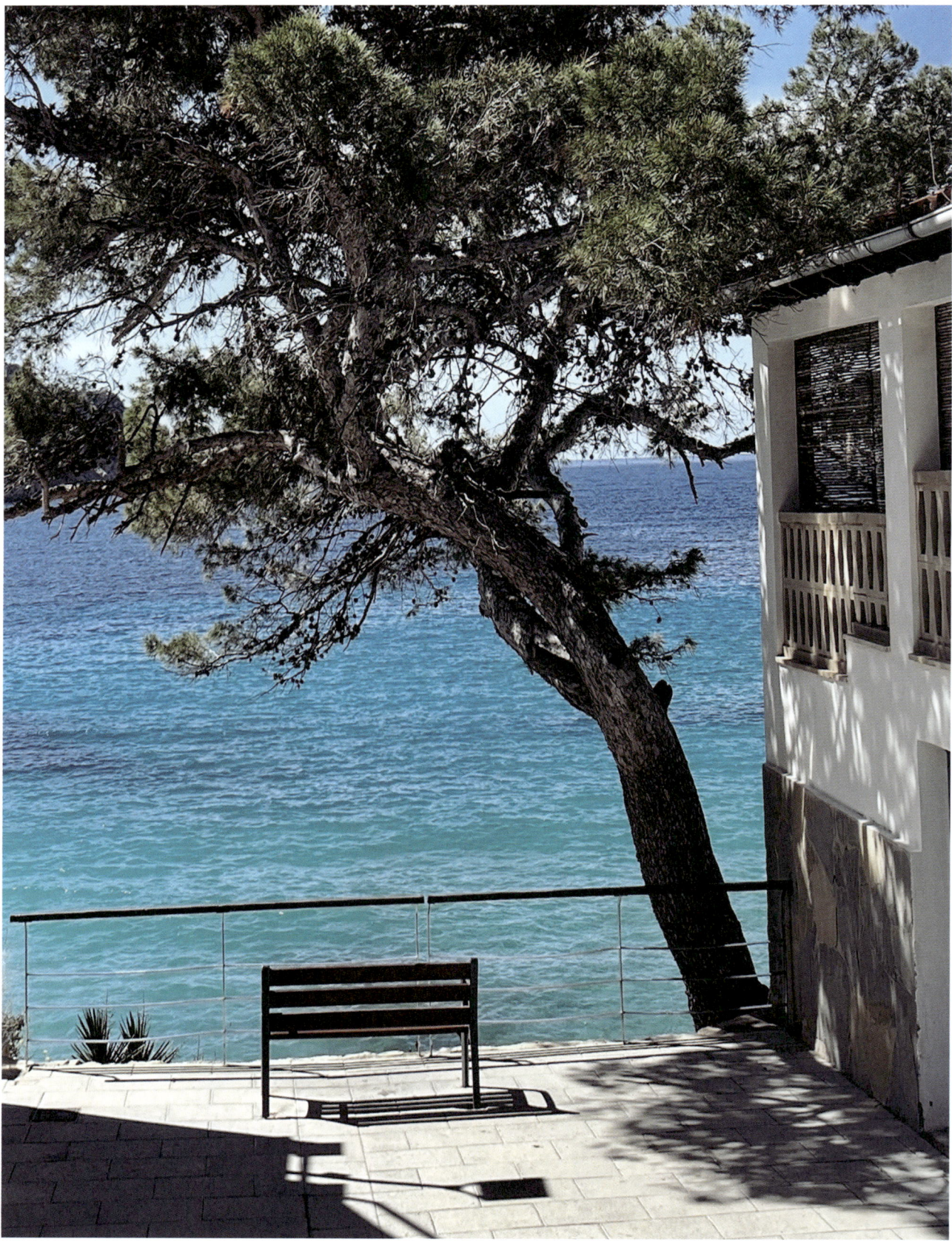

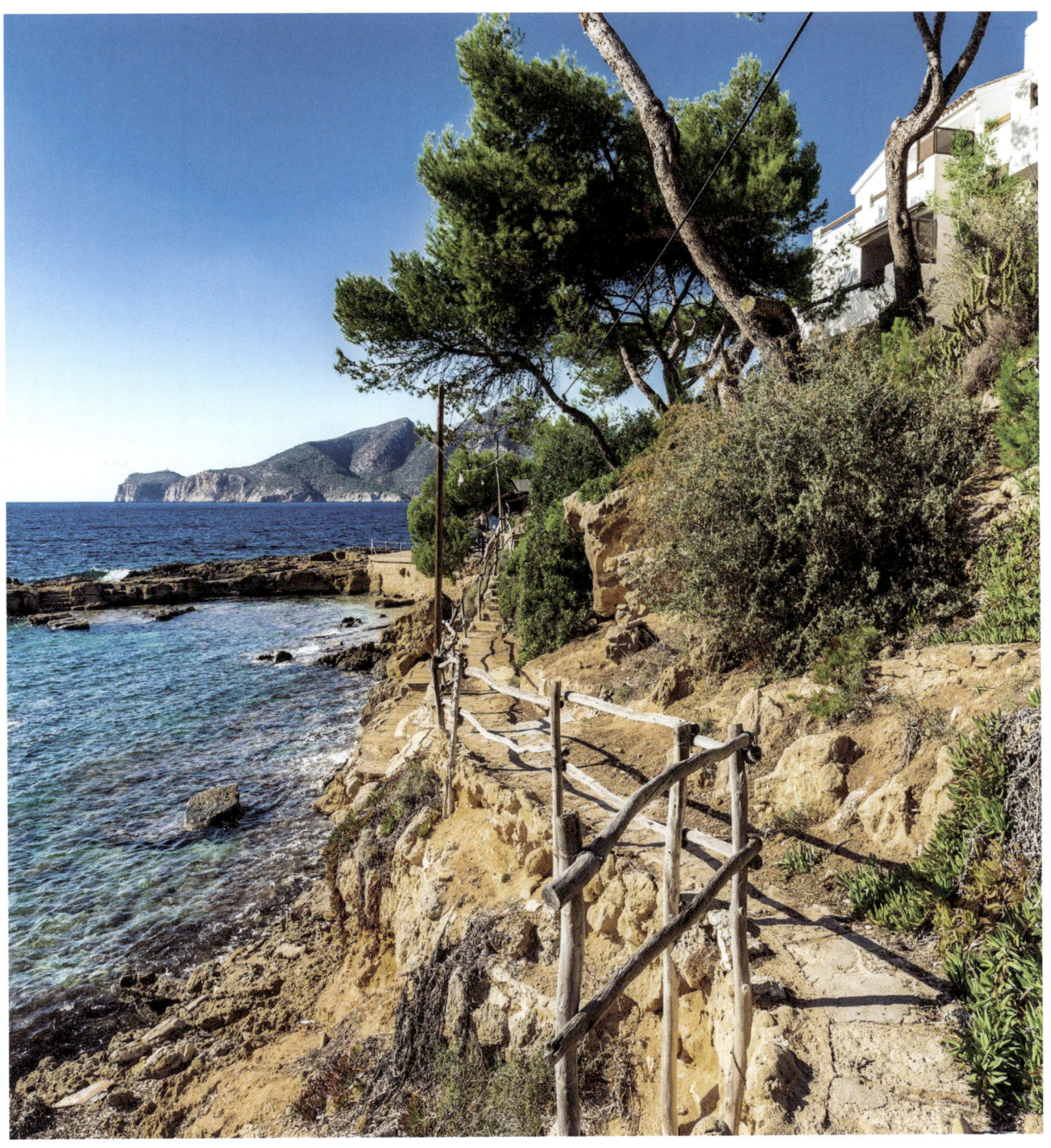

ABOVE AND LEFT: *The park bench with perhaps the world's most beautiful view stands in Sant Elm, a fishing village at the island's southwestern tip. This remote village was once a pirate stronghold, surrounded by rocky hideaways and smugglers' paths still accessible today. From here, the view of the uninhabited island of Sa Dragonera is spectacular.*

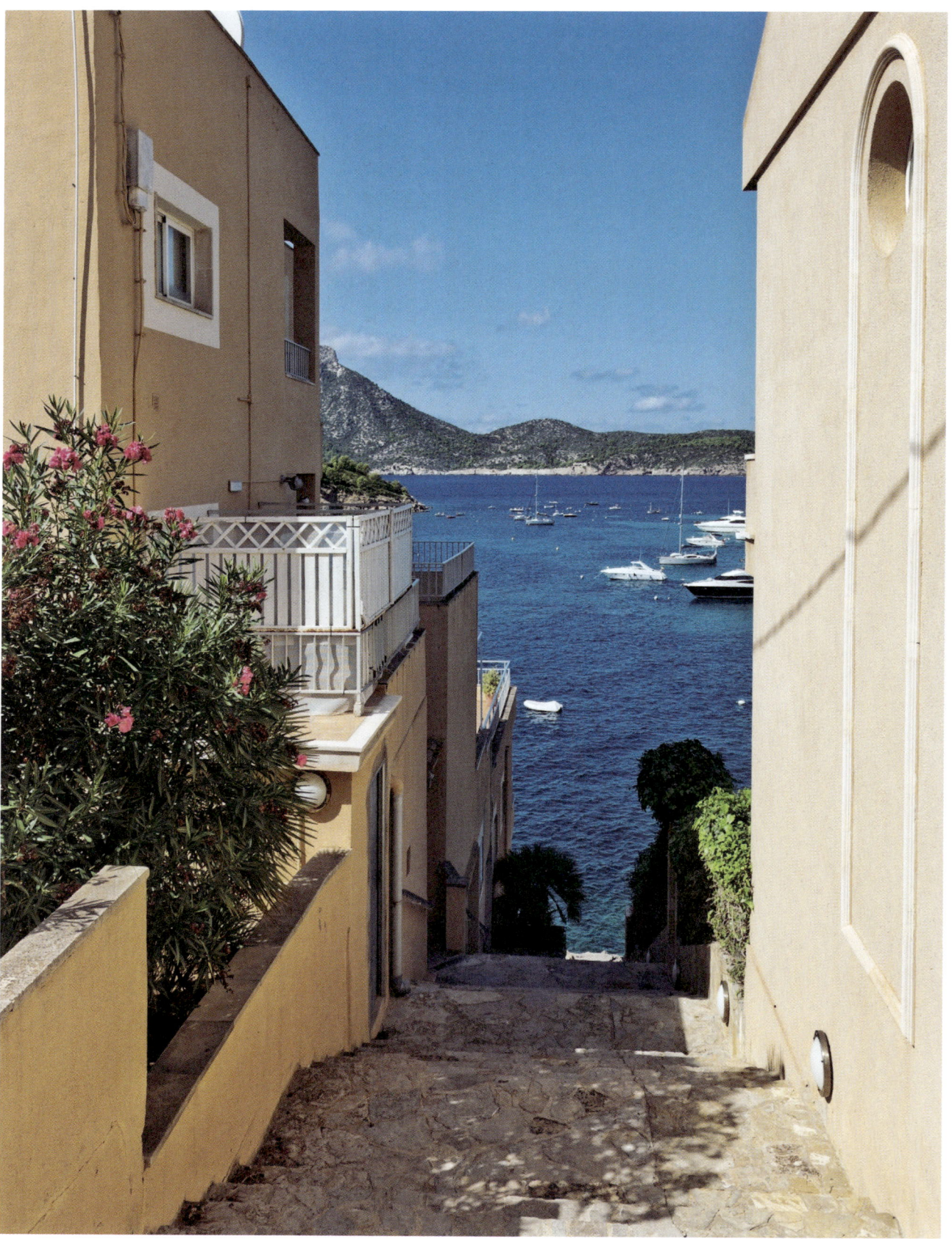

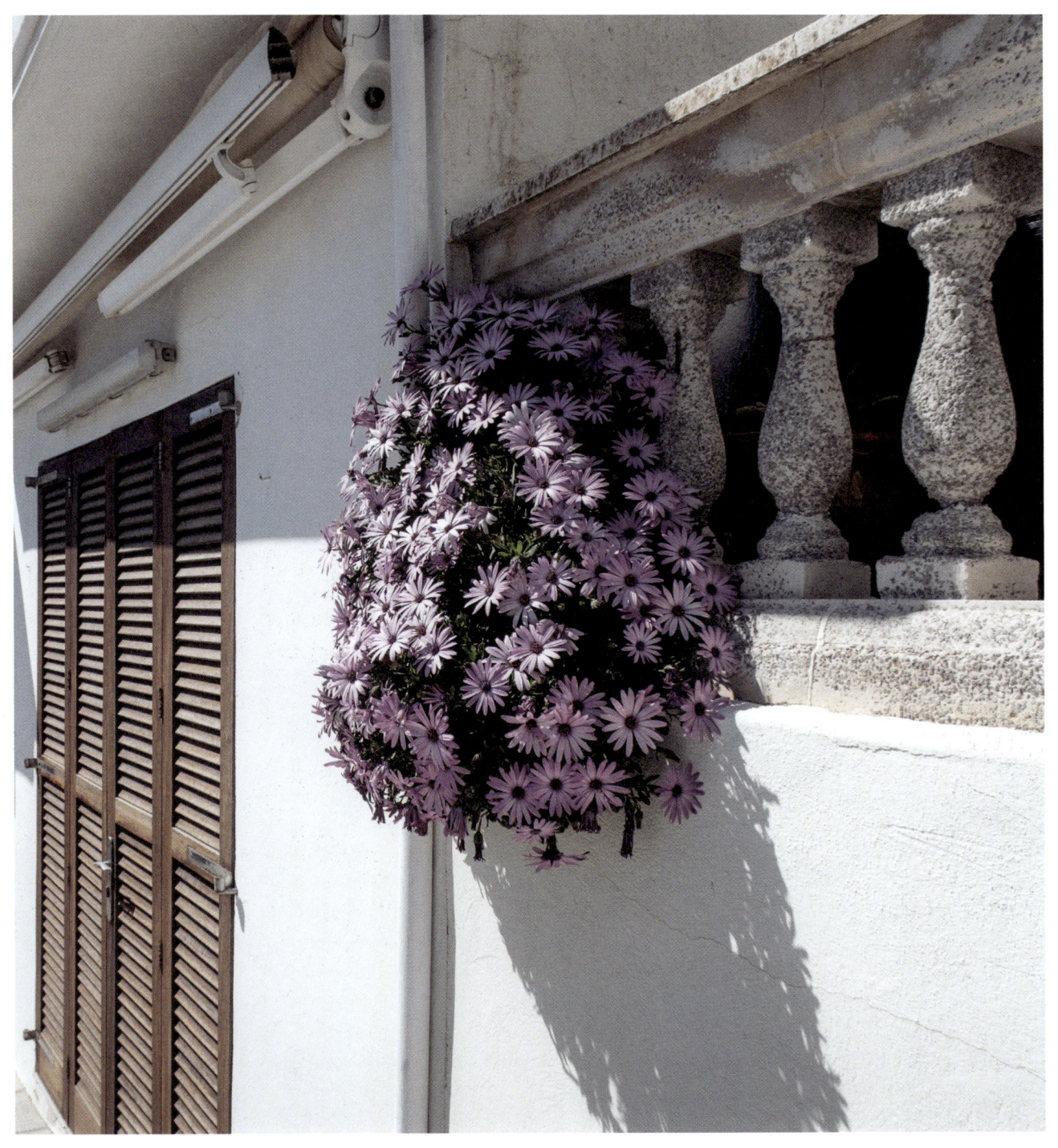

ABOVE AND RIGHT: *Otherworldly, laid-back Sant Elm stands at the foot of the Tramuntana range, reached by a winding road from Andratx, with a small promenade and a handful of restaurants.*

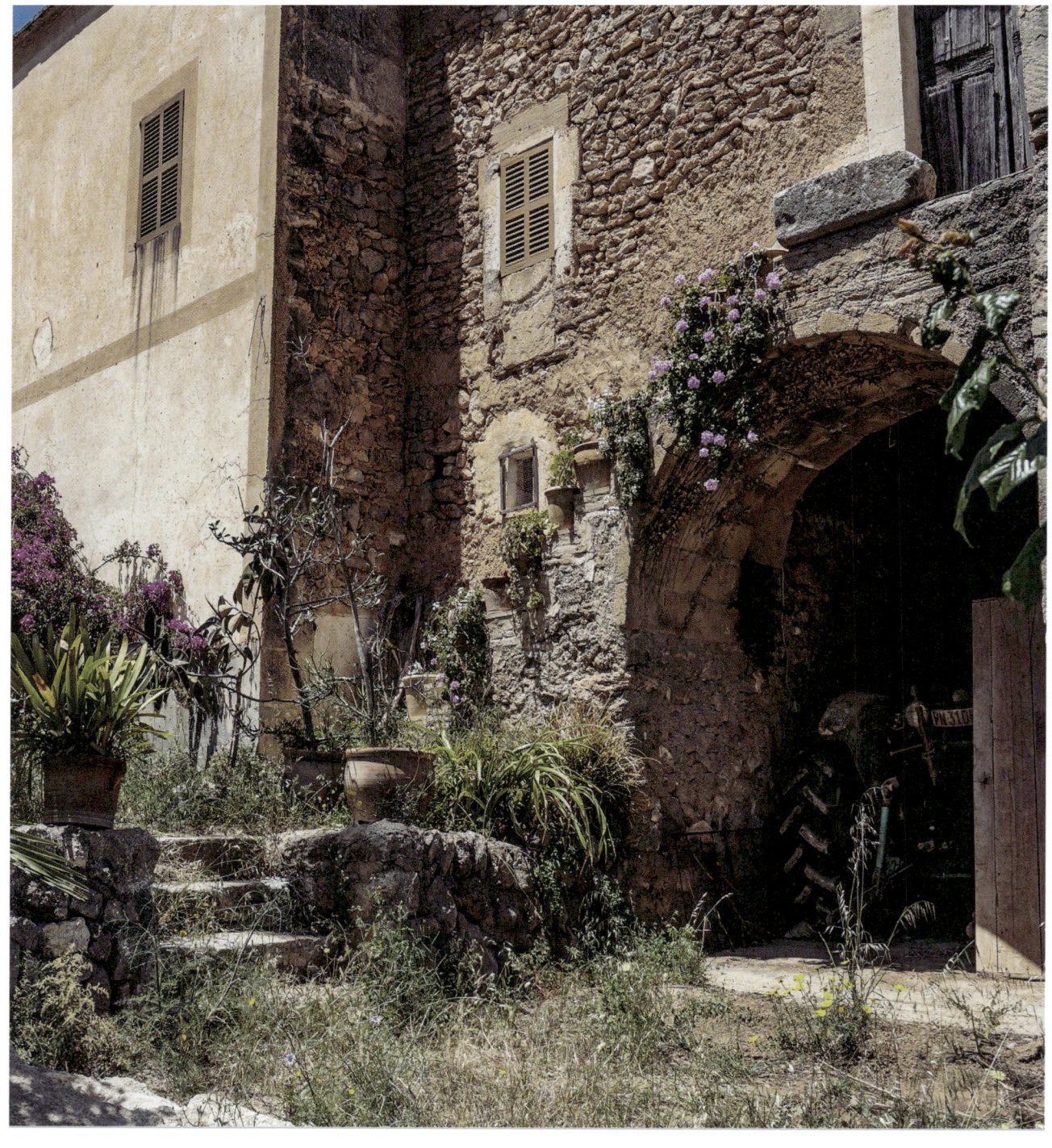

ABOVE: *Like something out of a fairy tale: the enchanted garden of a village farmstead in Felanitx in the island's southeast.*

RIGHT: *The Font de Santa Margalida, a fountain hidden at the base of a stairway inside the parish church of Sant Miquel in Felanitx.*

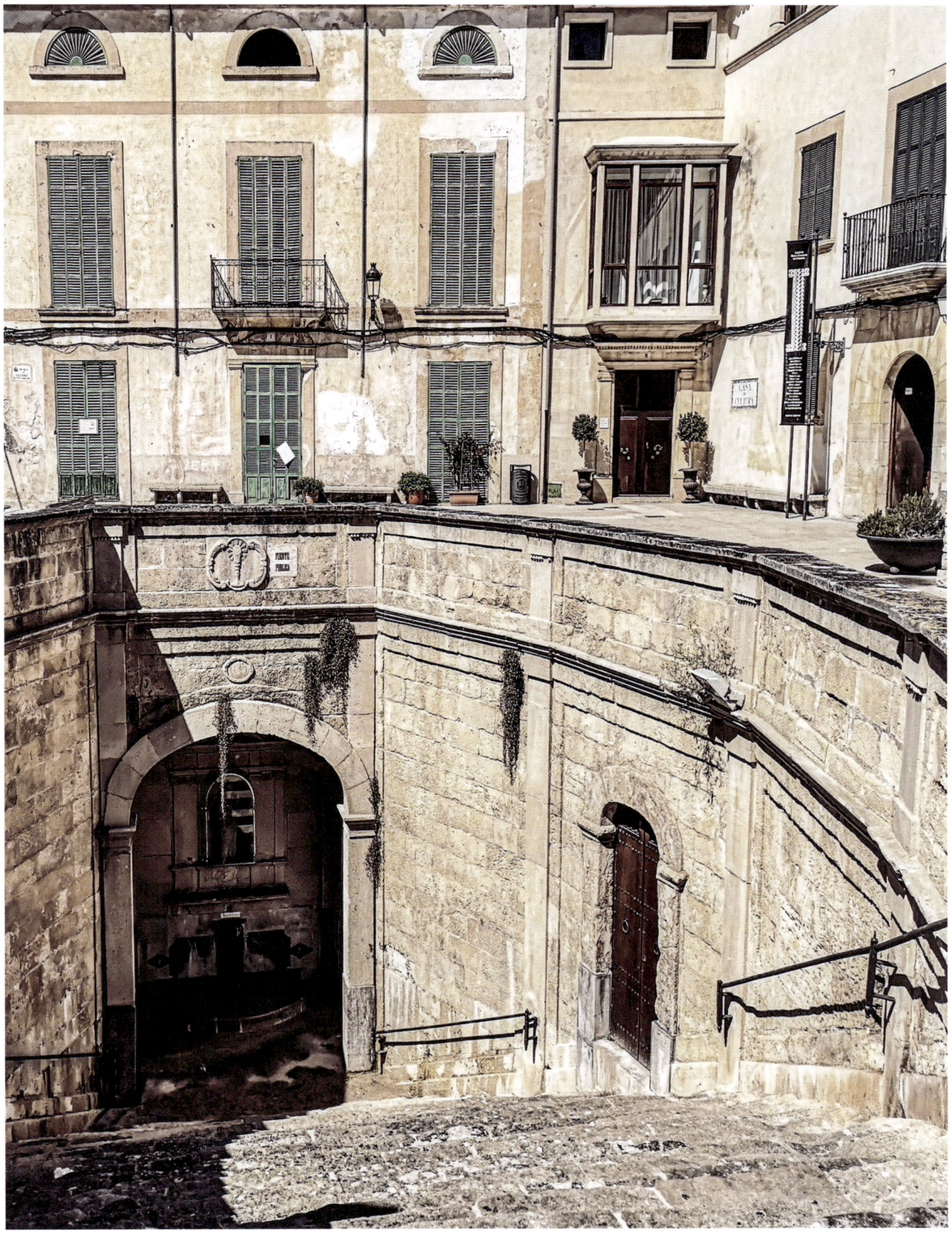

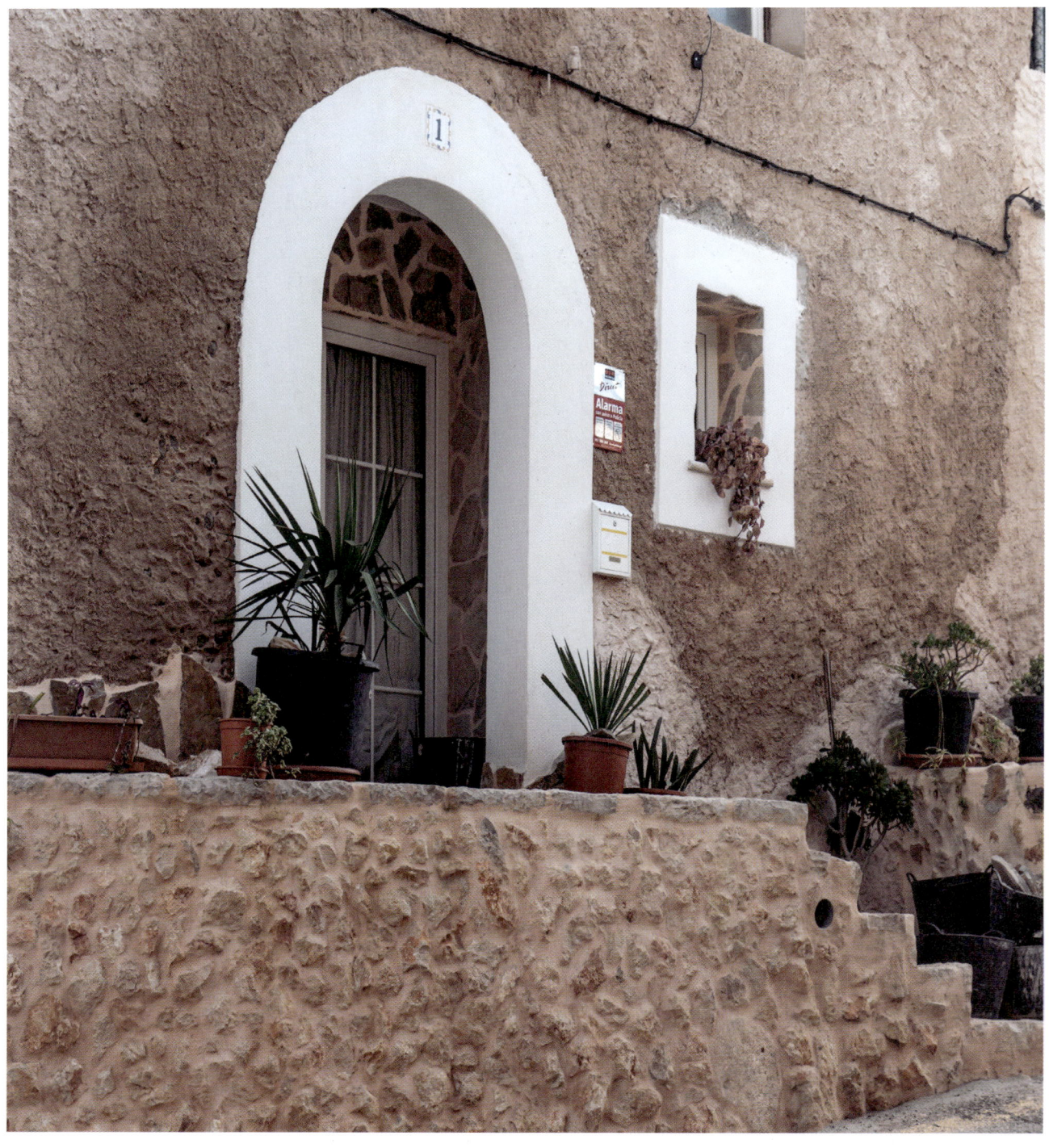

ABOVE: *Sandstone façades in Felanitx at dawn, with soft earth tones coloring the early morning village streetscape.*

RIGHT: *Bar Sa Recreativa on Plaça Arraval in Felanitx, with strong coffee and clattering plates—a place where neighborhood gossip has been exchanged for generations.*

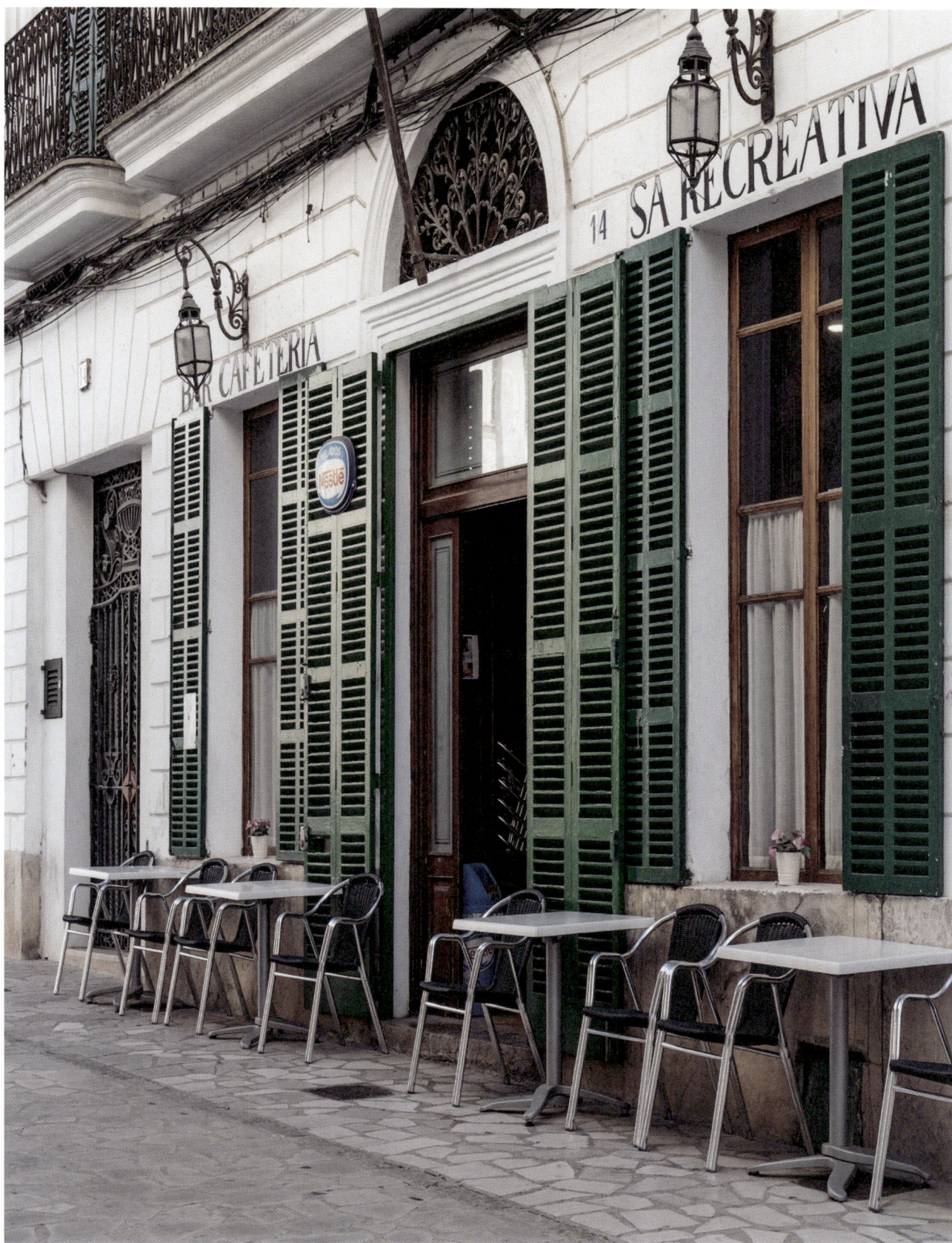

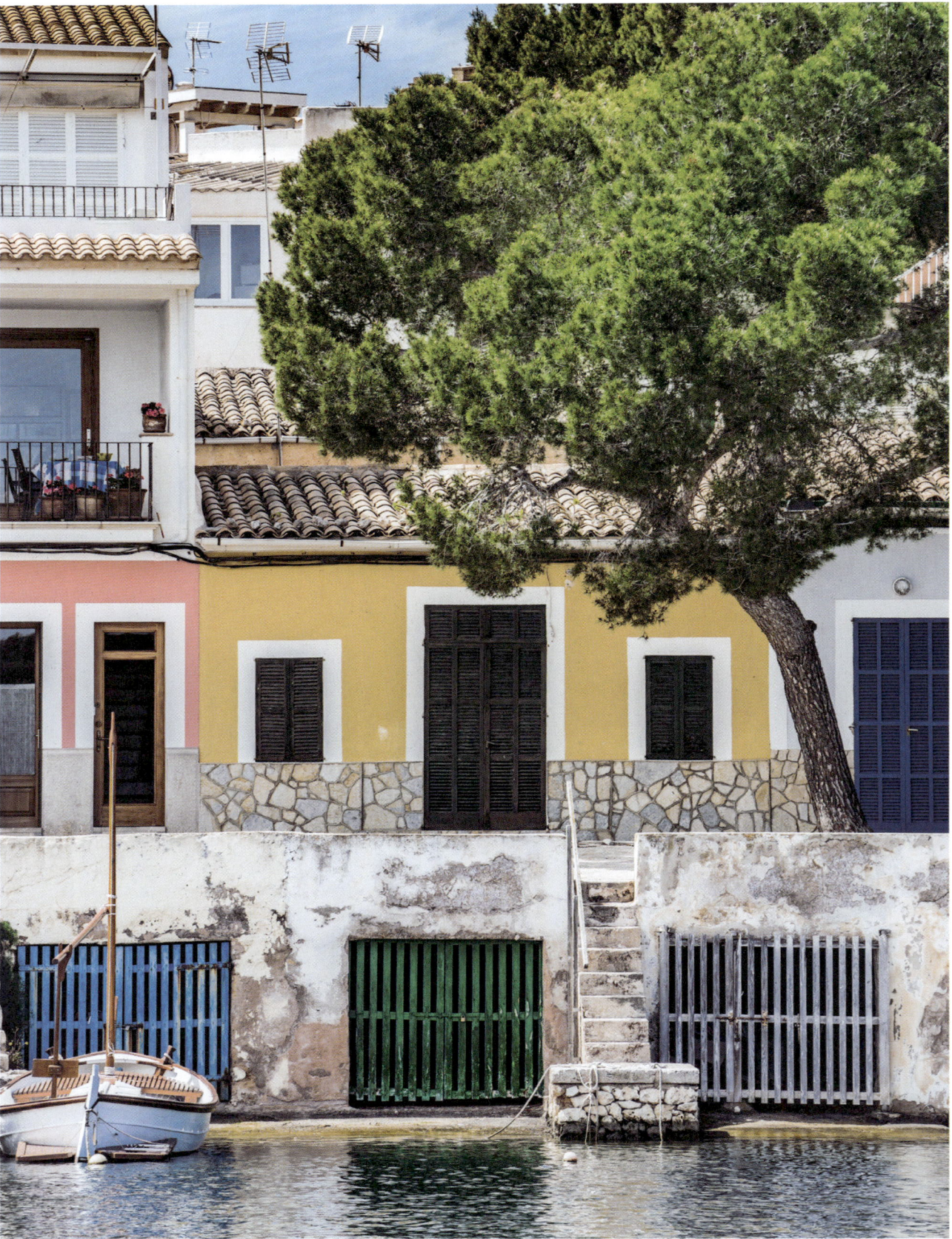

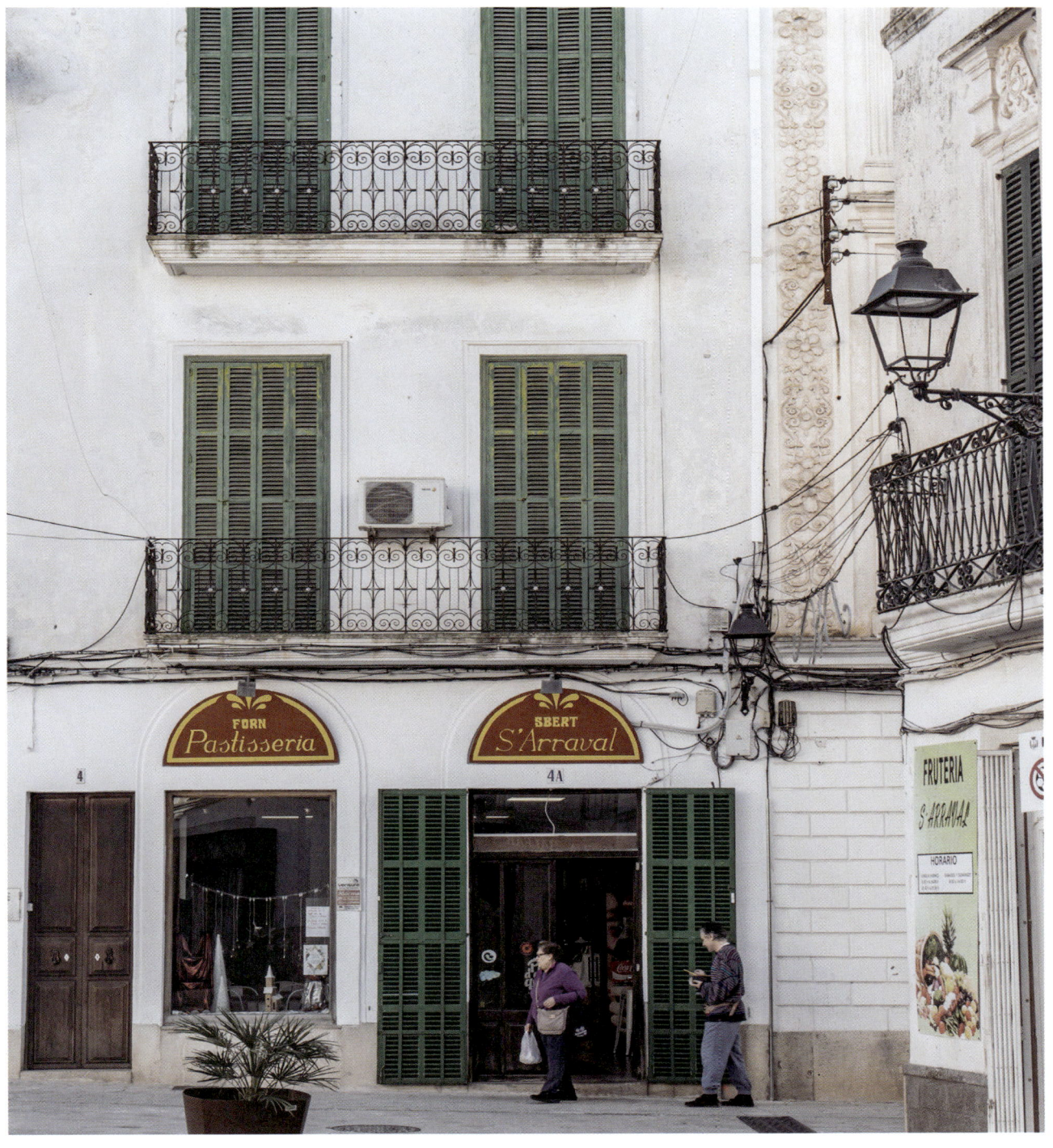

ABOVE: *Simply divine: stopping for a meringue puff pastry or an* ensaimada *to go, then continuing to stroll through the old town. The S'Arraval bakery on the eponymous square in Felanitx.*

LEFT: *Local lore holds that the picture-perfect fishing village of Portocolom, part of the municipality of Felanitx, is the true birthplace of Christopher Columbus.*

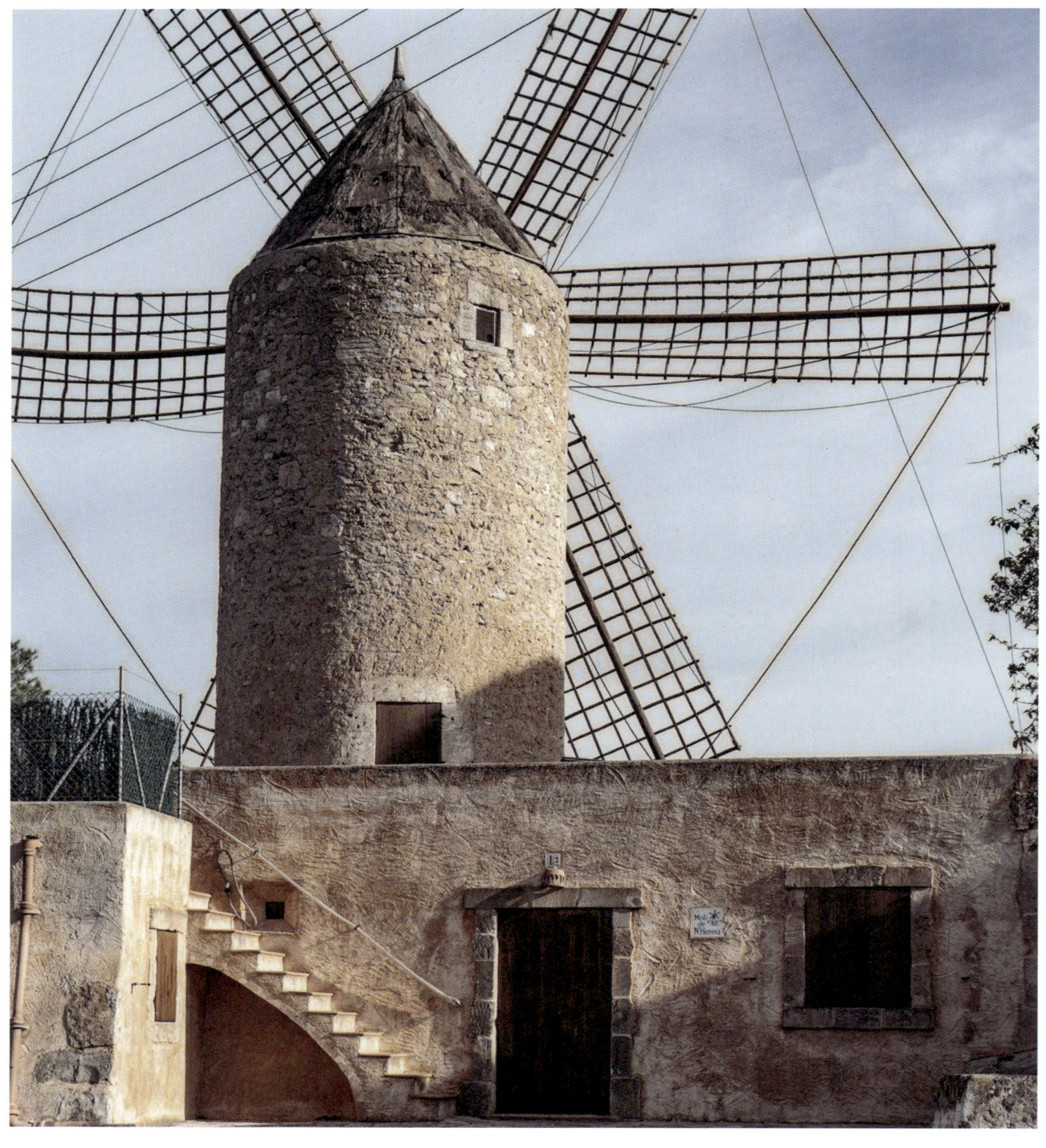

ABOVE: *An old windmill in Felanitx adapted for residential use is an example of the island's spirit of reusing historic structures everywhere.*

RIGHT: *A village with a distinct presence: the streets of Felanitx, with narrow alleyways, small stairways, and typical residential buildings.*

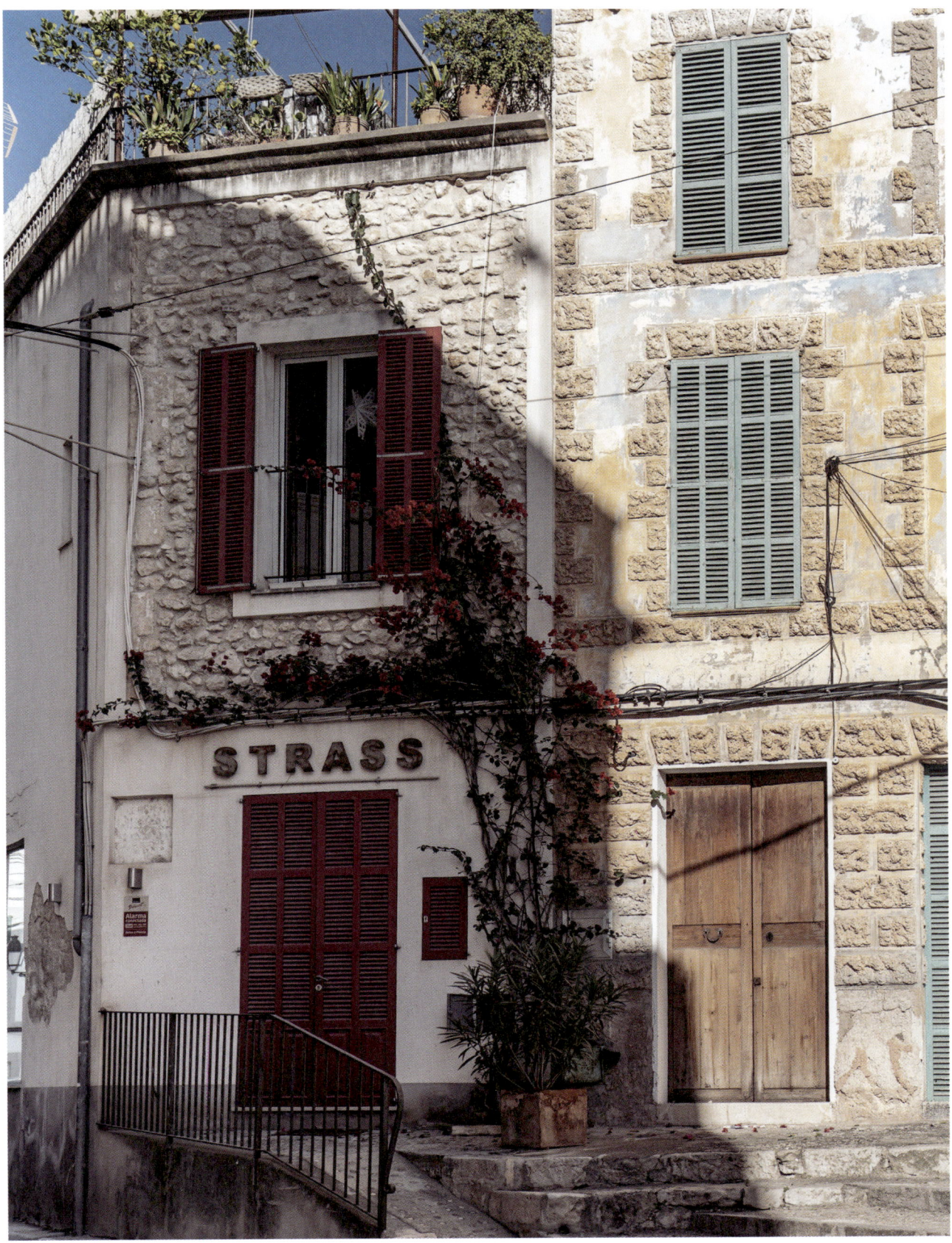

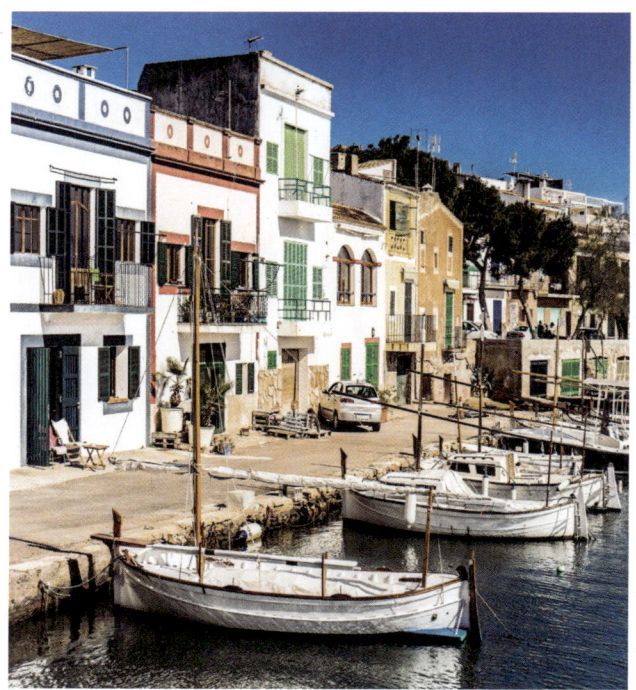
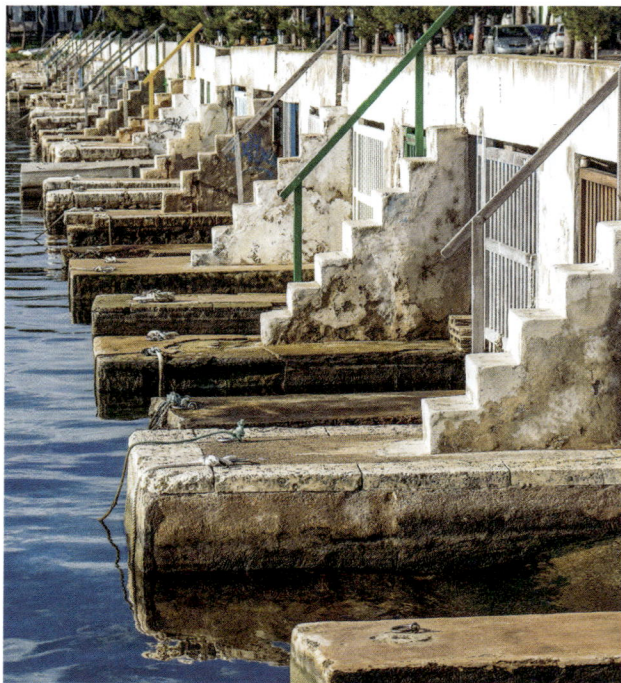
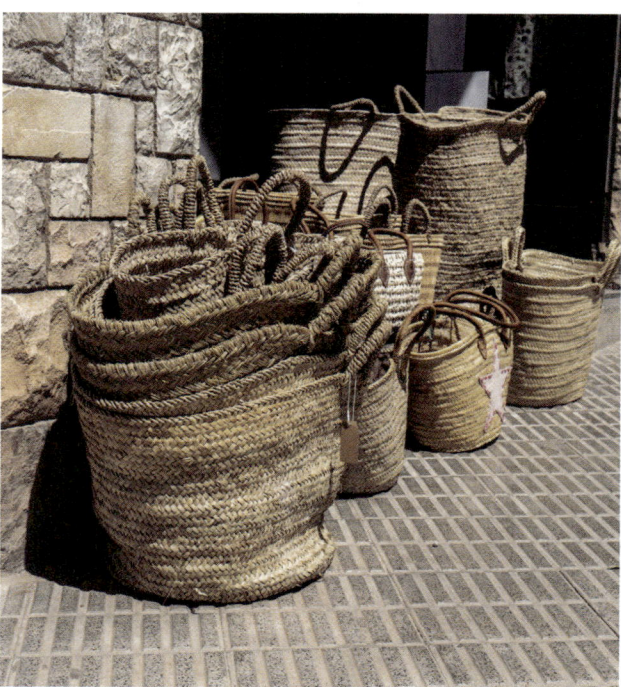
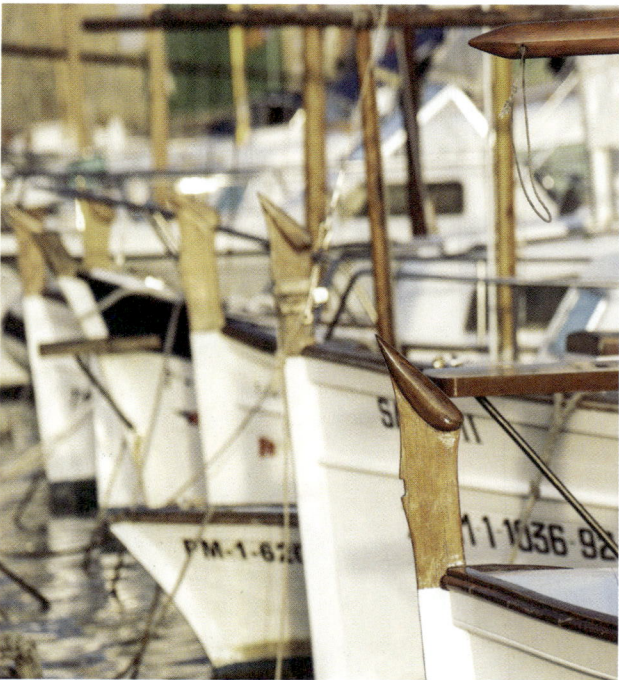

ABOVE: *The traditional, sturdy Balearic fishing boats, built to withstand every wave, are known as* llaüts. *Particularly fine examples can be seen in the small harbor of Portocolom. Bottom left: Basket bags woven from local dwarf palm leaves, still made by hand in parts of the island.*

RIGHT: *The old town of Felanitx, located roughly twenty minutes inland from the harbor of Portocolom.*

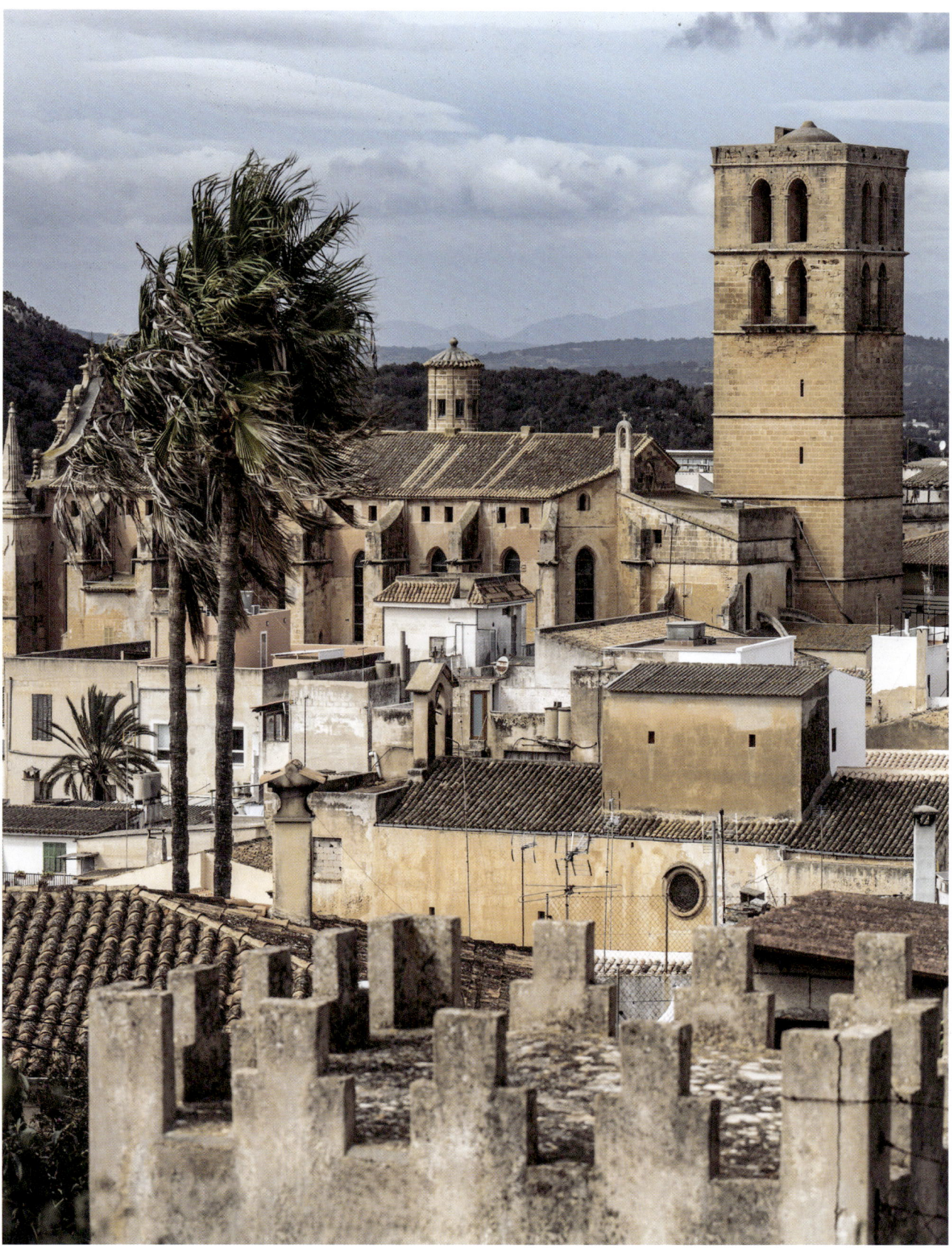

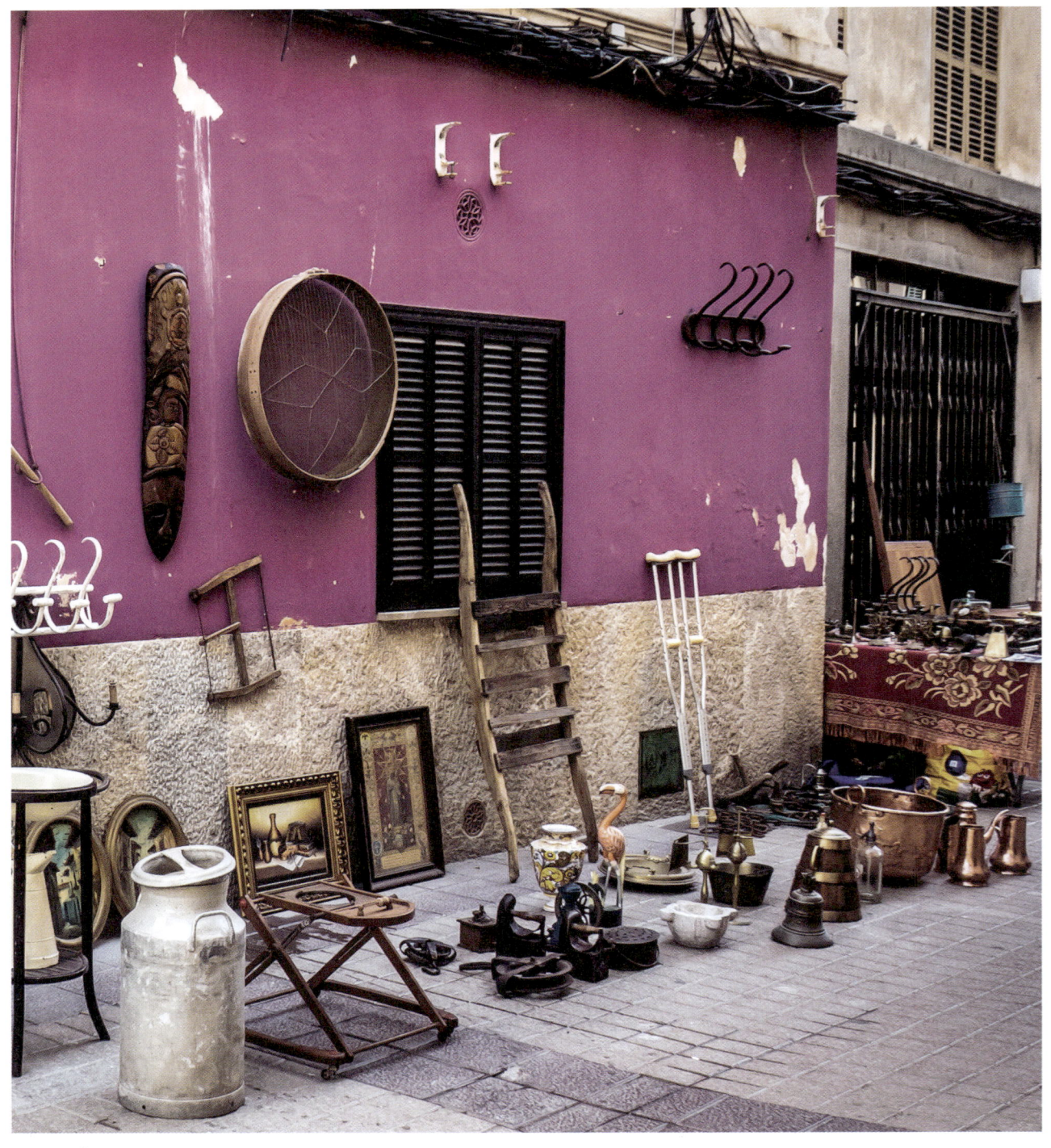

ABOVE: *The weekly flea market and produce market in Felanitx, held Sundays from 9 a.m. to 2 p.m., with stalls offering quirky finds, clothing, antiques, ceramics, crafts, food, and local specialties. Not your average faux-hippy commercial market.*

RIGHT: *Up and down the stairways and narrow passageways in the old town of Felanitx.*

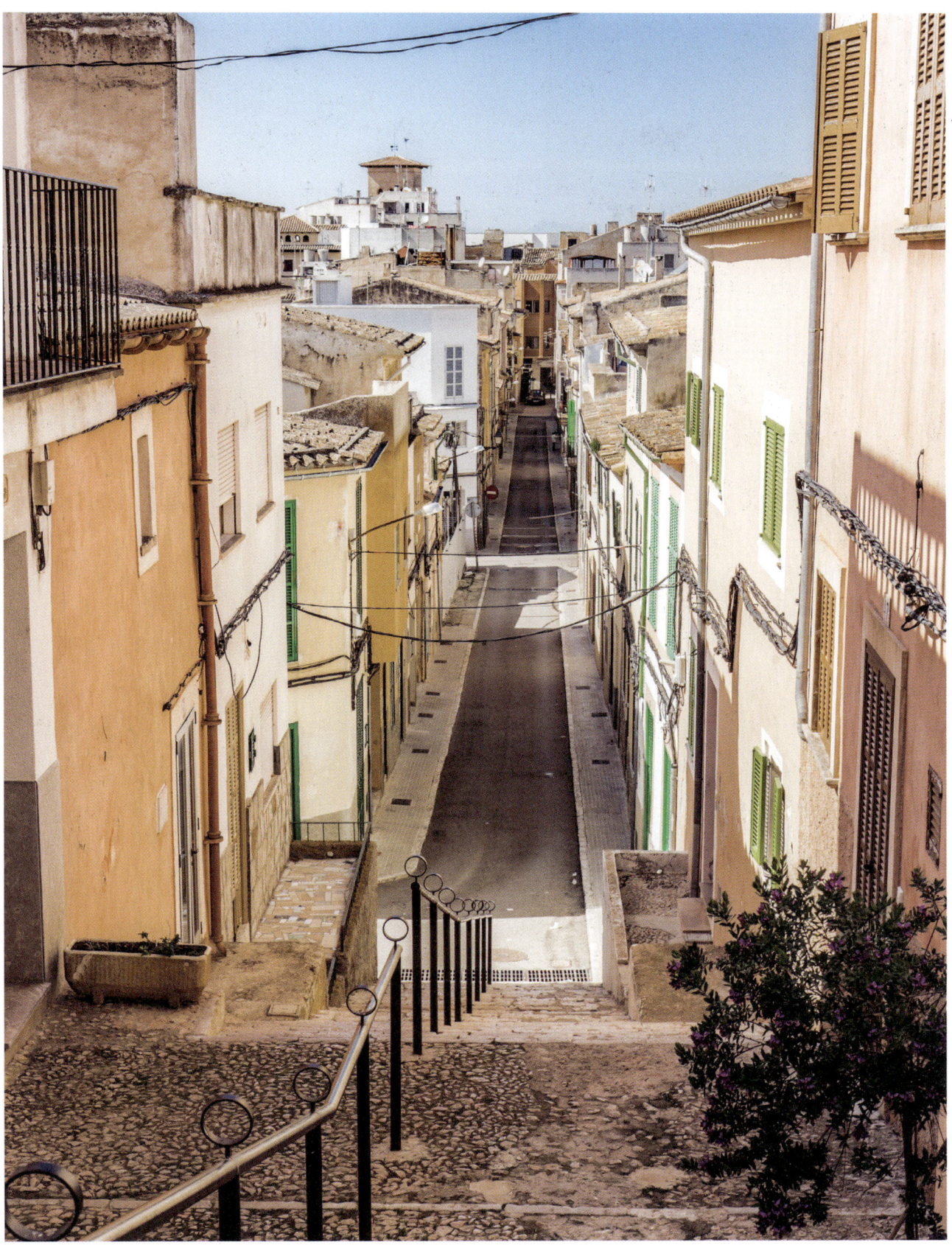

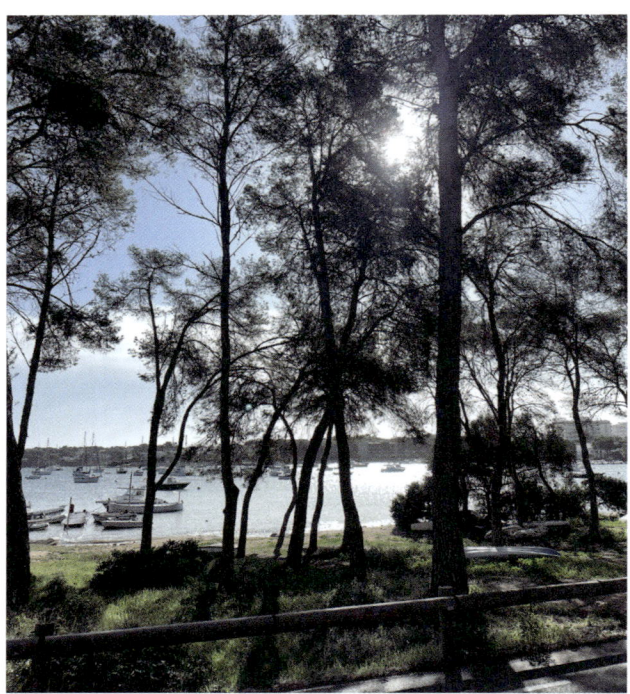
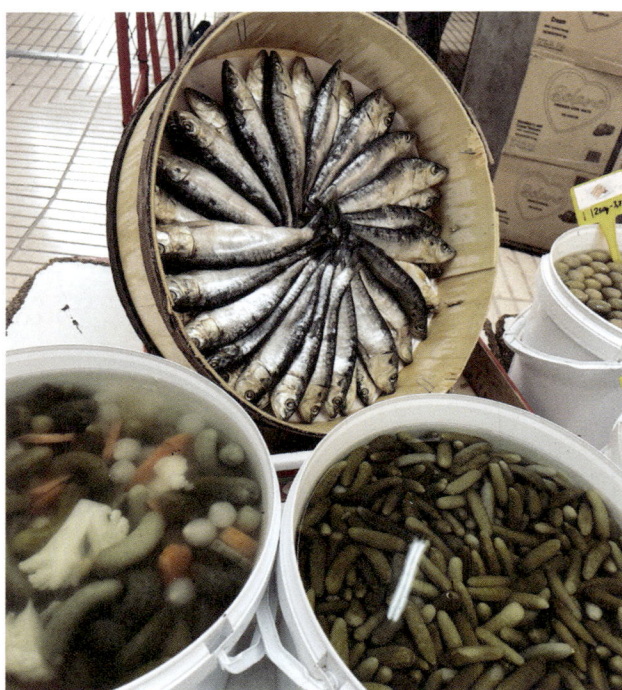
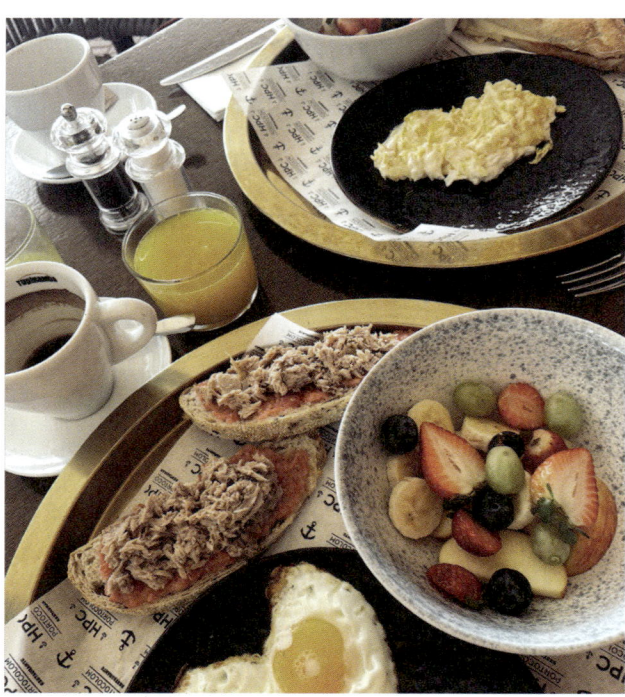
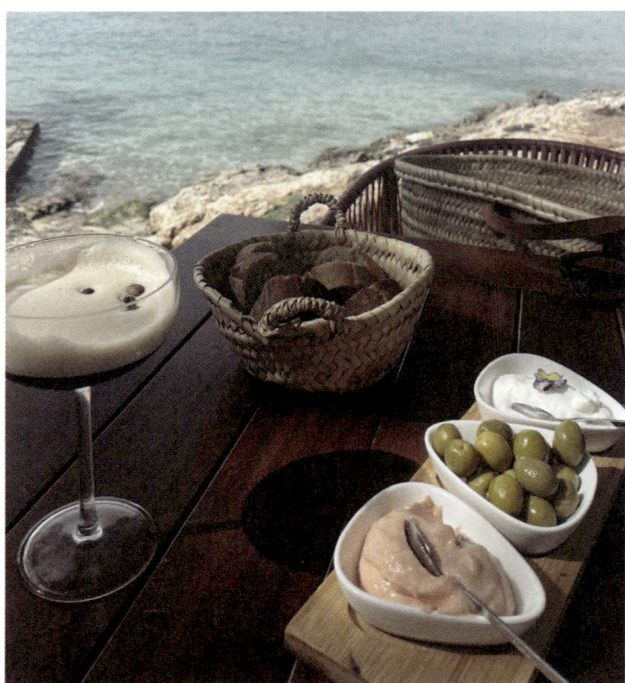

ABOVE AND RIGHT: *An ideal day in the southeast of Mallorca, with breakfast in Felanitx (below left), lunch at the Mercat Municipal (above right), a walk along the bay of Portocolom (right and above left), and an evening espresso martini at the Blue Bar.*

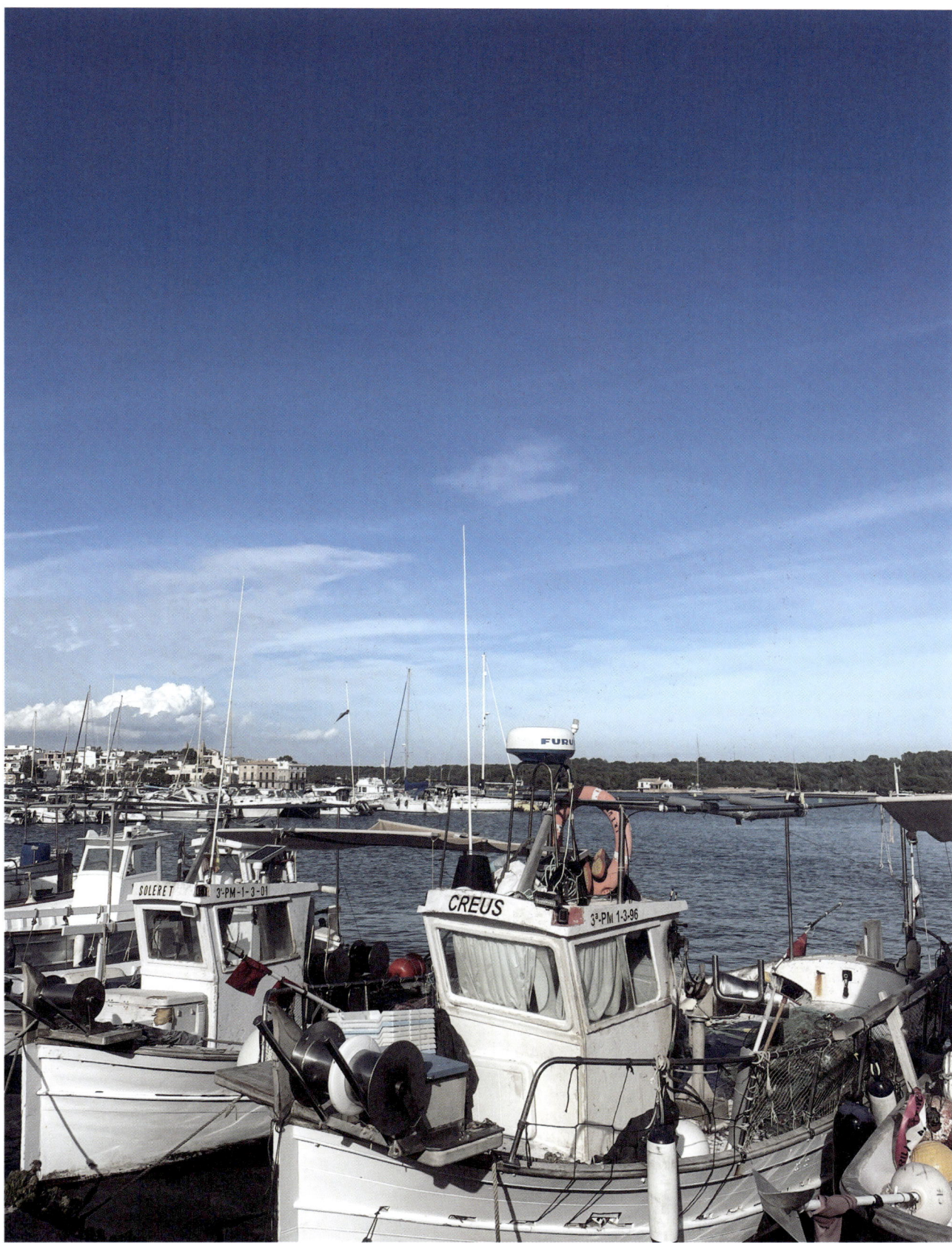

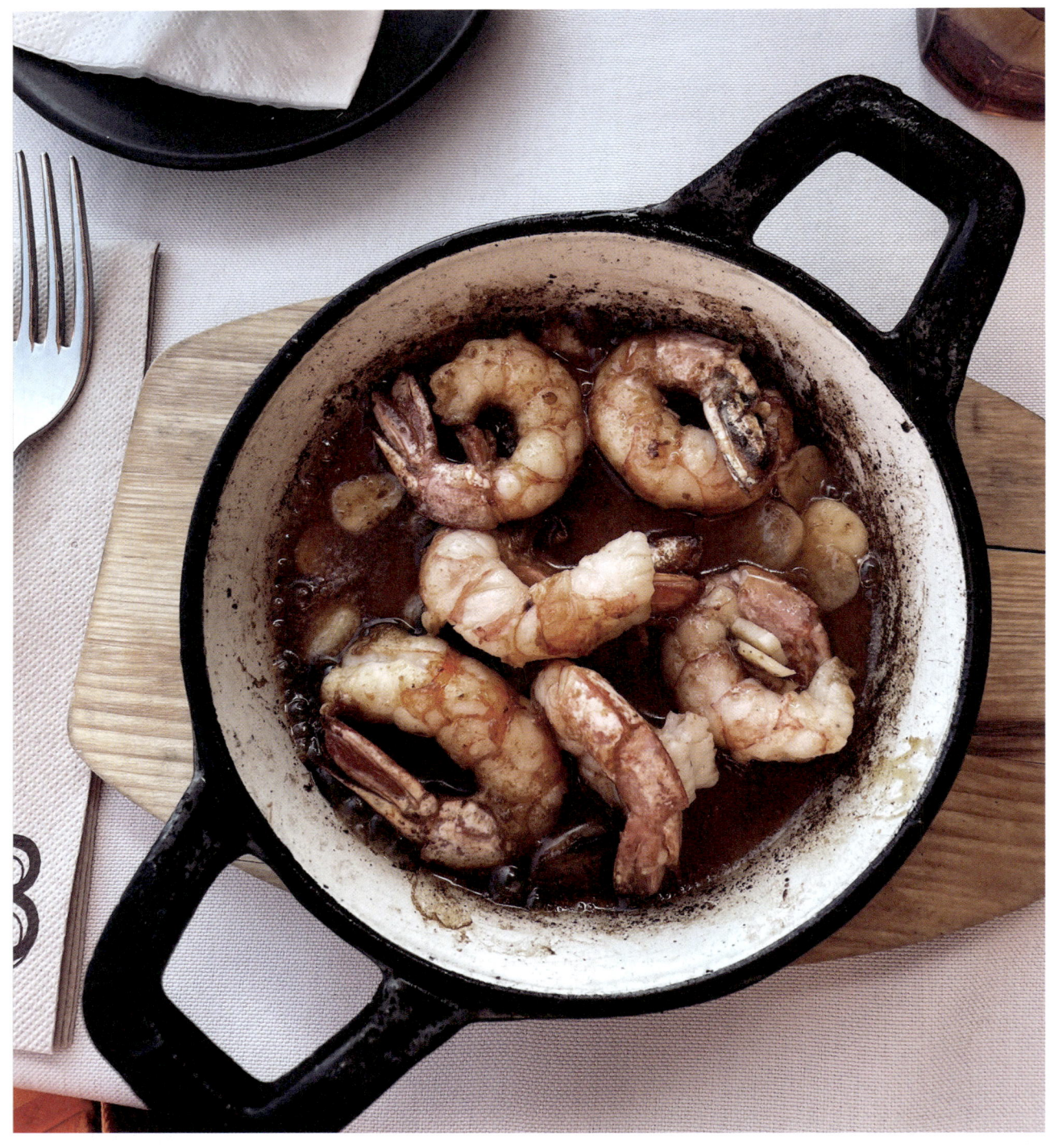

ABOVE: *The best tapas:* gambas al ajillo *served in hot oil. The best part is using bread to mop up the leftover sauce.*

RIGHT: *The Ca n'Angela fish shop in Portocolom offers the daily catch and fantastic poke bowls to go, a fact not only the yacht crowd will gladly confirm.*

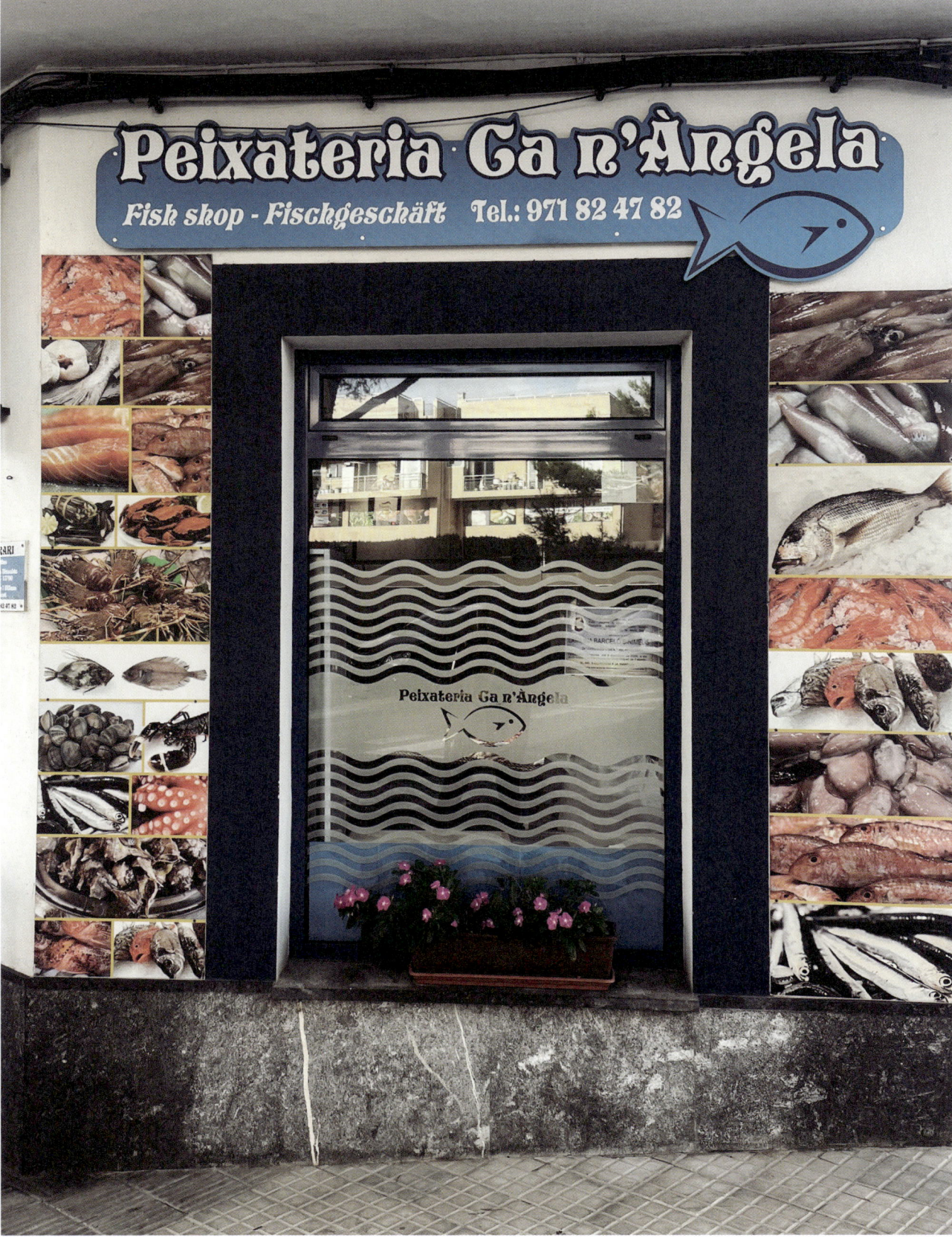

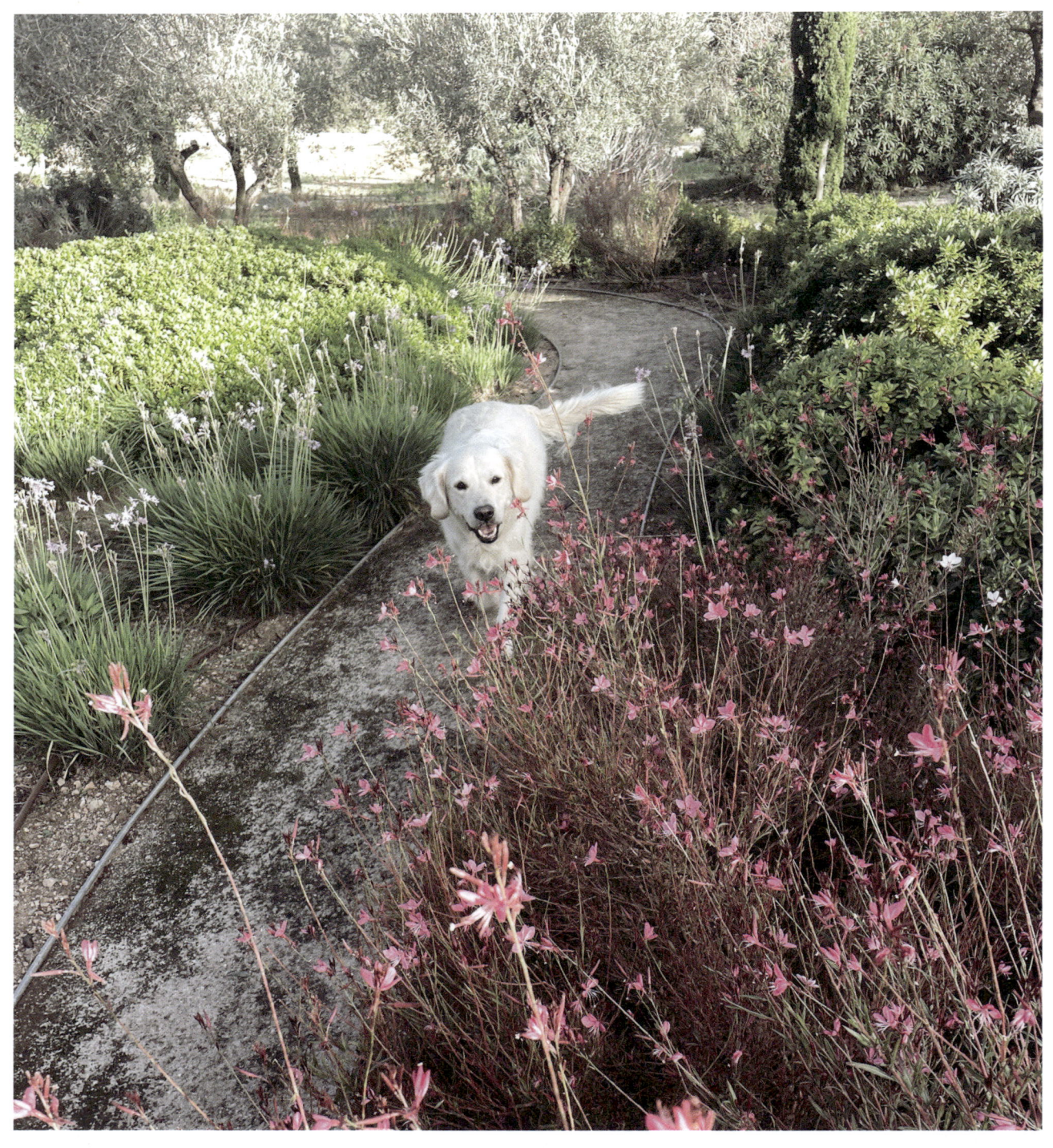

ABOVE AND RIGHT: *A country estate in the southeast of the island, representative of modernized agricultural properties now used as vacation homes. Golden retriever Carlos is lucky to be spending his vacation here.*

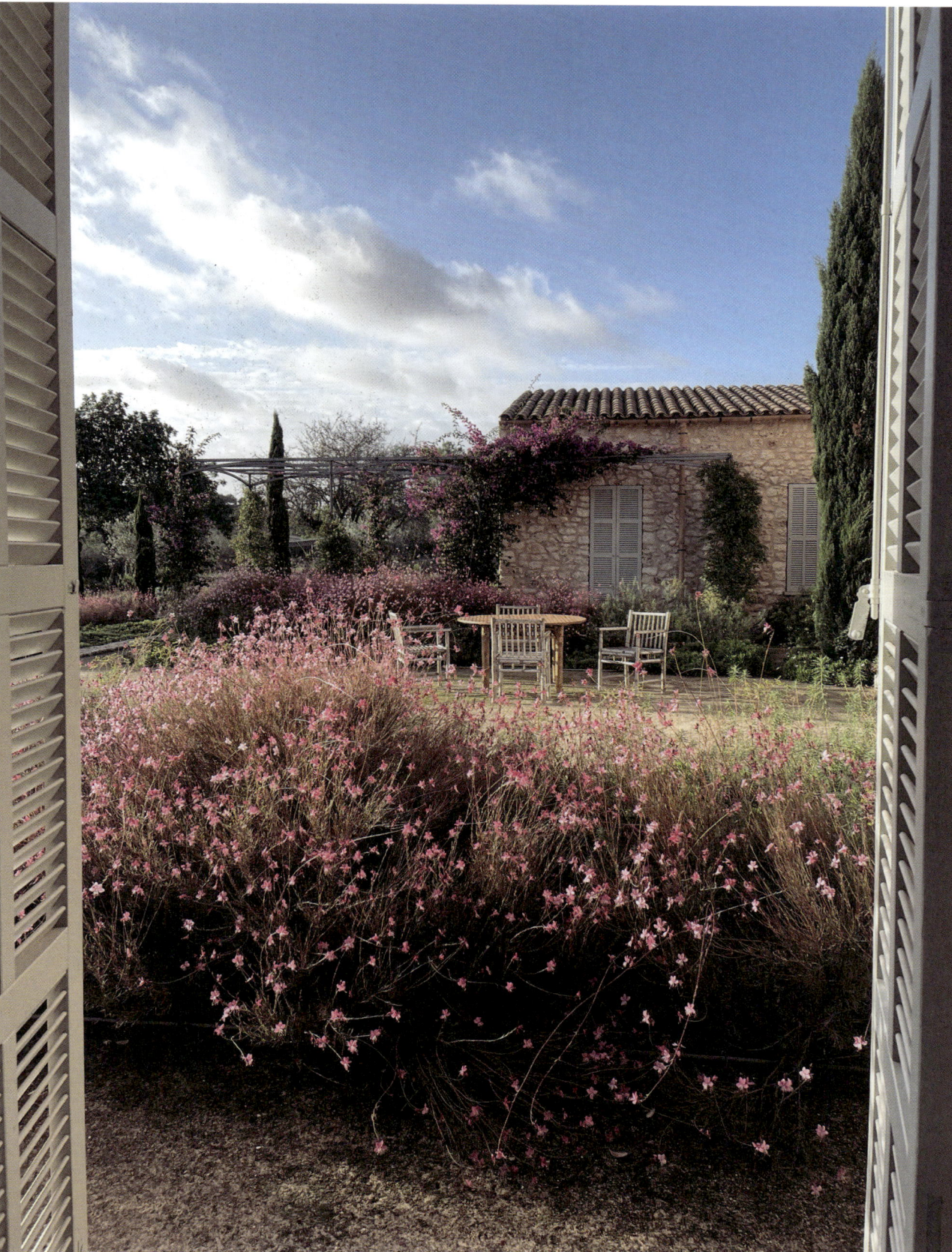

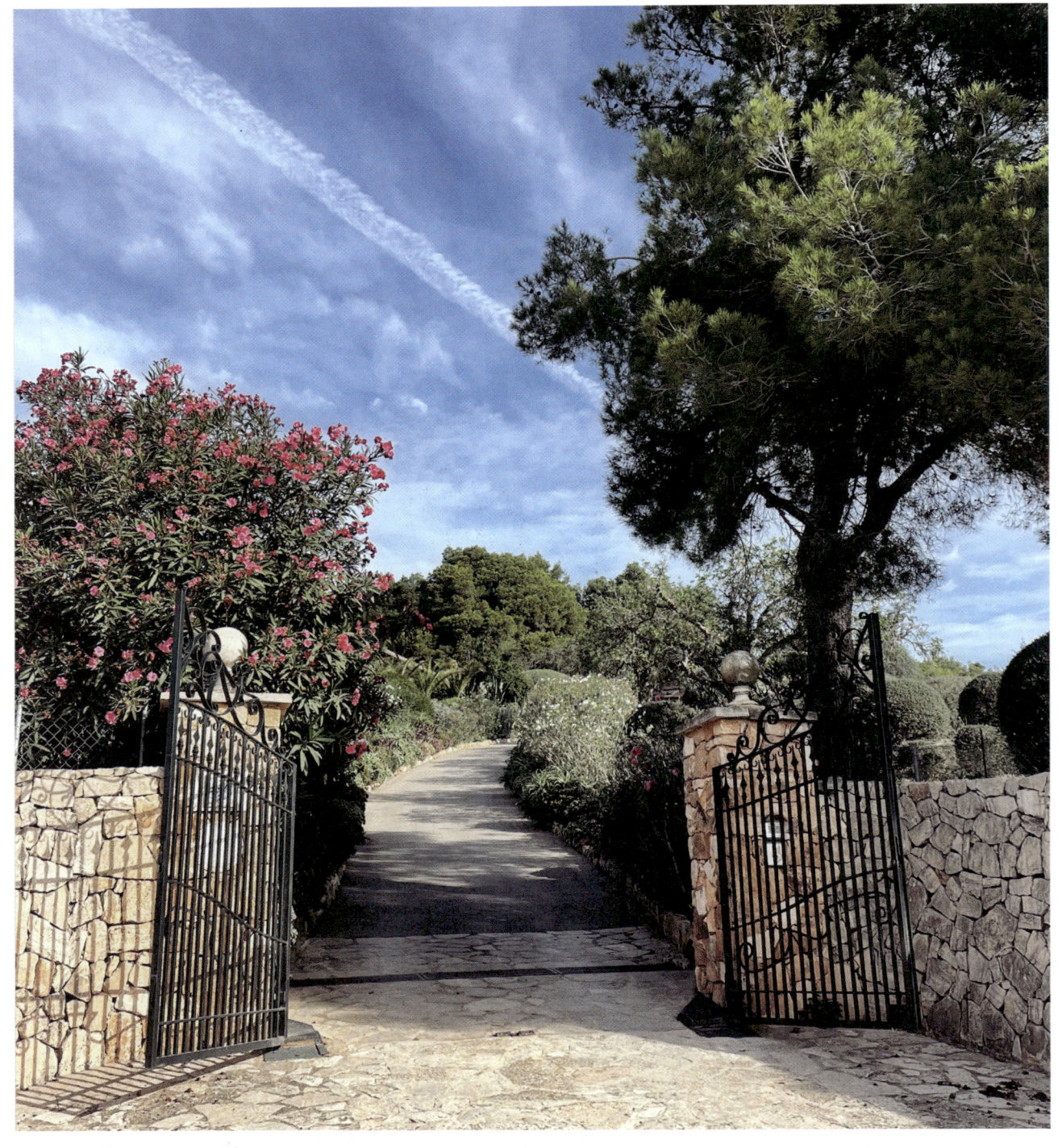

ABOVE: *Finca architecture, with natural stone walls assembled piece by piece, lend many rural estates their distinctive character. This technique is continued in modern homes.*

RIGHT: *Siesta time, with the louvered doors closed for several hours as life slows to a pause.*

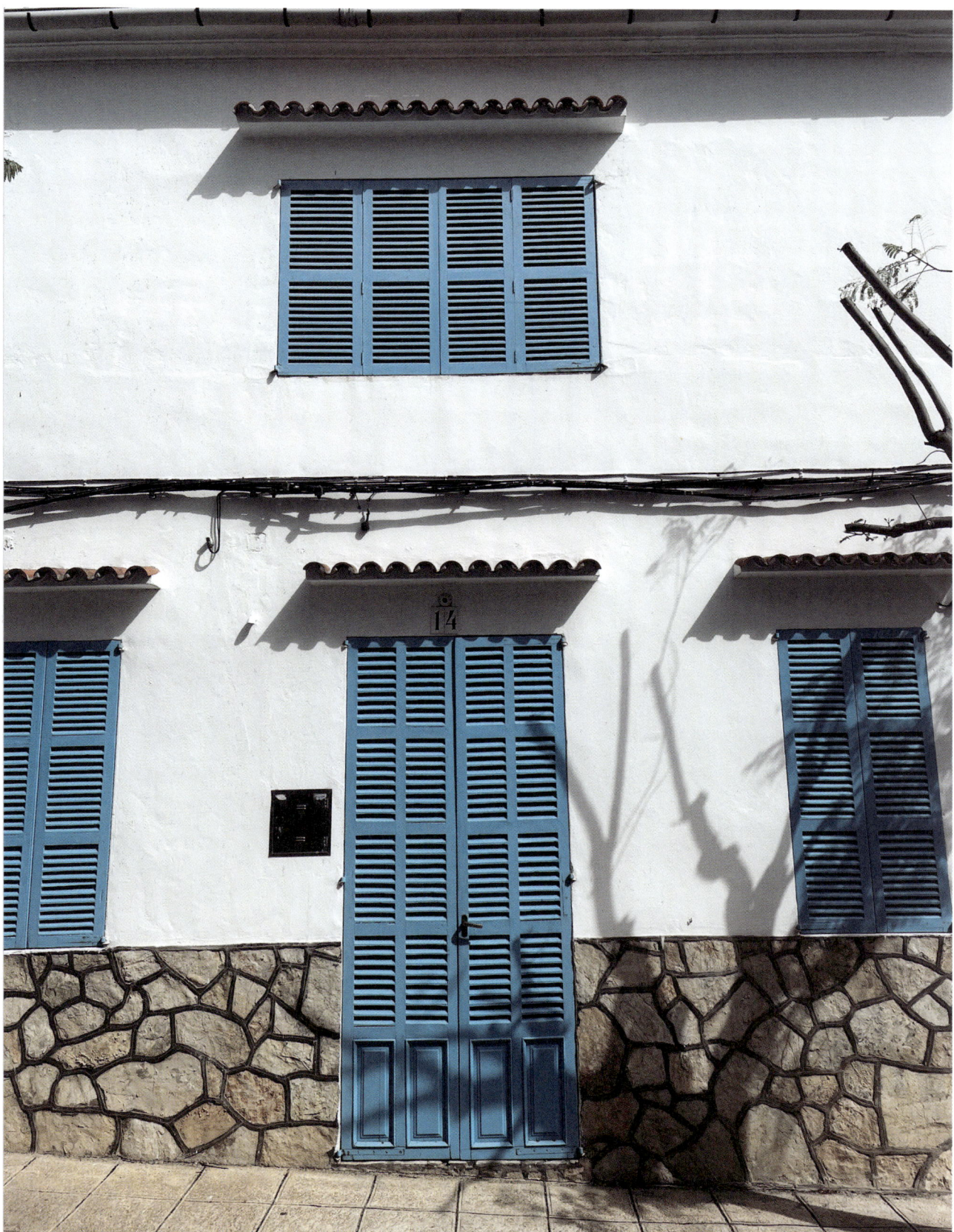

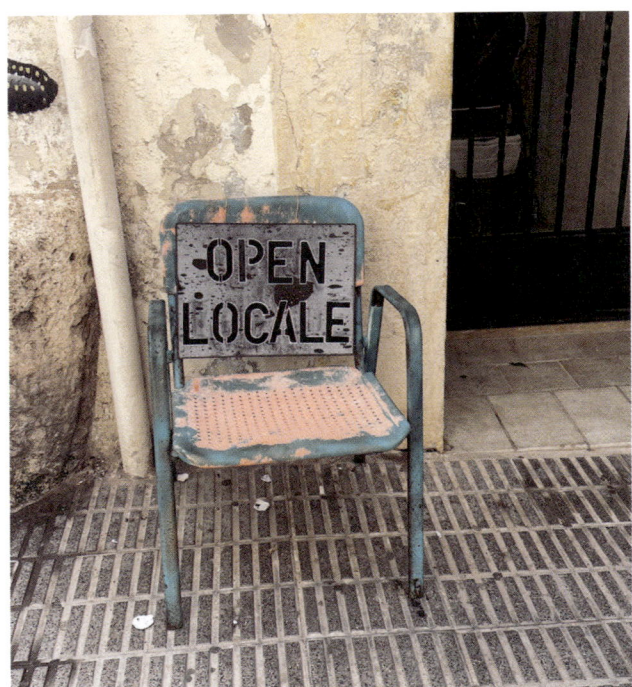
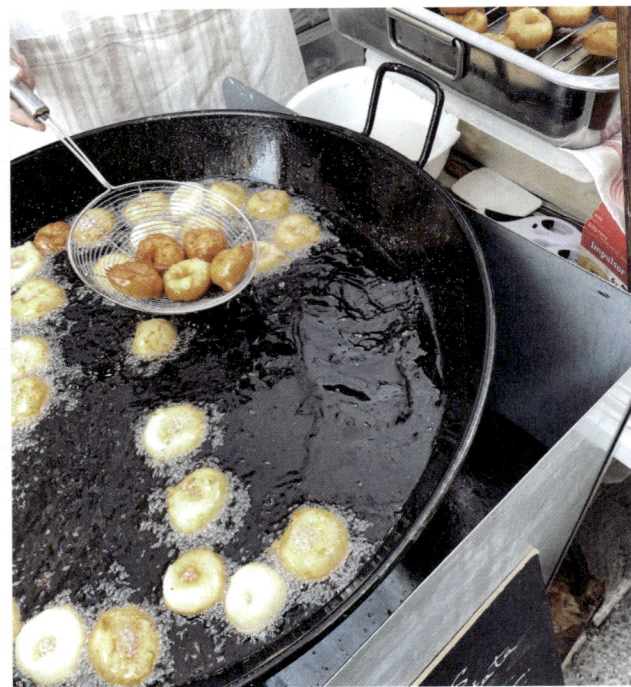
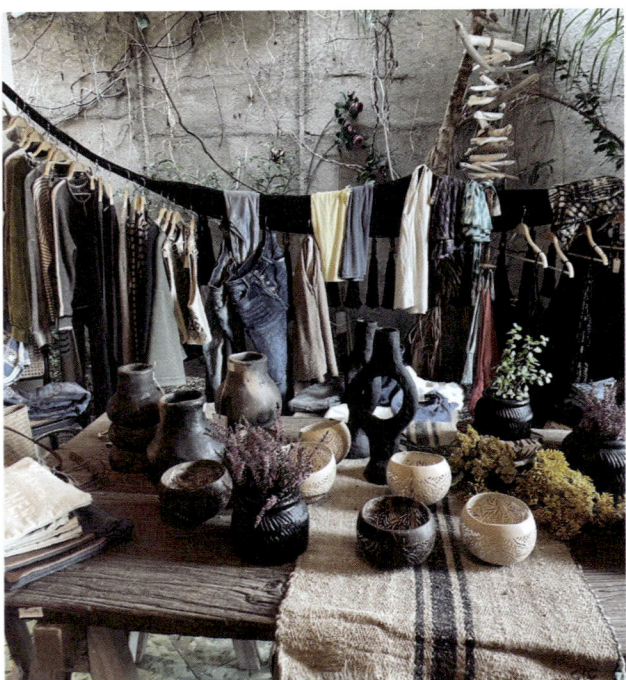
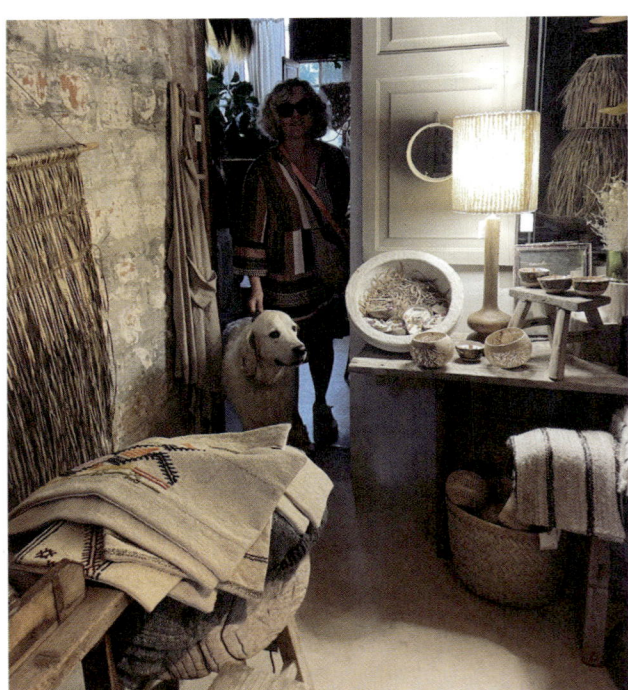

ABOVE: *An afternoon in Portocolom, with pastries, a walk through town, and a visit to the tastefully curated shop at the Barefoot Hotel, featuring various local products.*

RIGHT: *An abandoned building in Felanitx with Moorish arches and a neo-Mudéjar decorative façade lies dormant.*

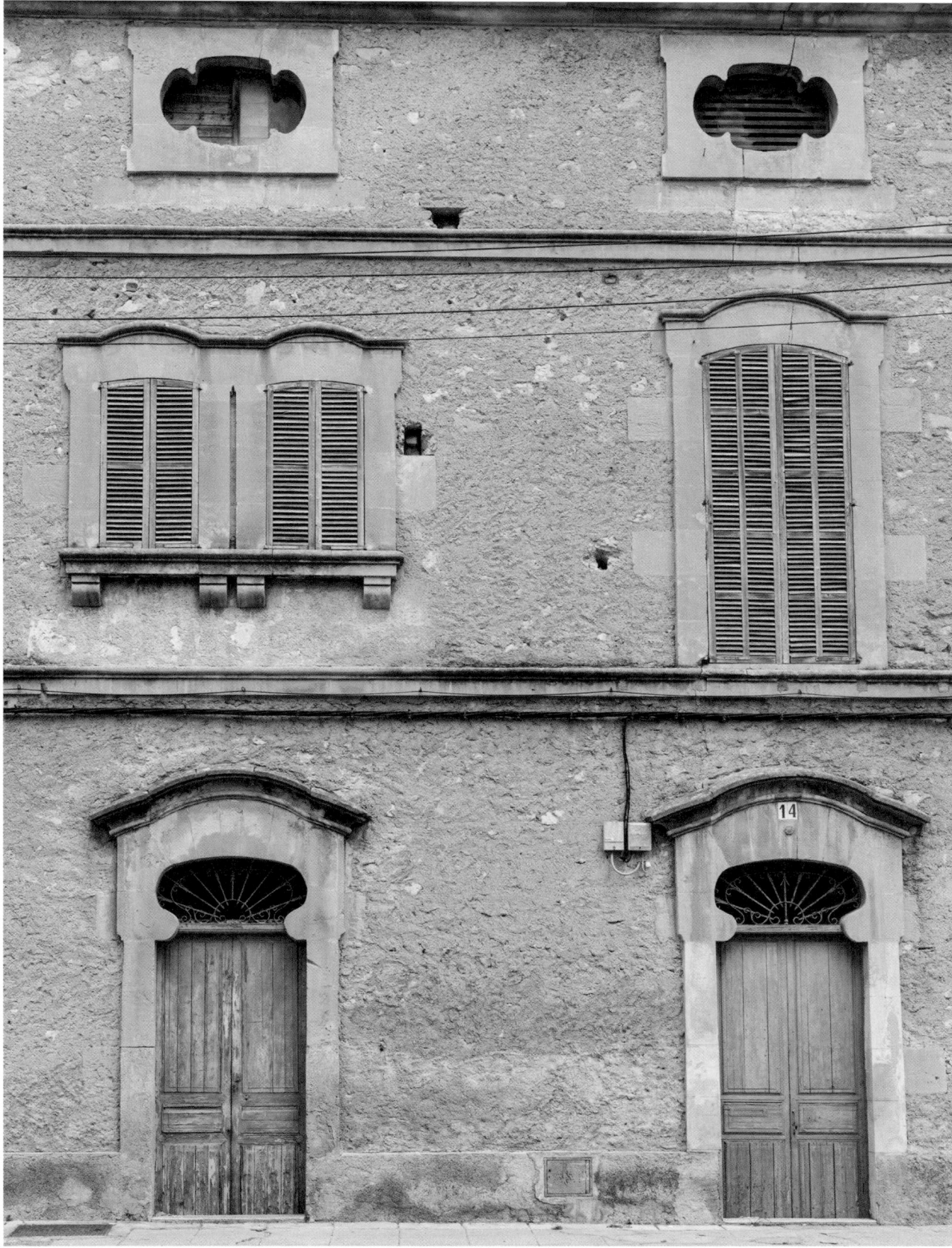

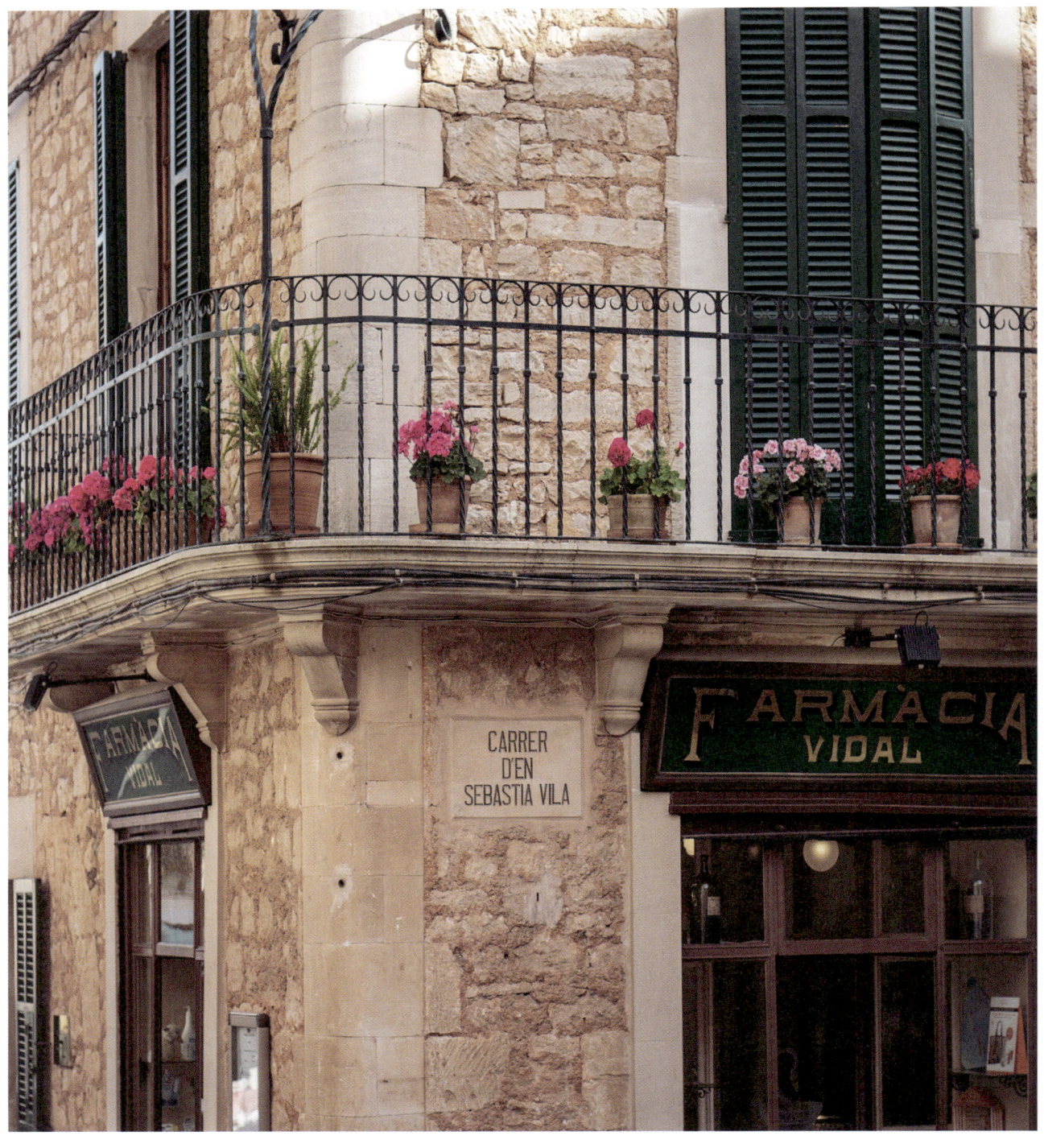

ABOVE AND RIGHT: *The area around Santanyí is known for golden-brown stone used in major buildings across the island, including Palma's cathedral. The town itself has a distinctive charm: craftsmanship, art, and tradition are held in particularly high regard here.*

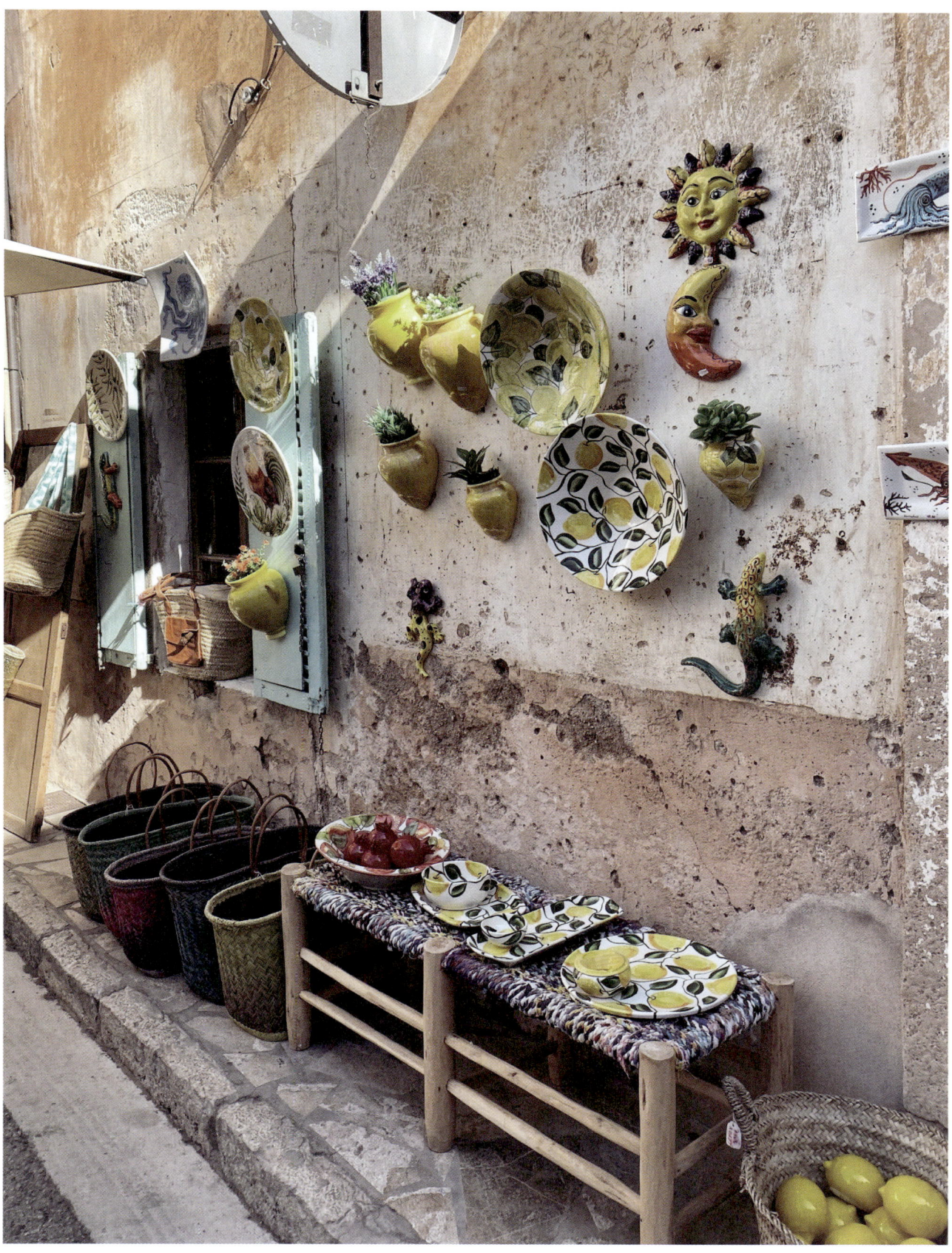

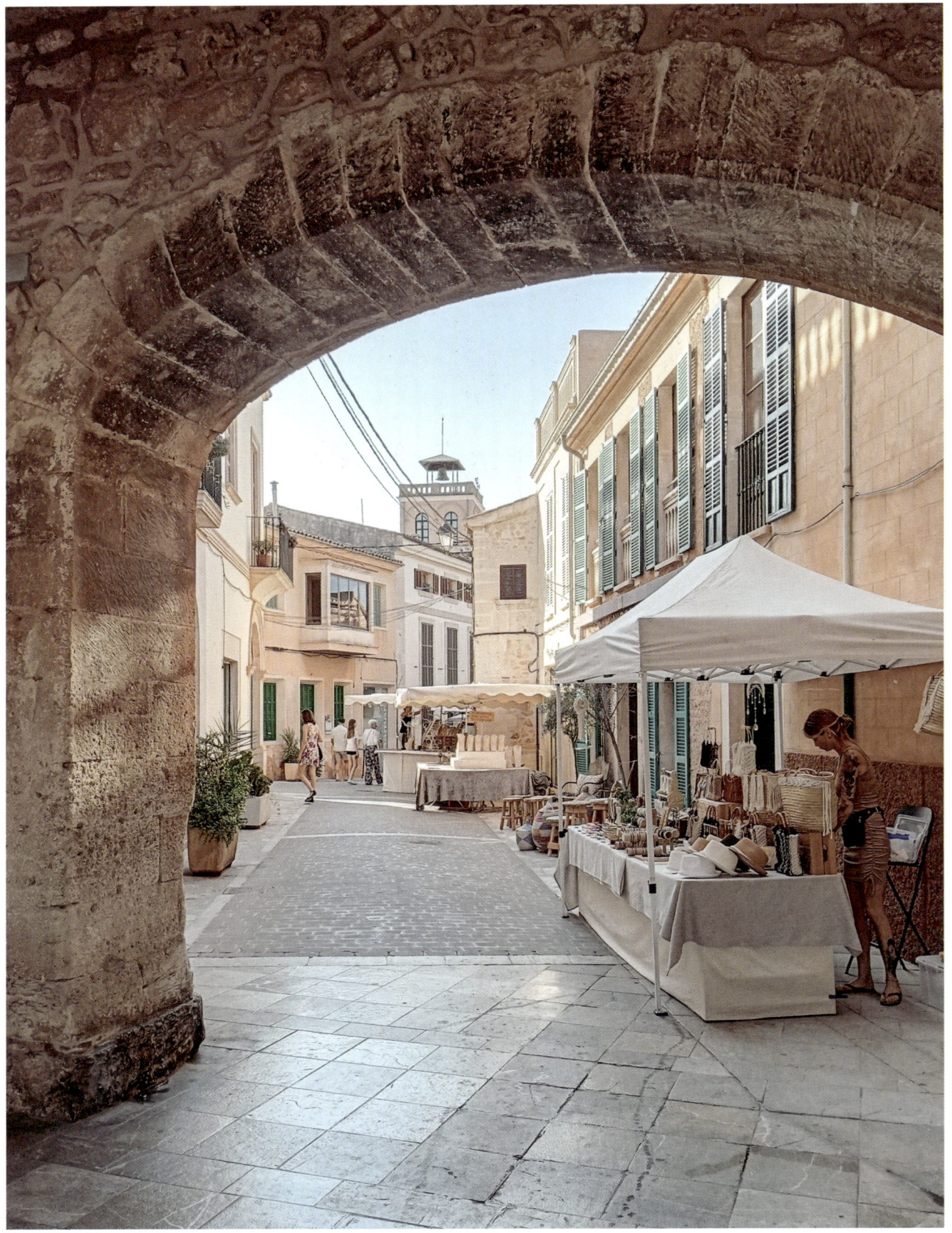

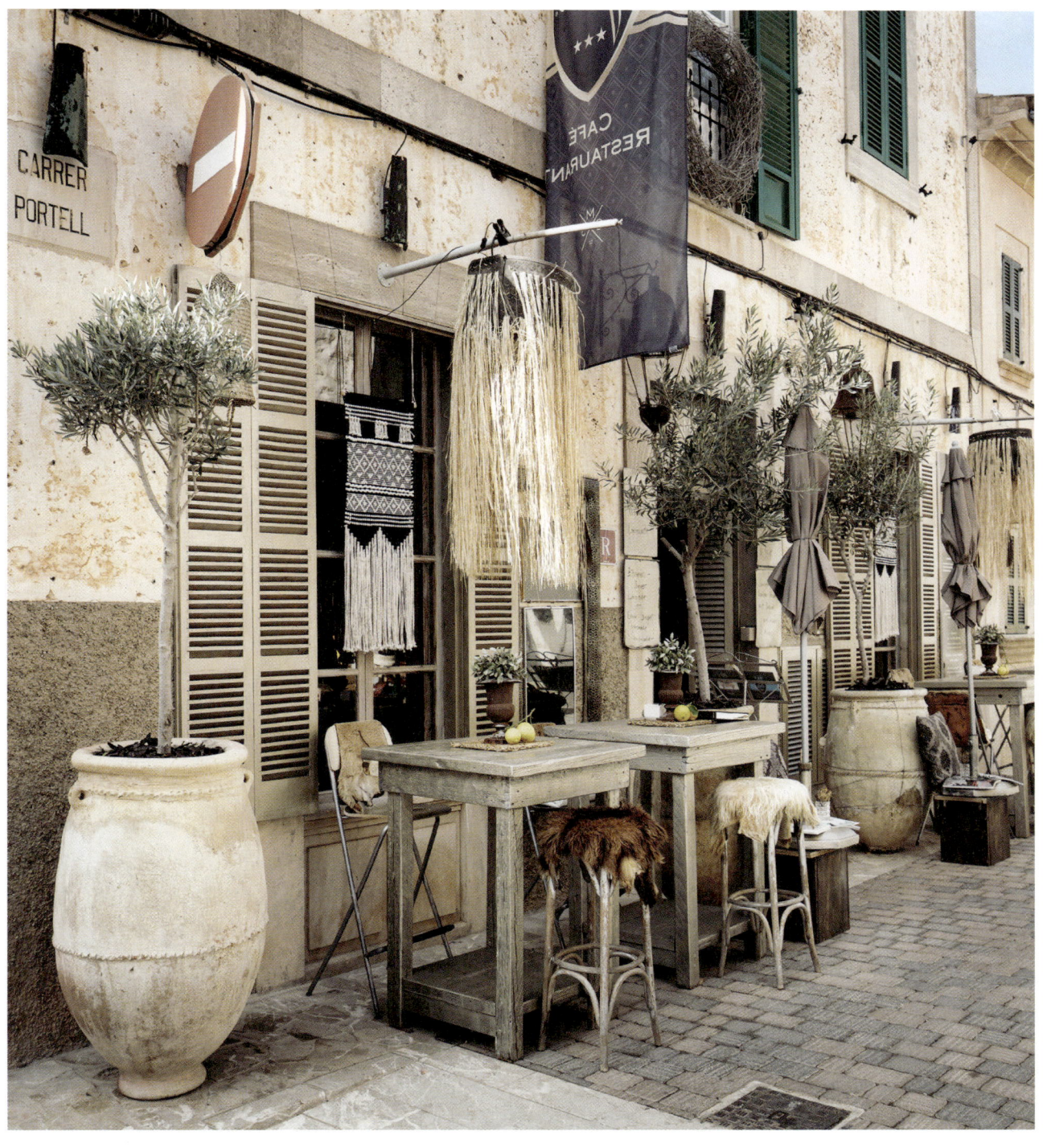

ABOVE AND LEFT: *The twice-weekly market in Santanyí, offering crafts, ceramics, jewelry, cheese, wine, fruit, and vegetables on Wednesday and Saturday mornings. For the local cafés and bars, this is always a welcome opportunity to offer a few light bites at lunchtime.*

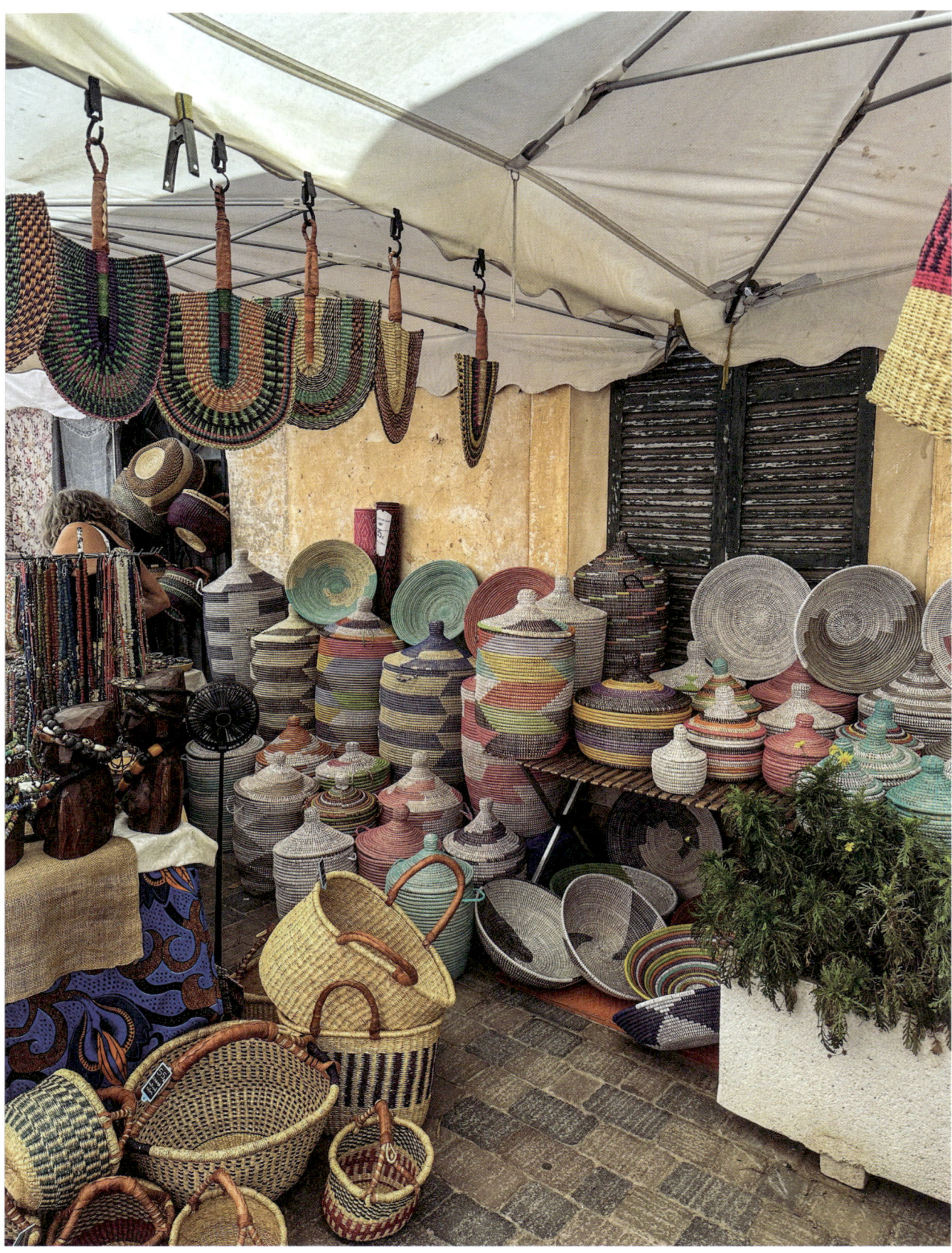

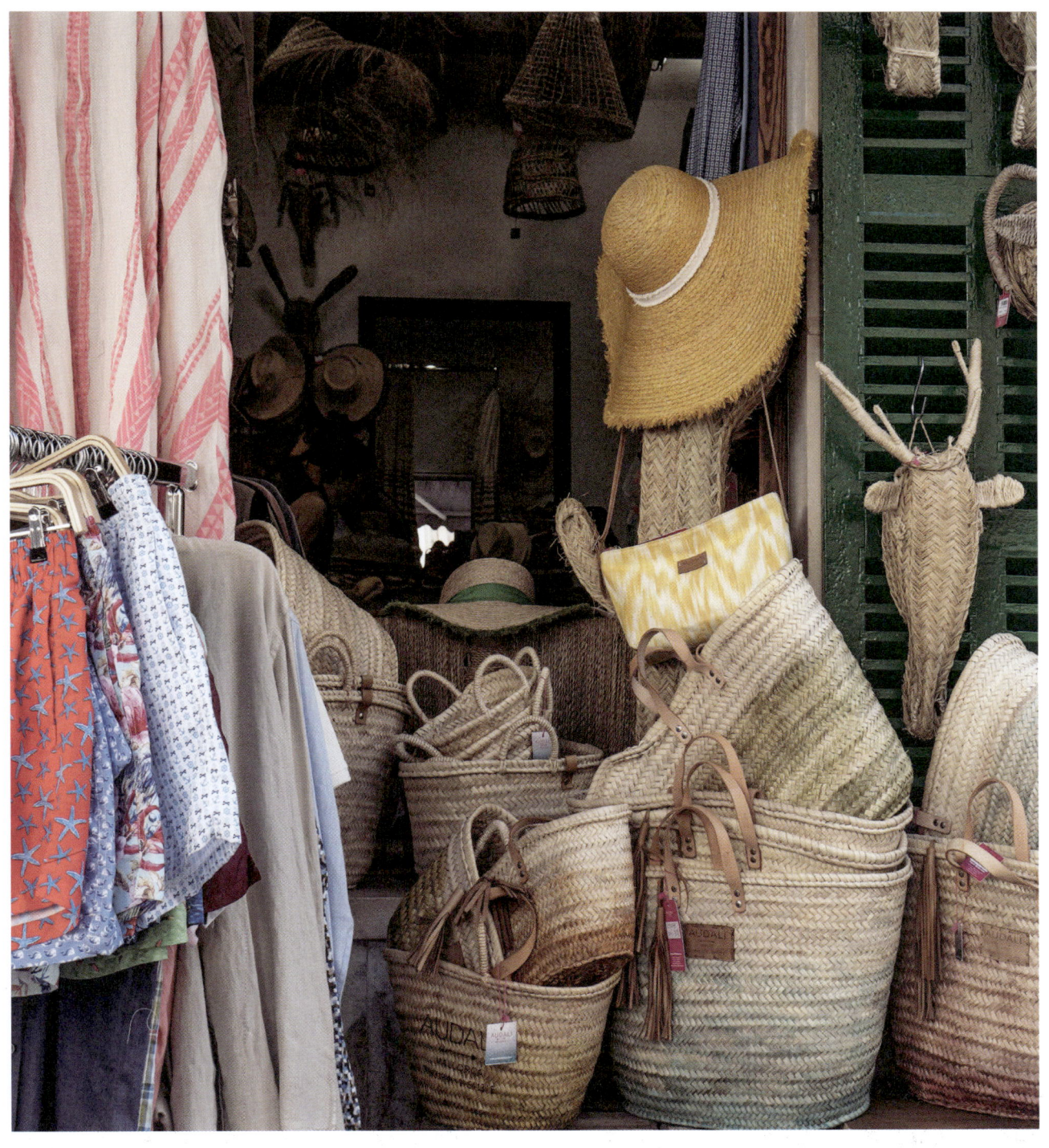

ABOVE: *Not a market day? Santanyí still has a lot to offer with high-end crafts including baskets, and hand-made clothing. Traditions are carried forward in the spirit of soft tourism.*

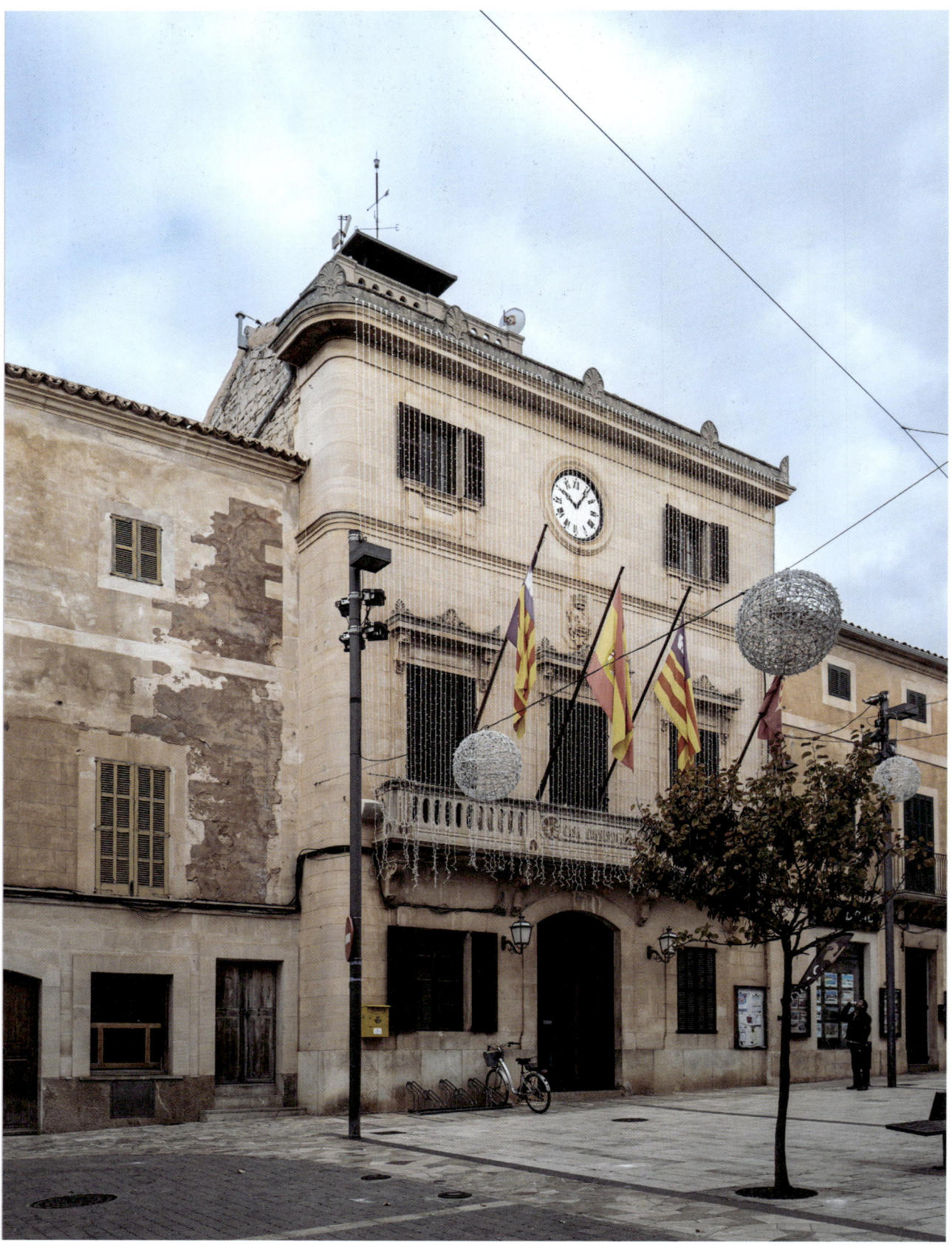

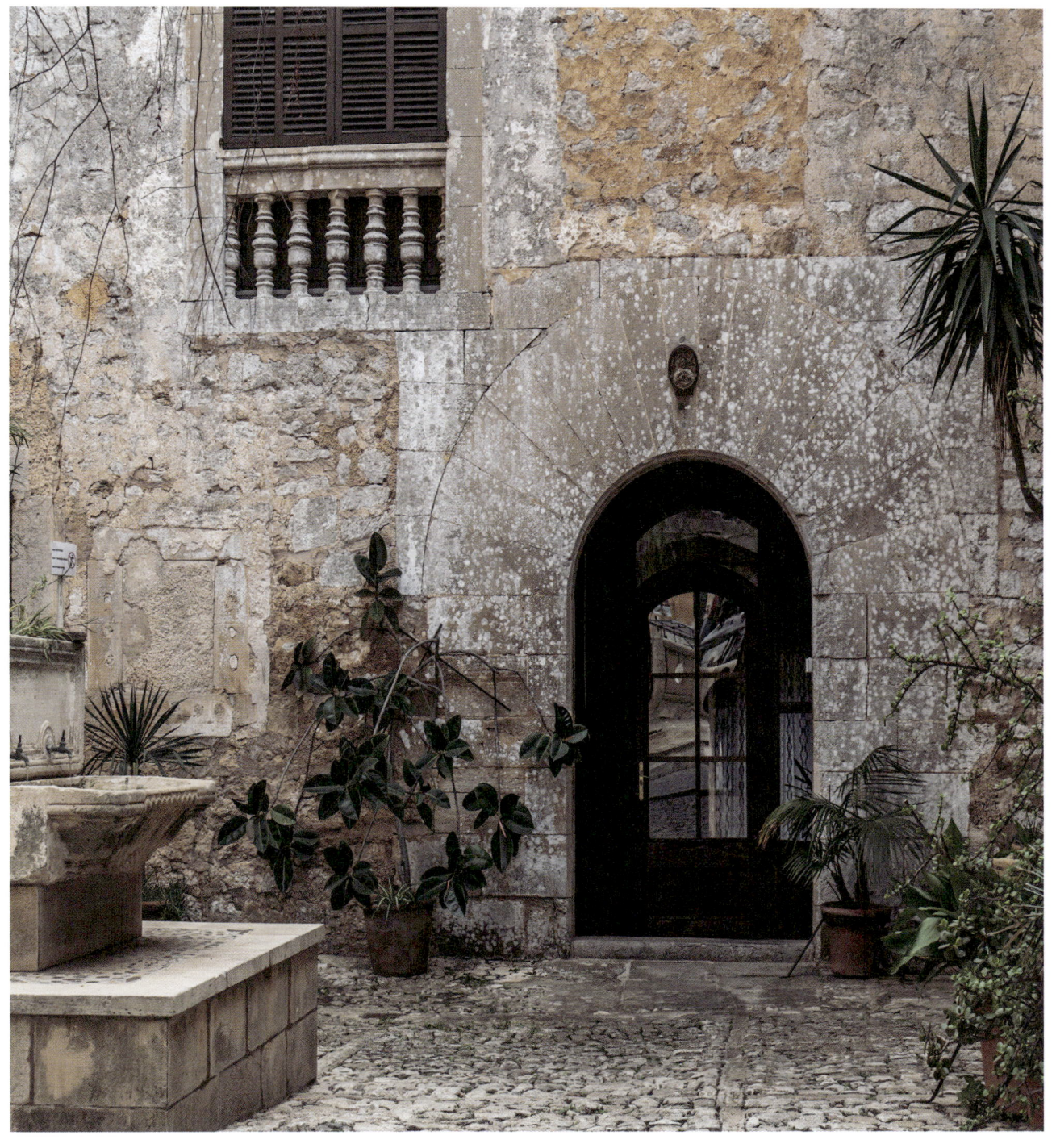

ABOVE: *In Santanyí, history becomes the backdrop, where discoveries await at every turn, reaching far beyond Roman times. Enchanted courtyards, old cobblestones, and mansions tell the stories.*

LEFT: *The Art Nouveau town hall with its bell tower on Plaça Major in the heart of Santanyí's historic old town.*

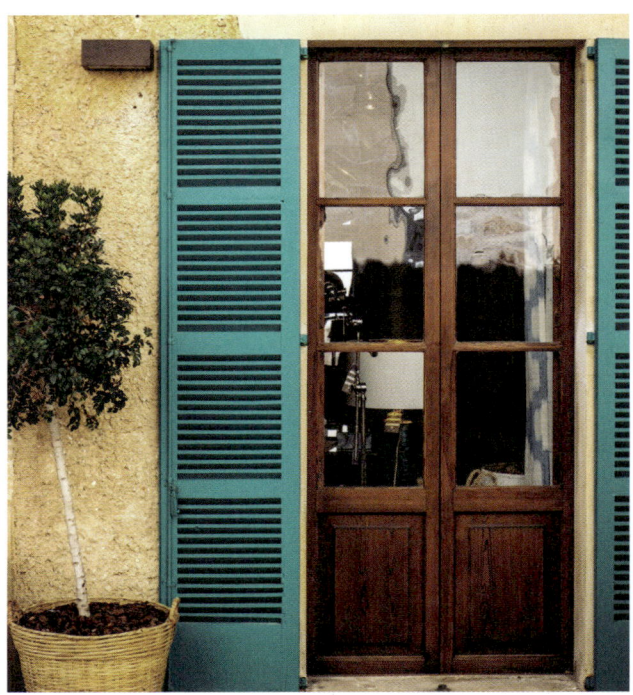
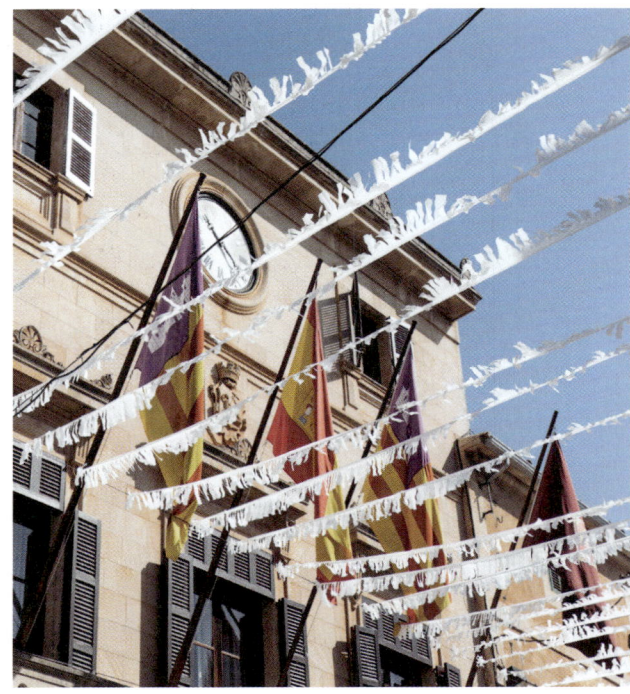
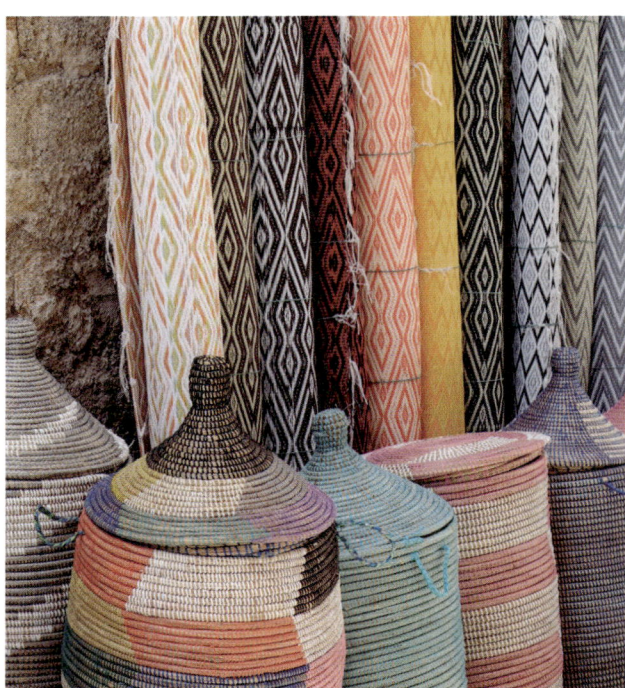
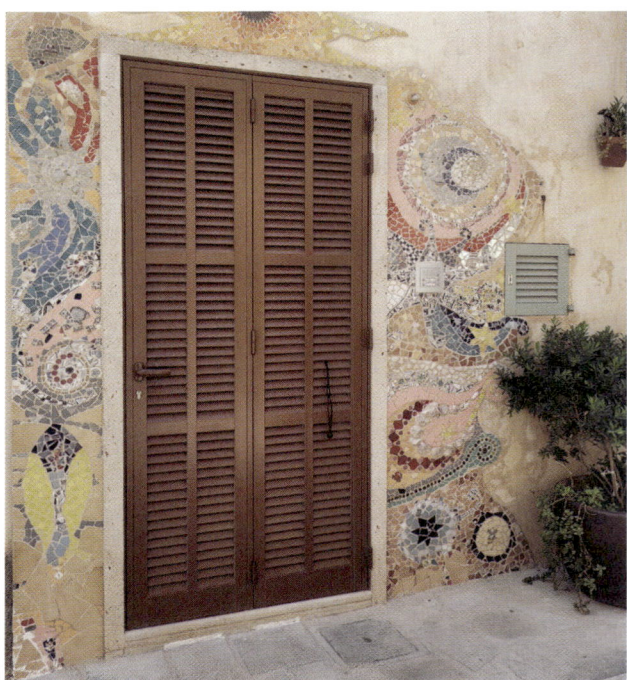

ABOVE AND RIGHT: *The faces of Santanyí throughout the year are so colorful and diverse that a visit is rewarding during any season. Street festivals in front of the town hall on Plaça Major (above right) and the colors and decorations of the town's shops, galleries, and restaurants offer inspiration in endless supply.*

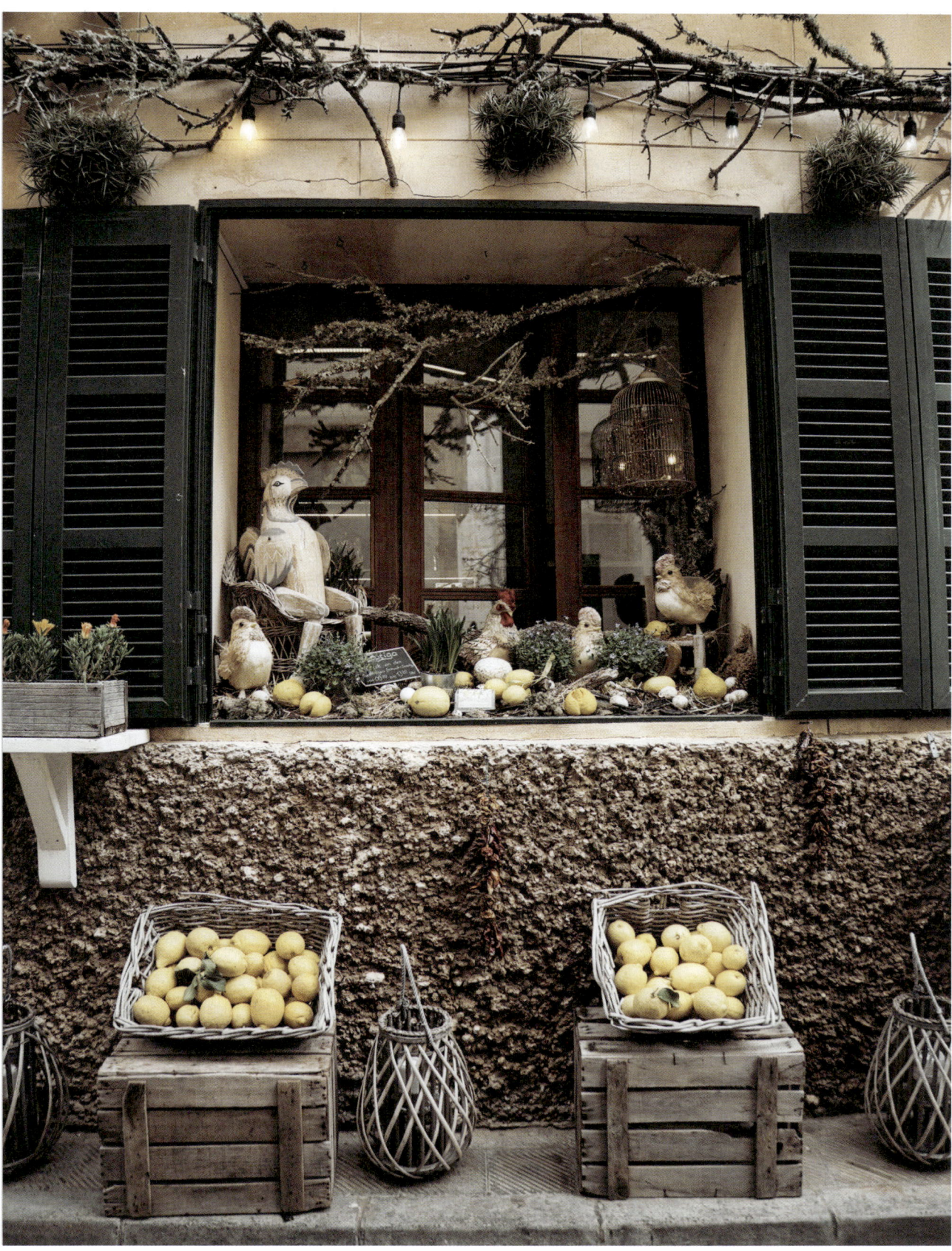

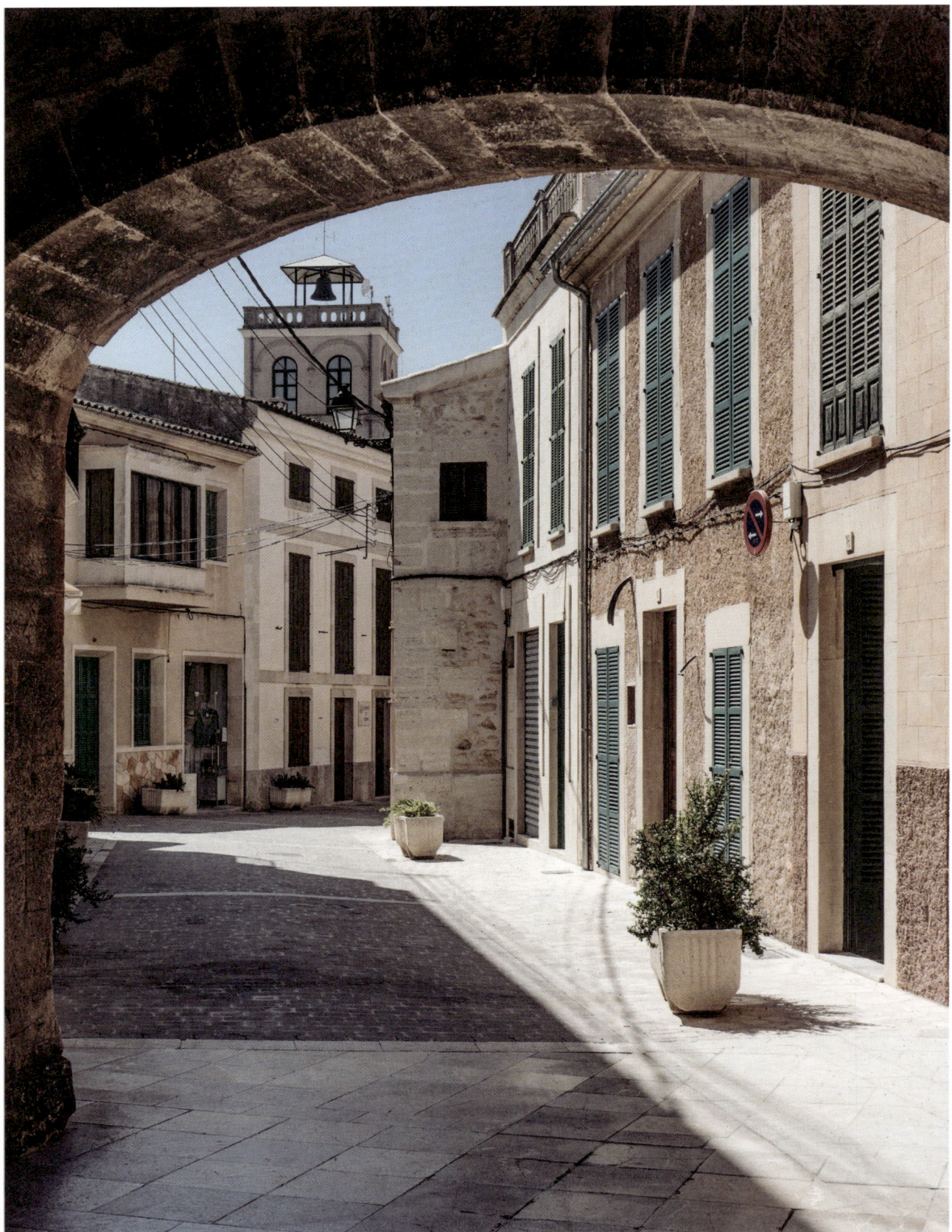

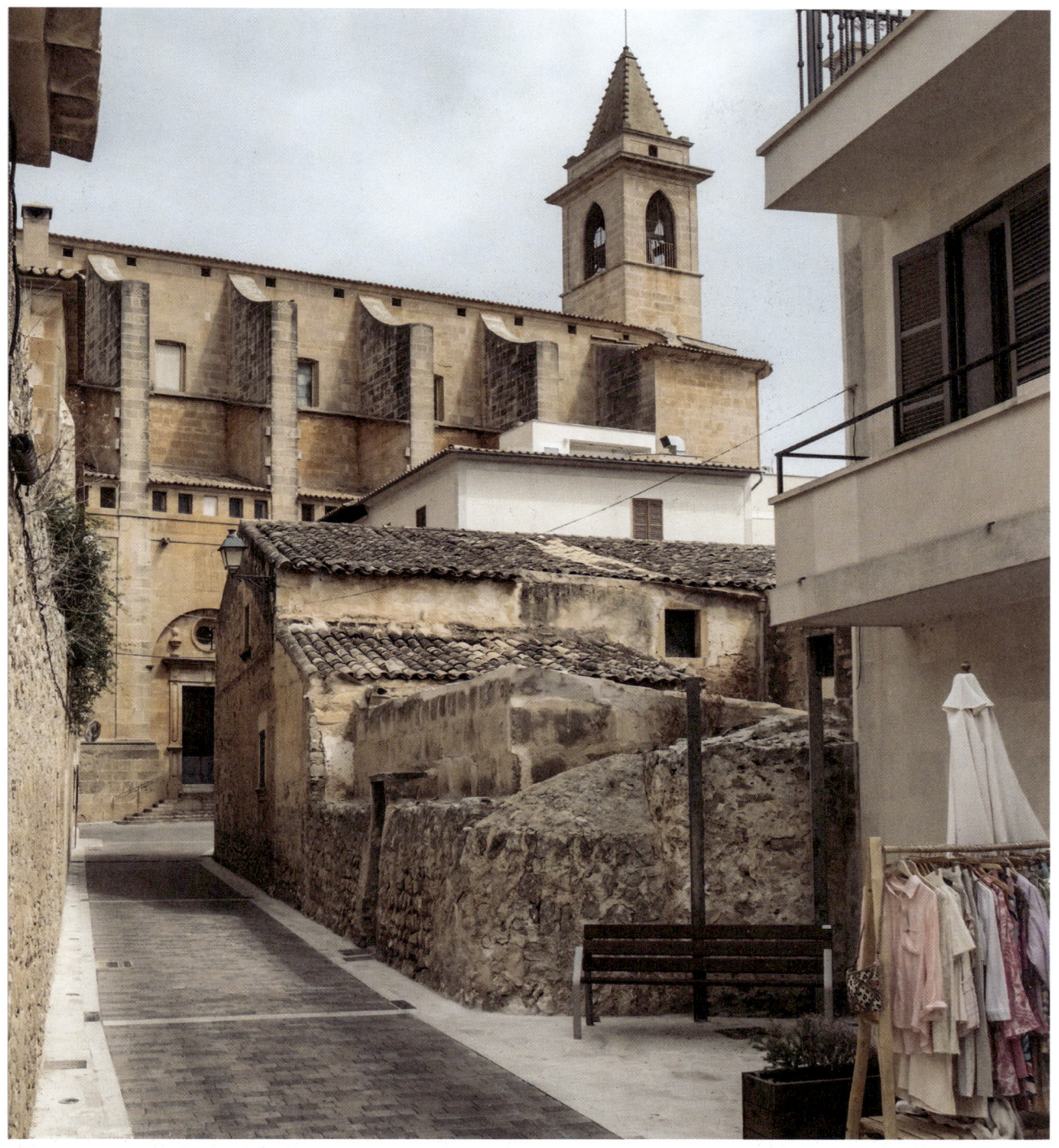

ABOVE: *The narrow but cozy network of streets in Santanyí's historic center, with the parish church of Sant Andreu on Plaça Major in the background.*

LEFT: *The view through the city gate toward the center of Santanyí that never grows tiresome.*

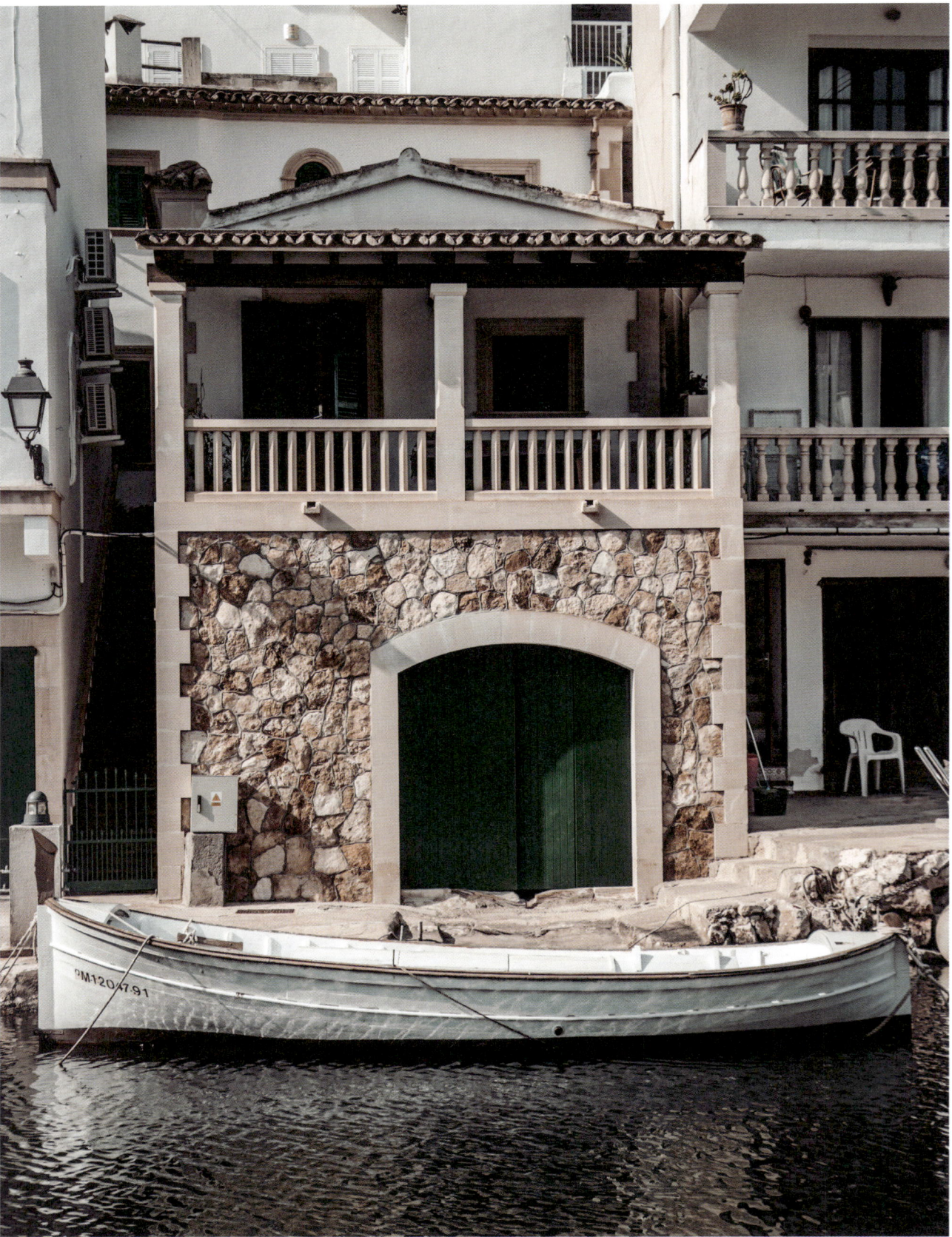

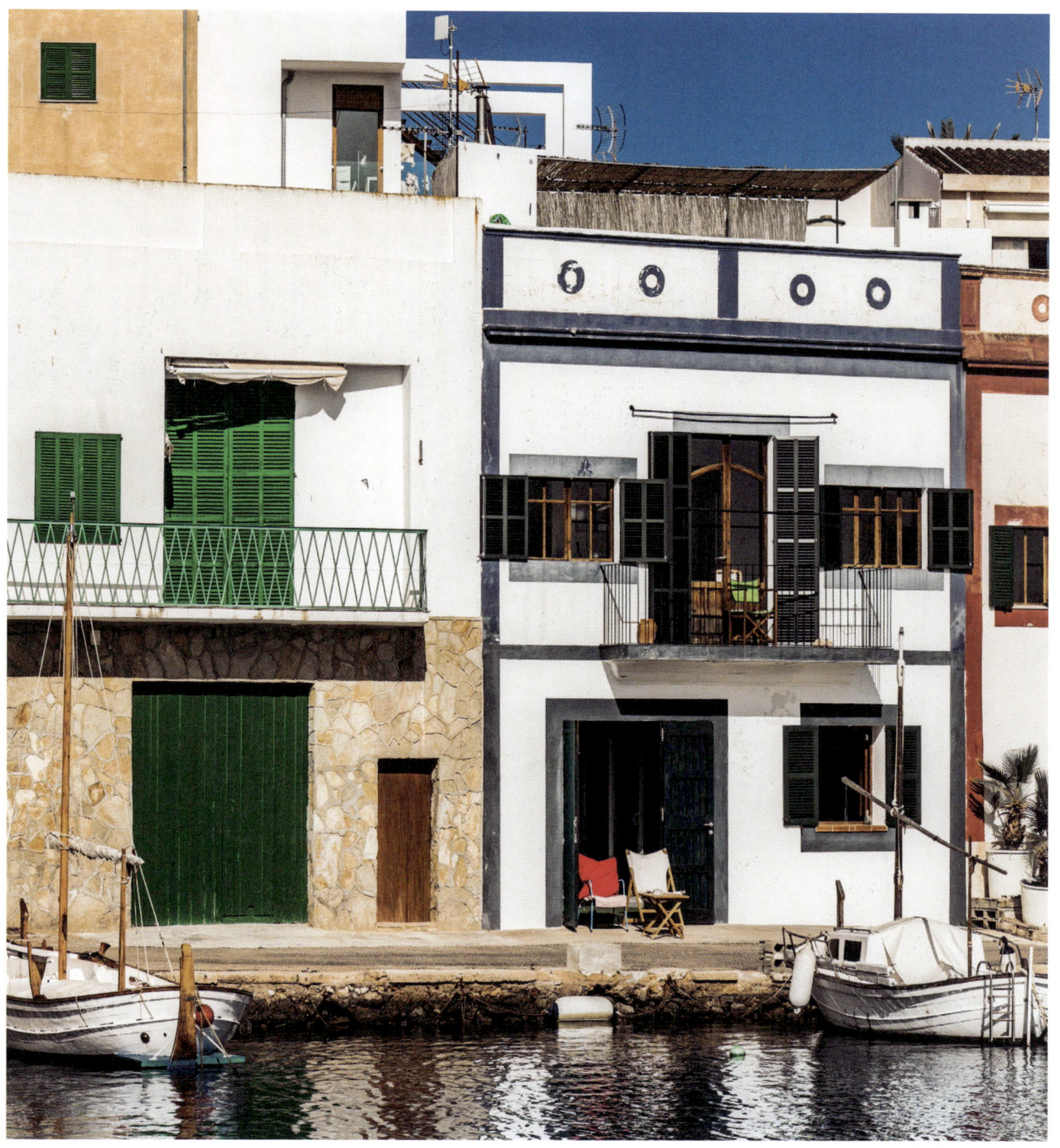

ABOVE: *Laid-back Portocolom, where small boats are moored just outside the door, resting in the calm of a protected bay that resembles a natural harbor.*

LEFT: *Cala Figuera near Santanyí, an idyllic-looking working fishing village set among rocky outcrops. Families here still make a livelihood from fishing.*

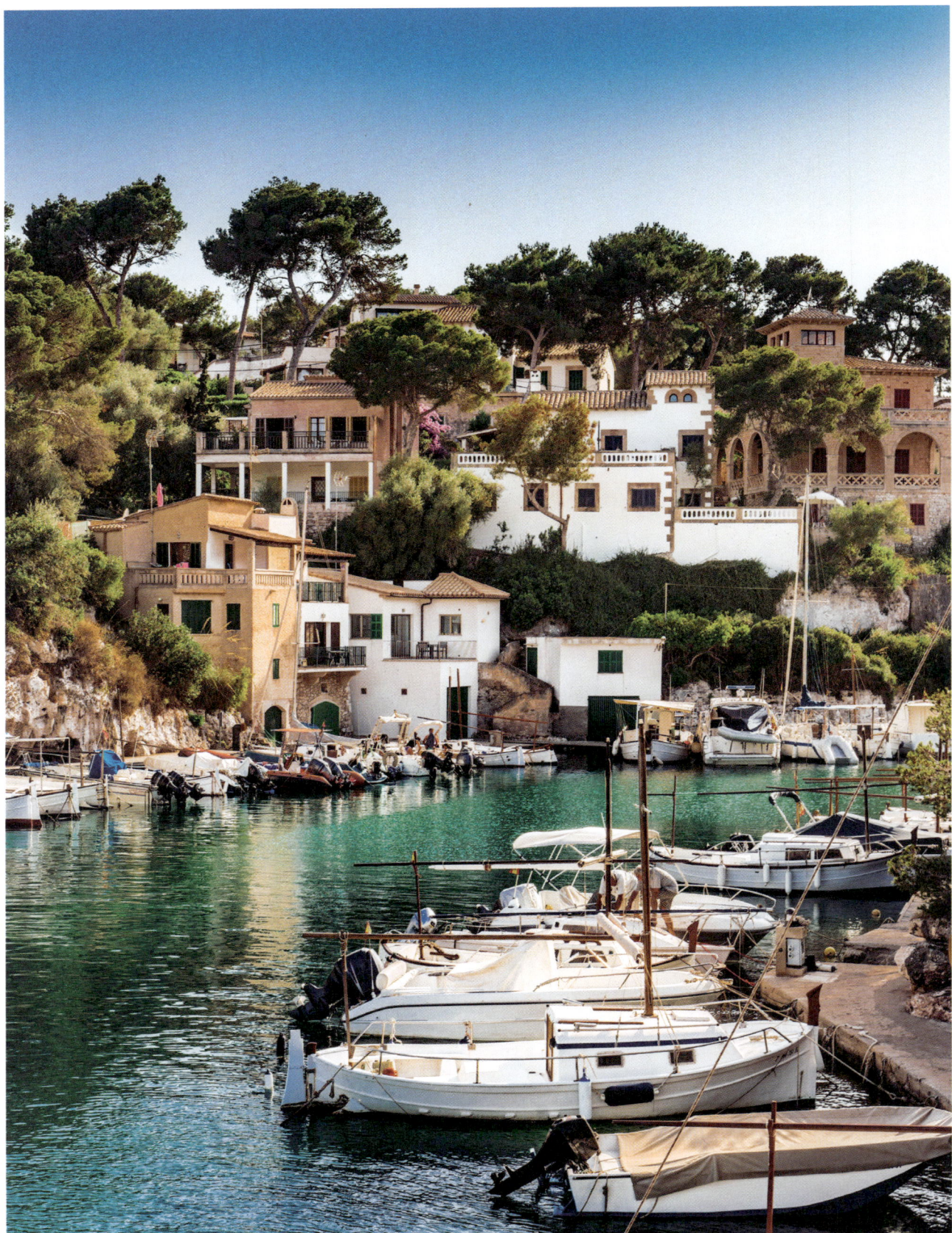

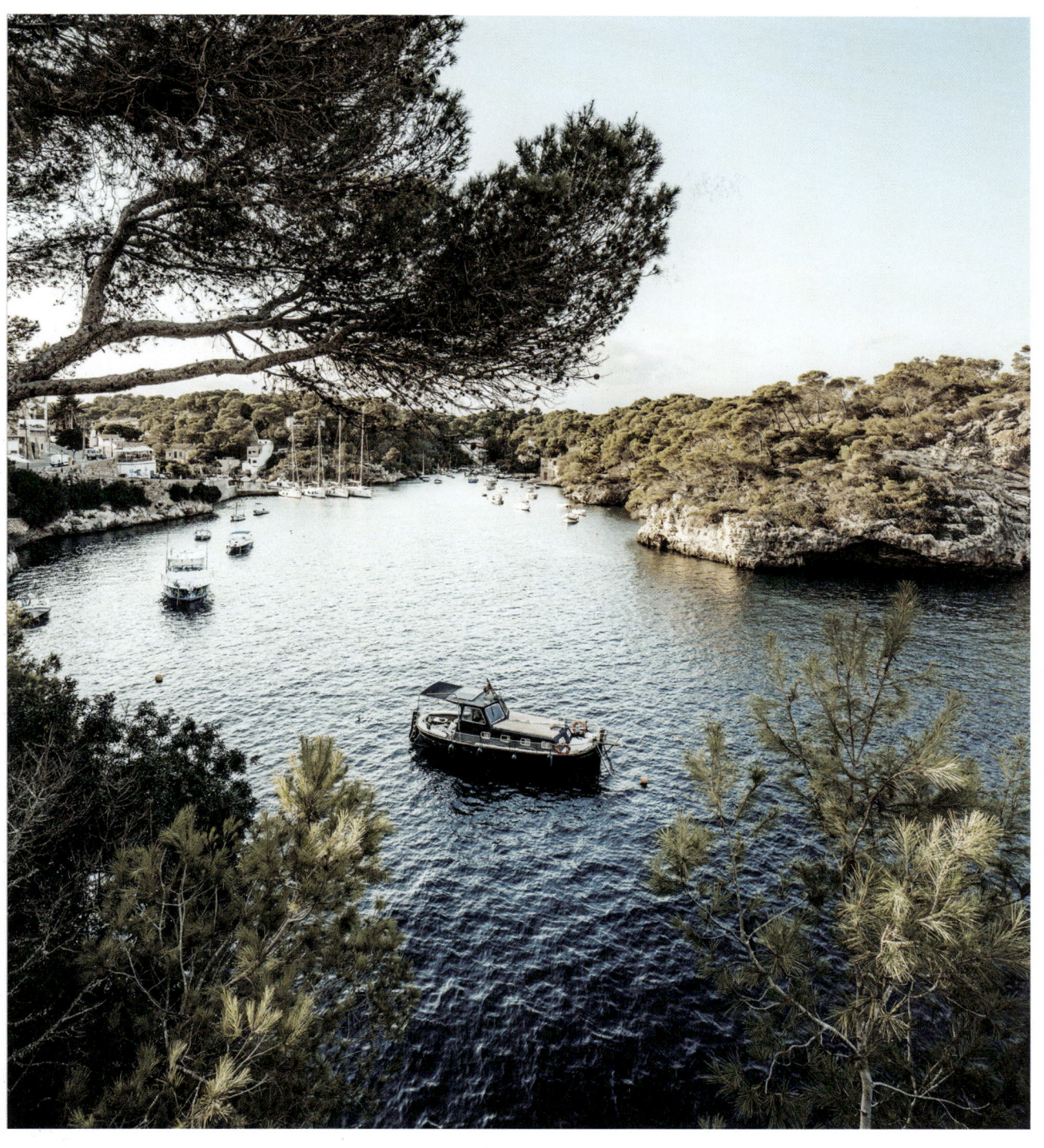

ABOVE AND LEFT: *Cala Figuera is a fjord-like natural harbor, with turquoise water and rocky inlets, surrounded by pine and fig trees for which the bay is named.*

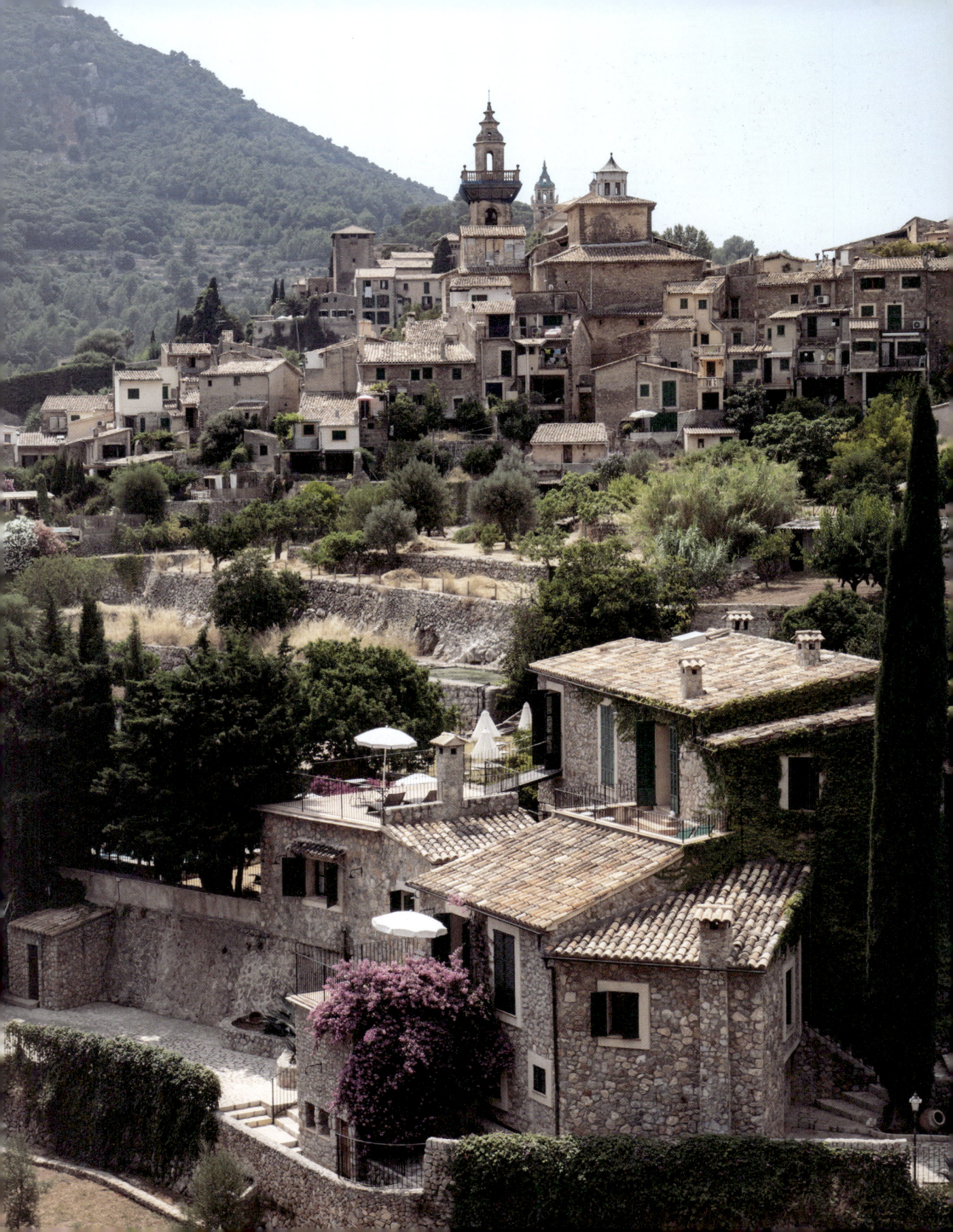

VALLDEMOSSA

A SMALL TOWN IN A RUGGED LANDSCAPE LONG ASSOCIATED WITH INSPIRATION, NOT ONLY FOR ARTISTS

Valldemossa is tied to a particular love story. The composer Frédéric Chopin and the writer George Sand spent the winter of 1838–39 here living in an abandoned monastery. Chopin, weakened by asthma and tuberculosis, had hoped the mild Mediterranean climate would aid his recovery. The couple also wanted to enjoy their early relationship far from the scrutiny of Parisian society. That was the intention. The reality proved harsher. Cold weather, constant rain, and daily life in the drafty monastery took a physical toll on the composer. Relations with the local population were strained. The traveling party, which included Sand's two children from her first marriage, met with reserve rather than warmth. An unmarried patchwork family raised suspicions. Sand herself stood out. She wore men's clothing, smoked in public, and expressed feminist views that caused offense. Accommodation options were limited; they found nowhere to stay outside the monastery.

In her book *A Winter in Majorca*, Sand offered a sharply critical portrait of the Mallorcans, but her account also shows affection for the island, its landscape, and its natural abundance. For Chopin, the stay was physically exhausting but creatively productive. In cell number 4, he composed many of his best-known piano works, including the "Raindrop Prelude." Those who travel through Valldemossa and its surroundings will be rewarded if they are attentive. The place tends to leave a lasting impression.

LEFT: *The hamlet of Valldemossa in the Serra de Tramuntana, in its center the monastery where Frédéric Chopin and his lover George Sand spent a winter. They lived and worked out of cell 4, now part of a museum at the monastery.*

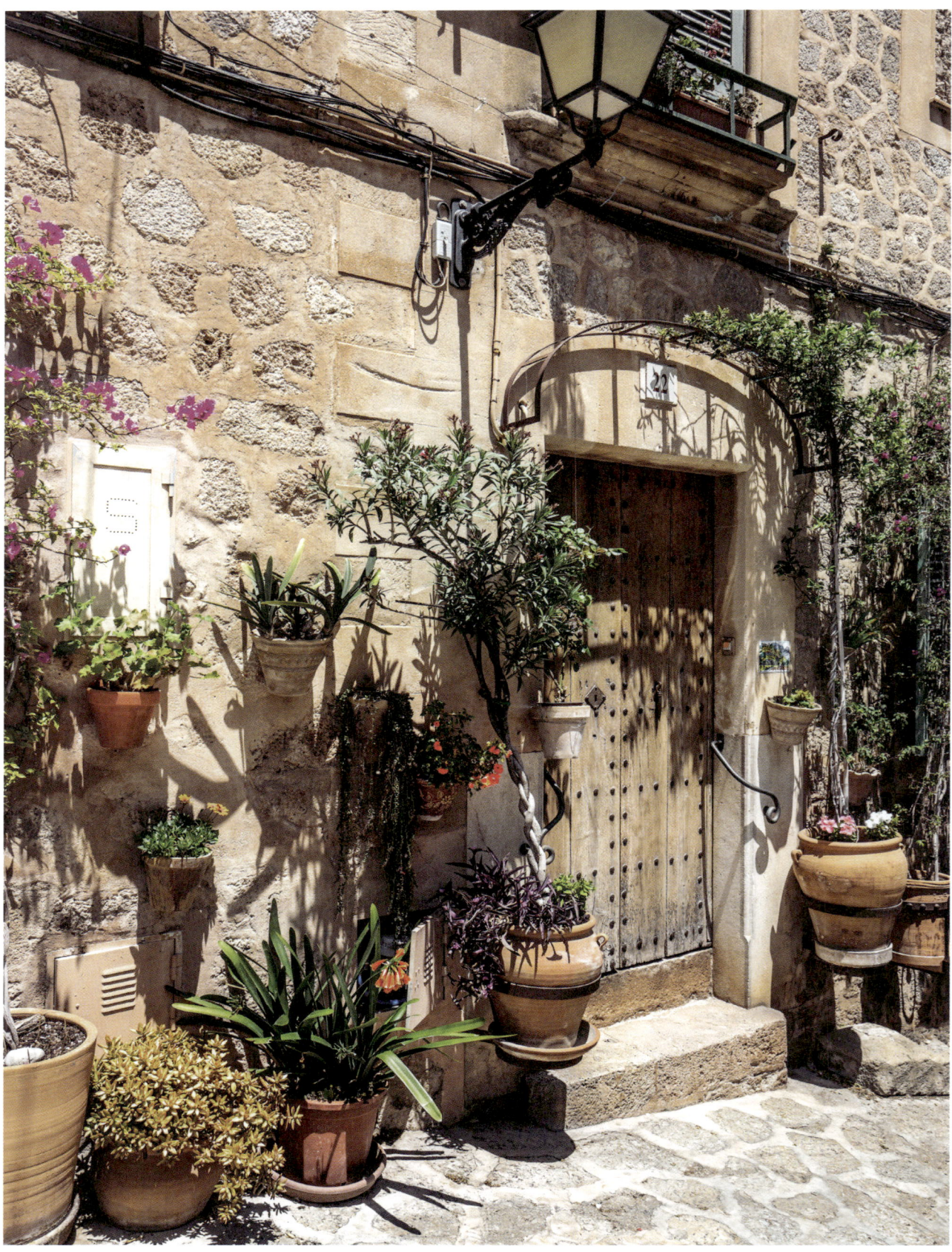

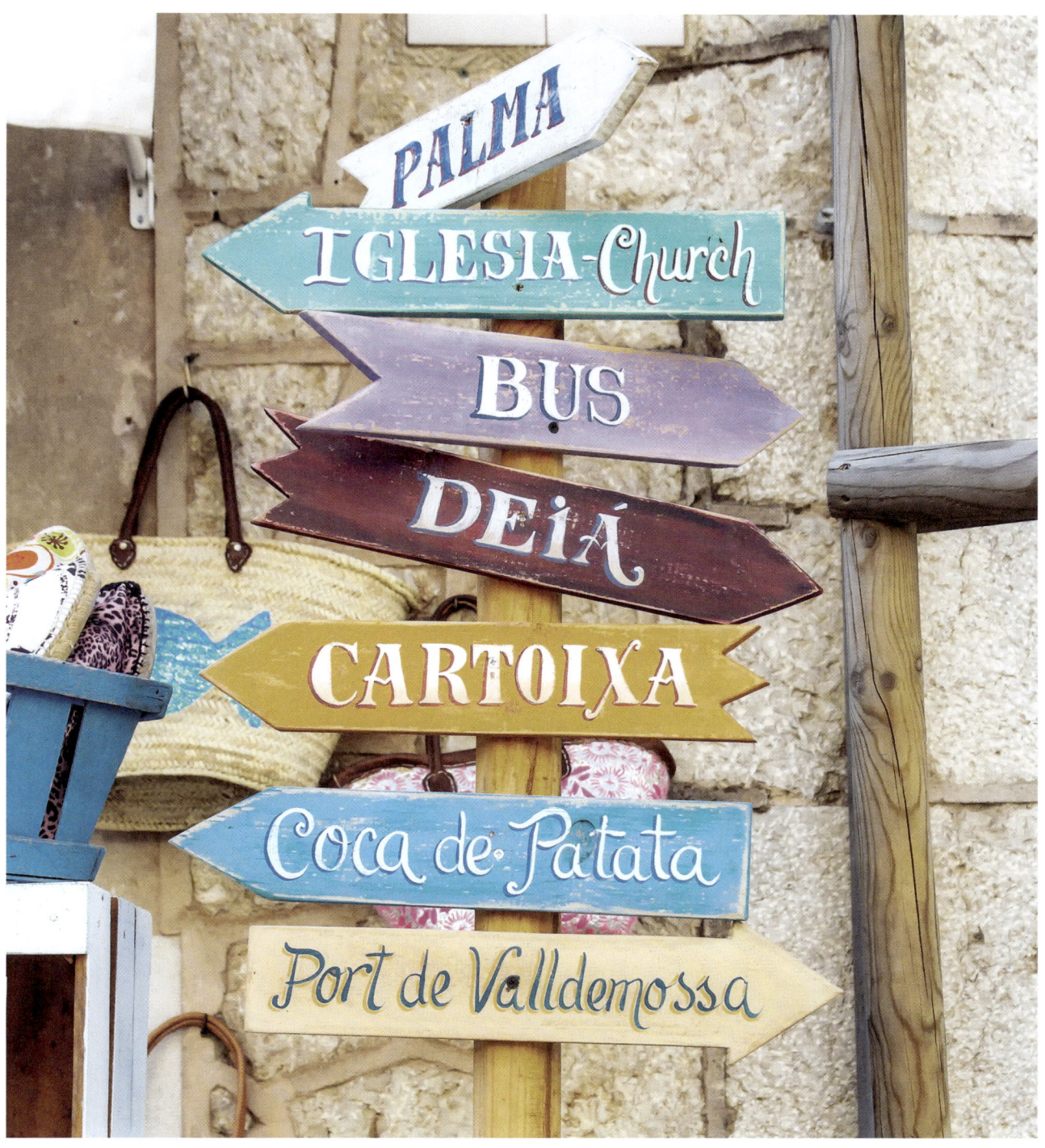

ABOVE AND LEFT: *The narrow streets of Valldemossa are wildly irregular; they run up and down, crisscrossing this way and that, as colorful as this signpost. Small surprises abound in roadside flowerpot gardens, hidden boutiques, and small cafés.*

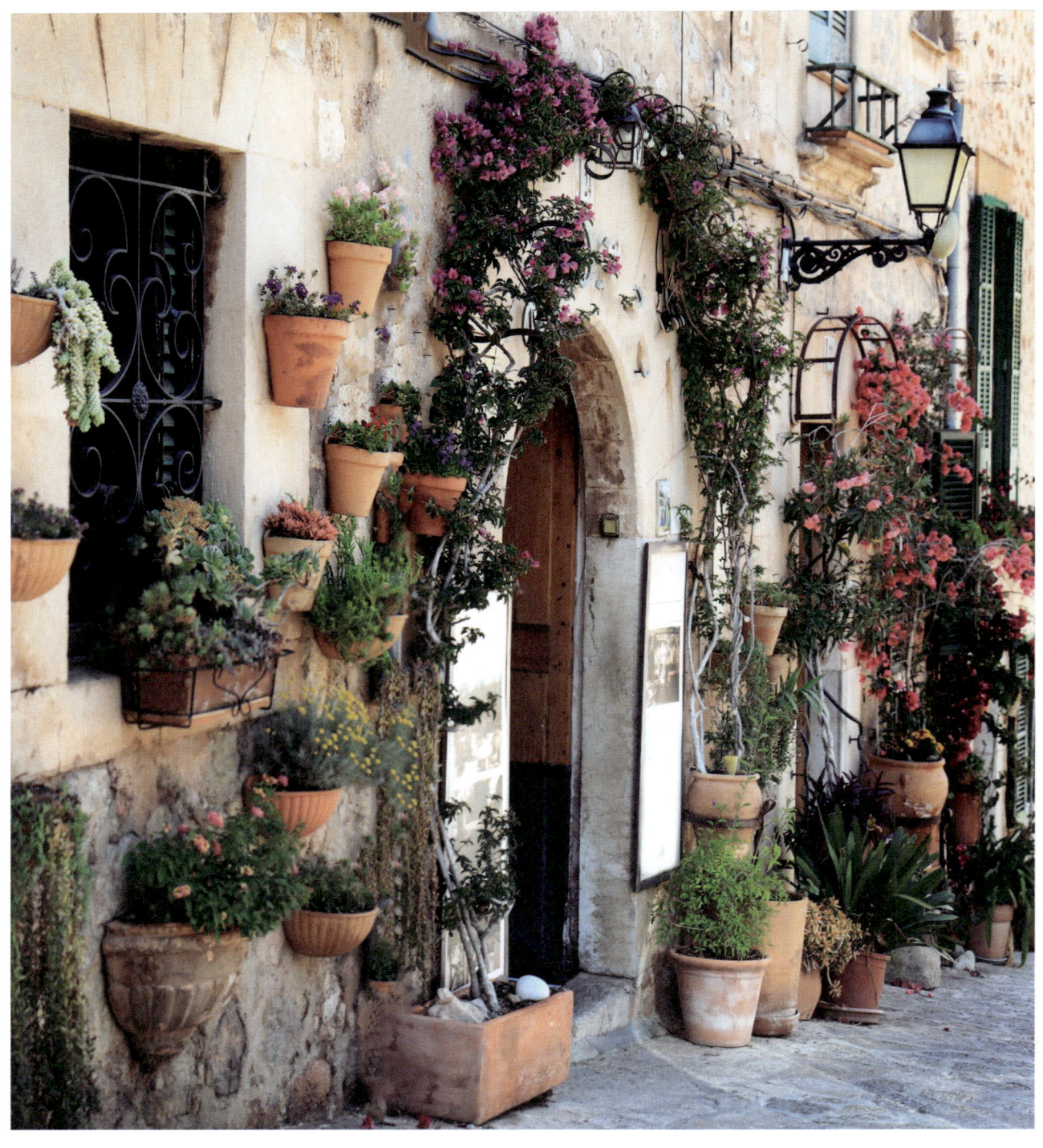

ABOVE AND RIGHT: *Flowerpots adorning the cobbled streets are a tradition in the town of Valldemossa, nestled among olive and almond groves, and pine and oak forests. Even though the island's most-visited village is no longer an insider's secret, it reveals a quite different side of Mallorca.*

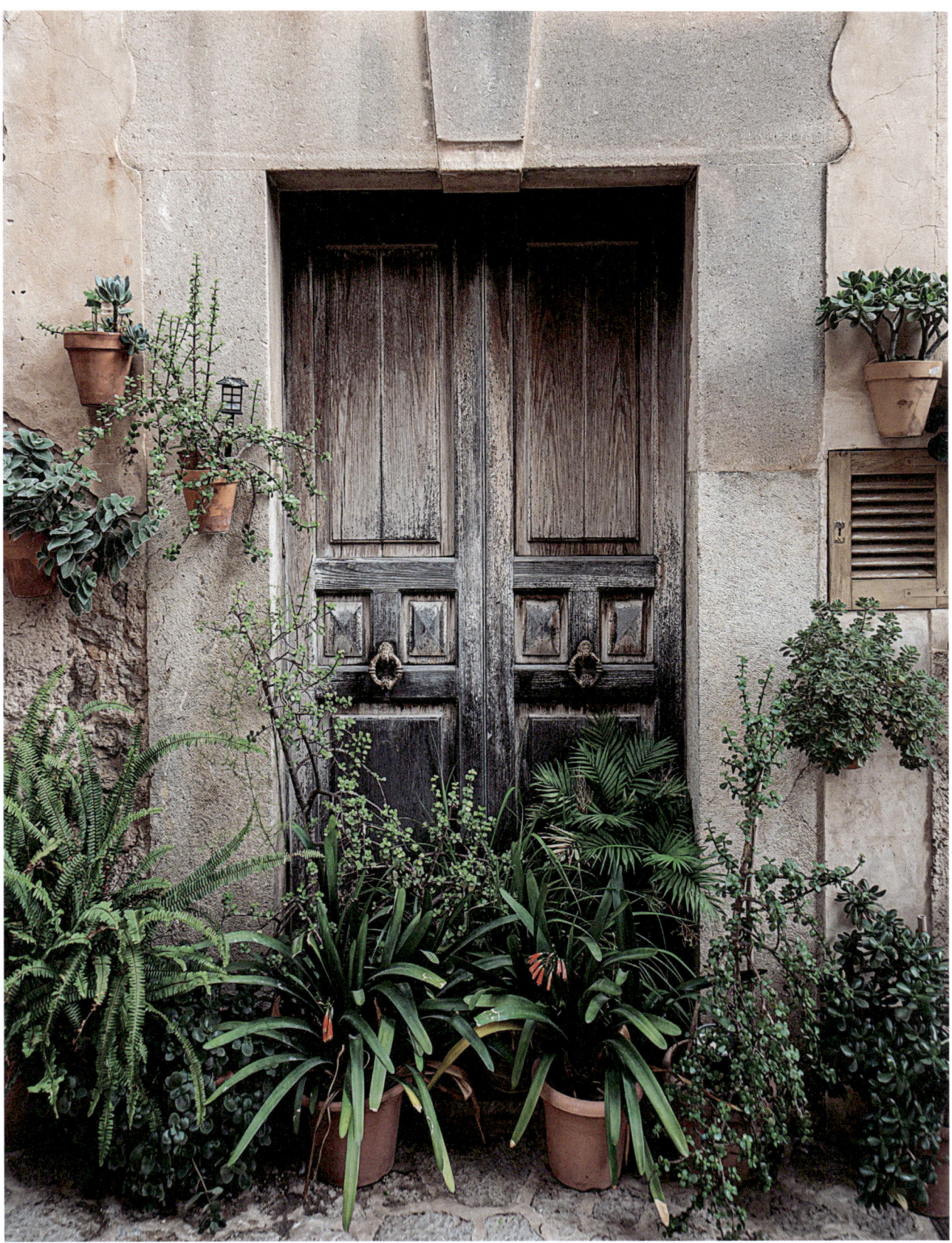

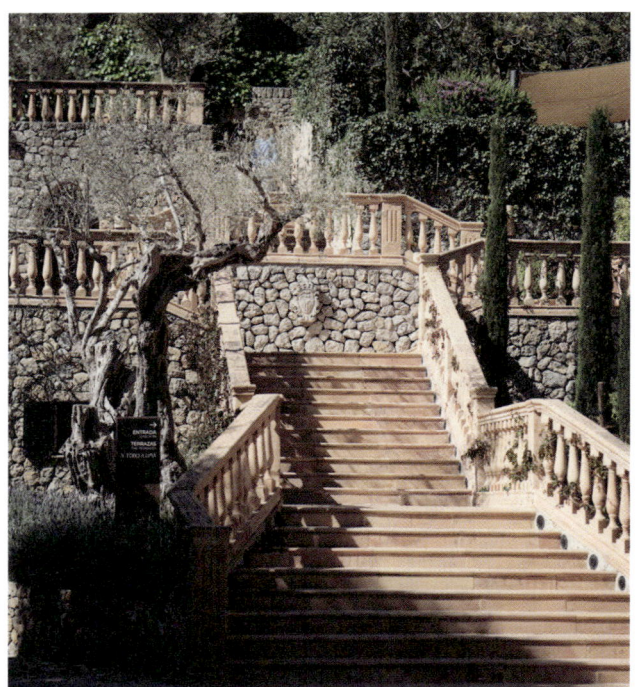
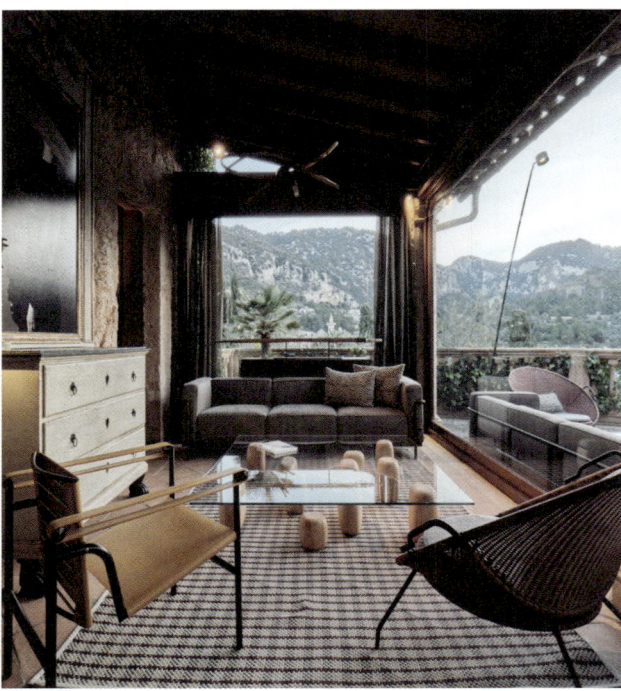
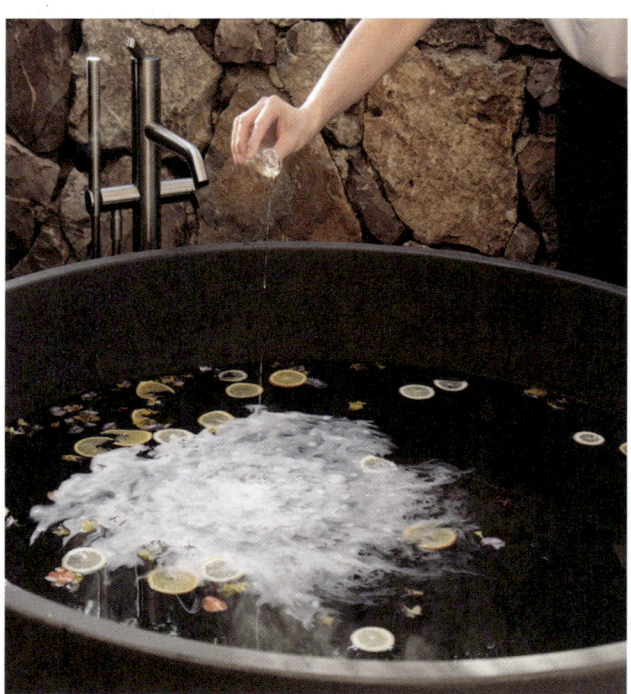
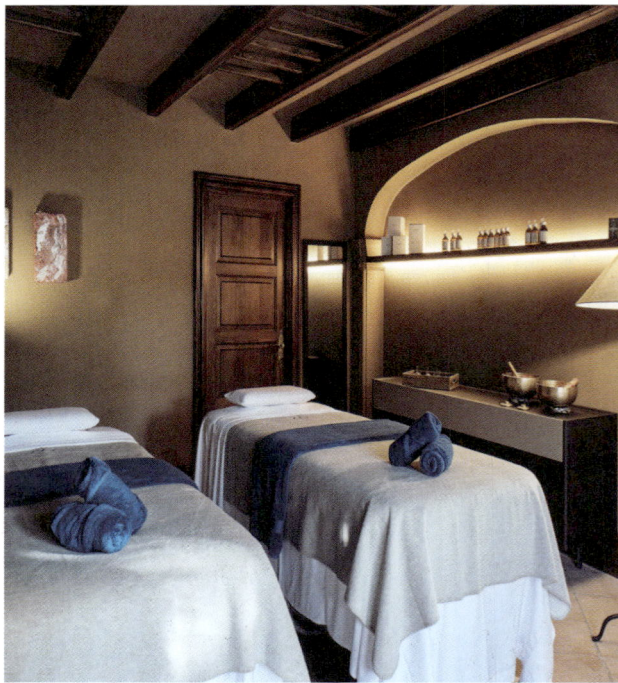

ABOVE AND RIGHT: *Hotel Valldemossa is housed in two nineteenth-century buildings just outside the center of town. Its Santuario health spa offering medical treatments, its outstanding restaurant, and its private atmosphere are among its draws.*

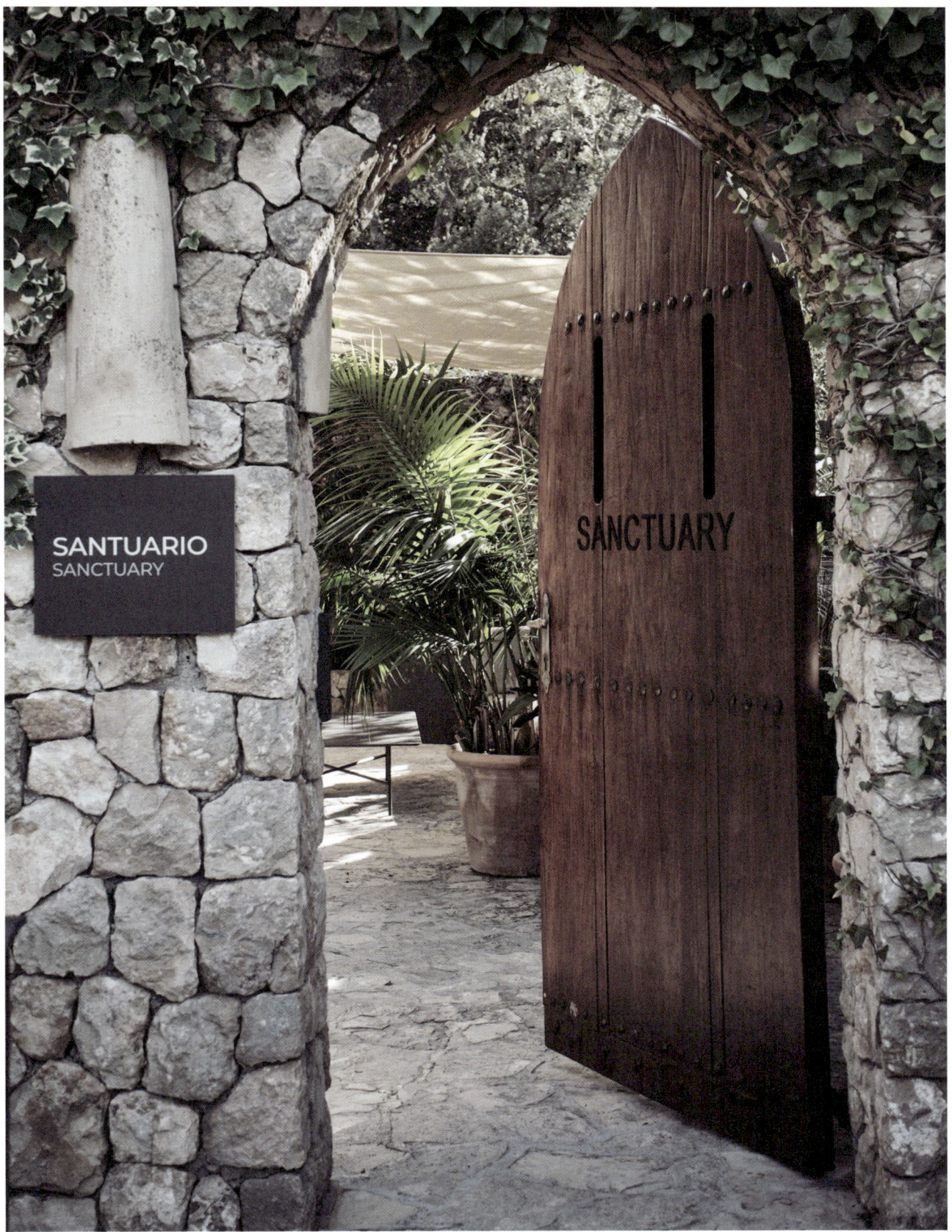

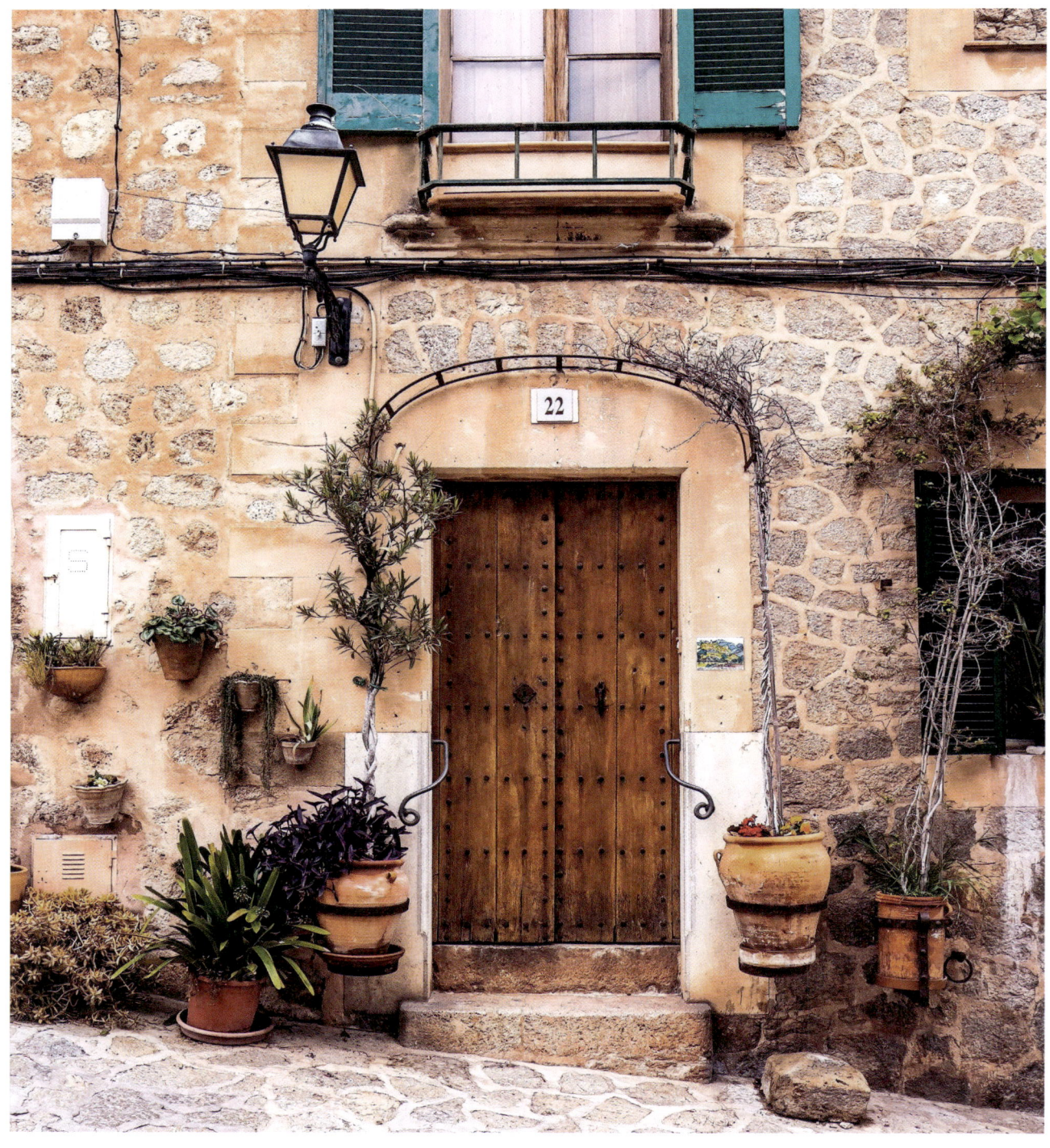

ABOVE AND RIGHT: *Valldemossa is a UNESCO World Heritage site and one of the most beautiful villages in the world according to National Geographic. No doubt about it.*

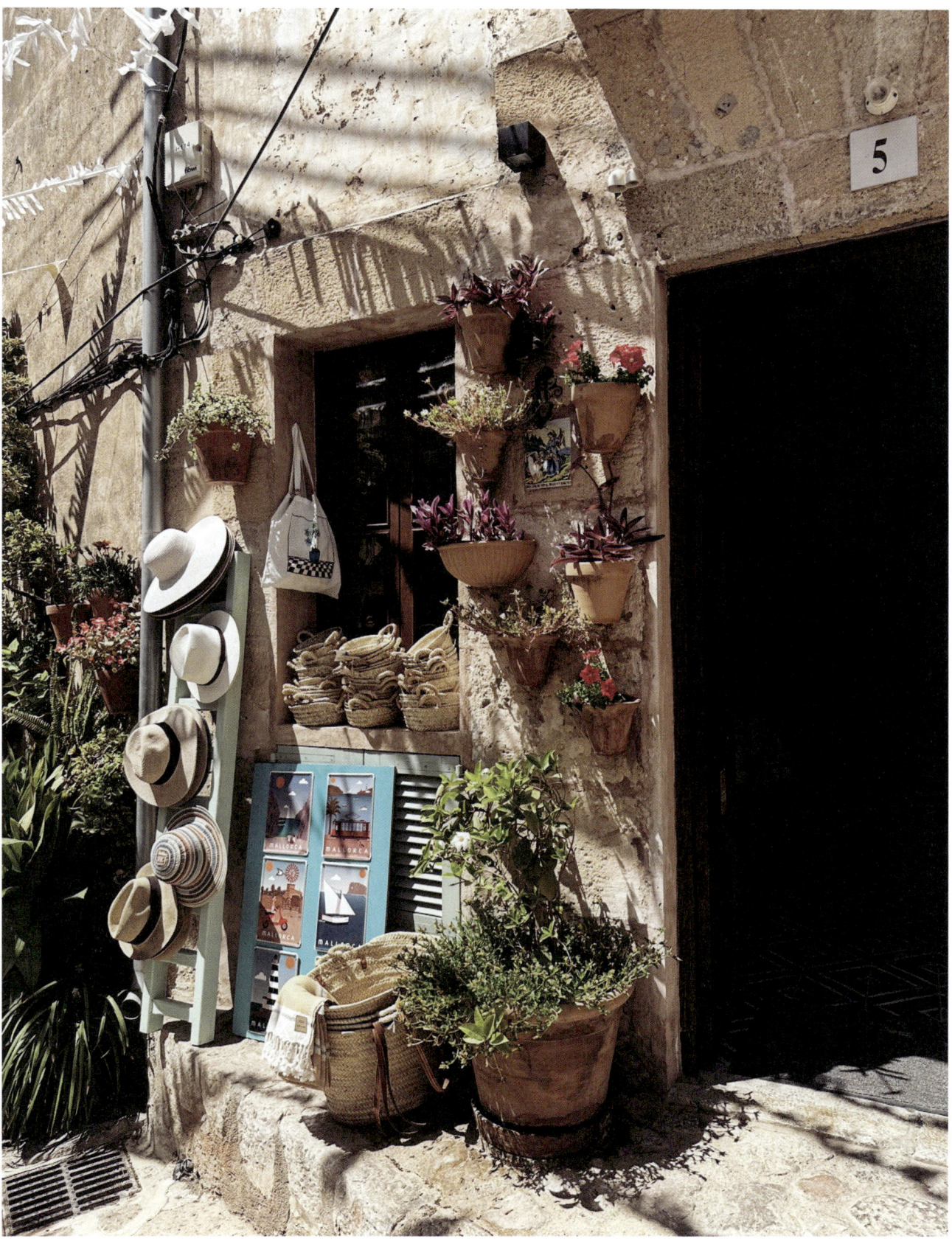

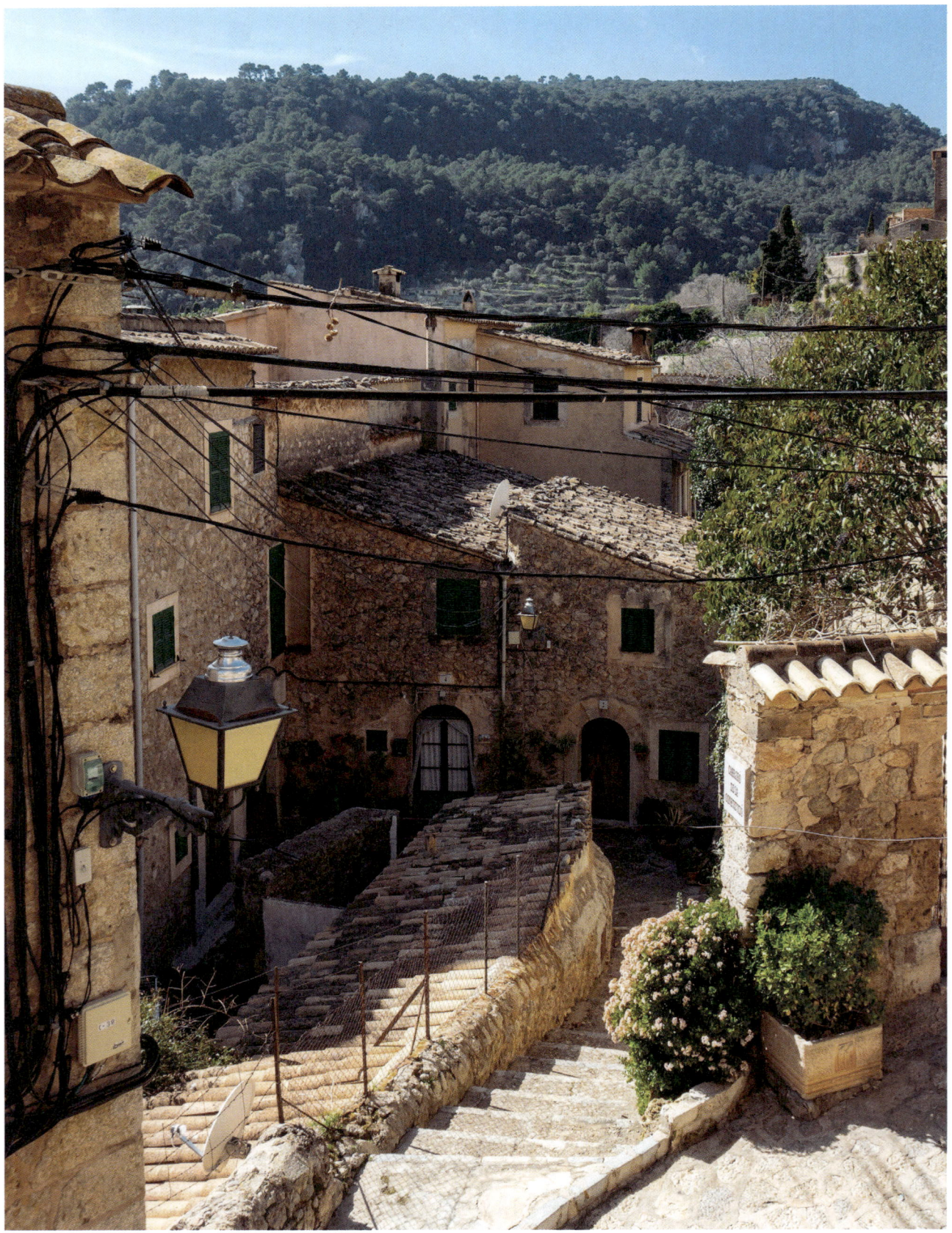

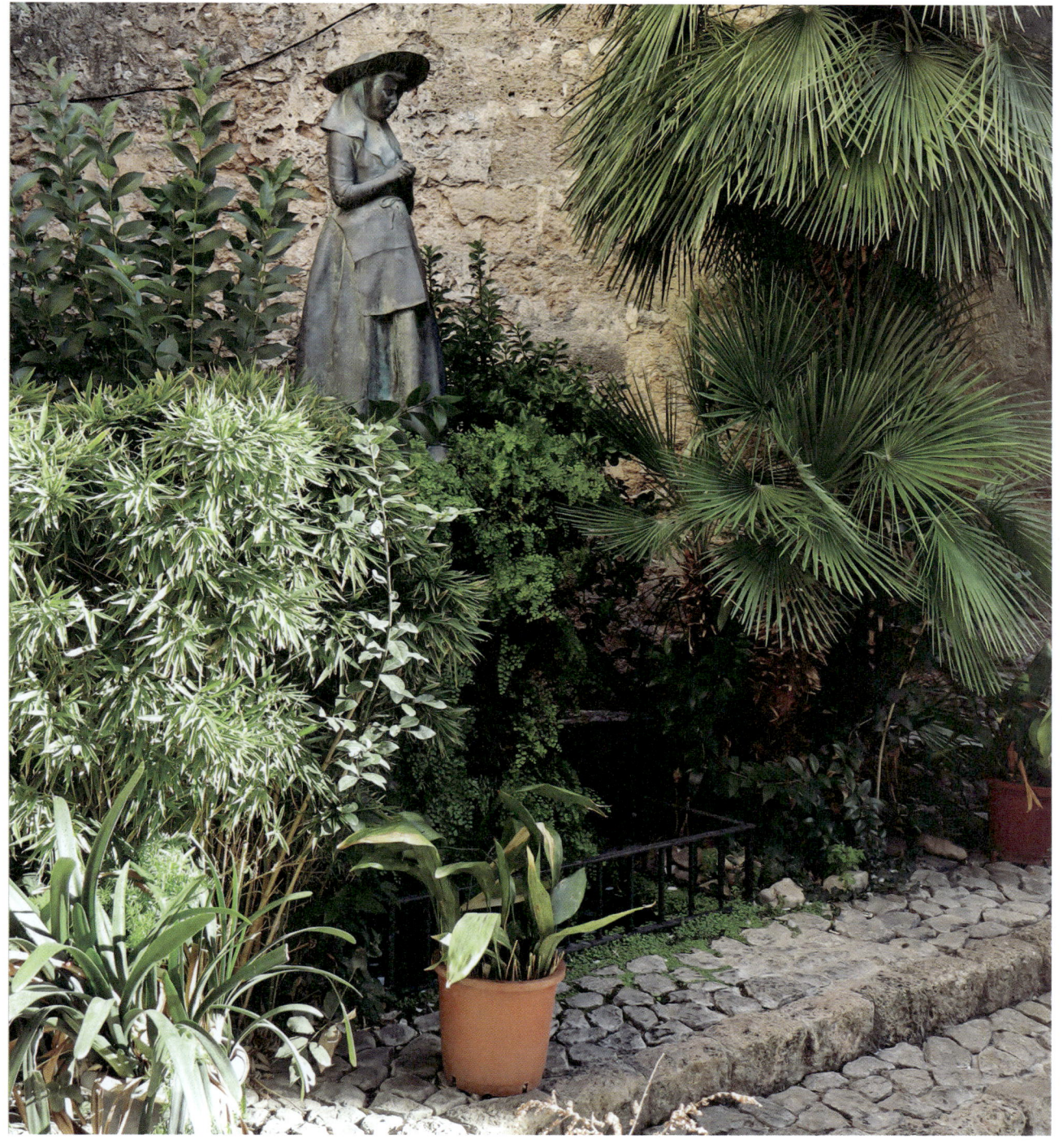

ABOVE: *A sculpture of the nun Catalina Thomàs, a saint born in Valldemossa in 1531. Saint Thomàs is revered as the patron saint of Mallorca, which shows in the many ceramic-tile depictions of her on local houses.*

LEFT: *Seclusion at its most beautiful: Valldemossa lies in a gently rolling valley framed by the Tramuntana mountains, with spectacular views in all directions.*

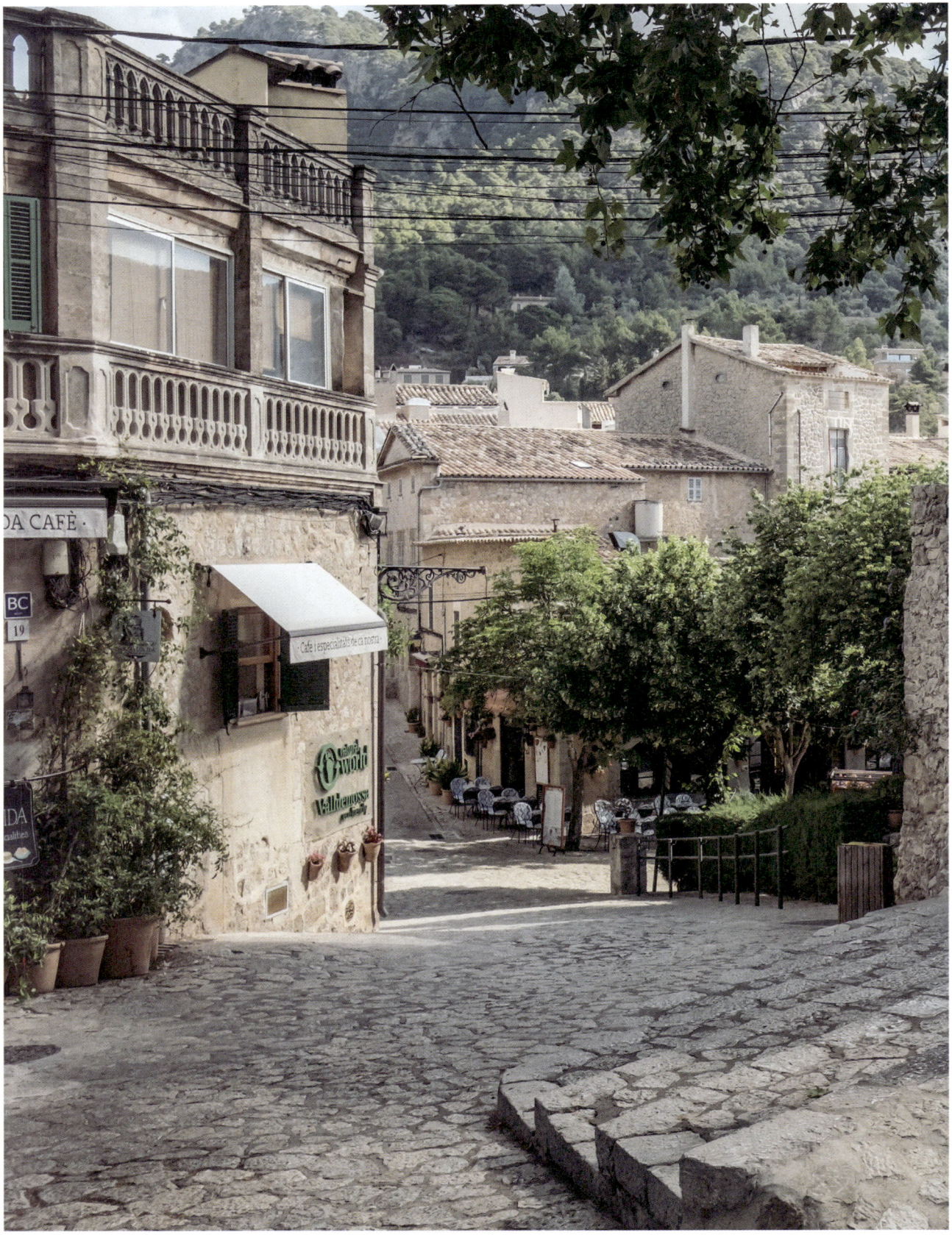

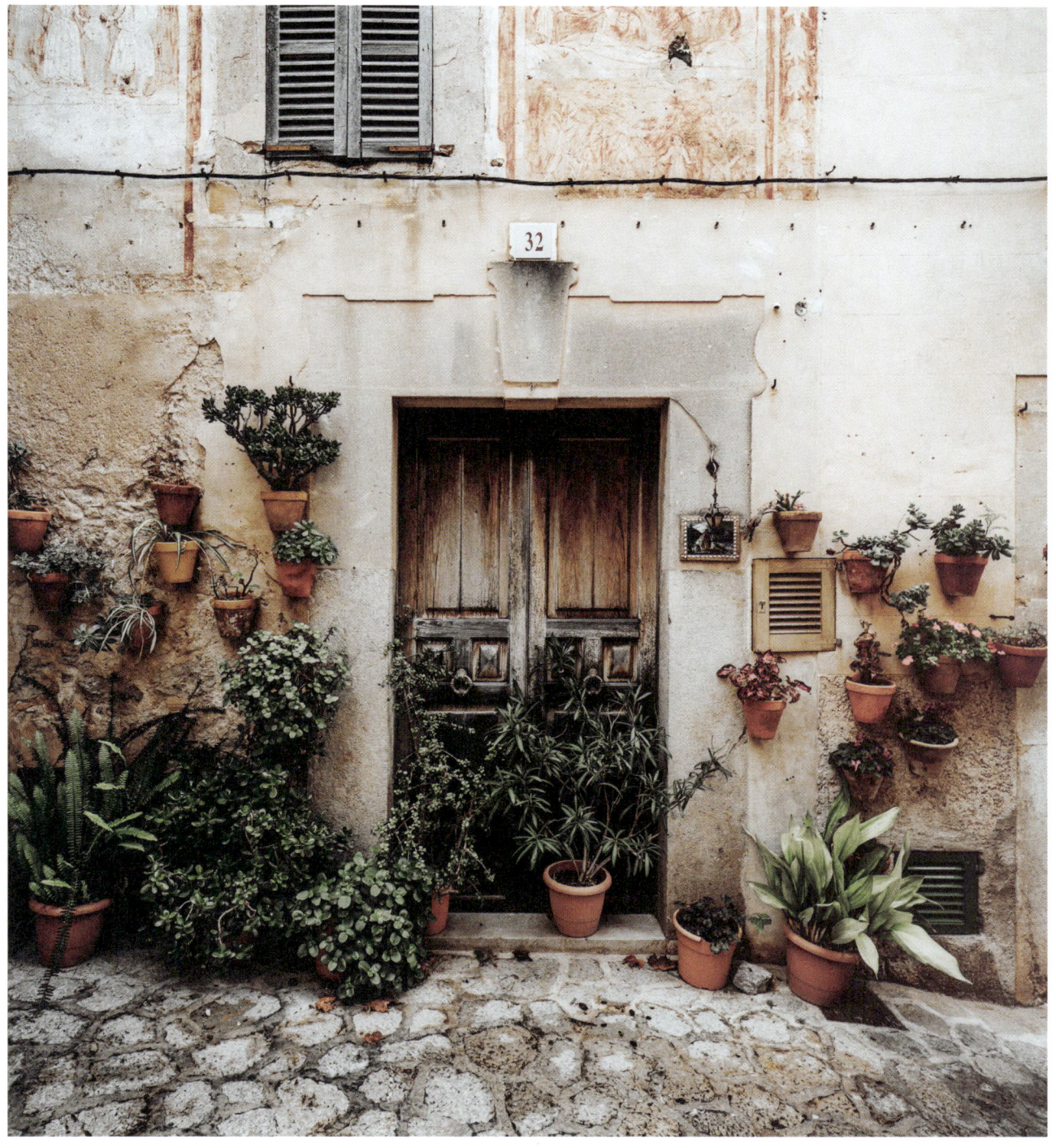

ABOVE: *A part of what makes Valldemossa special is that despite the town's popularity with visitors, many houses remain charming and largely unaltered.*

LEFT: *View from Plaça Cartoixa. This spot offers cozy cafés and restaurants, the perfect places to linger and settle into George Sand's* A Winter in Majorca.

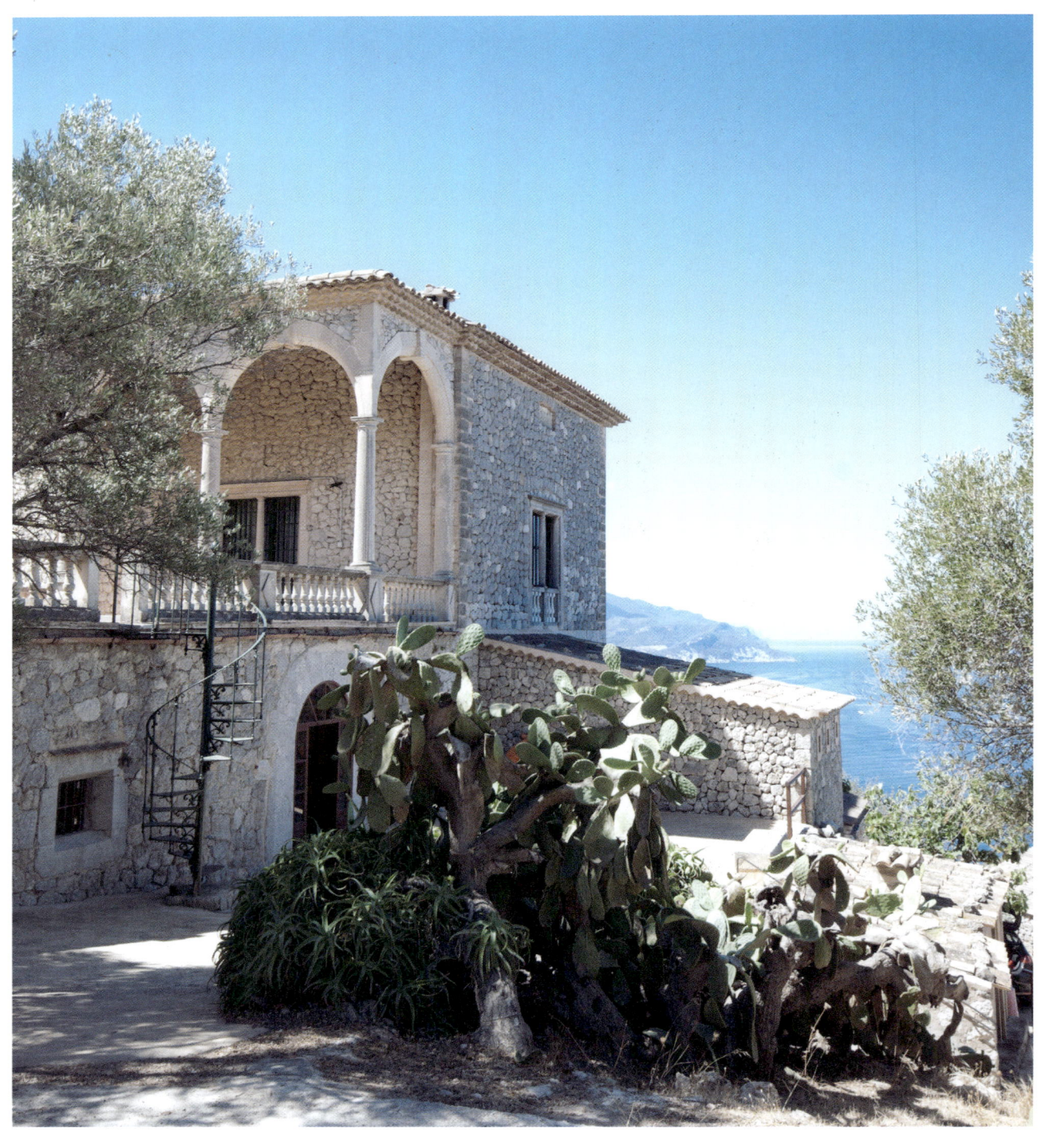

ABOVE AND RIGHT: *Between Valldemossa and Deià lies Son Marroig, once the country estate of the Austrian Archduke Ludwig Salvator and today a historic museum. From its pavilion, even his well-known cousin, Empress Elisabeth of Austria—Sisi—once admired the breathtaking view.*

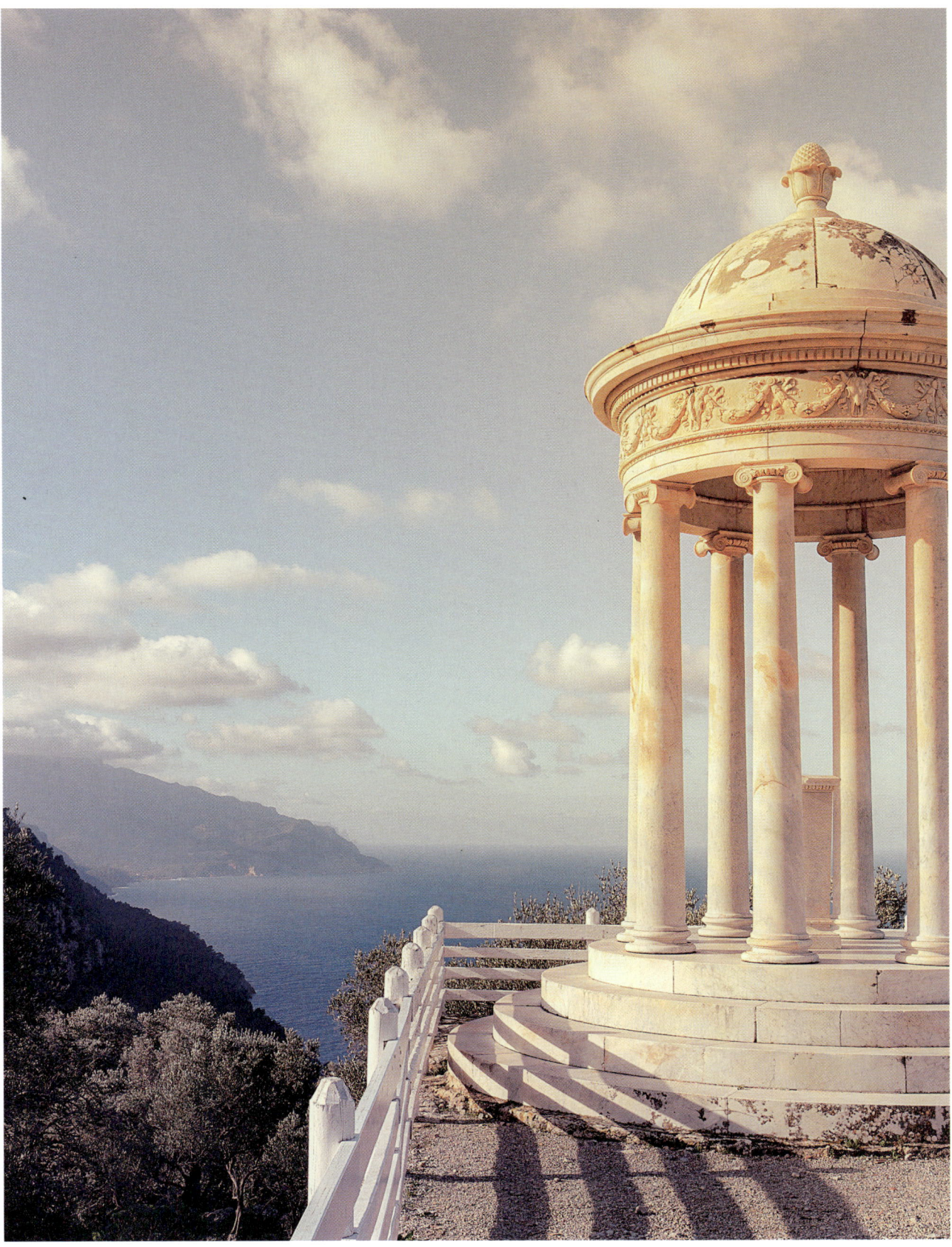

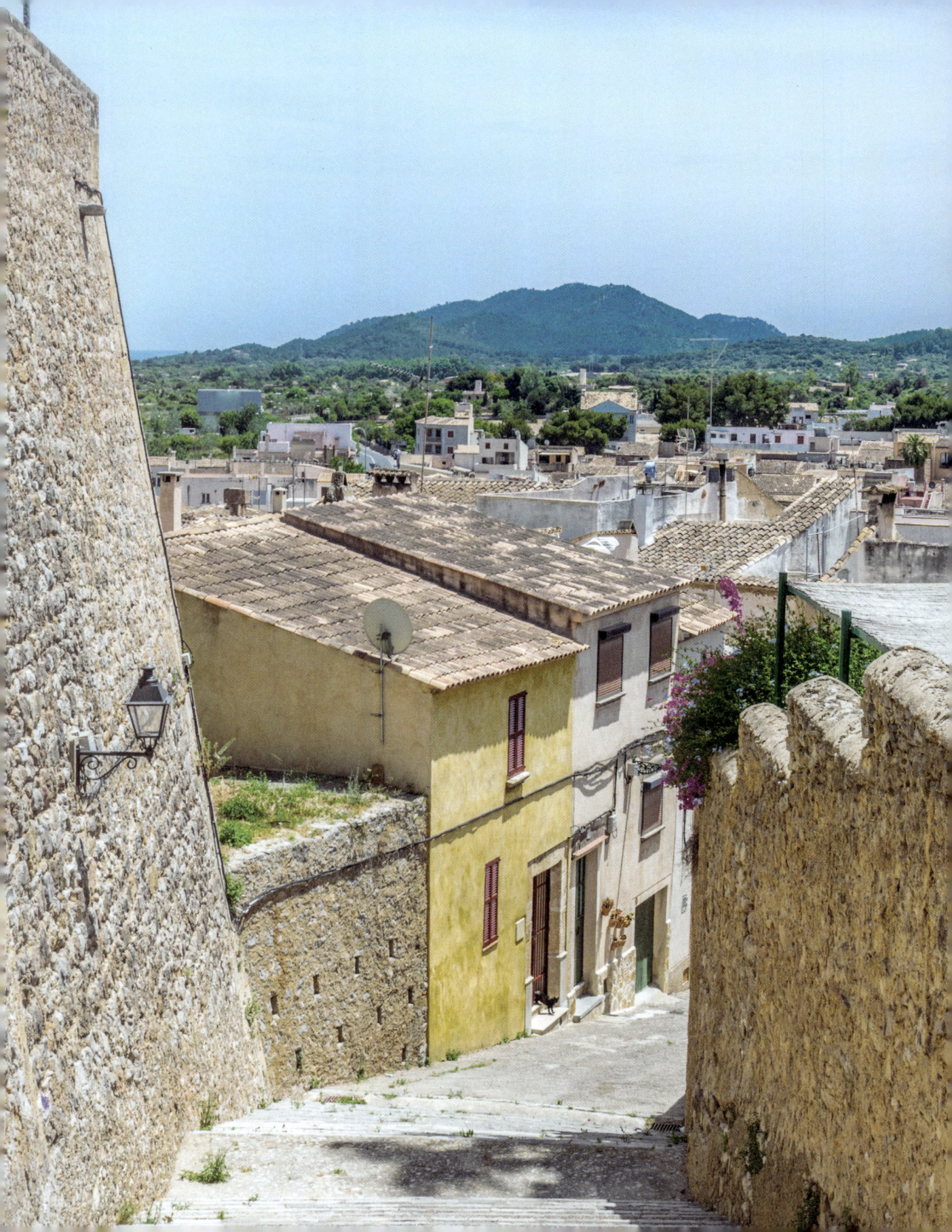

THE EAST

AWAY FROM THE CROWDS: MALLORCA'S VILLAGES WITH CHARACTER AND HISTORY

Do authentic villages even have a future on a vacation island? Places where workshops, small manufactories, and studios line the streets instead of cheap souvenir shops? With small tapas bars and cafés instead of obviously overpriced tourist traps? Artà is a clear example of how authenticity can be maintained even where tourism is not a pastime but a mundane fact. The small town in the northeast of Mallorca keeps its distinct character, in part through sustained political engagement at the municipal level. For many years, local policy has focused on protecting regional culture, promoting local products, and supporting traditional handicrafts such as pottery and basket weaving. That commitment is why Artà is officially one of Spain's eight Slow Cities, a designation which stands for quality of life, sustainability, and preserving the fabric of the local community. Agriculture dominates the surrounding area. In the town center, people live and work. The streets echo with more than the clunky sound of vacationers hauling suitcases. The place is quite attractive. For those who have already deposited their own suitcases somewhere, a customary first walk leads up to the fortified church of Sant Salvador, from where the remains of an old fortress offer wide views across the landscape. From Artà, a drive of about twenty minutes to the northeast follows rural roads through olive groves and rows of almond trees. The medieval fortress of Castell de Capdepera comes into view long before arrival. In this hilly settlement overlooking the sea, Mallorca presents a fairly recognizable version of its older self. Several beautiful beaches nearby offer easy access to quieter stretches of coastline. Away from the main tourist centers—is that a description or an exhortation?

LEFT: *The eastern part of the island is also known as Llevant, the region where the sun rises. Here are a number of well-preserved towns, including Artà and Capdepera.*

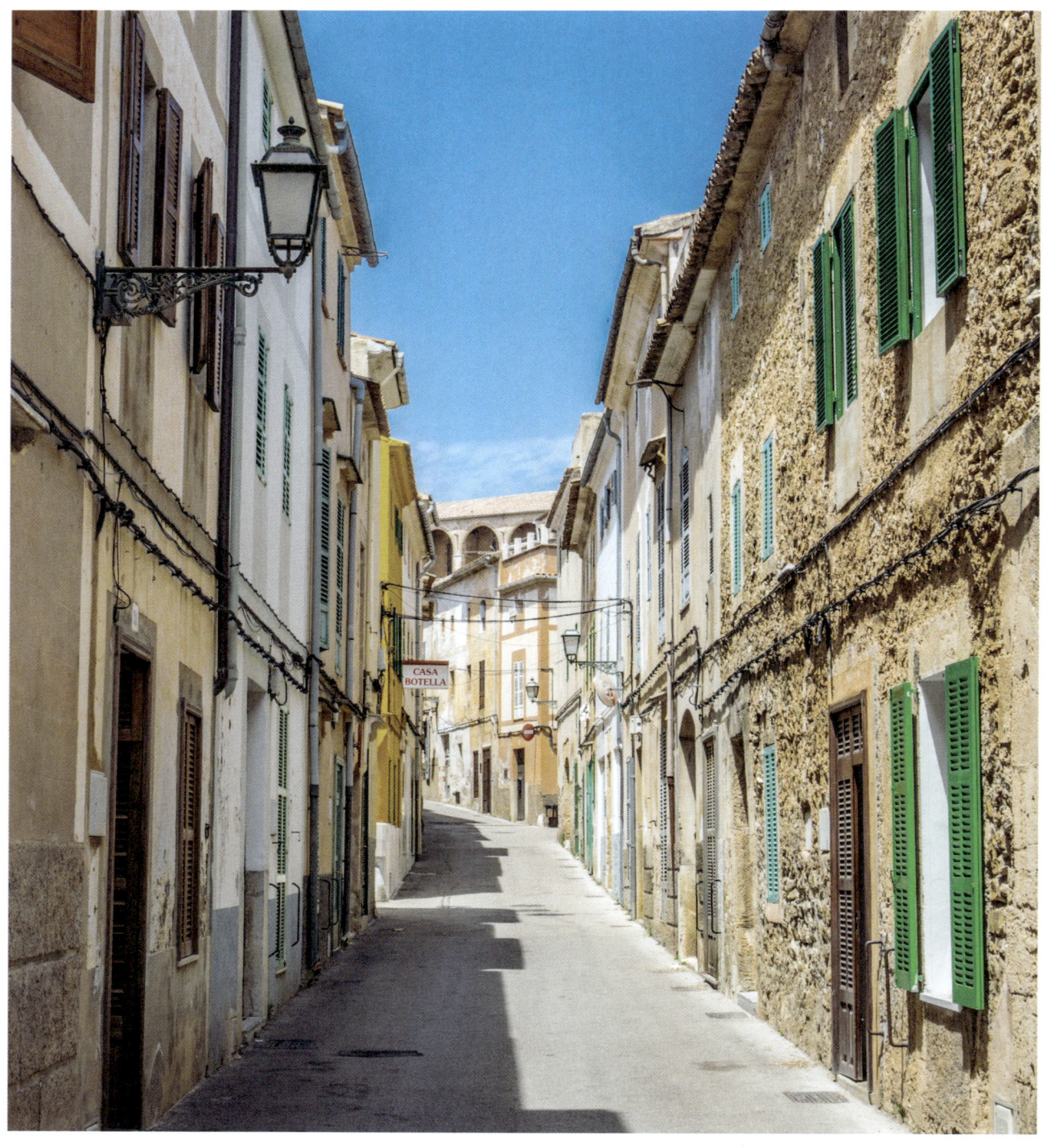

ABOVE AND RIGHT: *Many of Artà's old town streets offer beautiful sightlines. Perched on the hill, the church of Transfiguració del Senyor commands the town's skyline with its grand arches and stained-glass windows, visible from countless alleyways.*

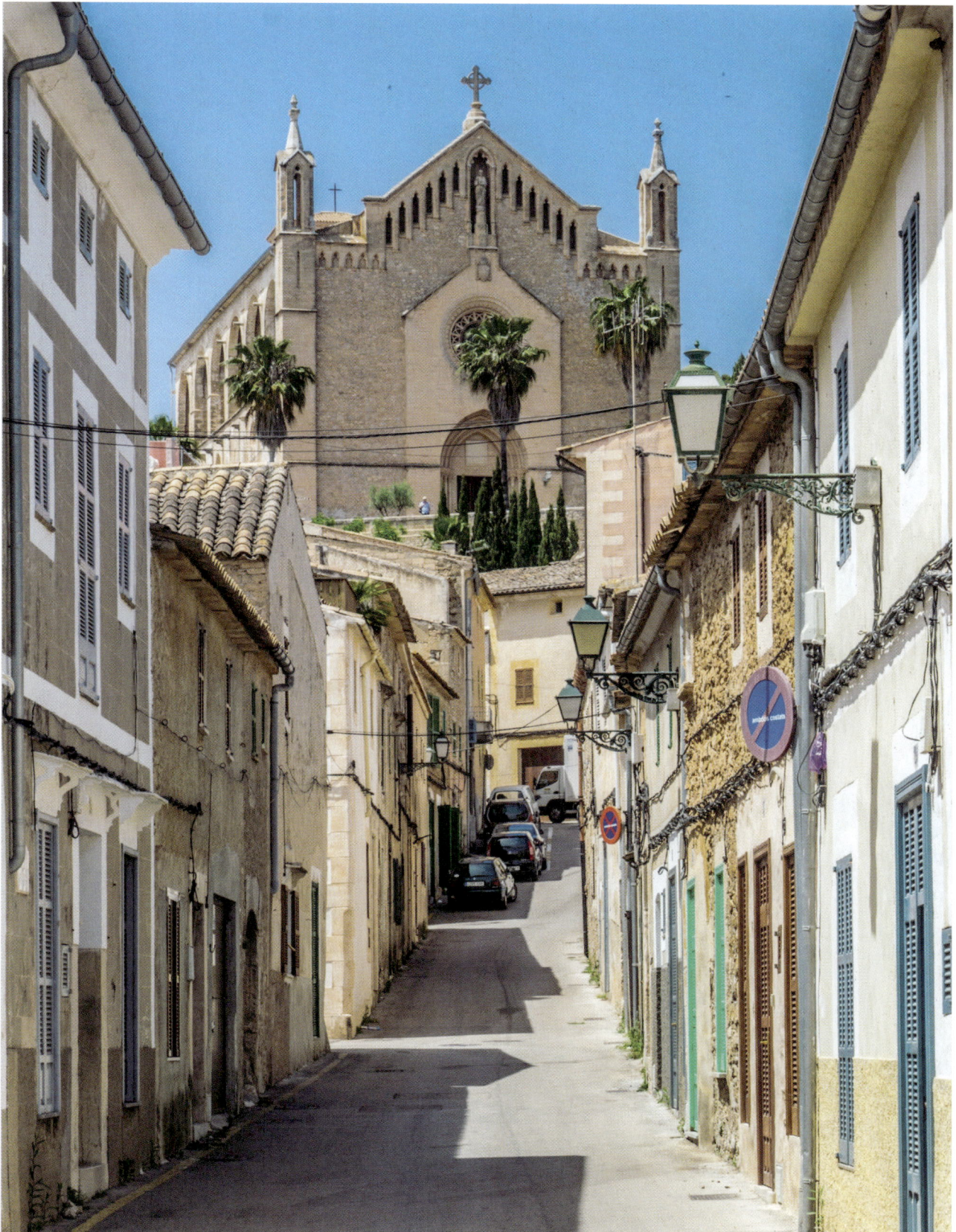

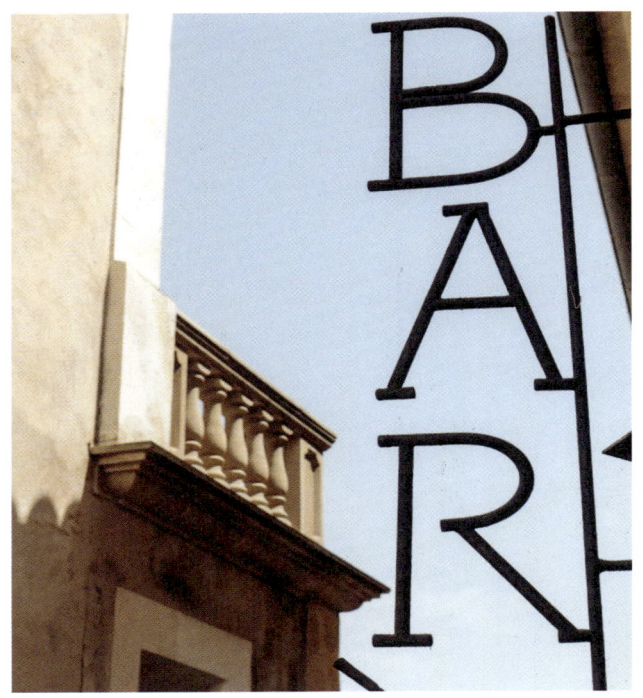
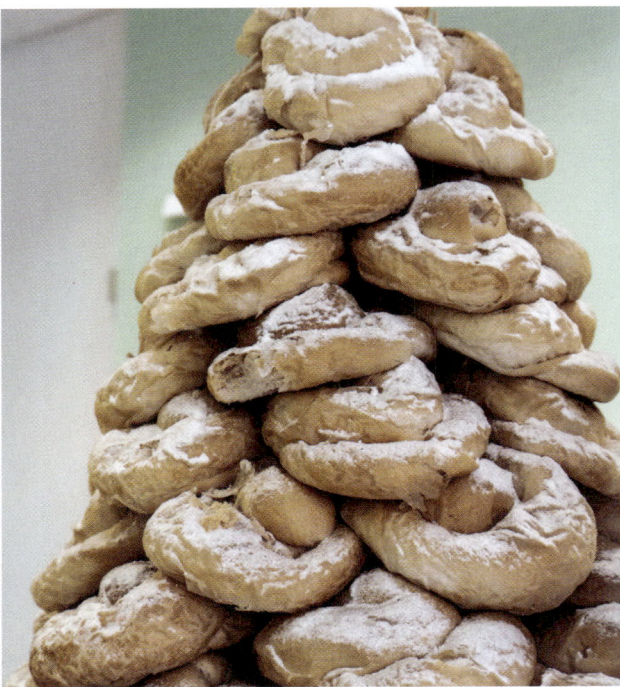
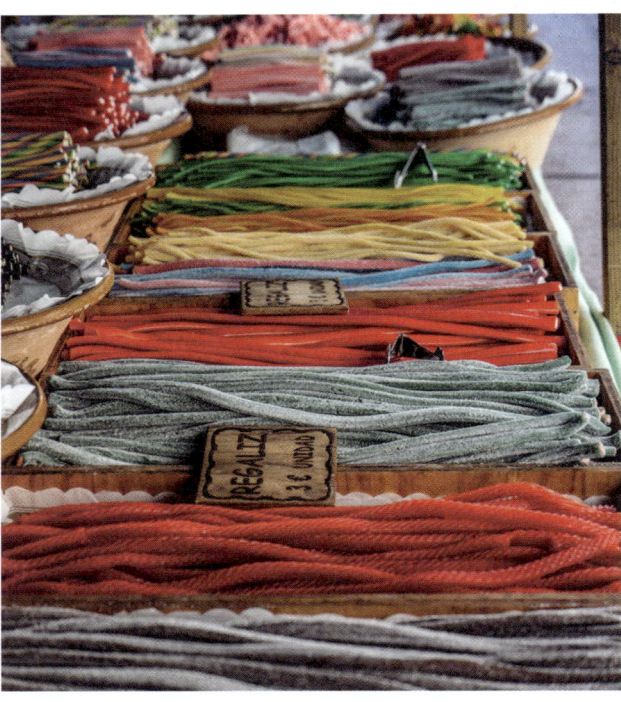
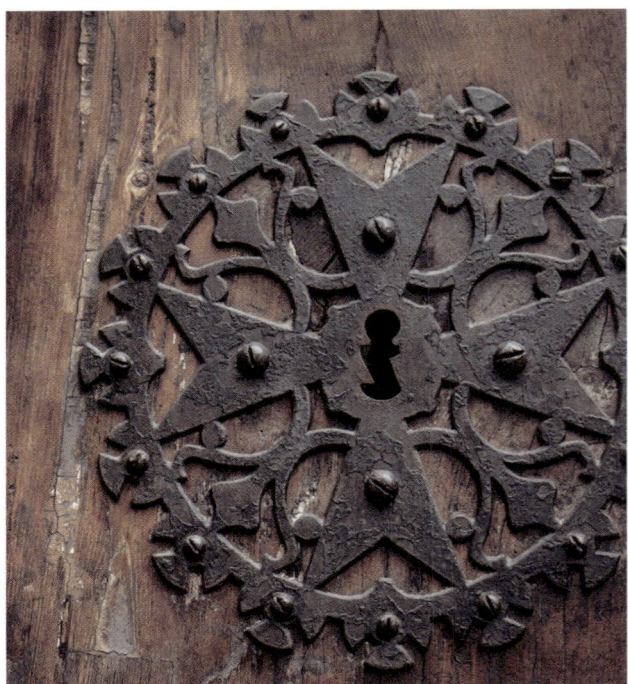

ABOVE AND RIGHT: *The streets and alleys of Artà are rich with detail. Homemade* ensaïmadas—*light, airy pastries, made with lard—are delicious any time of day. So are the brightly colored licorice specialties from the market. Details, like the keyhole set into the church portal of Transfiguració del Senyor, abound.*

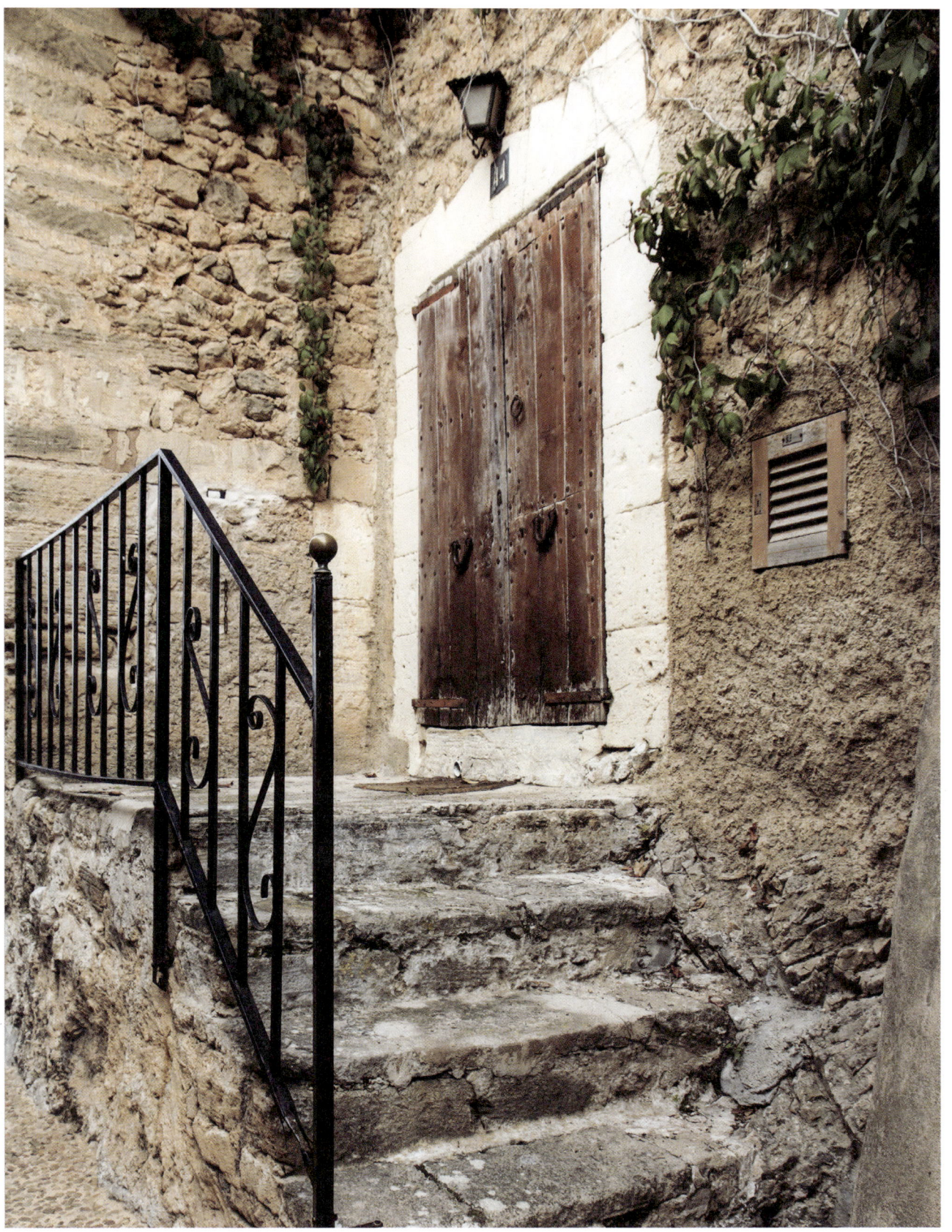

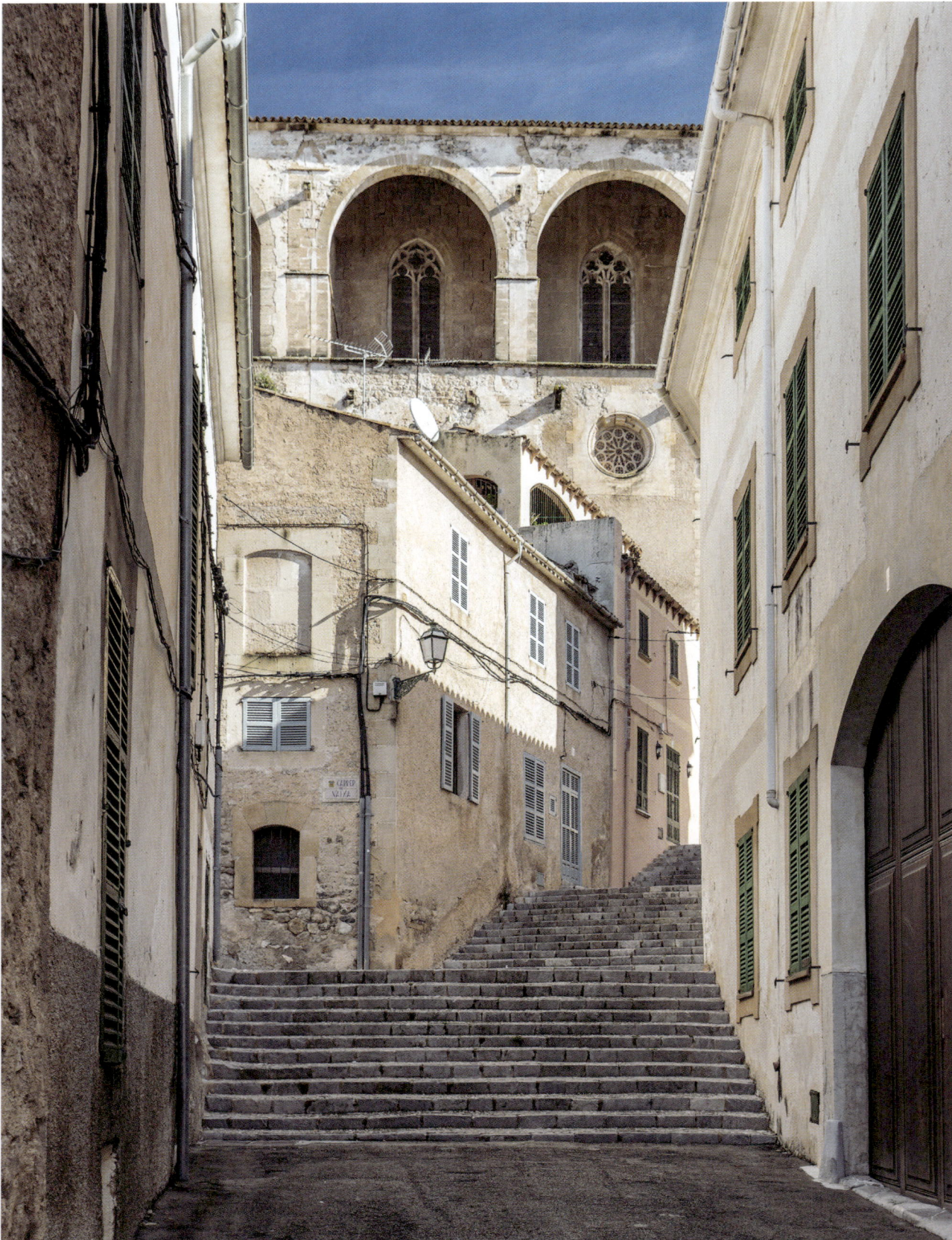

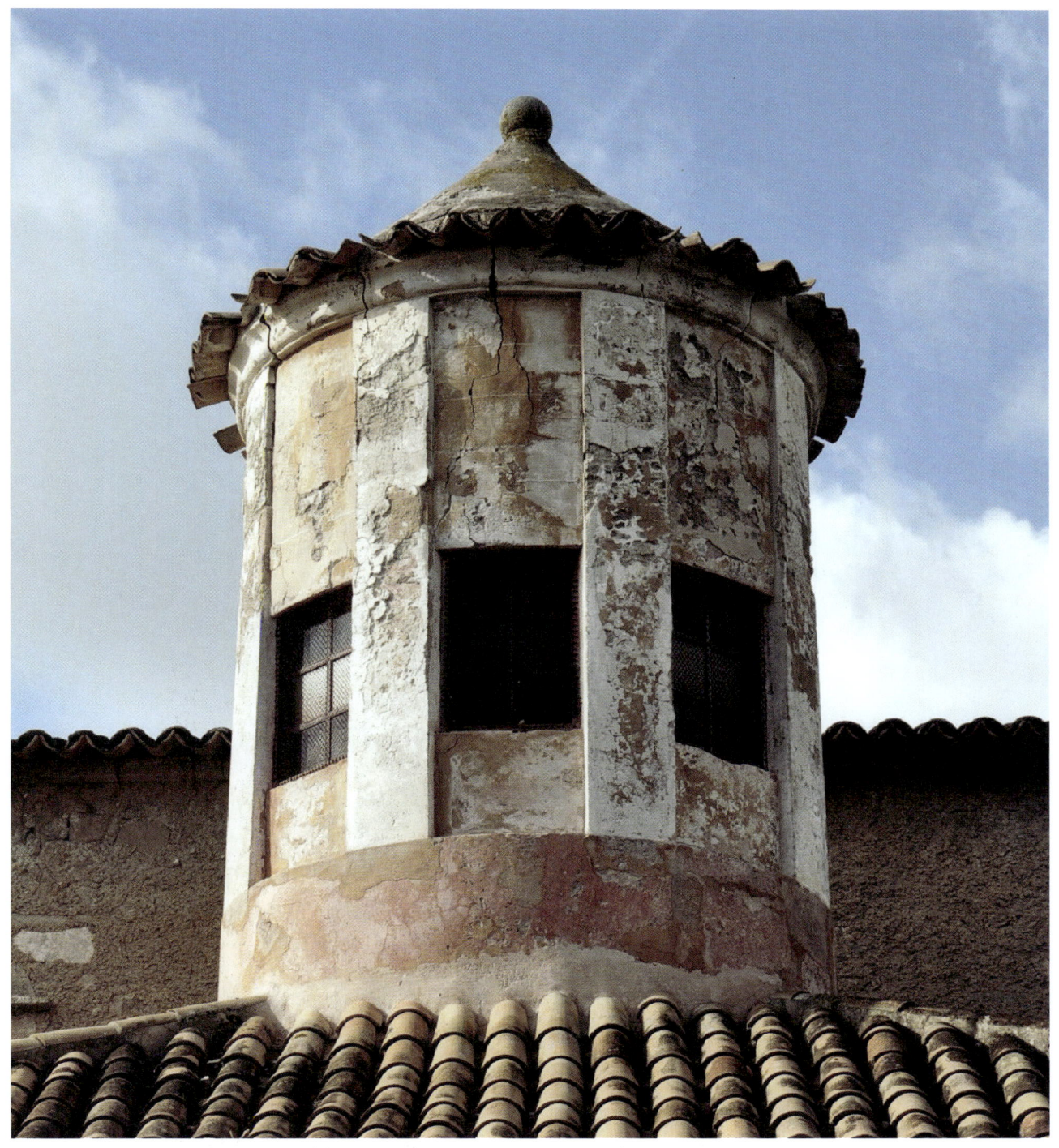

ABOVE: *Above Artà rises the medieval fortress of Santuari de Sant Salvador, and this chapel, with its tower, forms part of the complex.*

LEFT: *Every step is worth the climb: a steep alley stairway leading to the church of Transfiguració del Senyor.*

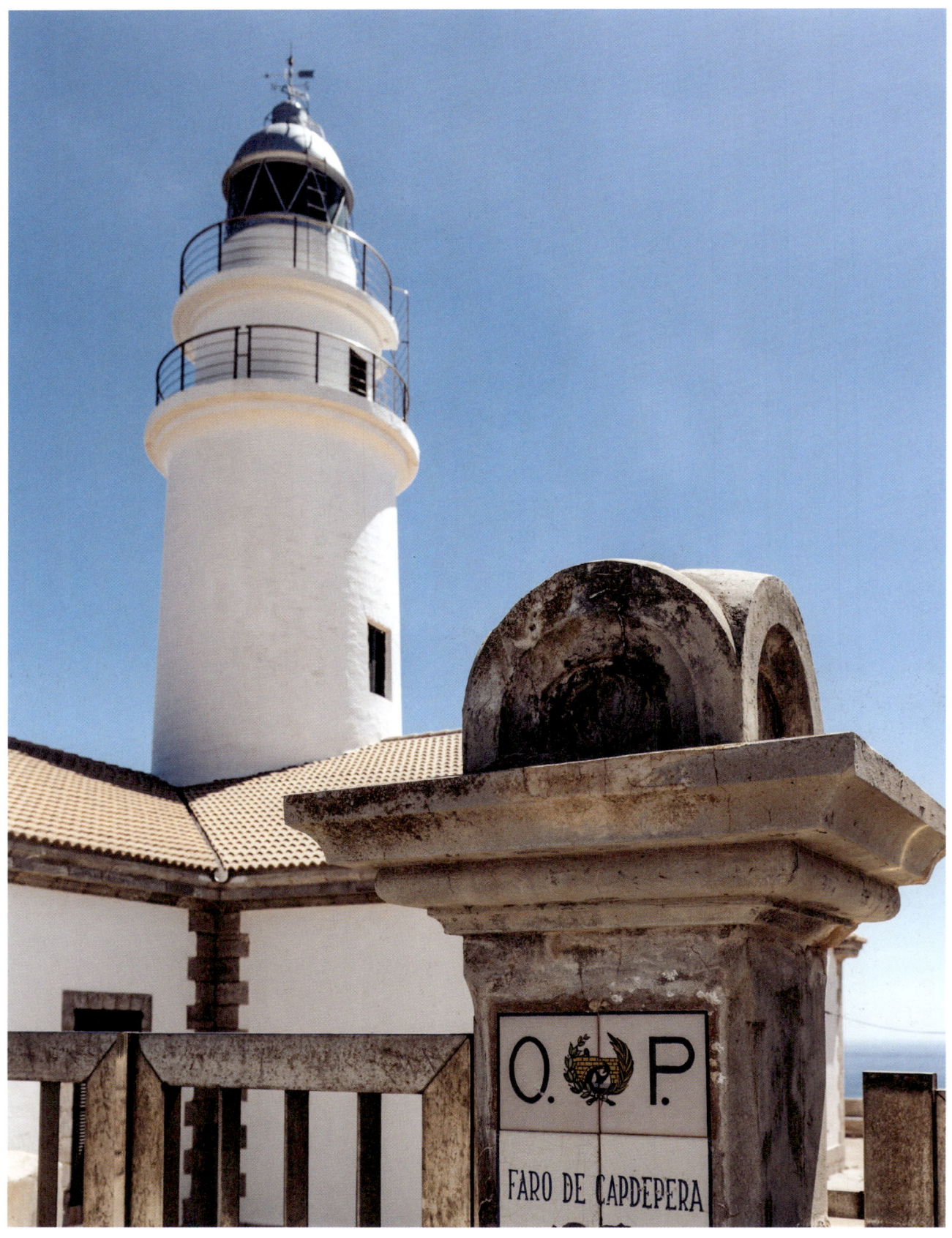

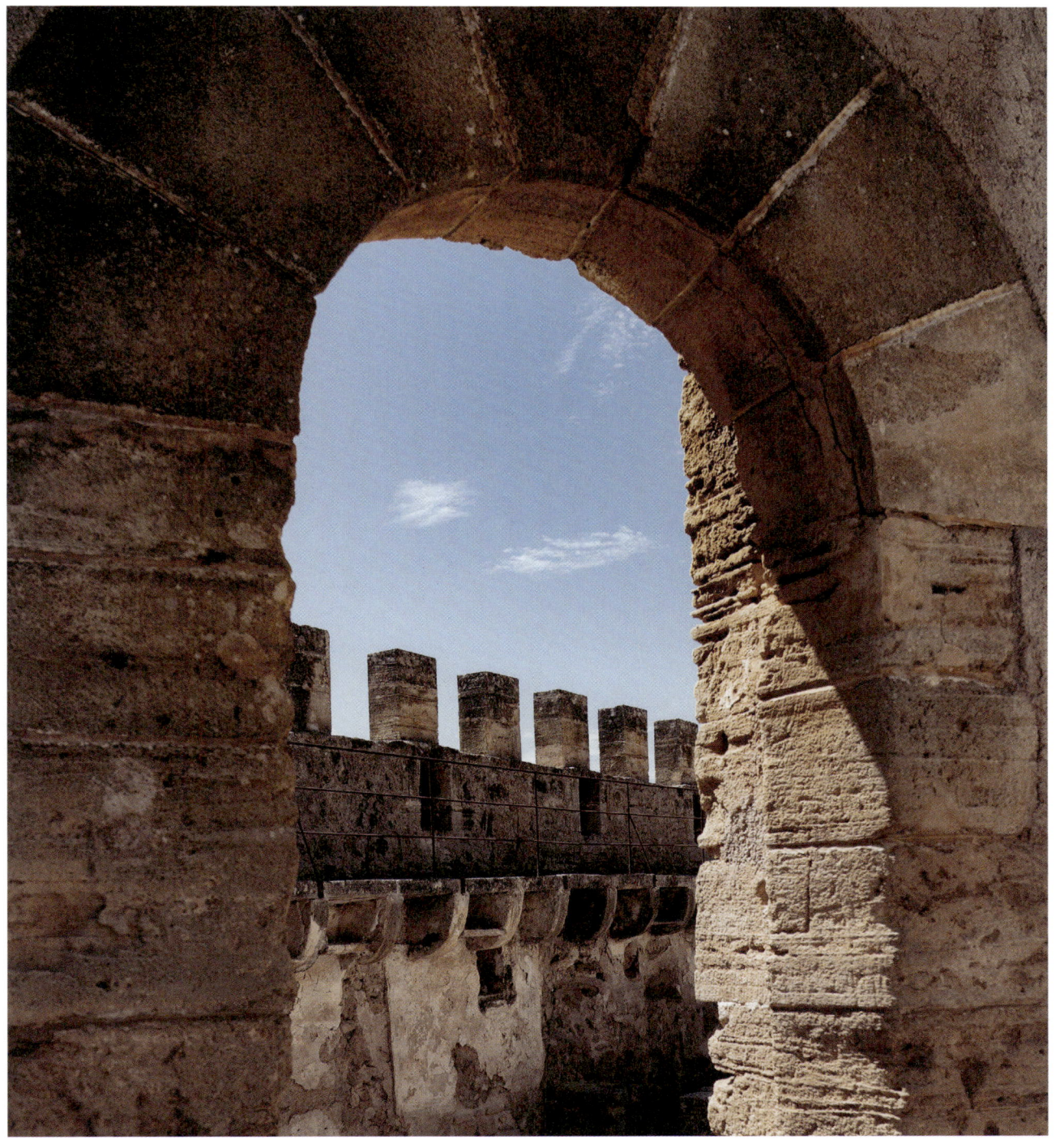

ABOVE: *The village of Capdepera not far from Artà, is likewise protected by a medieval fortress. The fort, with its round arches and crenellated walls, is among the largest and best-preserved castles on the island.*

LEFT: *Capdepera Lighthouse, a distinctive coastal landmark alone on a headland, is still in operation and a particularly rewarding destination.*

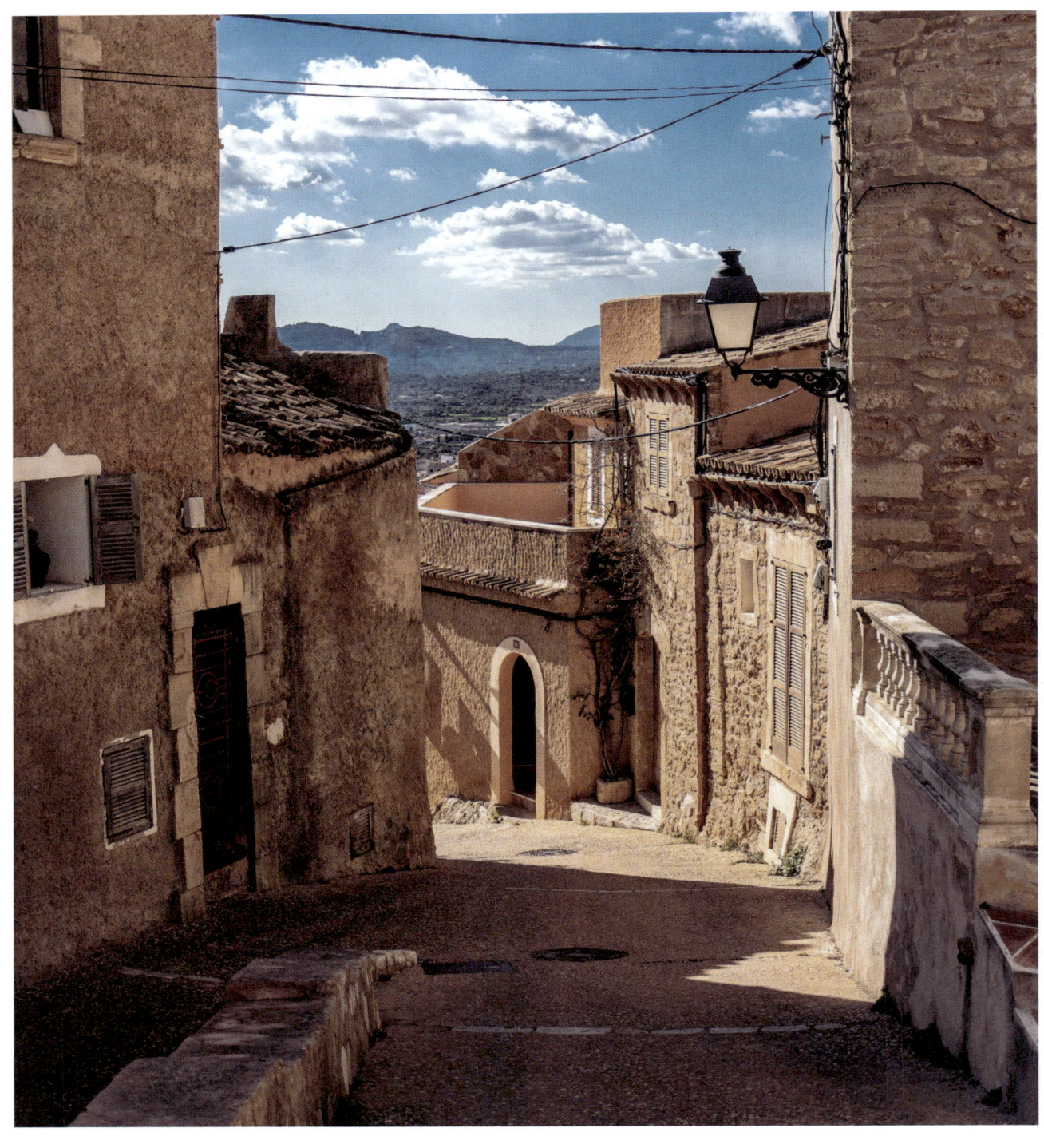

ABOVE AND RIGHT: *Capdepera is nestled into rolling hills, with winding alleyways running through the old town and a summit crowned by an extensive medieval fortress open to visitors—a fascinating place to visit, pirate stories included.*

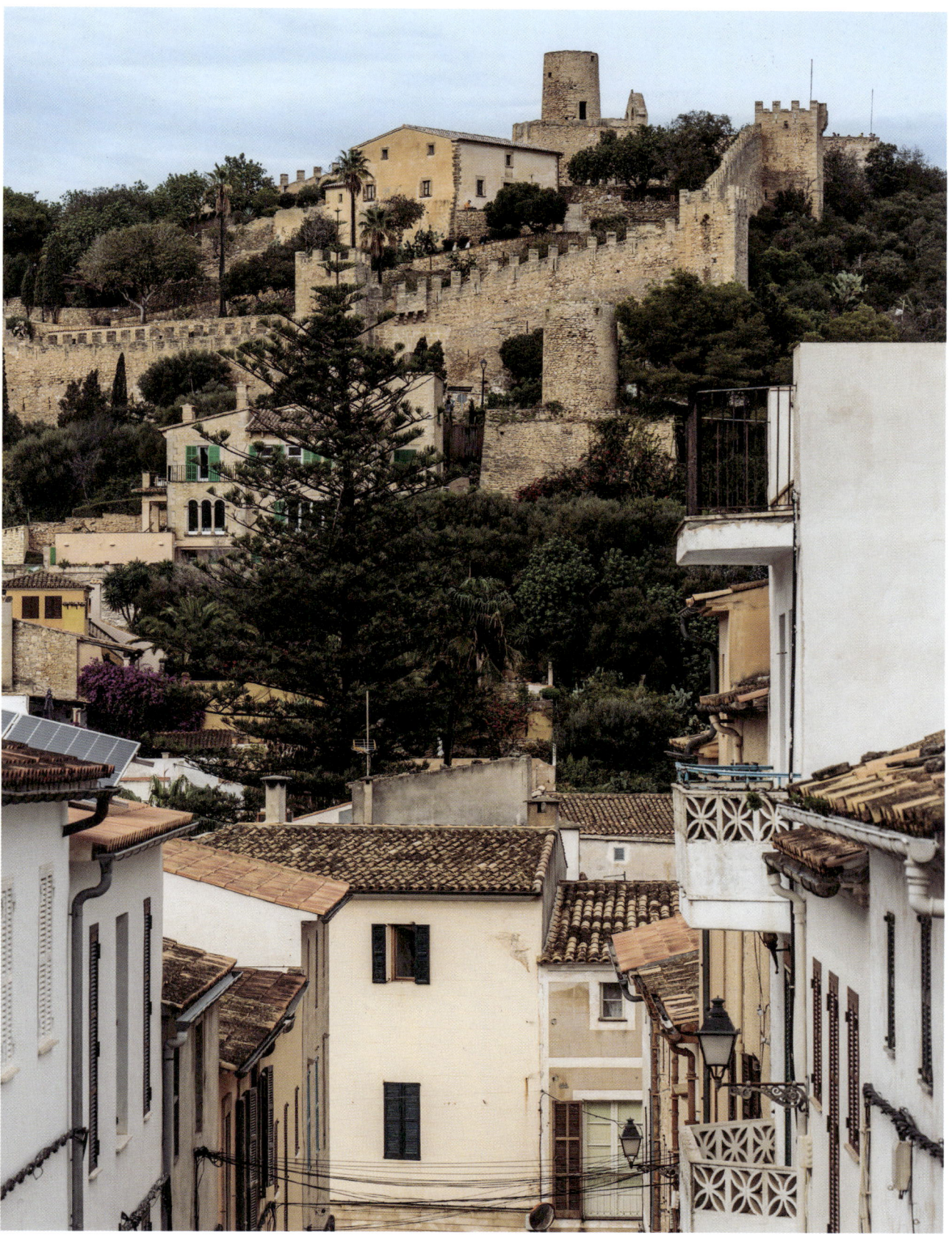

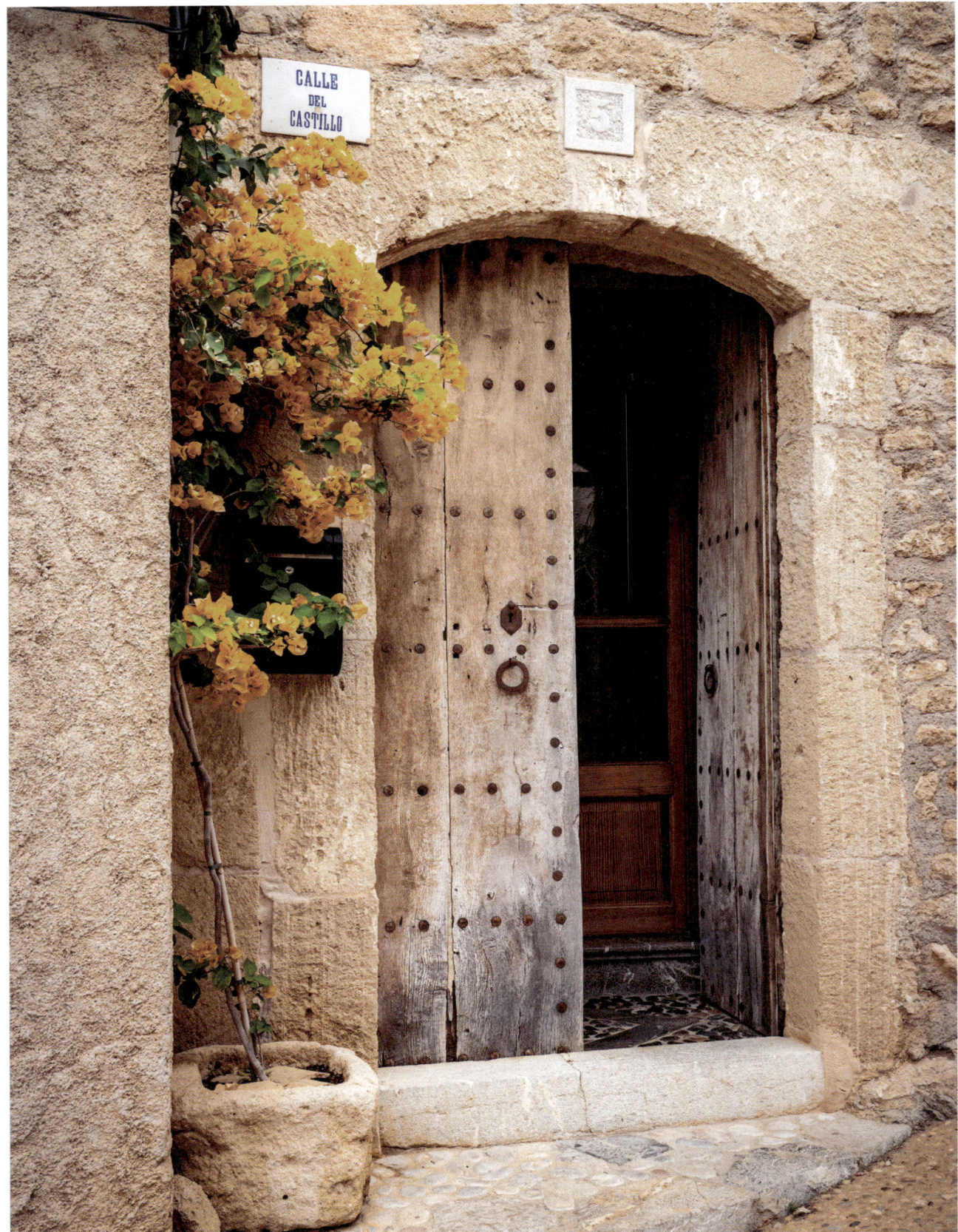

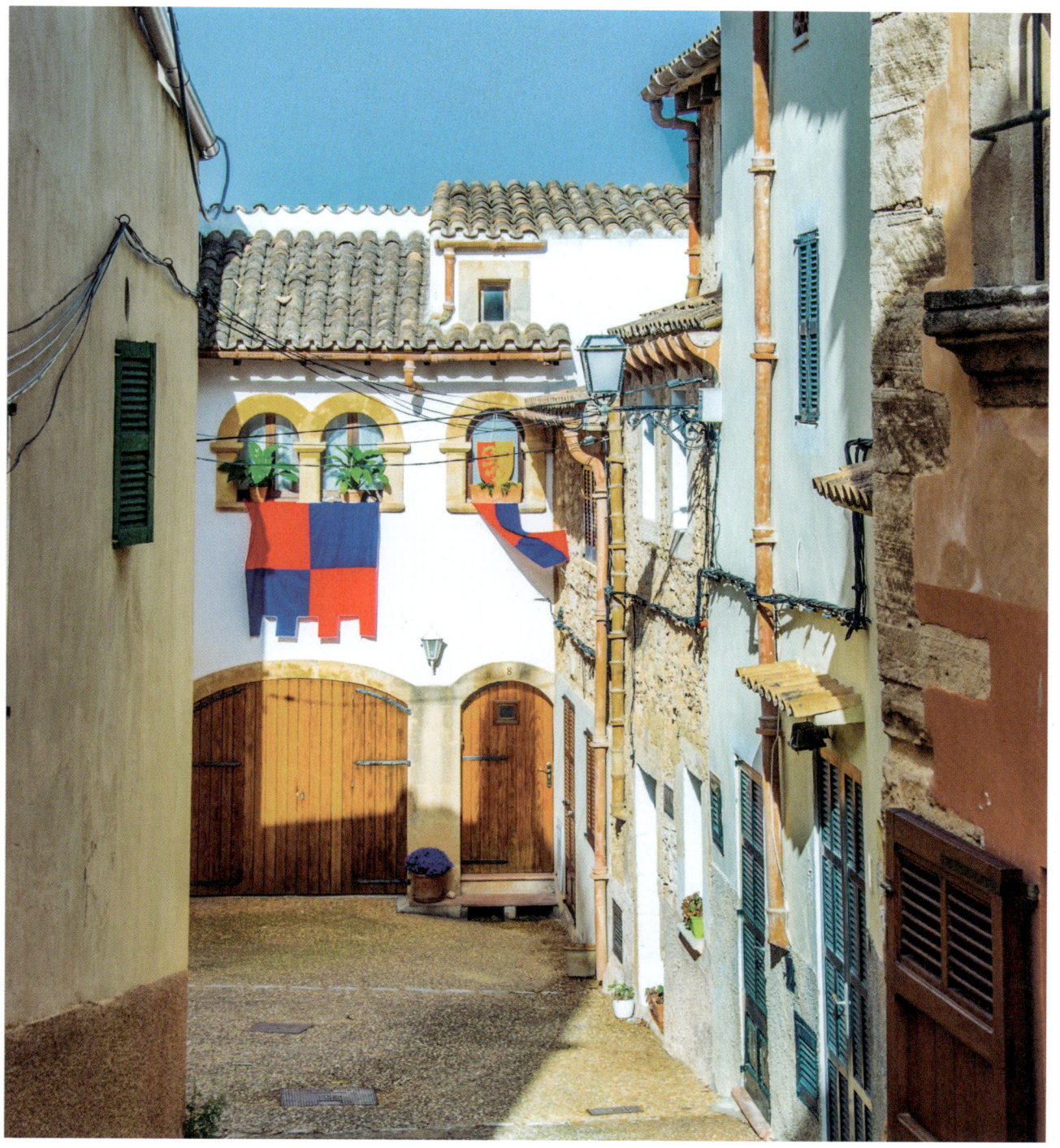

ABOVE: *Each May, Capdepera dons a costume, transforming into a medieval festival. Houses are decorated with colorful banners, historic market stalls set up in the streets, and performances all over town depict aspects of medieval life.*

LEFT: *Life within historic walls: a typical entrance in Capdepera.*

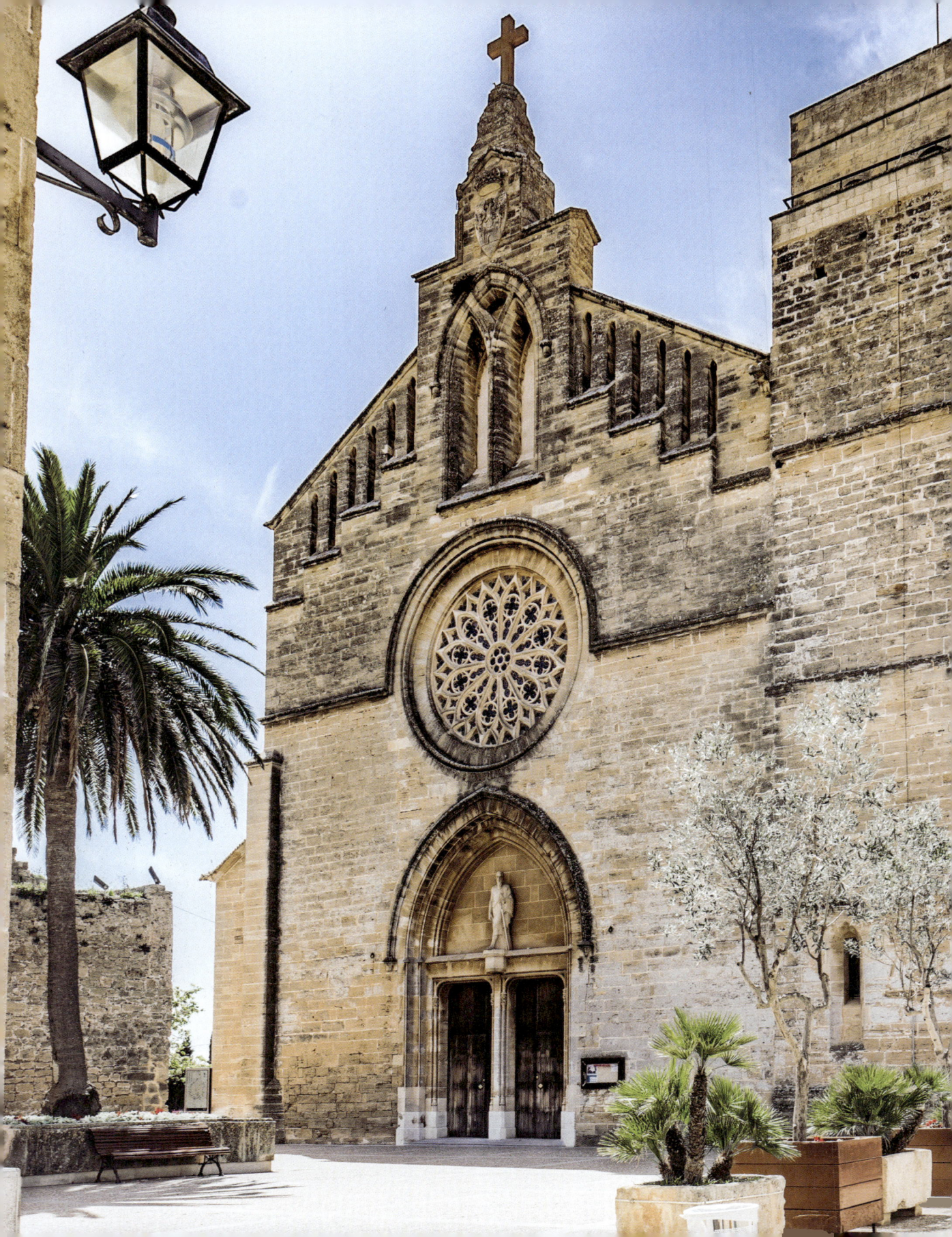

THE NORTH

ALCÚDIA AND THE SERRA DE TRAMUNTANA: HIDDEN PATHS, WIDE HORIZONS

The historic town of Alcúdia is close to the sea, surrounded by natural landscapes, sheltered coves with crystal-clear water and mostly pristine pine forests. Here, excellent restaurants invite lingering visits, narrow streets reward those who enjoy a stroll, and—often unexpectedly—archaeological sites point to the depth of the island's history. You can seize every opportunity, or simply enjoy being there.

The north is shaped above all by the Tramuntana mountains, which create their own distinct microclimate, with higher rainfall than in the south of Mallorca. This is what makes the landscape so unique, with waterfalls, wild goats, and vegetated mountain slopes. The Serra de Tramuntana range is a haven for hikers and cyclists. They seem drawn to restful characteristics like winding roads, wide sea views, and spectacular sunsets, with numerous villages like Sóller, Fornalutx, and Pollença set into the landscape, each with its own character.

LEFT: *An inviting park bench shaded by a palm tree is a pleasant spot to linger. The neo-Gothic church of Sant Jaume at the edge of Alcúdia's old town is incorporated into the historic city wall.*

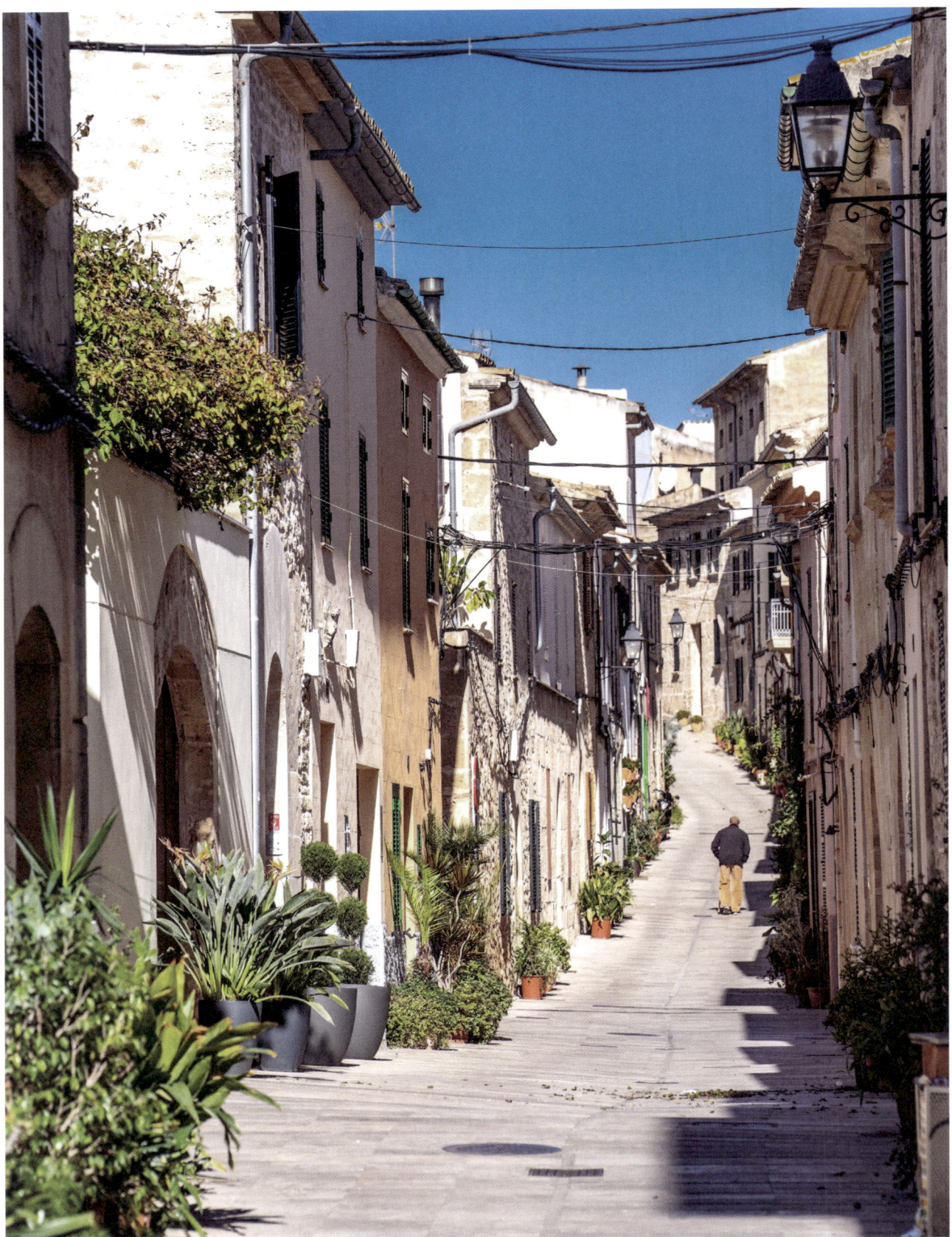

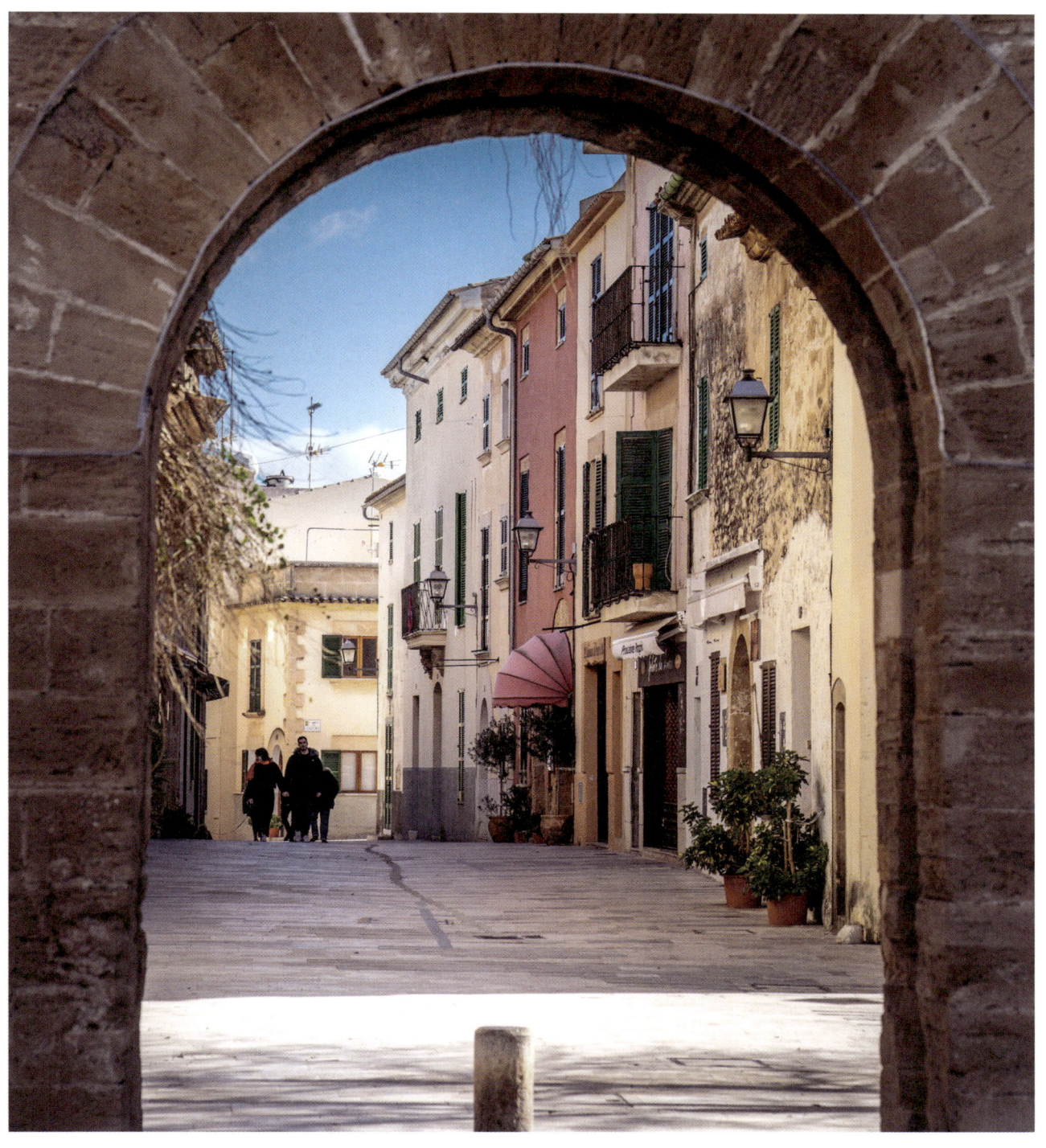

ABOVE AND LEFT: *Alcúdia sits on a small headland in the island's northeast, flanked by the bays of Alcúdia and Pollença. Its proximity to the sea makes this small town with its well-kept houses and bright streets particularly appealing.*

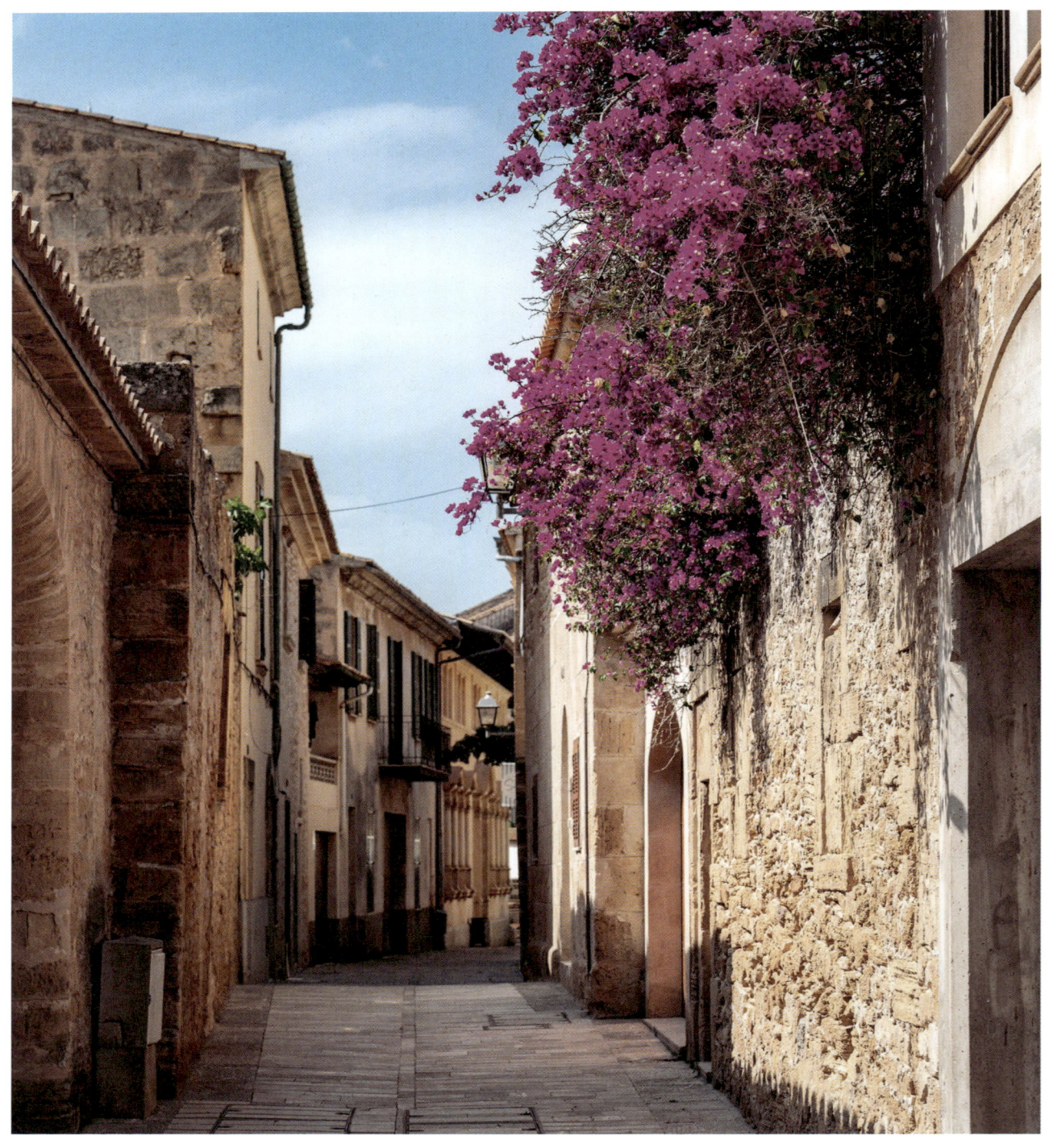

ABOVE: *Few pastimes are finer than wandering through these bougainvillea-draped alleys in Alcúdia.*

RIGHT: *Compact but richly decorated: Alcúdia's Renaissance town hall with its impressive clock tower and elegant portal on a small square in the heart of the old.*

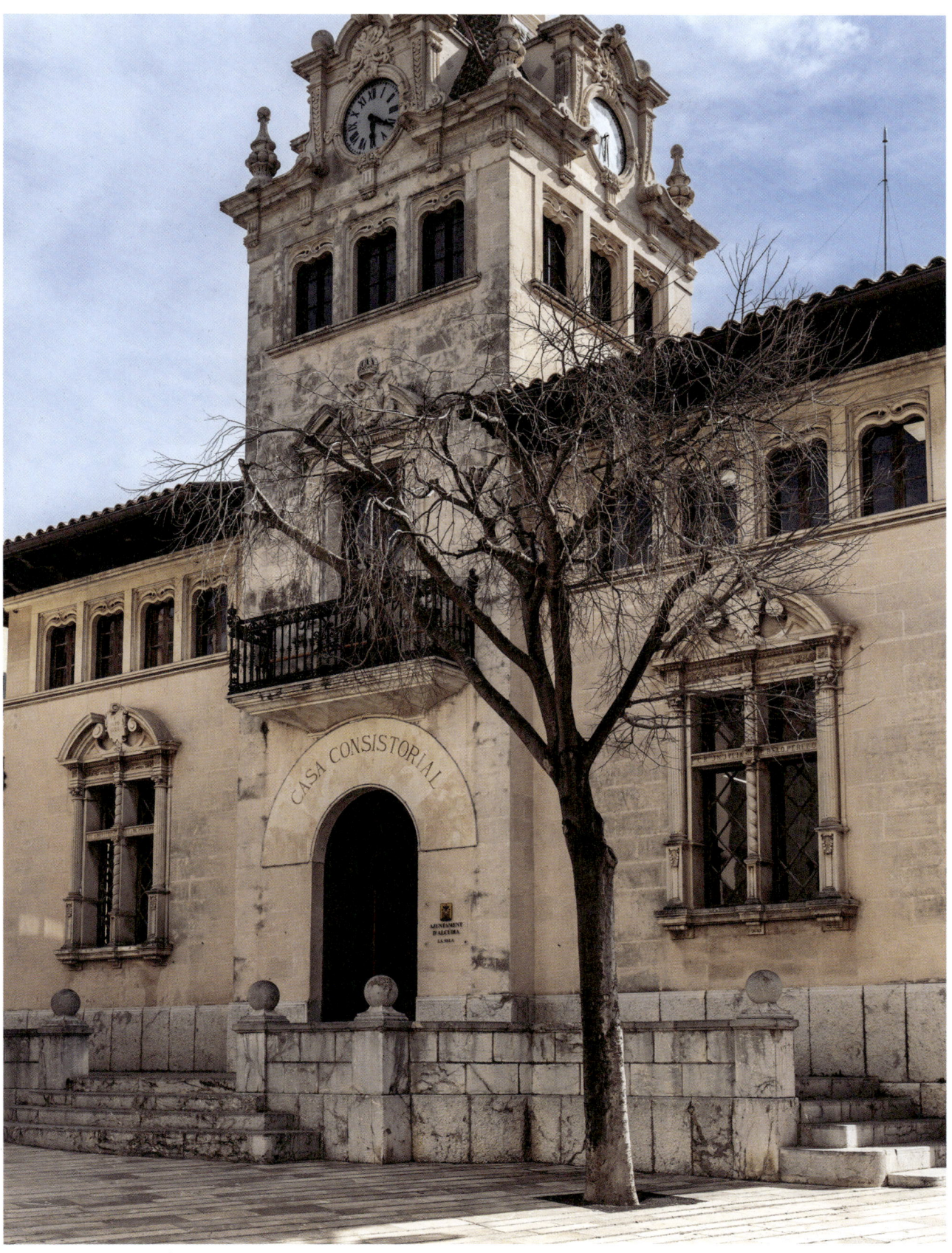

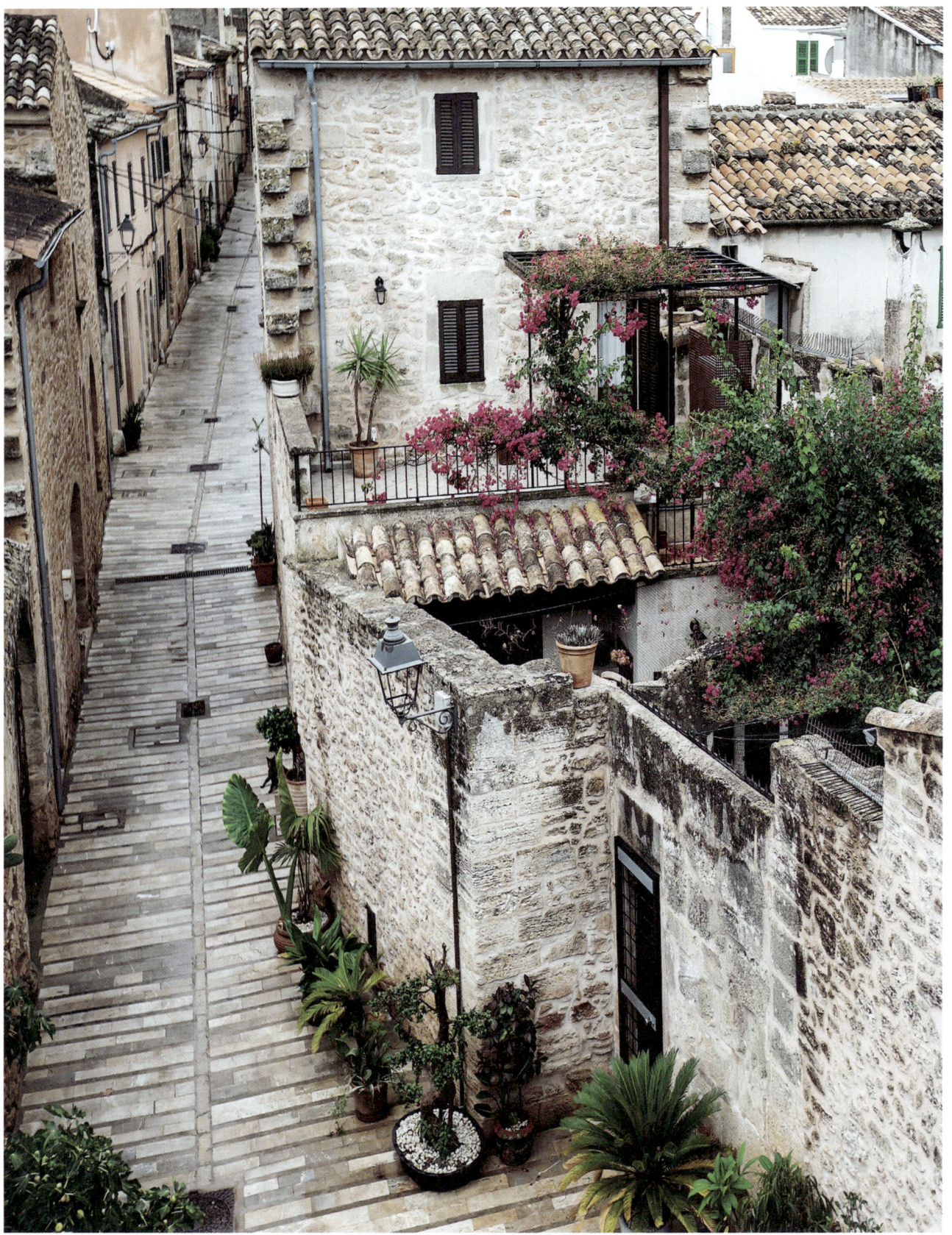

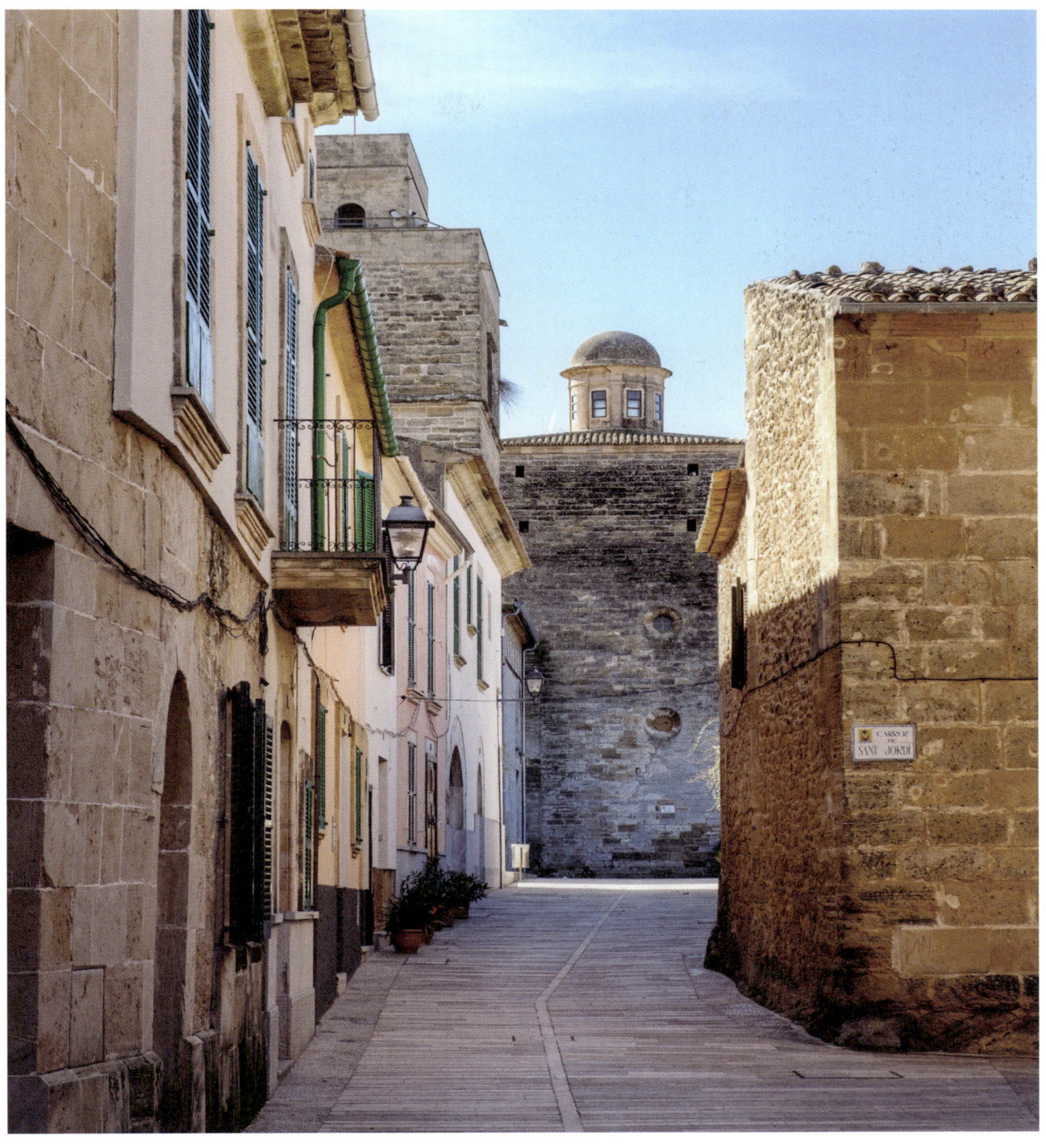

ABOVE: *Living, breathing history: the view from Carrer de la Rectoria toward the church of Sant Jaume and its small tower.*

LEFT: *You can spend hours in Alcúdia, strolling through the pueblo and taking in the historic architecture along narrow stone-paved streets.*

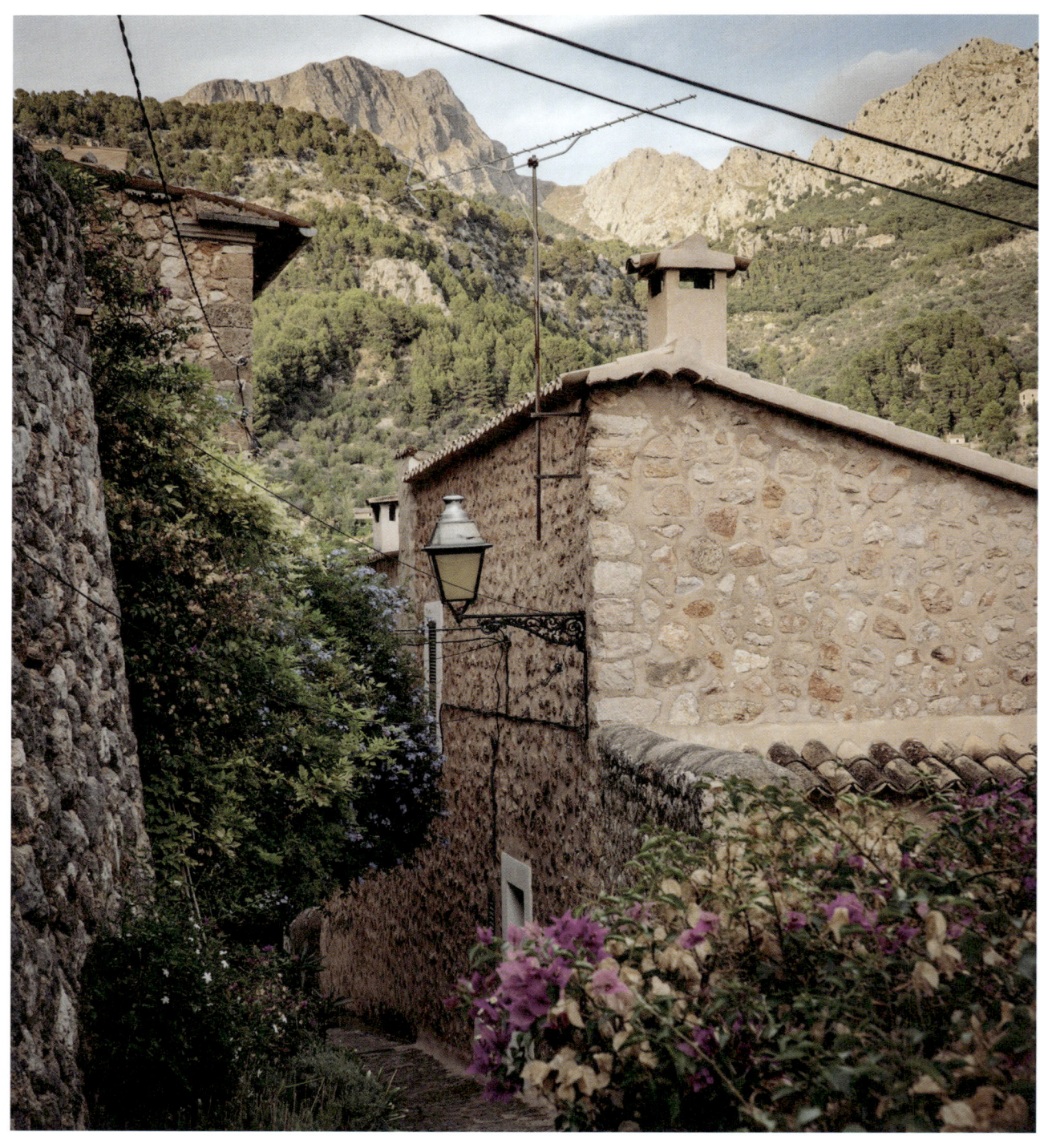

ABOVE AND RIGHT: *Stairways double as narrow passageways lined with plants and flowers and rustic stone houses. Time slows down in the perceived seclusion of the mountain village of Fornalutx, northwest of Sóller.*

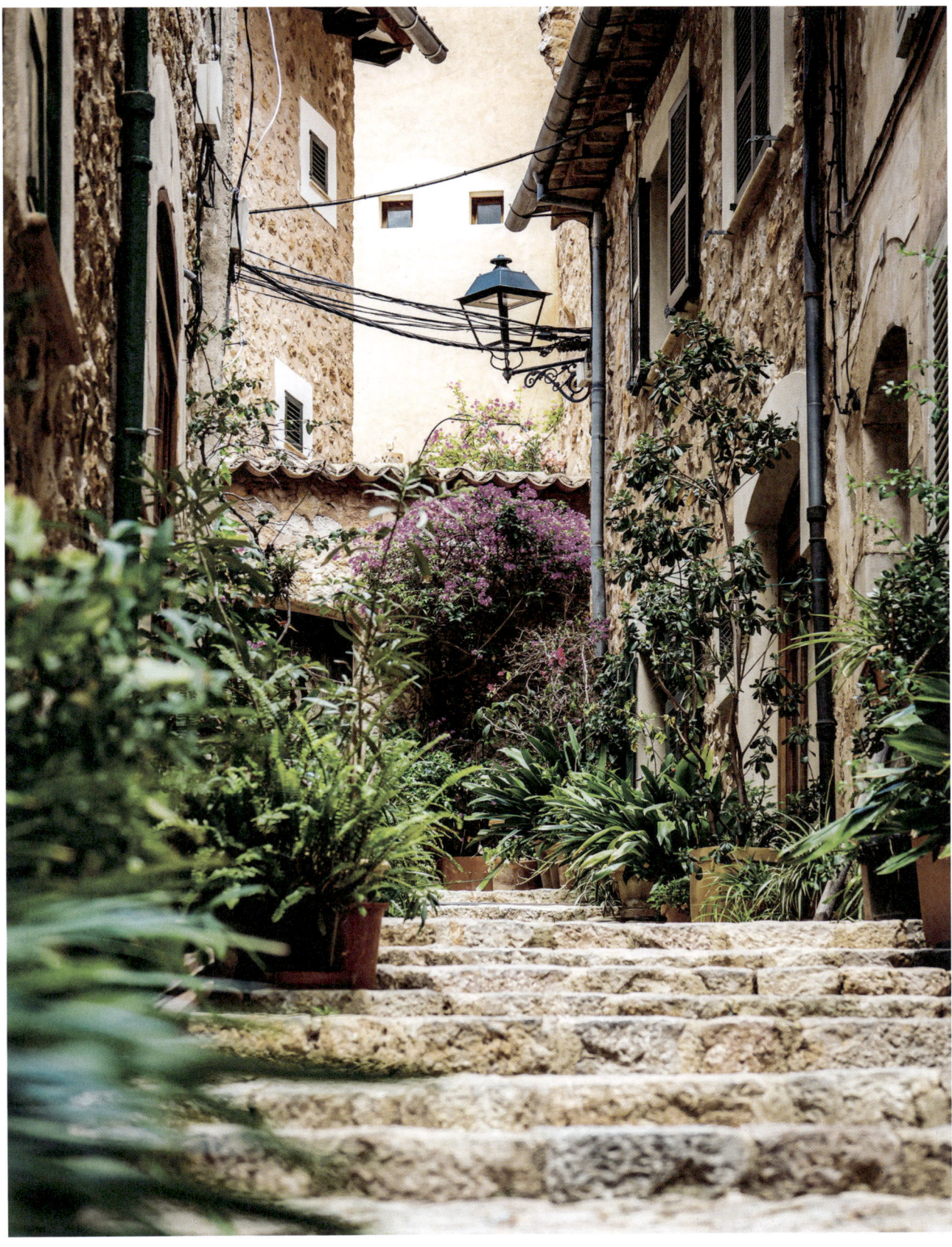

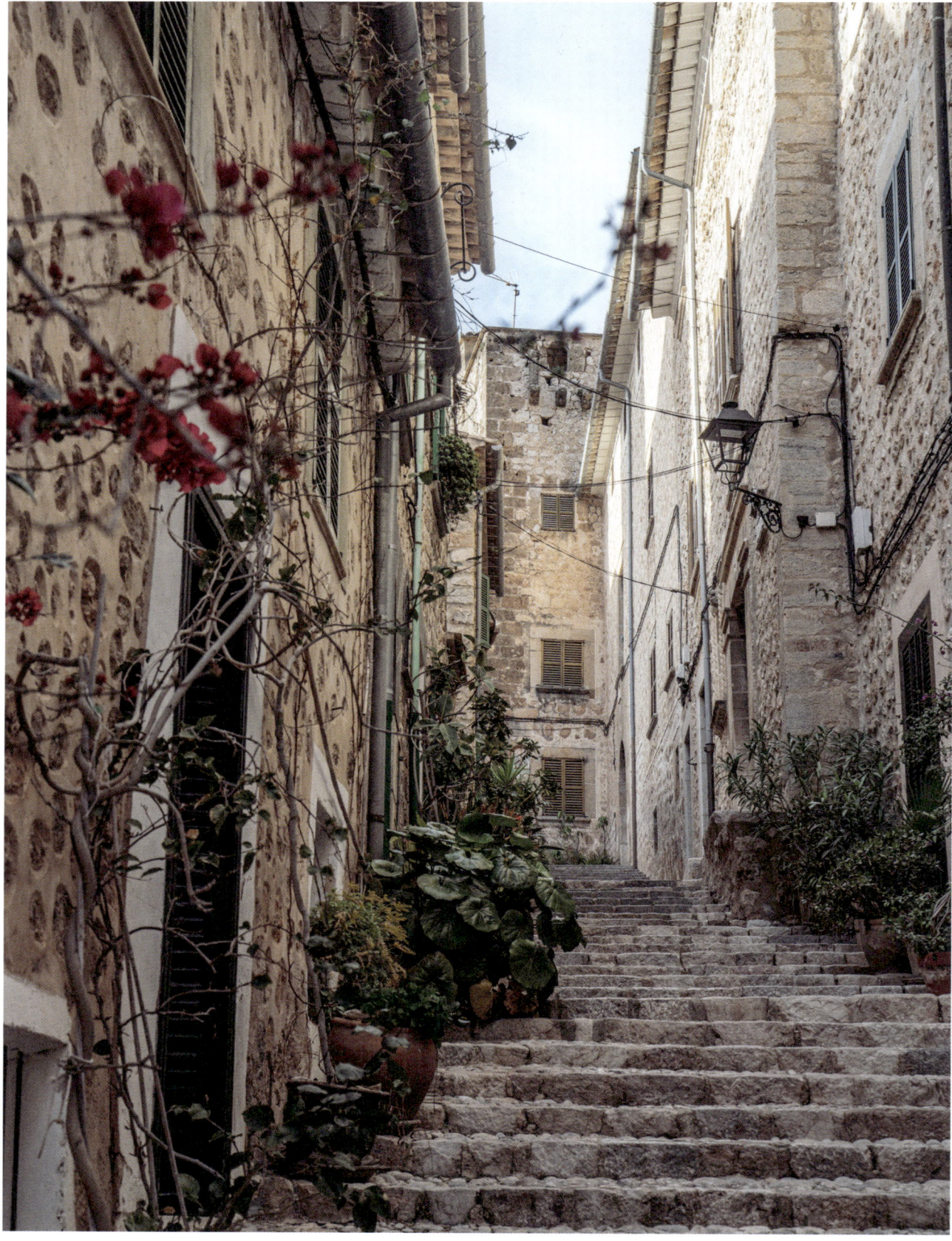

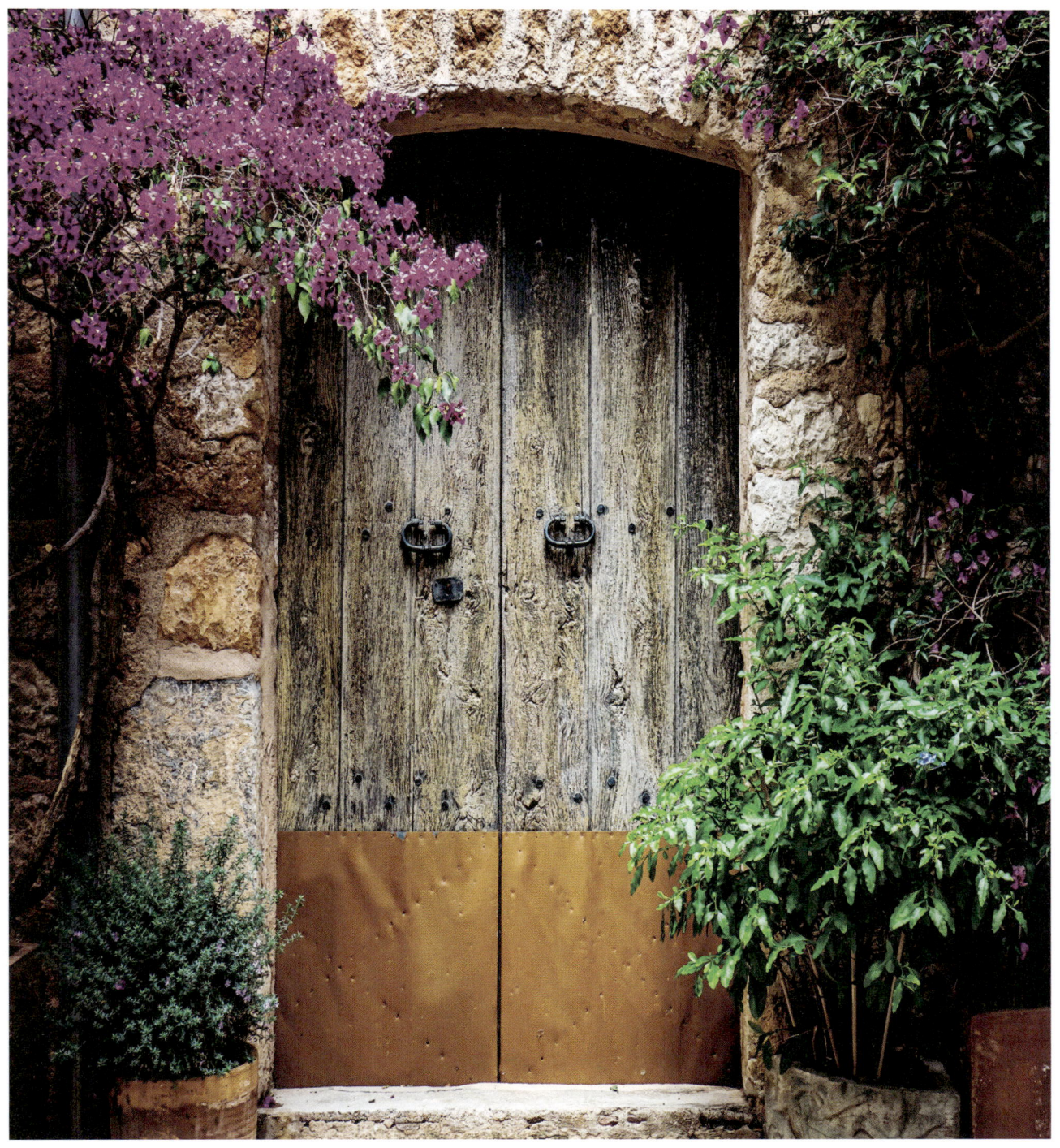

ABOVE AND LEFT: *Demanding but rewarding: Climbing the staircases and taking in Fornalutx's distinctive, closely spaced lanes. Everything here has aged gracefully and been charmingly preserved.*

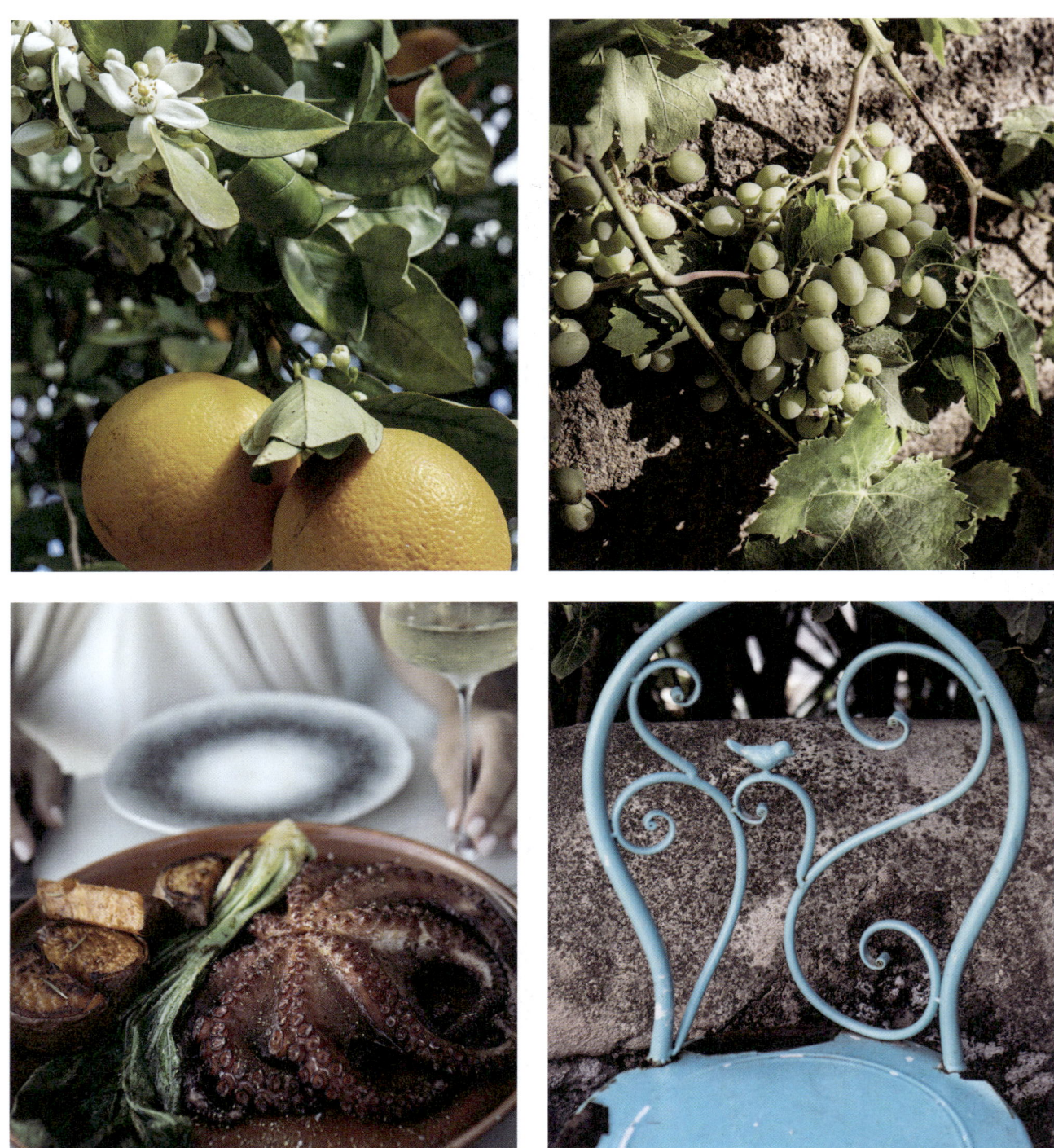

ABOVE AND RIGHT: *Tucked in a hillside garden behind a stone wall in Fornalutx, Ritmo is an intimate restaurant as rooted in local tradition as the village itself. Chef and proprietor Marcos Servera, the heart of this modern eatery, describes his cuisine as "nomadic cuisine": Mallorcan, traditional, and regional, with finest ingredients the Atlantic has to offer.*

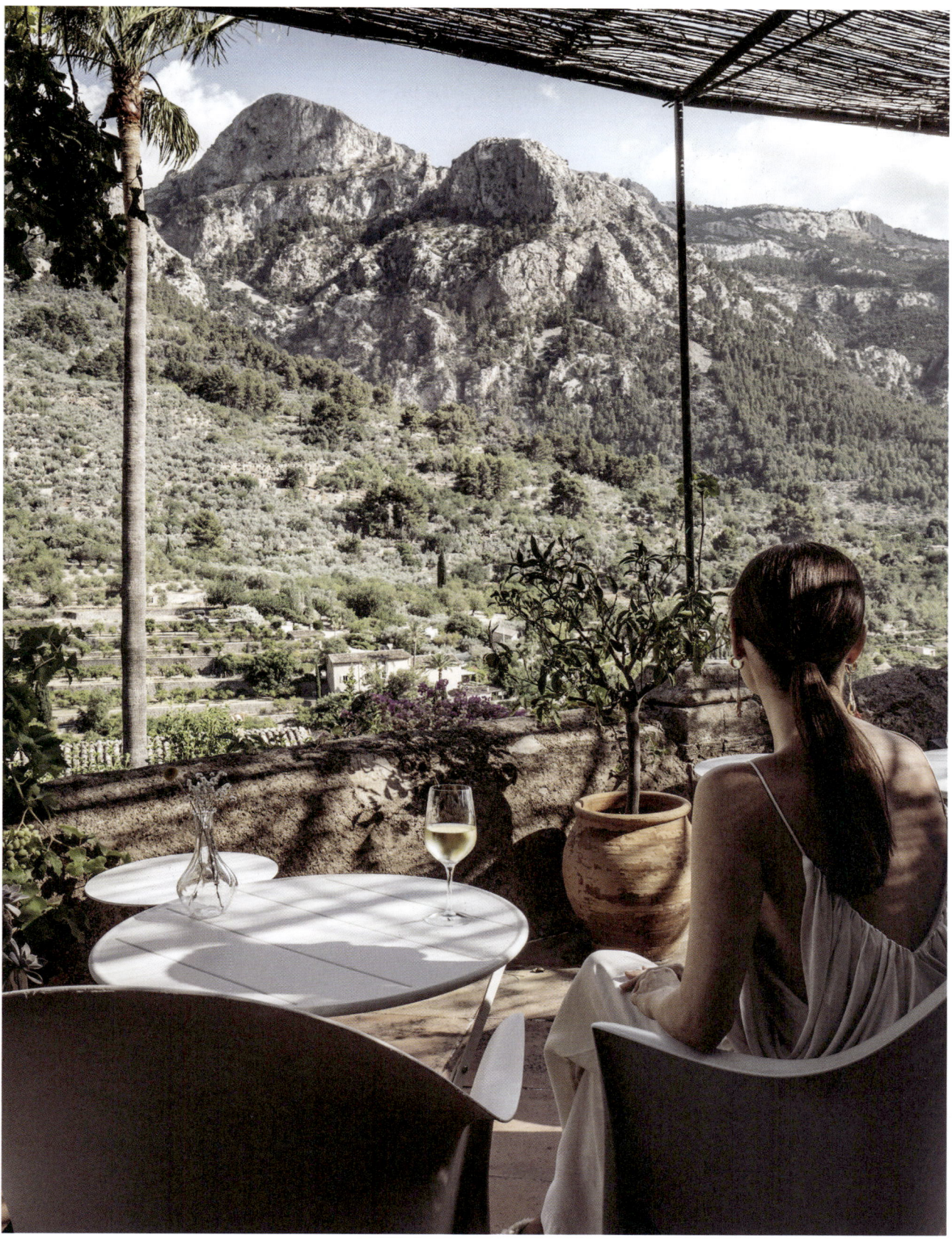

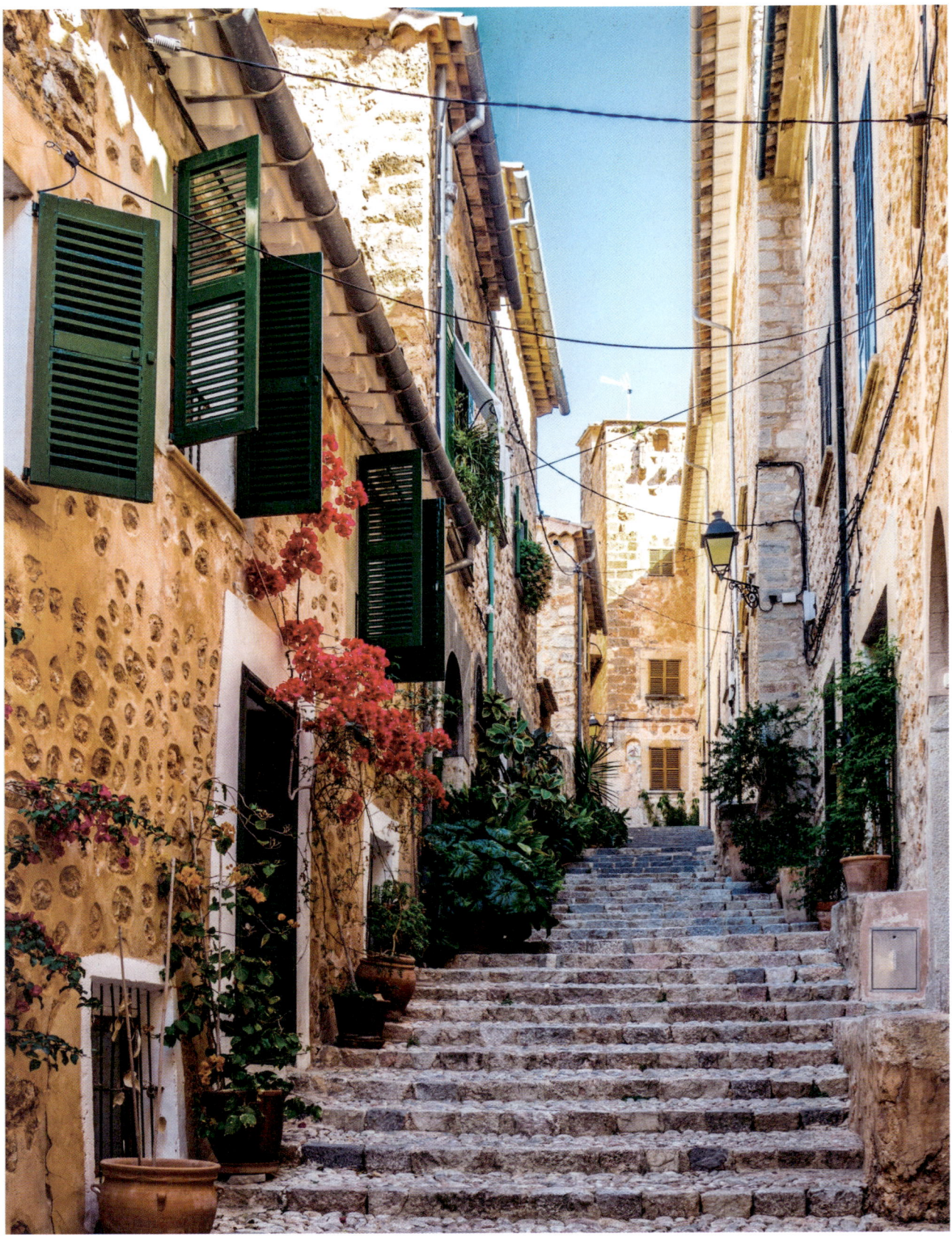

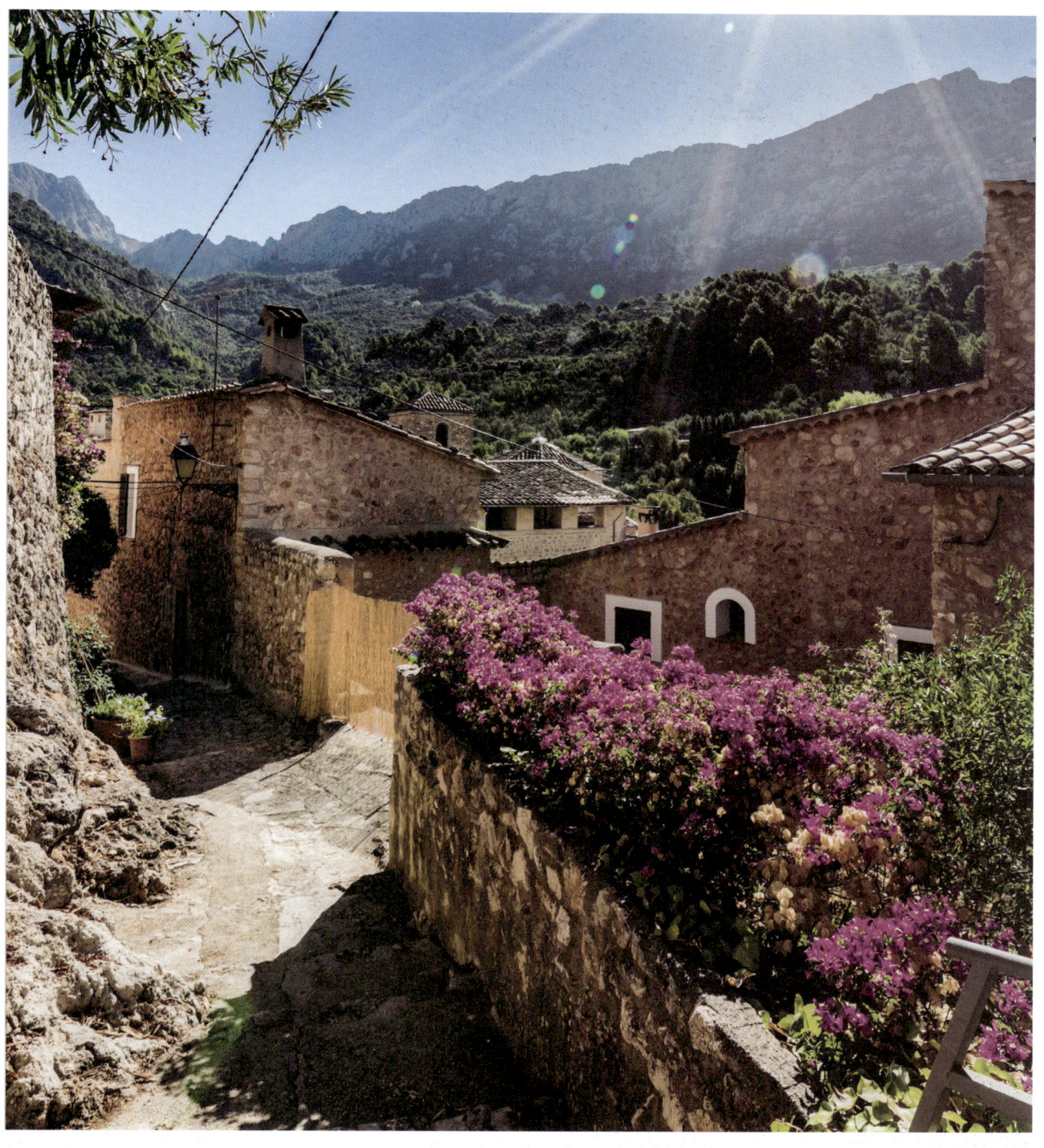

ABOVE AND LEFT: *No map or destination is needed in Fornalutx, just a bit of intuition. The best approach is to lose yourself in the narrow passageways, wandering freely where every turn reveals small casitas and stone huts clinging picturesquely to the rock.*

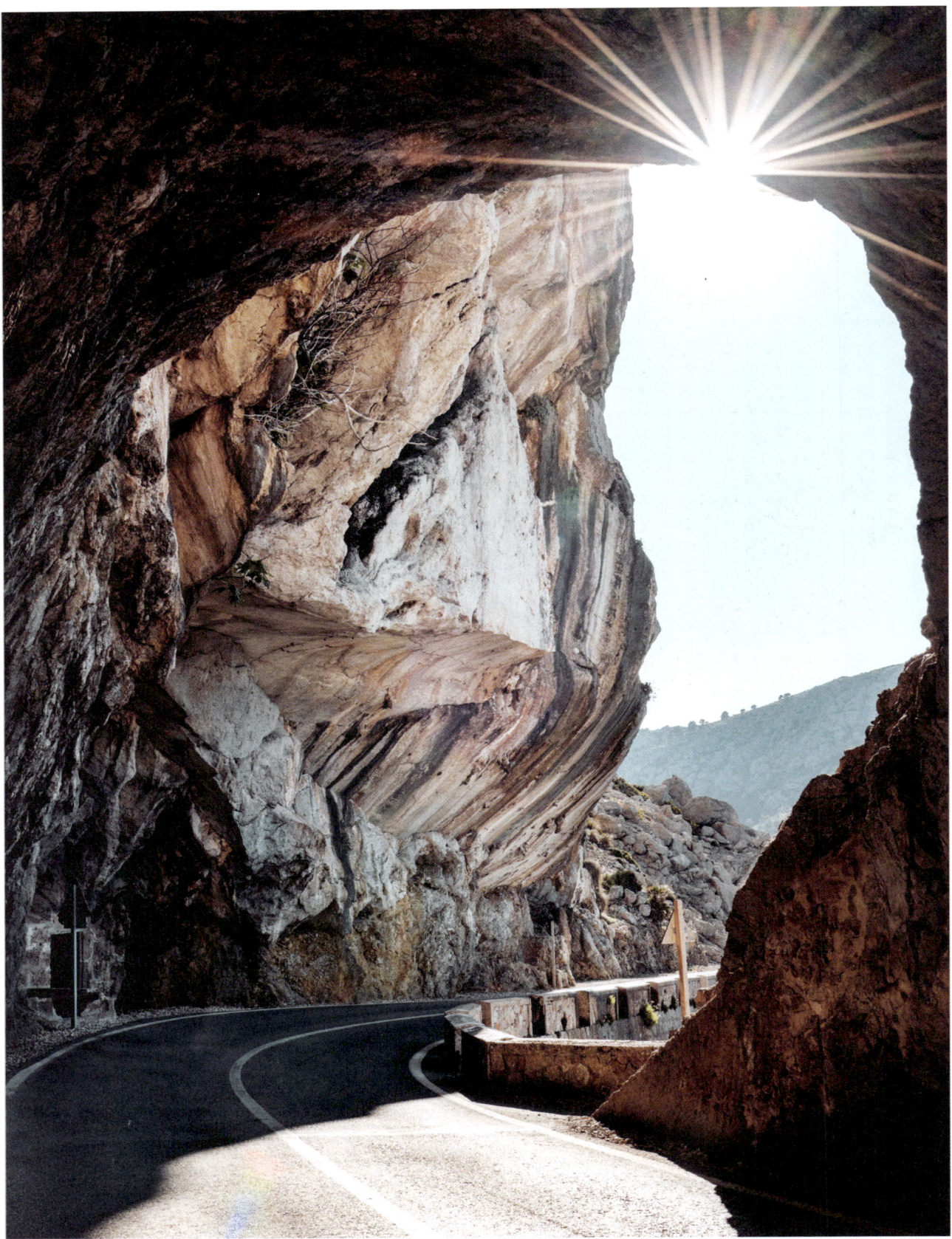

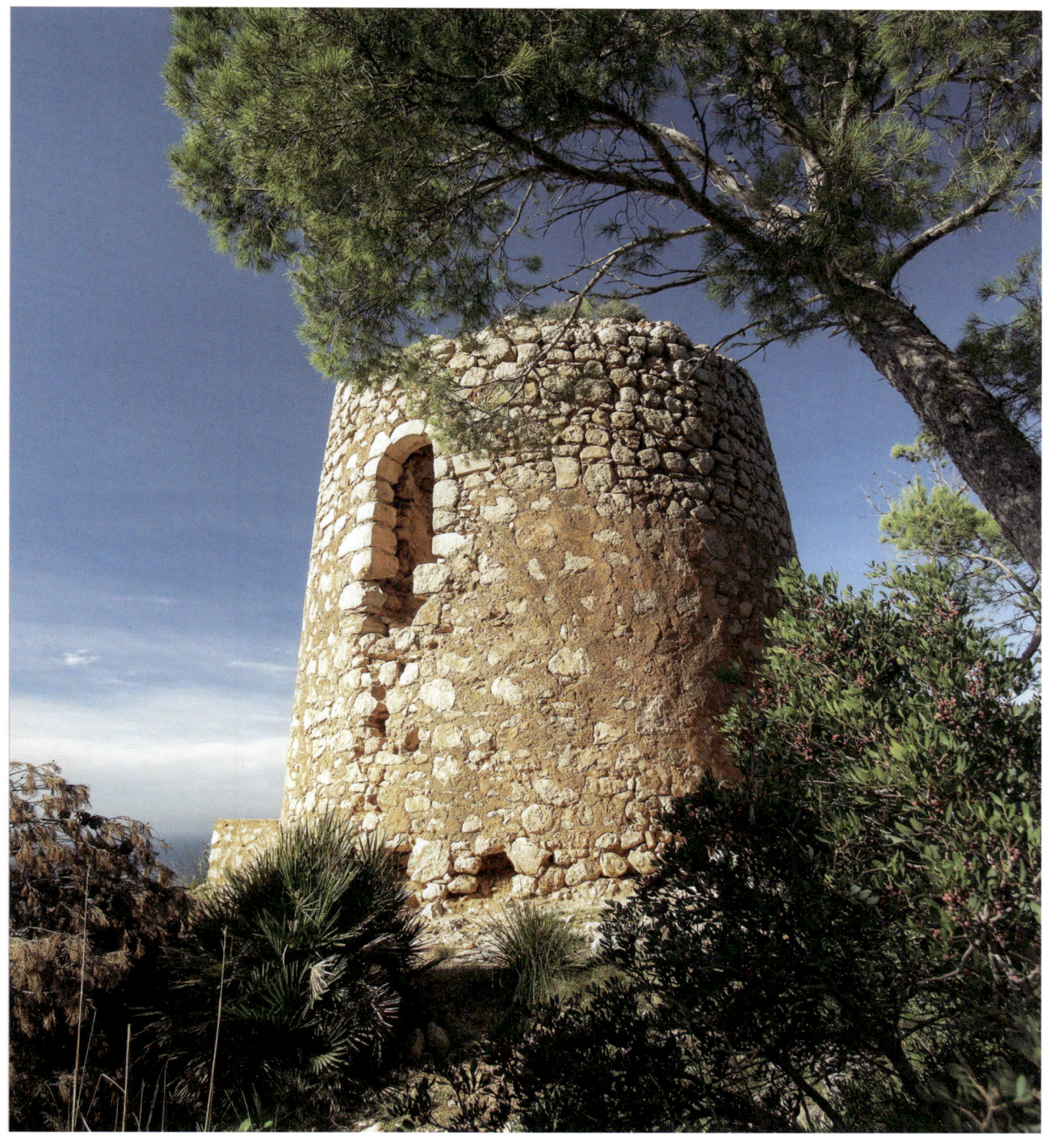

ABOVE AND LEFT: *The mighty Tramuntana mountains define Mallorca's northwest: World-famous serpentine roads snake through the hilly landscape, offering mesmerizing views. Medieval watchtowers can also be found throughout the region.*

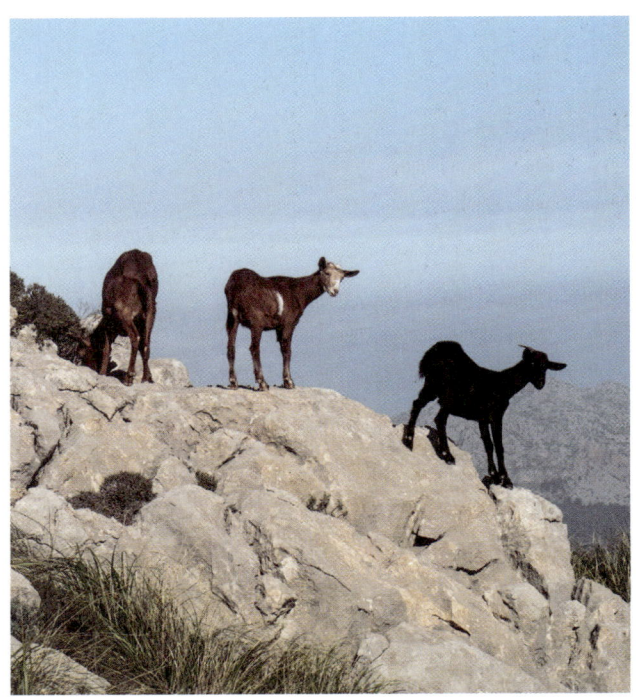

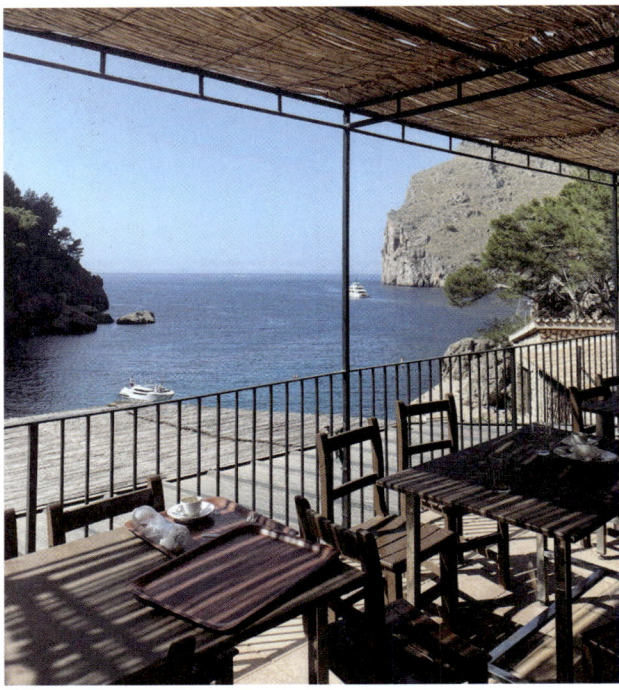

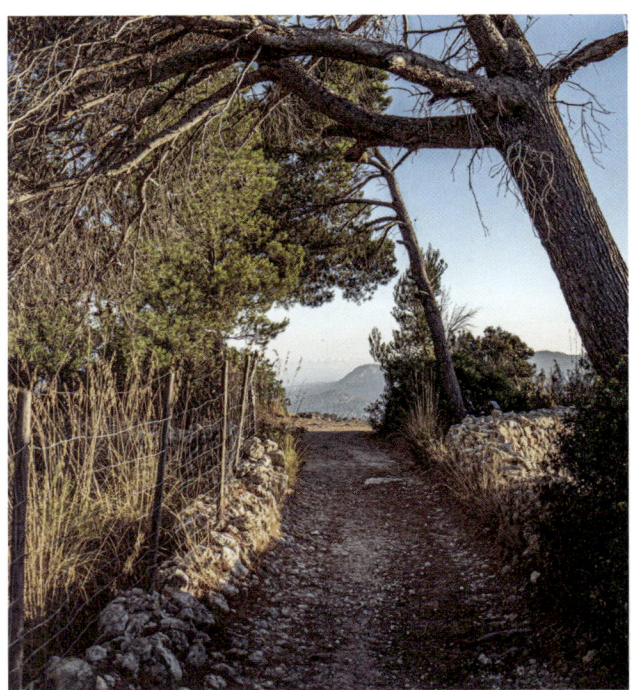

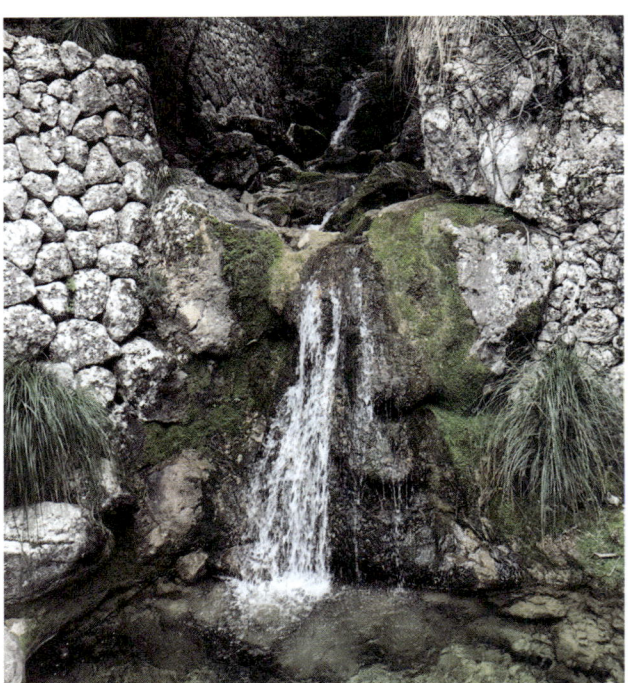

ABOVE AND RIGHT: *Mallorcan wild goats in the Tramuntana are a familiar sight, and vital to the ecosystem and the many creatures who live there, as they clear away flammable dry shrubs, grass, and undergrowth. Wild and romantic gorges and waterfalls also shape the mountainscape, like the Barranc de Biniaraix above Sóller. Echoes of a pirate past at sunset: the medieval Torre del Verger in Banyalbufar.*

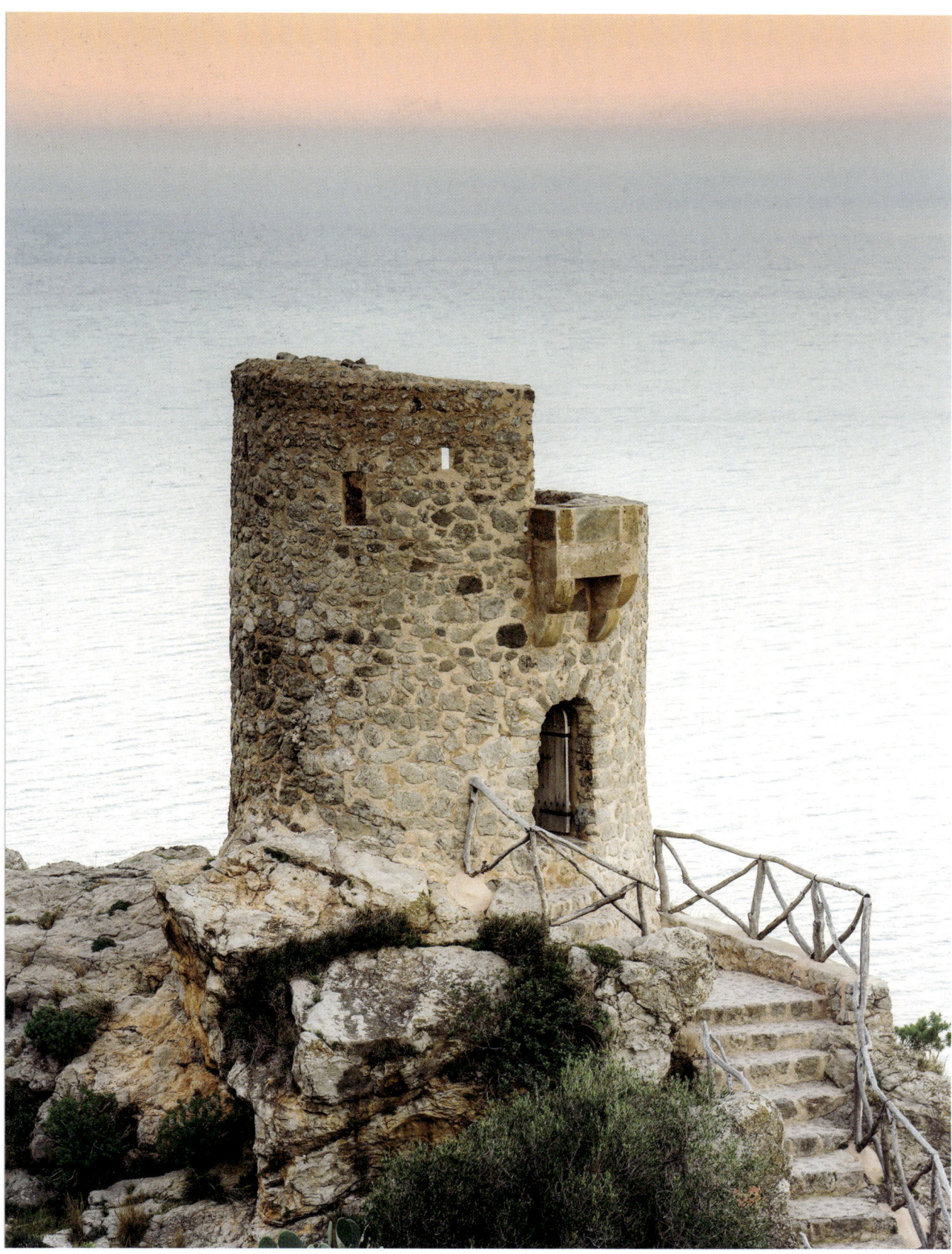

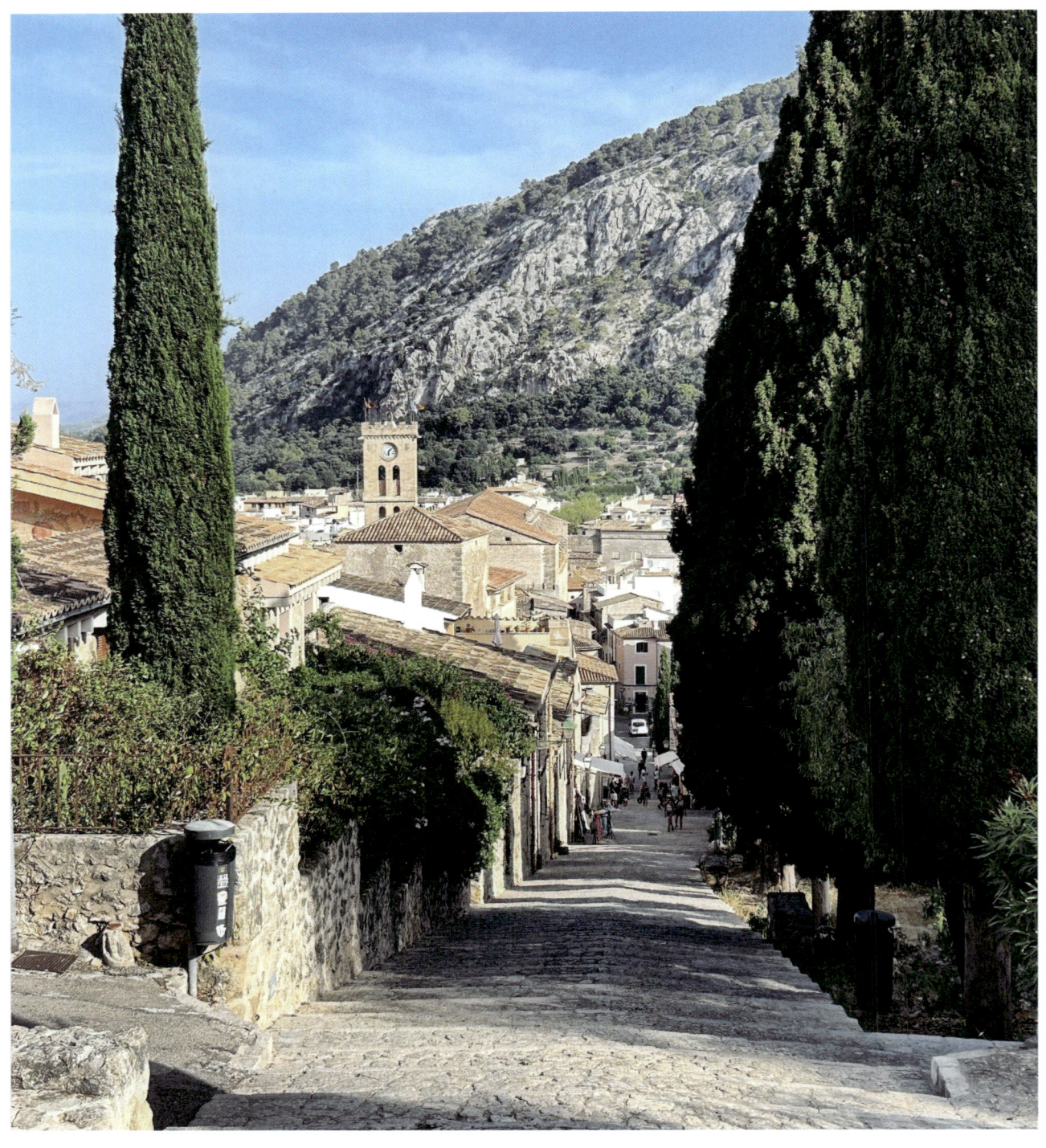

ABOVE: *The cypress-lined path leading up to Calvary in the old town of Pollença.*

RIGHT: *Legendary tapas, burgers, and small plates at Bar Tecun not far from the harbor in Port de Pollença.*
Live music every Friday, with good vibes guaranteed.

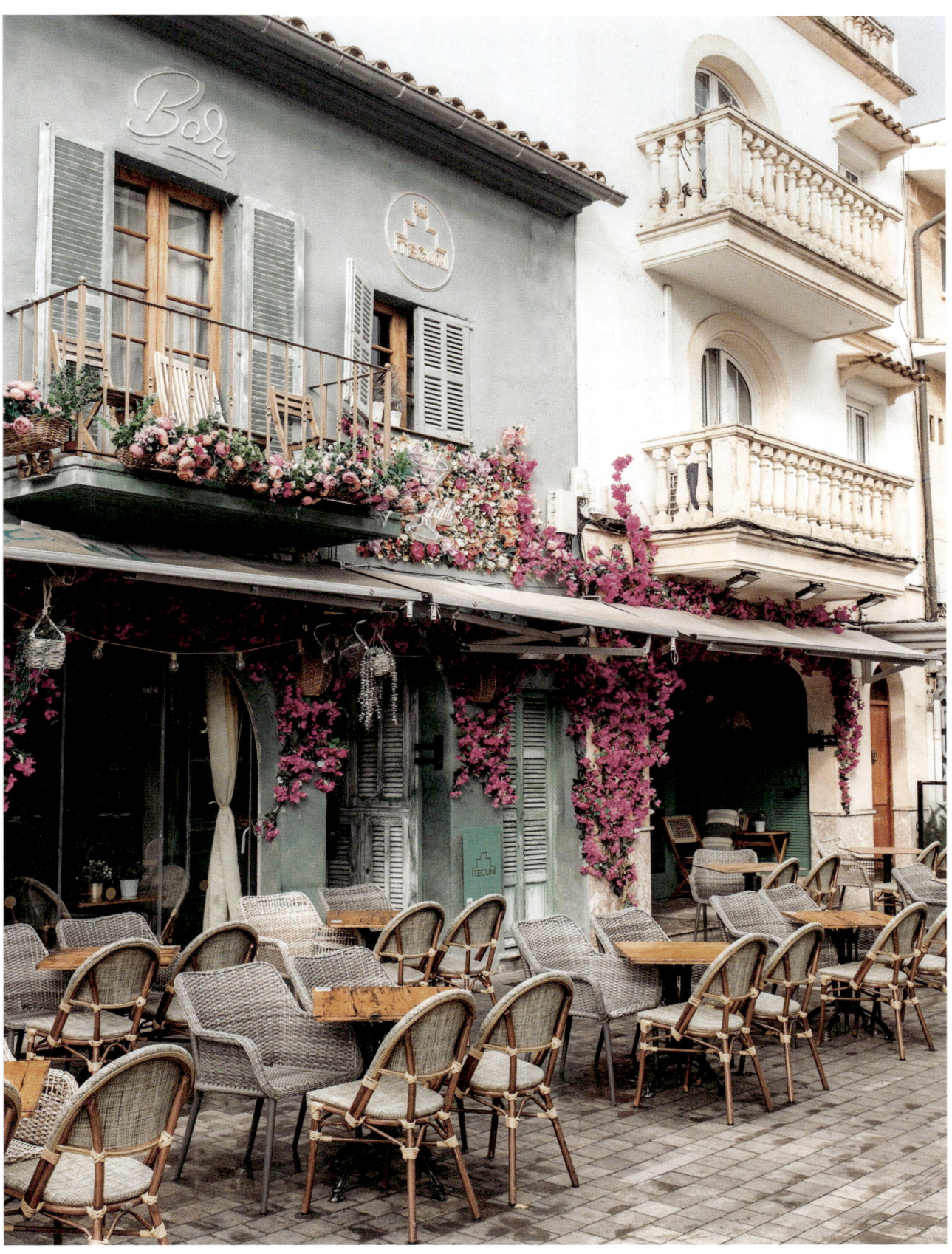

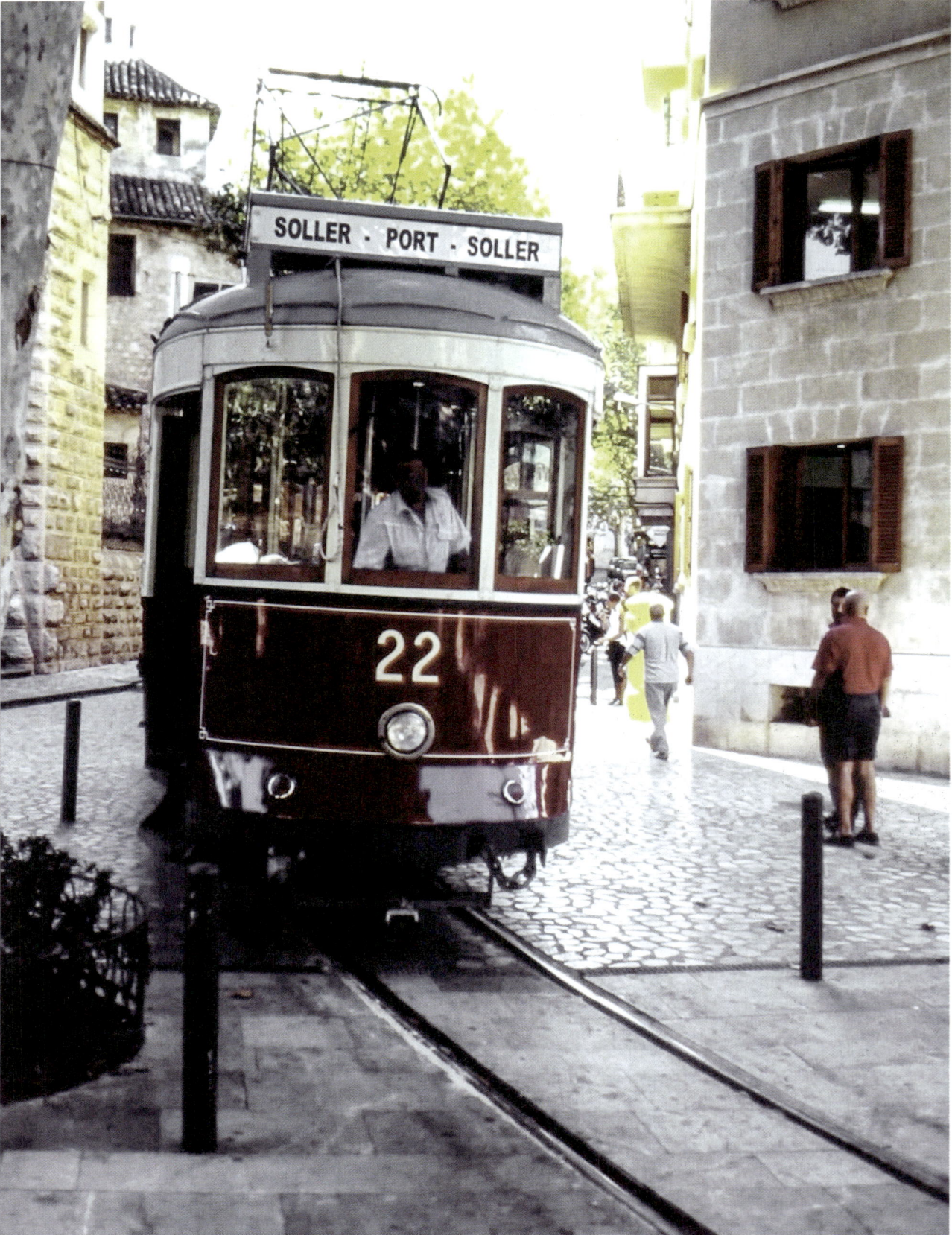

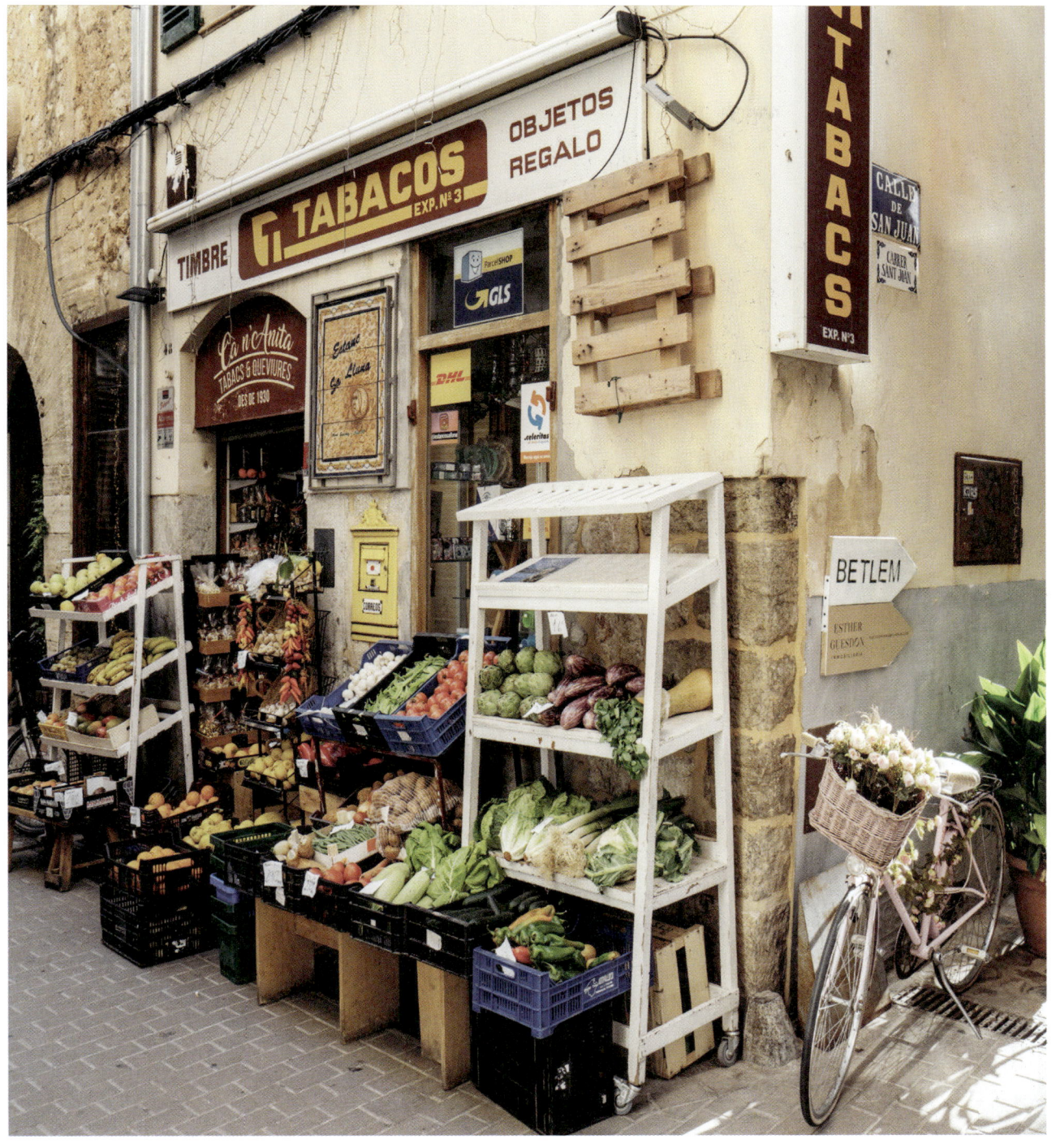

ABOVE: *The small town of Sóller is marked by Spanish Art Nouveau architecture and lies in the fertile "Golden Valley" of the Tramuntana, which gets its name from its many orange groves.*

LEFT: *The "Red Lightning" (Ferrocarril de Sóller) is a historic tram that winds its way through Sóller to the harbor at Port de Sóller, rolling past orange groves and pine forests on its hourlong journey.*

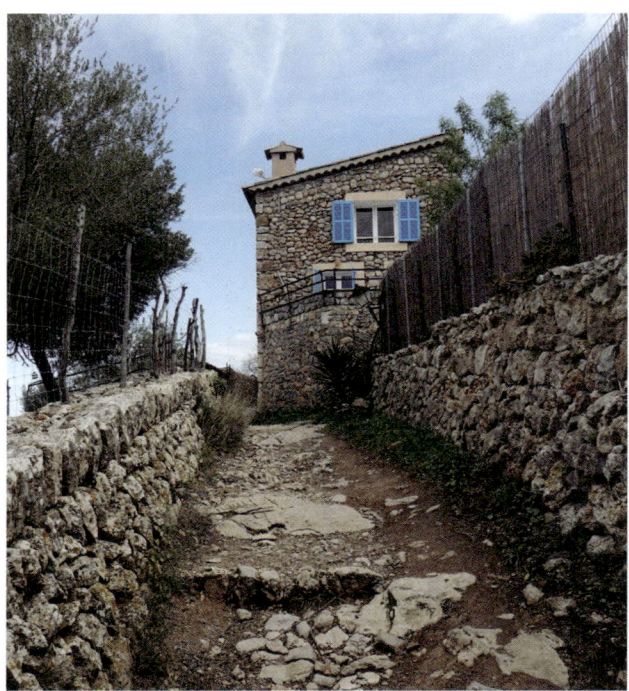

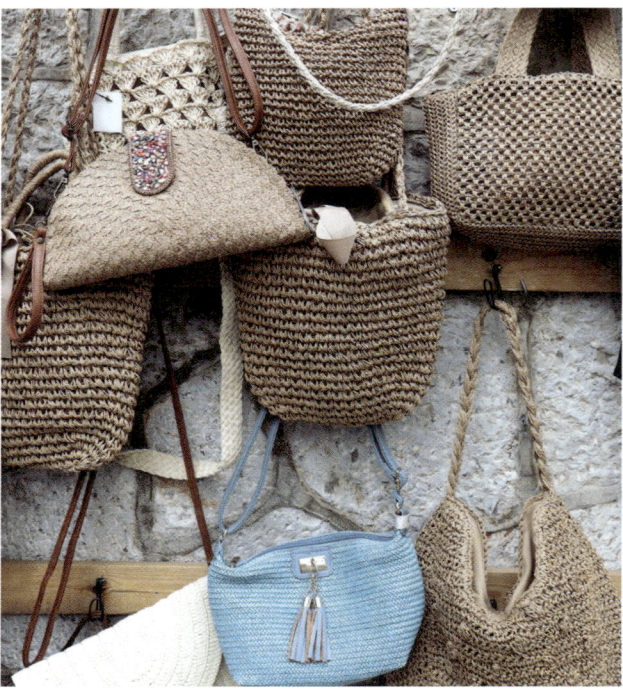

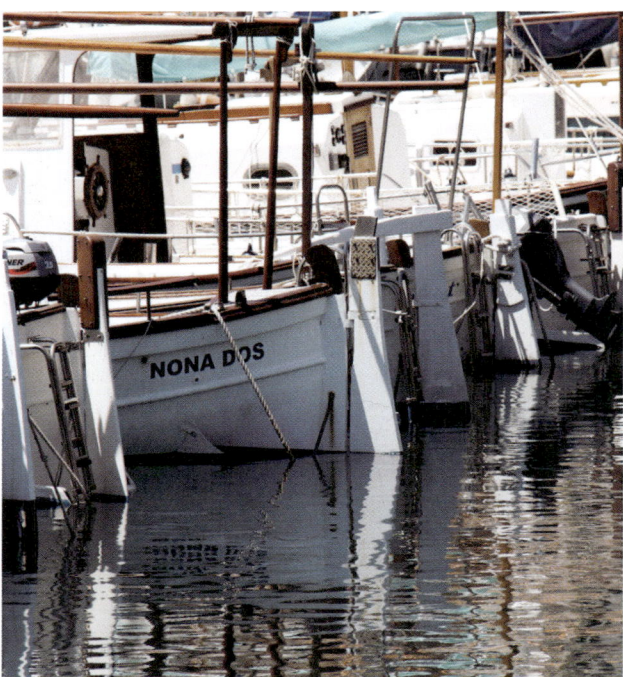

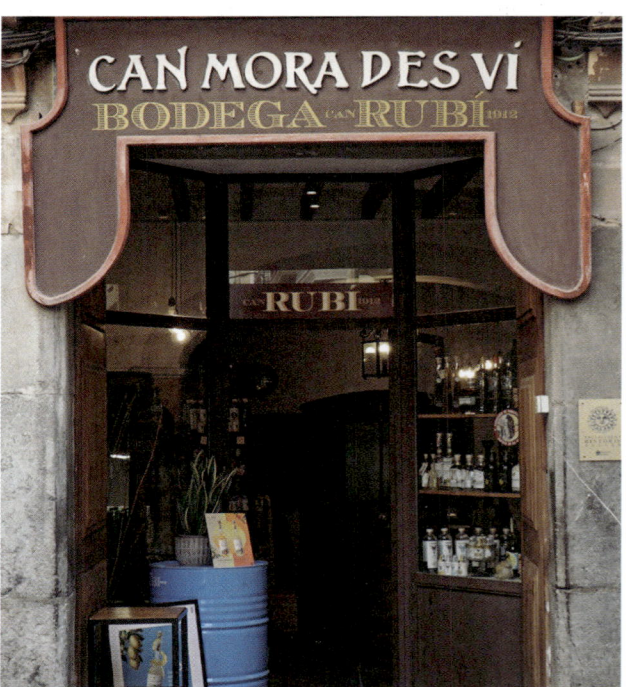

ABOVE: *Strolls here come highly recommended, as there is much to discover in the sheltered bay of Port de Sóller: bodegas, tapas bars, small shops, a fishing harbor, and traditional fincas nearby.*

RIGHT: *An ensemble of Modernisme: the church of Sant Bartomeu in Sóller set among beautiful Art Nouveau buildings.*

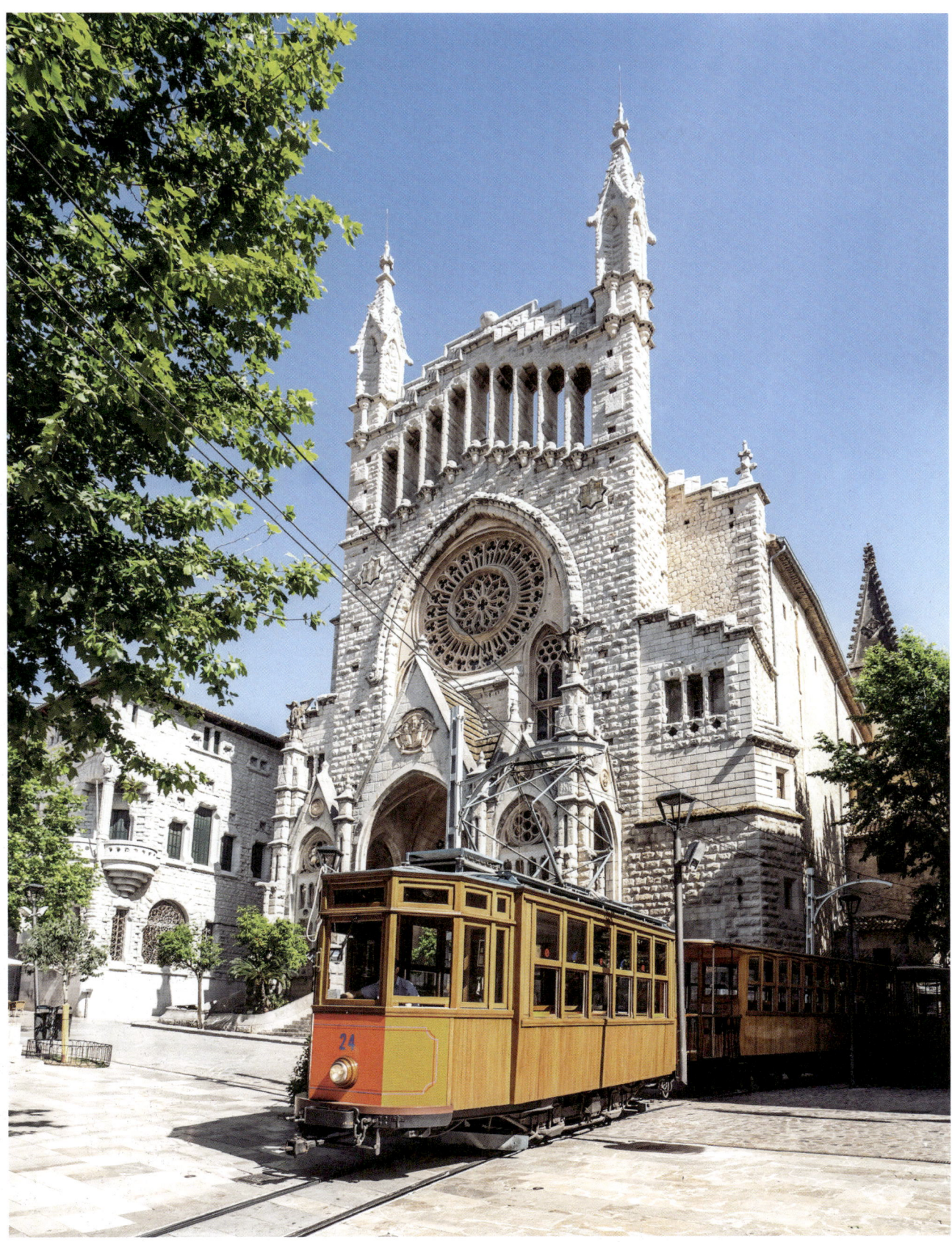

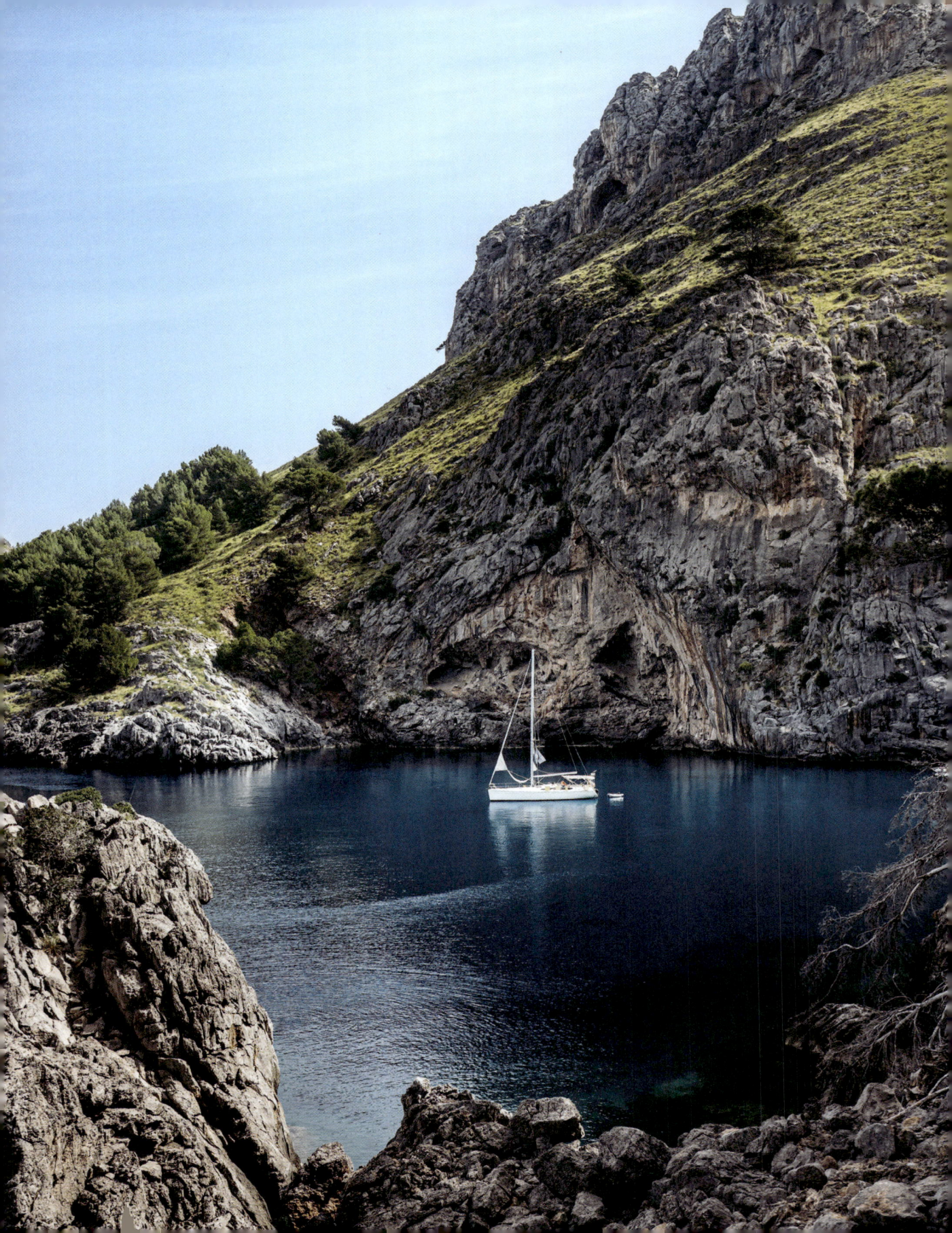

MALLORCA'S BAYS

GREETINGS FROM THE TURQUOISE REALM OF KING NEPTUNE

There are, of course, long sandy beaches. Some are quiet, others more animated with promenades, beach clubs, parties, and watersports. Almost more compelling, however, are the many large and small coves scattered around the island. Even trying to access them can be a challenge. The payoff, however, is getting to snorkel among the rocks and maybe watch a busy octopus or gaze at a school of fish. It's an experience you will surely want to repeat.

The water around the Balearic Islands is distinctive, significantly clearer than along the coast of the mainland, and the sight of its turquoise blue triggers an immediate sense of joy. King Neptune has endowed Mallorca and its neighbors with an endemic plant with unusual properties: *Posidonia*. Extensive underwater meadows of this seagrass surround the islands, filtering the water, binding carbon dioxide, producing oxygen, and sheltering numerous marine species. Also called Neptune grass, *Posidonia* is not a form of algae but a flowering plant, with roots and leaves that it sheds in autumn. Its importance to the marine ecosystem is considerable, and conservation efforts have ramped up in recent years. Measures include chasing away boaters who try to anchor over seagrass beds, which can tear up the plants. Encountering these seagrass leaves in the sea or on the shore is a quiet reminder of a natural wonder worth being grateful for.

LEFT: *Here, the journey is truly part of the destination: You can drive to the Cala de Sa Calobra in the northwest of Mallorca on an adventurous winding road, reach it on foot by following a spectacular hiking trail, or take a boat from Sóller.*

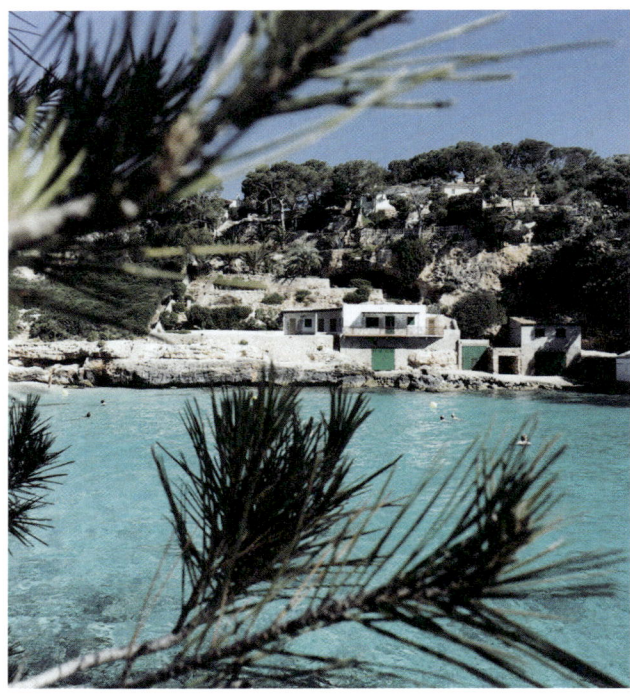

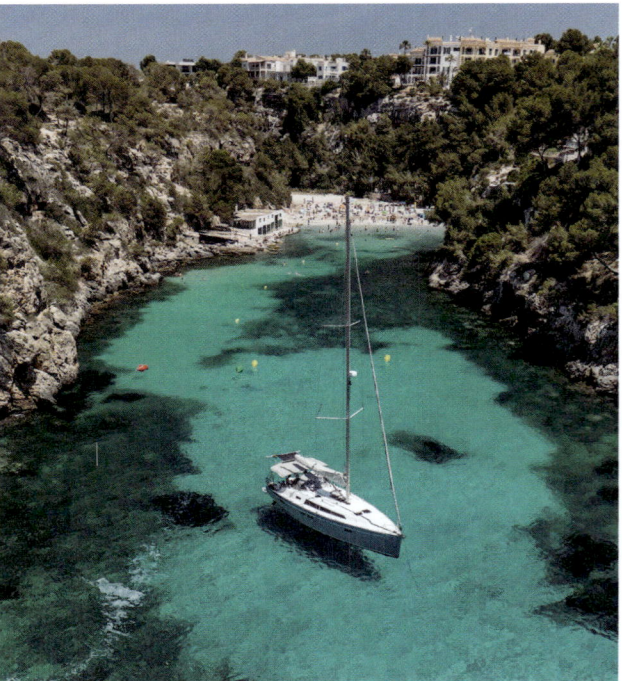

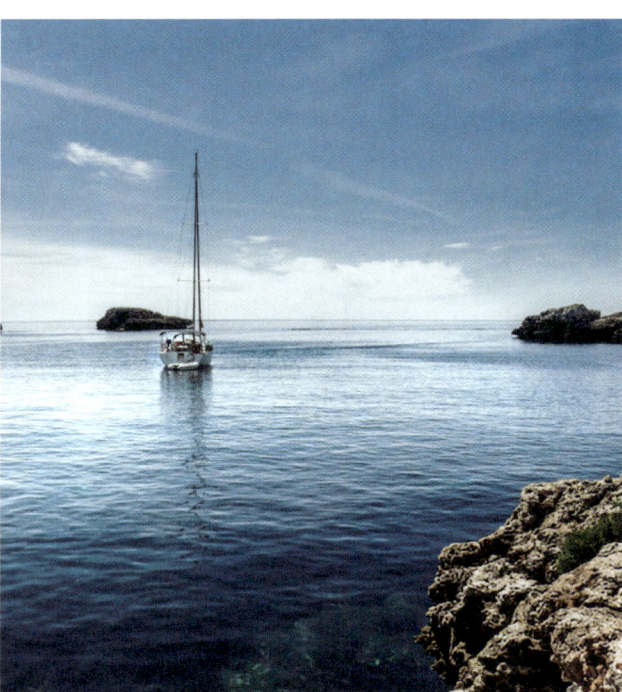

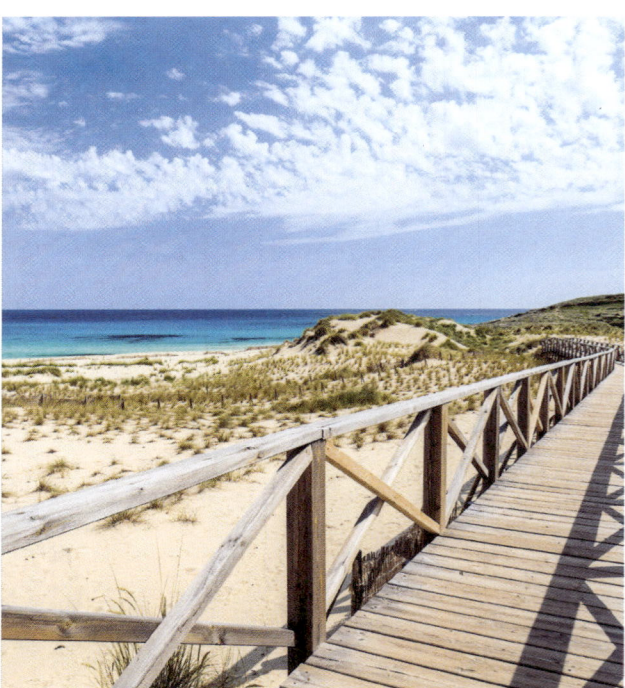

ABOVE: *How clear can water be? Mallorca's bays have an answer: Cala Llombards (upper left), Cala Pi (upper right), Cala Ferrera (lower left), and Cala Mesquida (lower right).*

RIGHT: *The almost meditative view of the rock arch Es Pontàs near Cala Santanyí.*

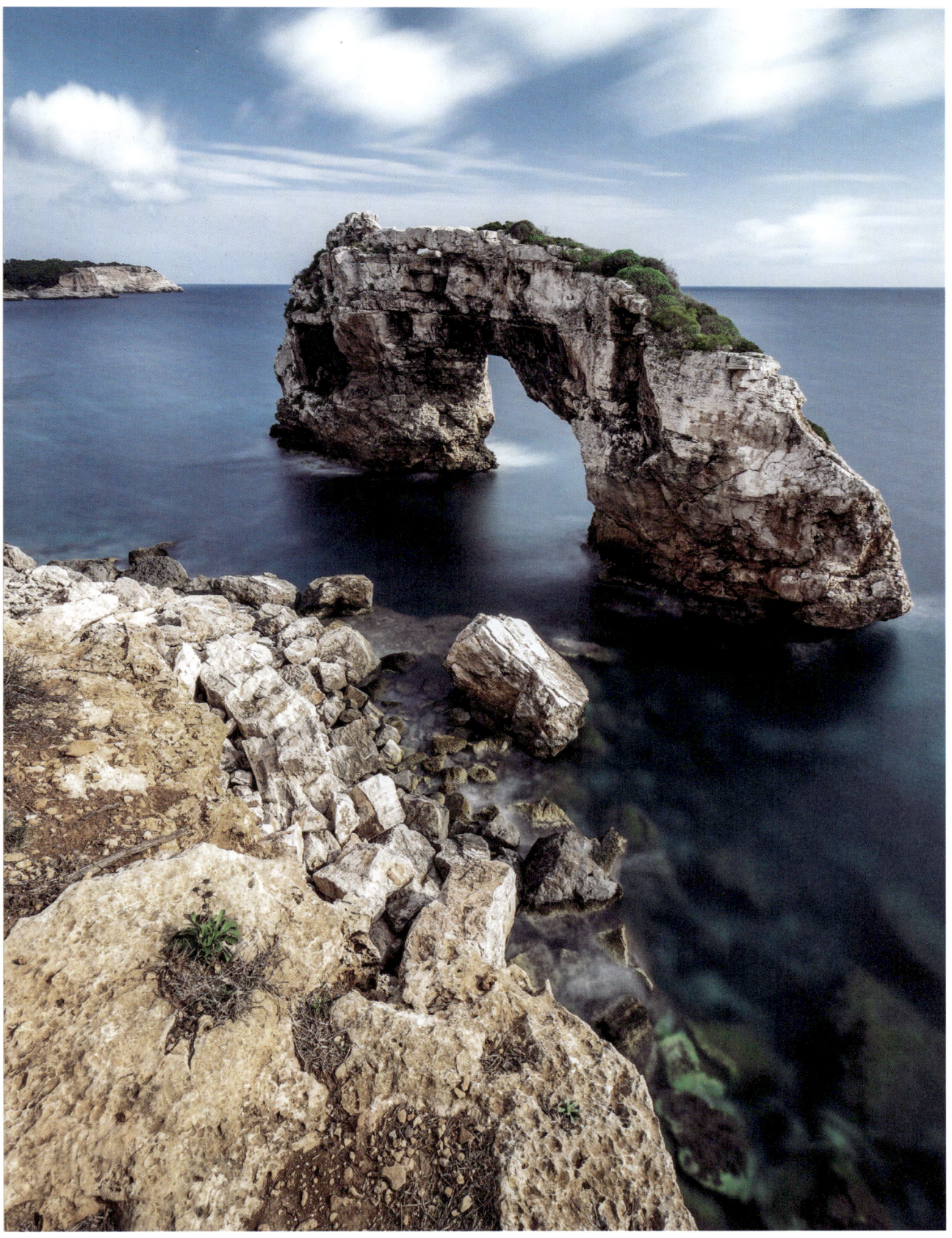

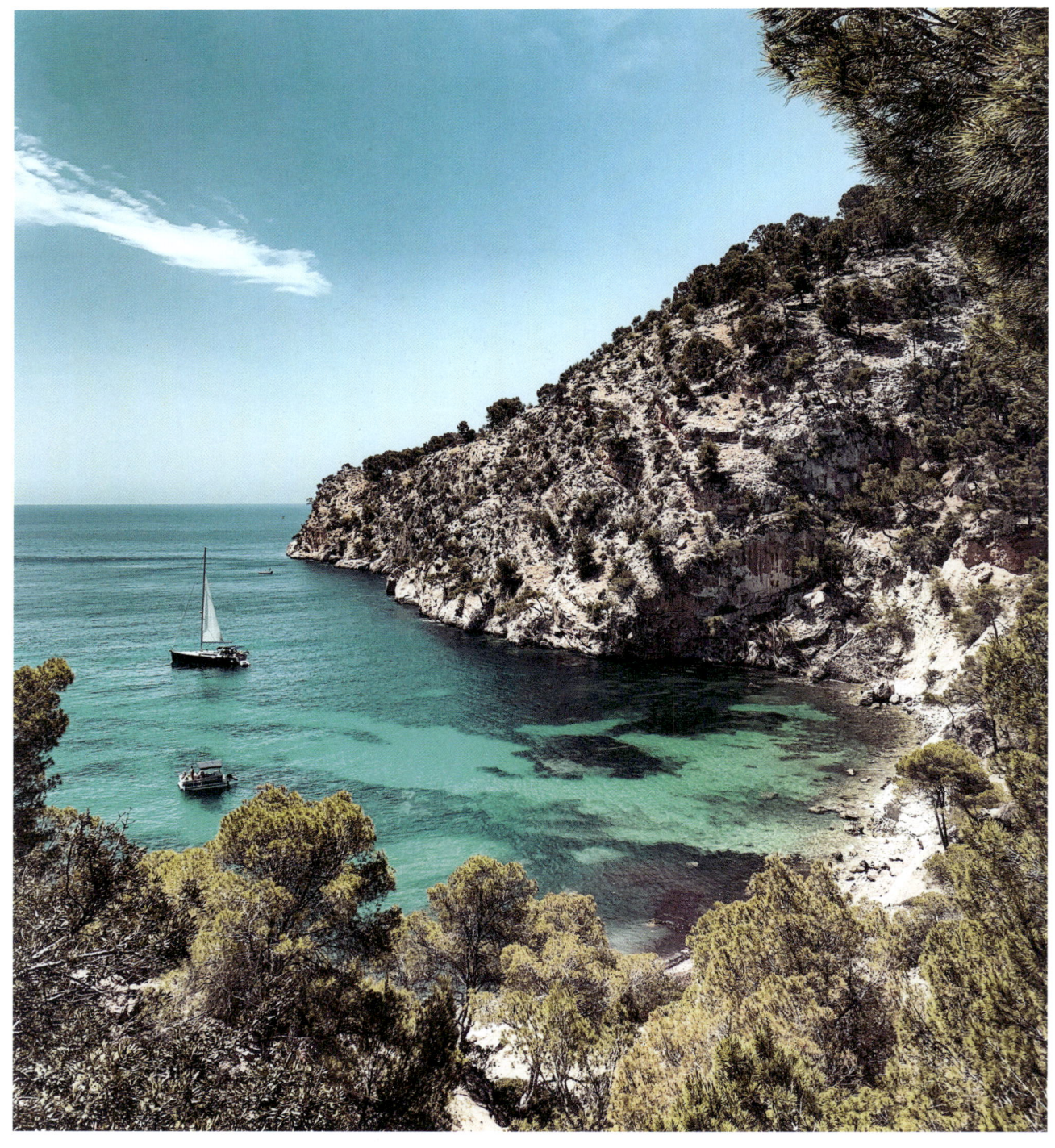

ABOVE: *Pristine beauty: Cala Blanca near Andratx is a small, rocky cove that remains lightly frequented even in summer. Dog owners especially love this cozy spot, as four-legged friends are welcome on the beach here year-round.*

RIGHT: *The beach at Cala Mesquida, in the east of the island, is part of a nature reserve with wild dune landscapes.*

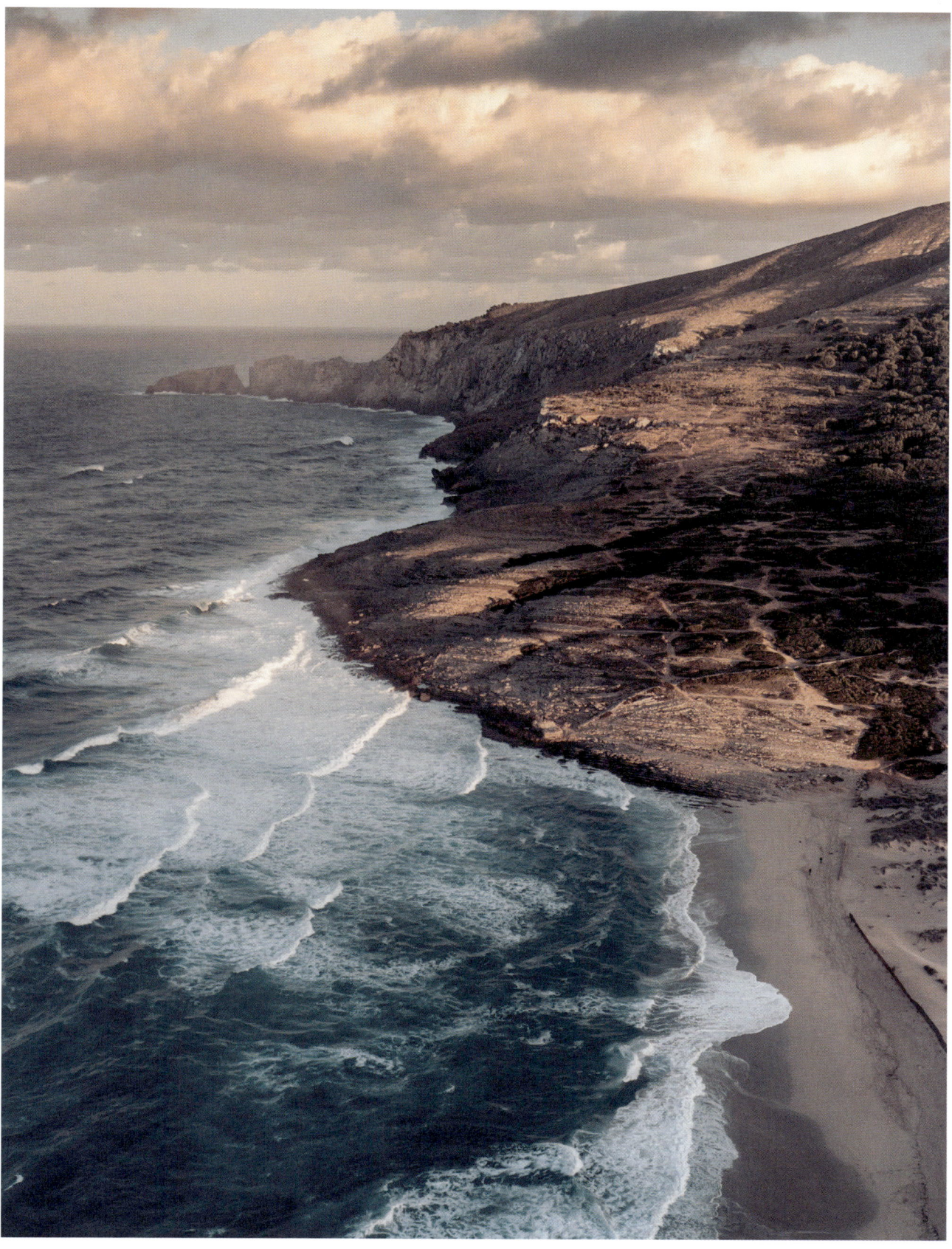

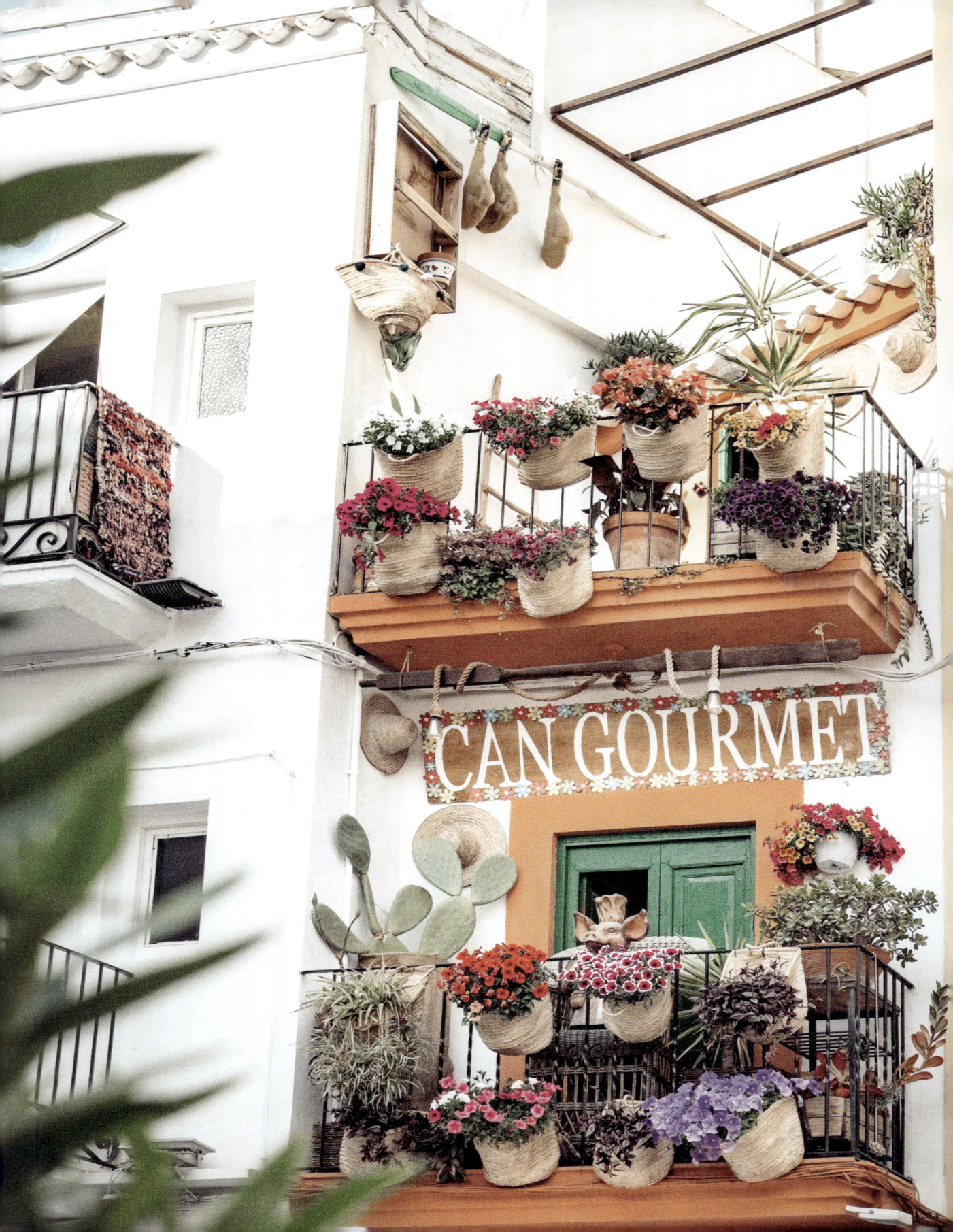

IBIZA TOWN

THE ISLAND'S LAID-BACK GUIDING PRINCIPLE: LIVE AND LET LIVE

Mallorca has a markedly independent sister island in Ibiza. The two Balearic islands share a similar history and related roots, but Ibiza—known in Catalan as *Eivissa*—has long been somewhat wilder, less conformist, and more enigmatic. Ibiza was settled by Phoenicians, Romans, and Moors, and later reconquered by the Catalans. Watchtowers, fortresses, and fortified churches followed. In many respects, the smaller island has retained the character of a defiant pirate stronghold. Mallorca, by contrast, developed into a center of trade and tourism.

In the 1950s, during the Spanish military dictatorship under Francisco Franco, Ibiza was impoverished and agrarian. While the regime on the mainland maintained strict control, Ibiza largely escaped attention. This drew artists and social outsiders to the island, where a countercultural milieu began to form. Word spread that the cost of living was extremely low. American conscientious objectors and peace activists went into hiding here. Hippies explored ideas of freedom and spirituality inspired by the Phoenician island deities Bes and Tanit. Pragmatism held sway between local residents and the flamboyant newcomers as long as they could pay their way. Live and let live remains part of Ibiza's social fabric.

This is evident on an initial walk through *Dalt Vila*, the island's old town. The area contains numerous expressions of bohemian life: unconventional boutiques, gay clubs, artists' studios, and bars. Everyday openness is visible in the streets between souvenir shops and high-end fashion stores. Here, personal difference draws little attention.

LEFT: Muy auténtico: *Enjoy award-winning sandwiches, a glass of red wine, and an eclectic crowd at the bodega Can Gourmet on Carrer de Guillem de Montgri, one of the small shopping streets behind the harbor promenade.*

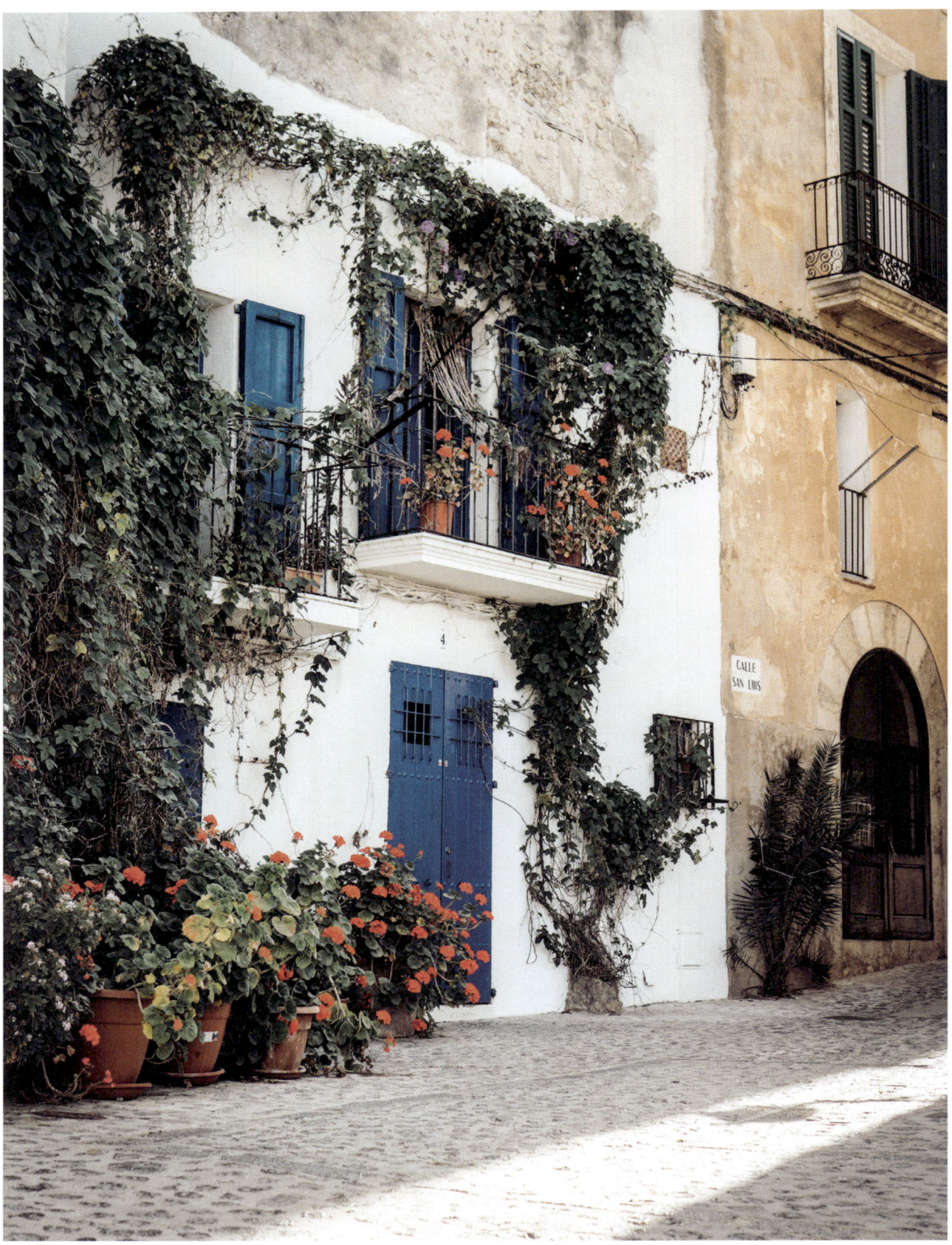

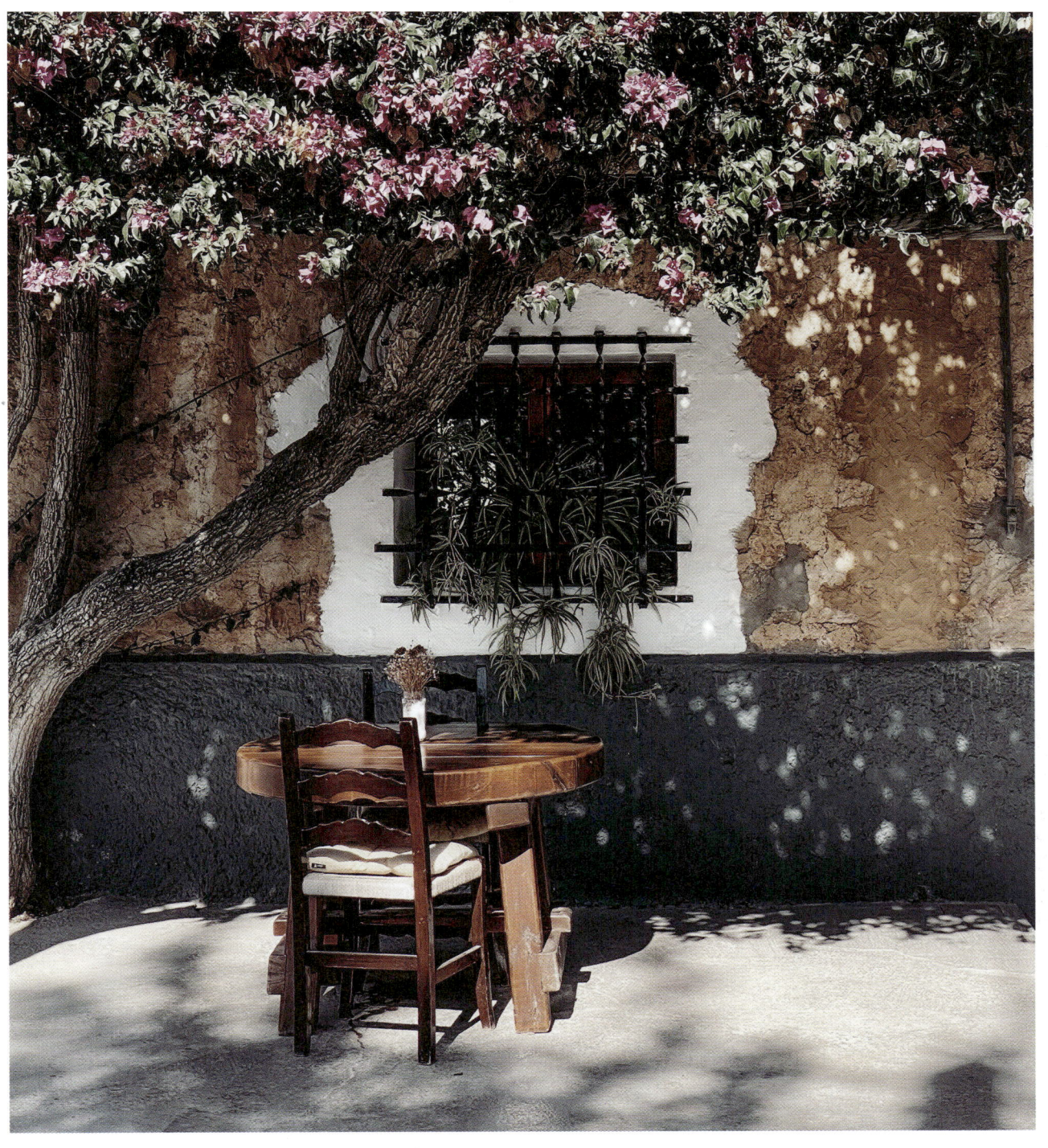

ABOVE AND LEFT: *If you only have a few hours to spend on Ibiza, a walk along the streets of the old town, up to the fortress walls, and on to the cathedral reveals the many sides of the island, with picturesque corners at every turn.*

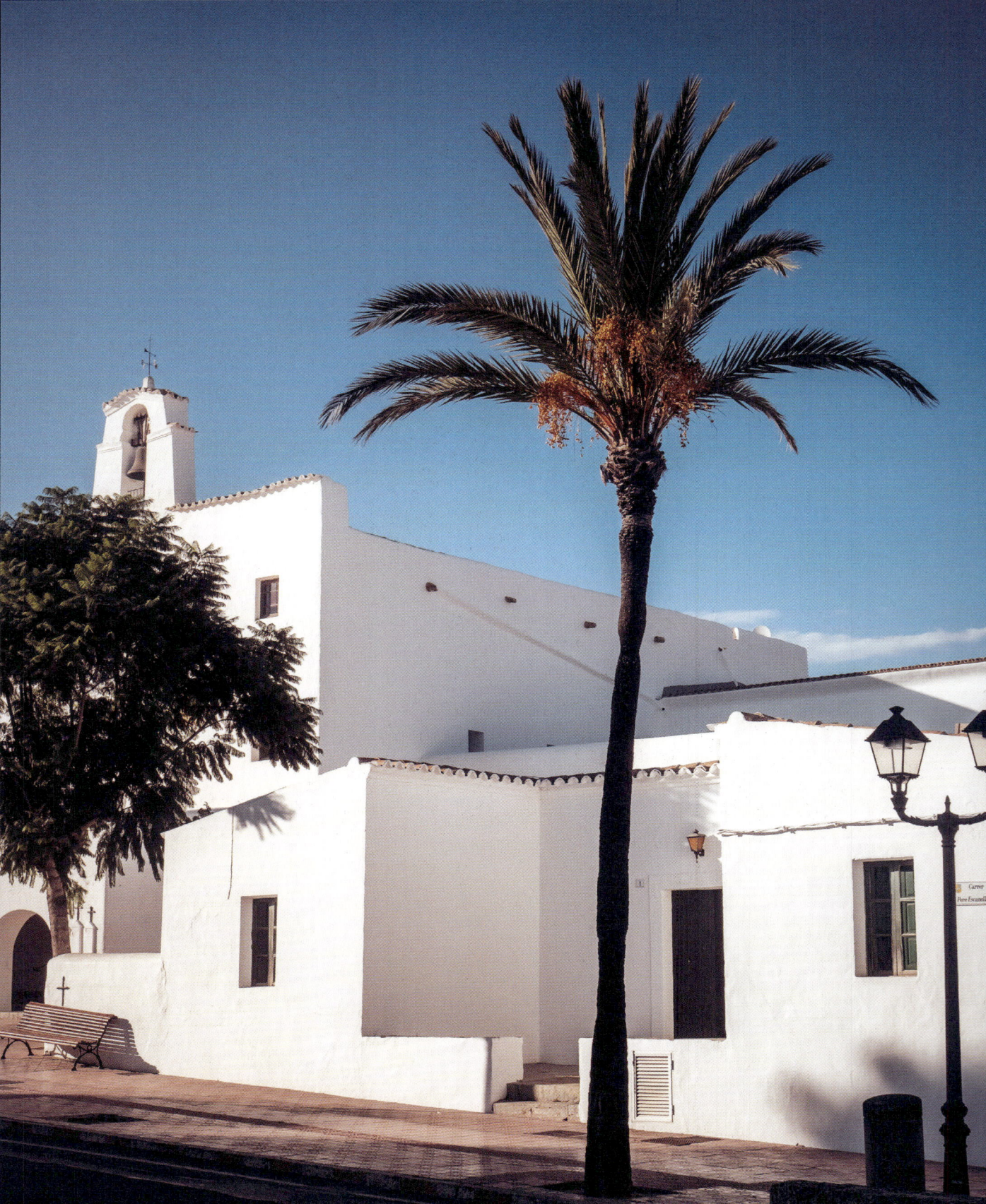

THE SPIRIT OF IBIZA

BAUHAUS, NIGHTS OUT AT THE CLUB, AND MYTHS ABOUT HIPPIES

Dazzling white façades and minimalist designs with cubic elements make Ibiza's architecture markedly different from that of Mallorca. Some say that the purism and bold lines of the churches and fincas was what inspired modern architects like Le Corbusier and Bauhaus founder Walter Gropius to trim down to the essentials. The small, one-story farmhouses still feel modern and are everywhere on Ibiza.

A lot of clubs, like Pacha or Amnesia, got started in a traditional finca. Today they have become mega venues, but the thick walls of the original structures still stand. In the old days people would drive from the beach to the disco in a Renault 4, barefoot the whole time. Today what would have been the same people have to buy tickets to "events" at the clubs and they show up in a "VIP" shuttle. But they're still going to the same party. Parties on Ibiza are different. There are no ages or questions or limits; it's just the here and now. People do not tend to express regret about hitting a club like Amnesia or Pacha or DC10 on a visit to Ibiza.

For those who persist in wondering what it was like here in the past, there are a few places where that spirit remains palpable. These places include the restaurant La Paloma, the paella place Can Salinas, and the cove of Cala Escondida, home to the coolest beach bar under the sun. And what about the hippie markets? That tradition is still kicking, too, a counterpoint to the commercialism of the rest. Vendors sell hand-made jewelry, tie-dyes, and other crafts. For their predecessors, who had a perhaps stronger claim to hippiedom, it was their only livelihood. The local farmers knew a good thing when they saw it and began selling their produce there too, continuing to do so to this day.

LEFT: *Decorative simplicity: the church of Sant Josep, a typical Ibiza structure. The whitewashed walls give off stunning light and shadows as sunlight floods across them.*

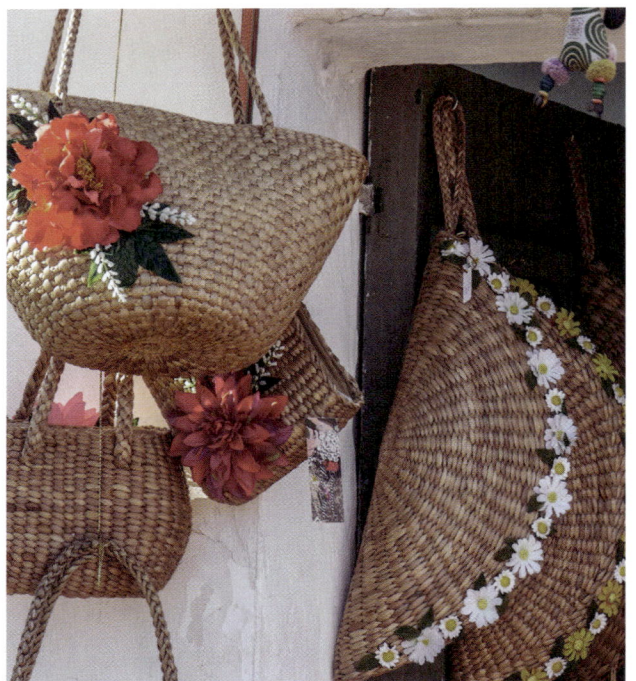
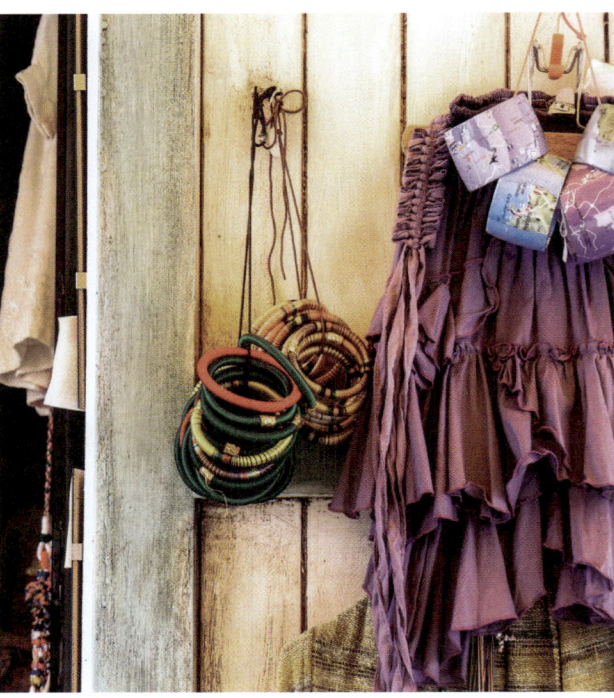
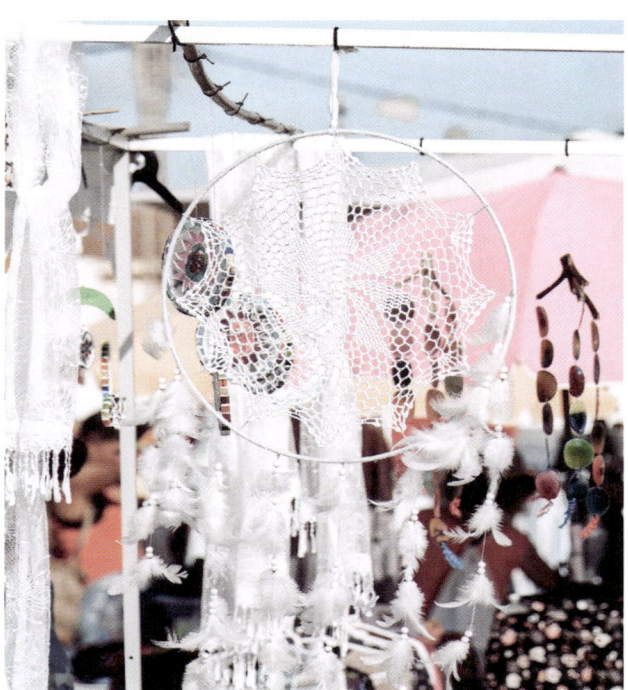
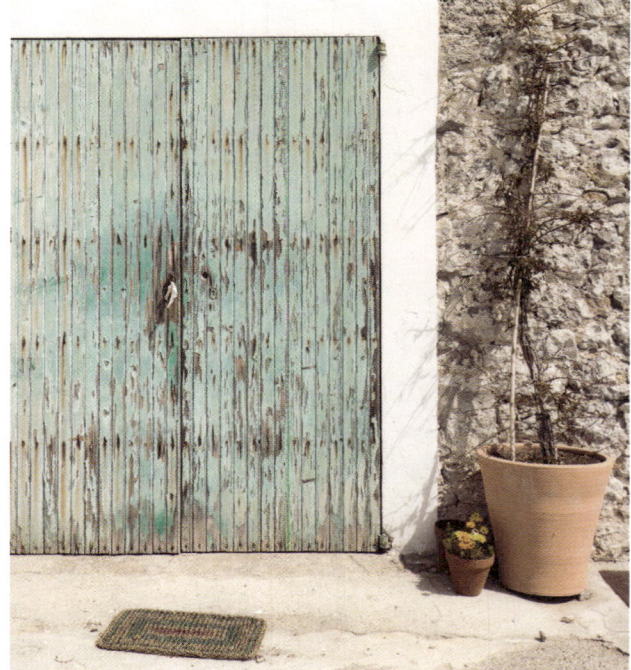

ABOVE AND RIGHT: *If you're on the lookout for those special hippie and boho pieces, the boutiques of Santa Gertrudis are a treasure trove (top). Then there's the original Mercadillo de Sant Jordi at the old horse-racing track, one of the island's most authentic hippie markets where people peddle crafts, vintage items, local fashions, and produce from their own farms.*

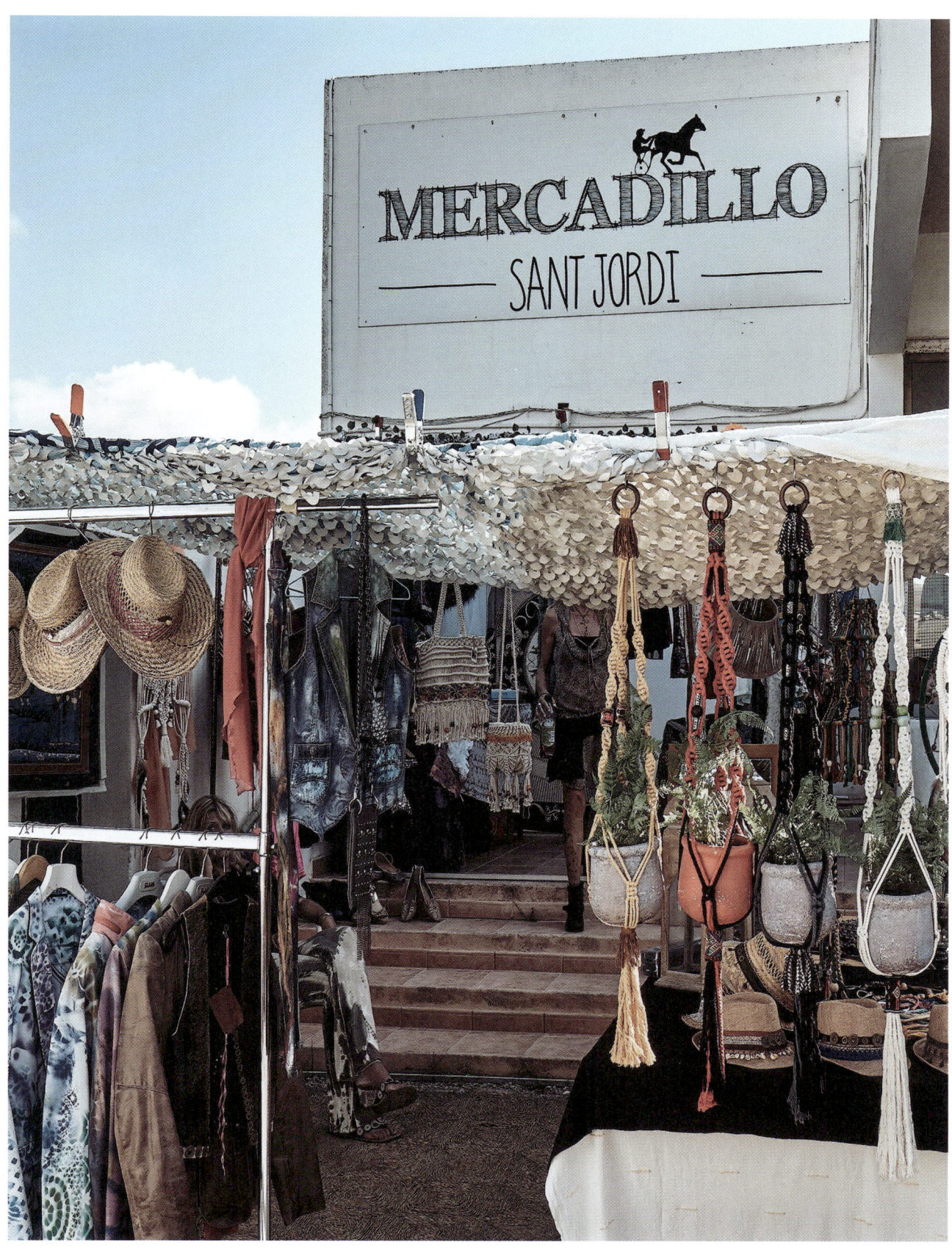

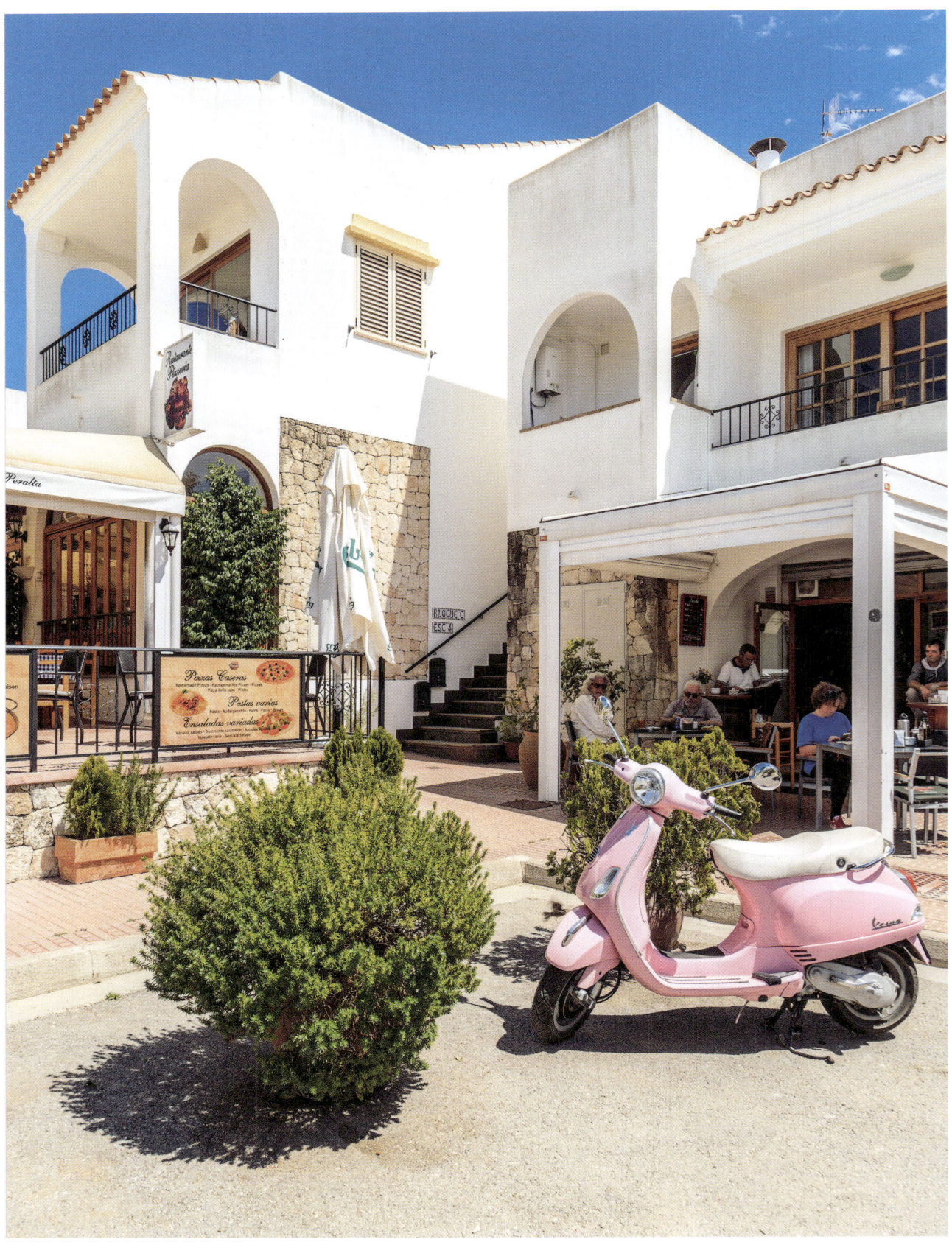

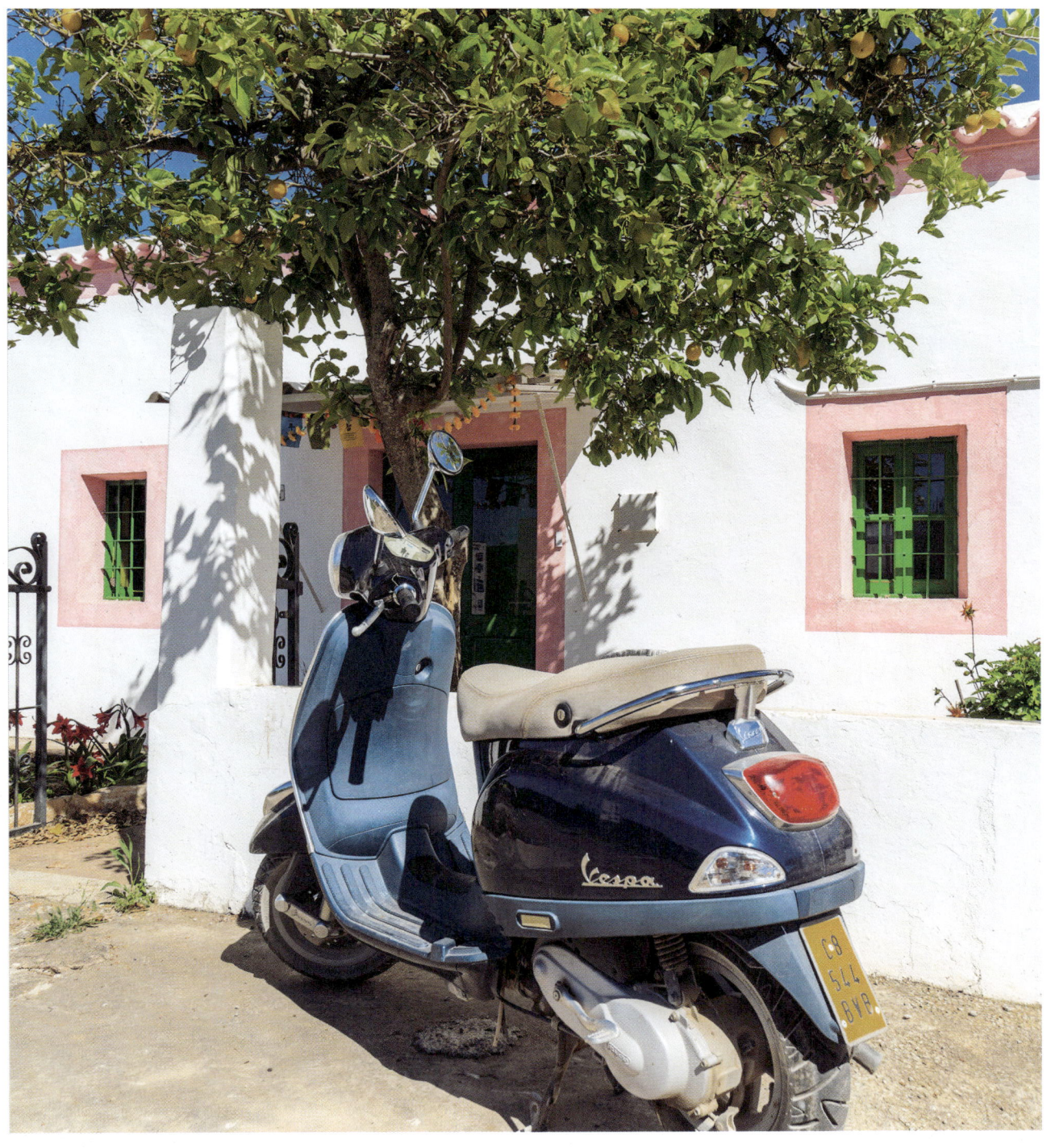

ABOVE AND LEFT: *A friendly, extroverted community: The village of Sant Carles north of Santa Eulària was a gathering spot for Ibiza's hippie scene in the 1960s and is still associated with alternative lifestyles. Nearby, visitors to the hippie market of Las Dalias will want to visit Bar Anita for a café con leche.*

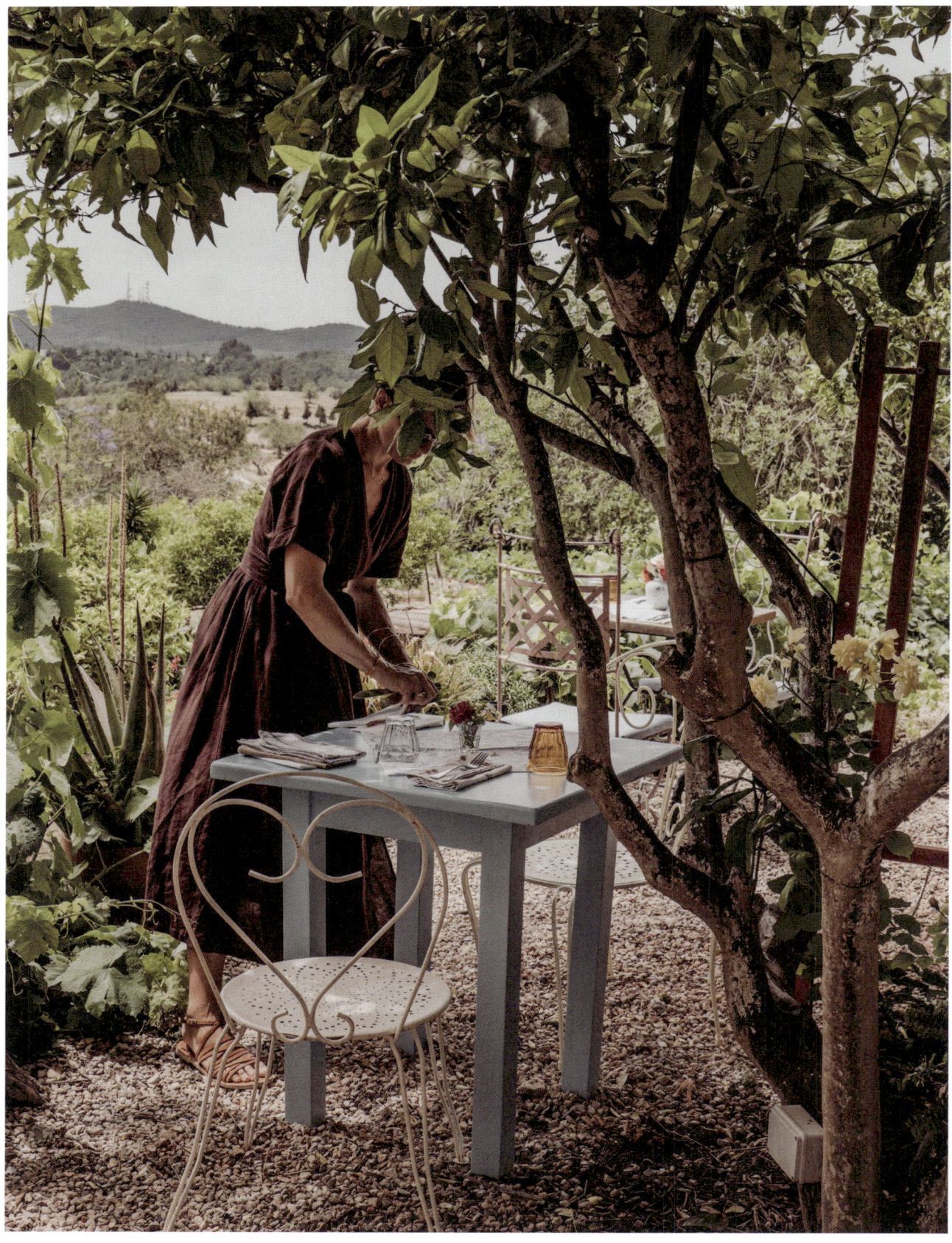

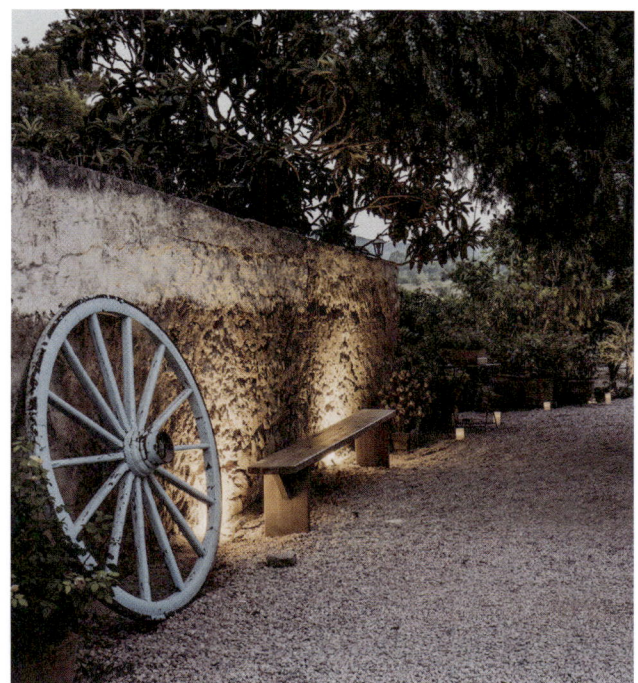

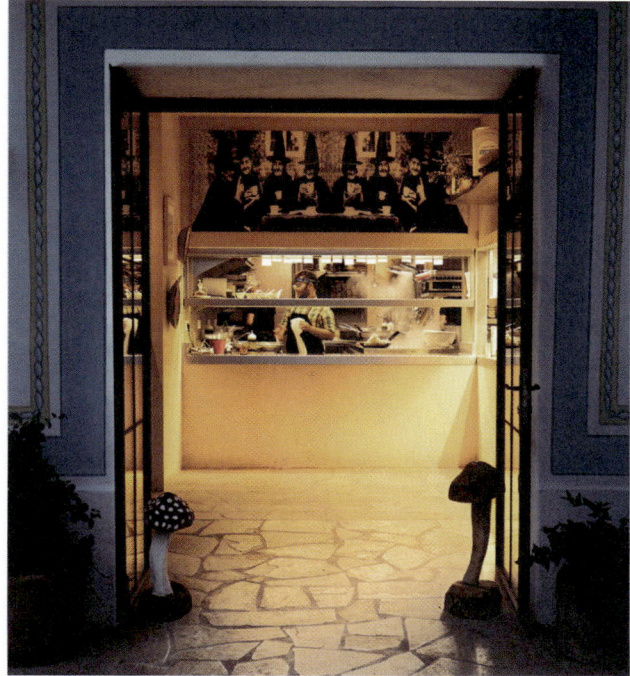

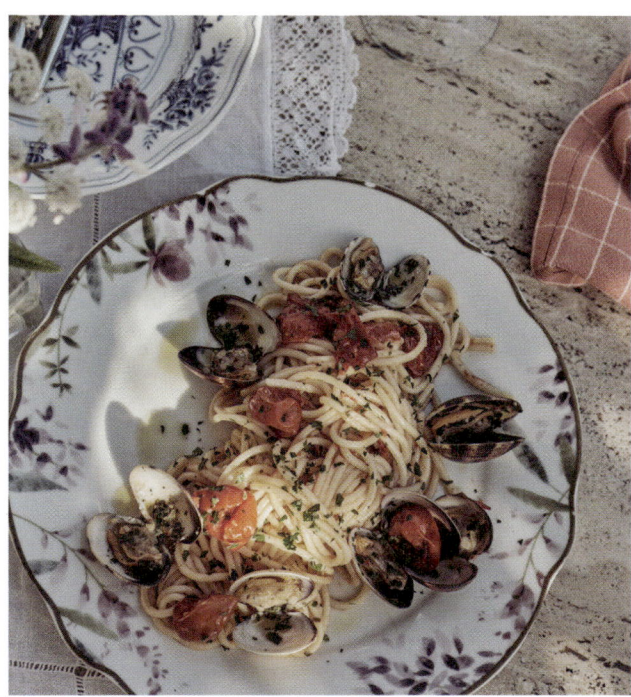

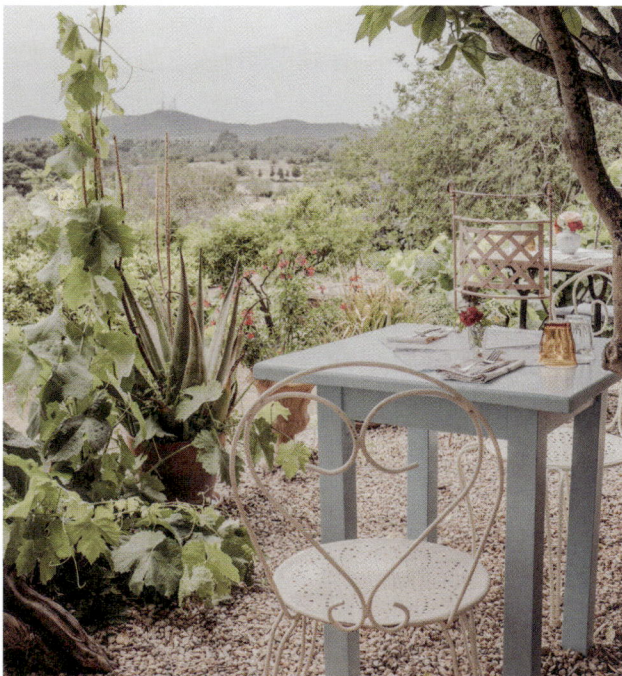

ABOVE AND LEFT: *Experience the real Ibiza while party people move between beach clubs and Ushuaïa Ibiza: Enjoy a relaxing lunch beneath fig and lemon trees at the intimate restaurant La Paloma in the inland village of Sant Llorenç de Balàfia—there's no rush, even during high season.*

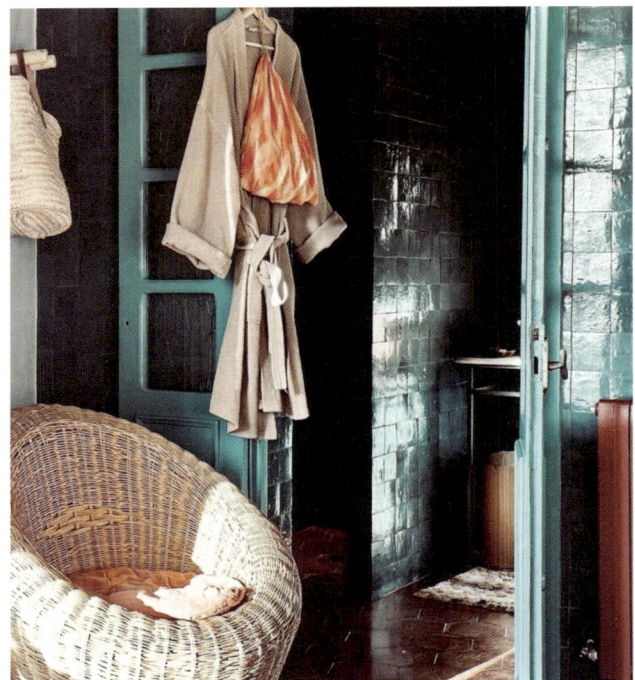

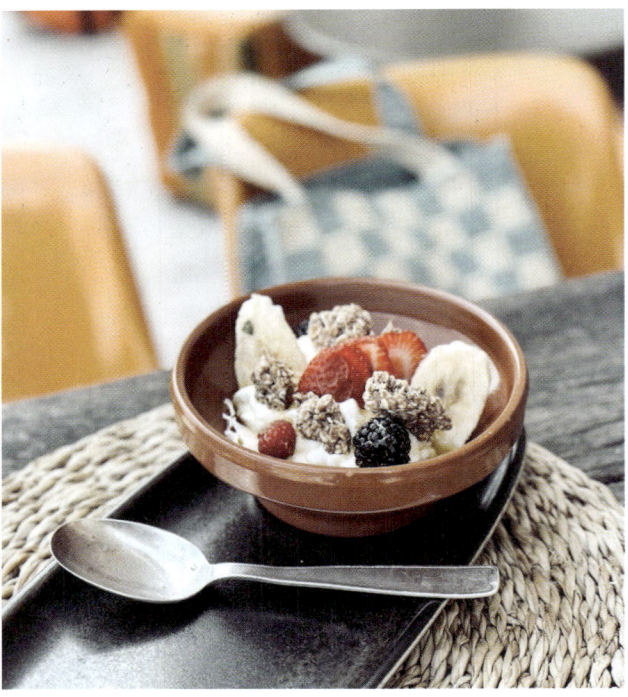

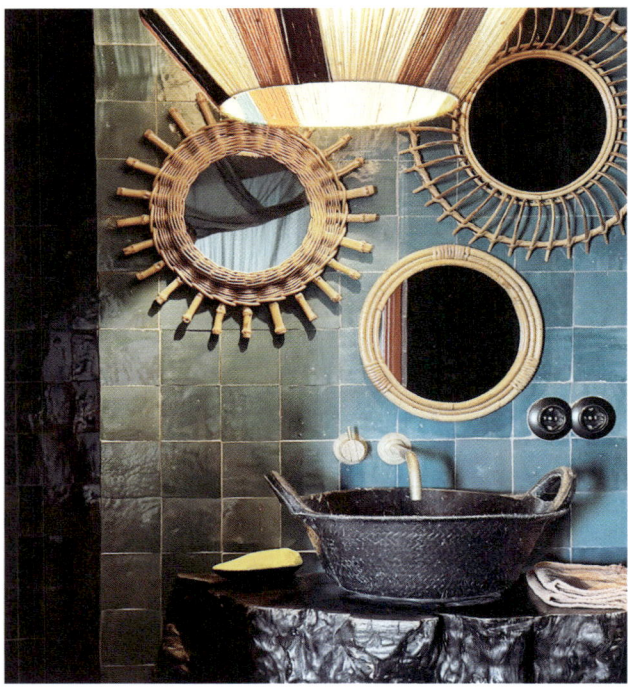

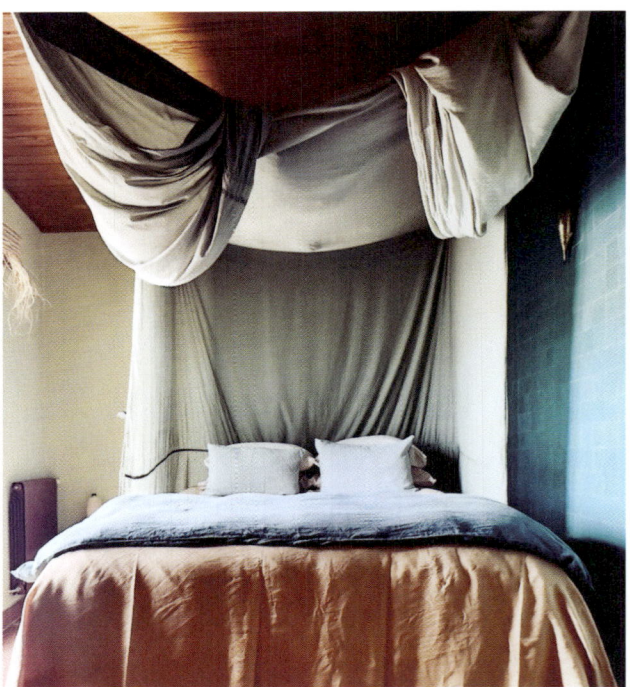

ABOVE AND RIGHT: *A familiar pattern on Ibiza: At the bay of Portinatx on the northern tip of the island, a once modest hostal has been given a face-lift. Now the Hotel Los Enamorados, it focuses on art, textiles, and design, with nine individually furnished rooms. The hotel's rooms, bar, and restaurant channel a bohemian vibe straight from the 1970s.*

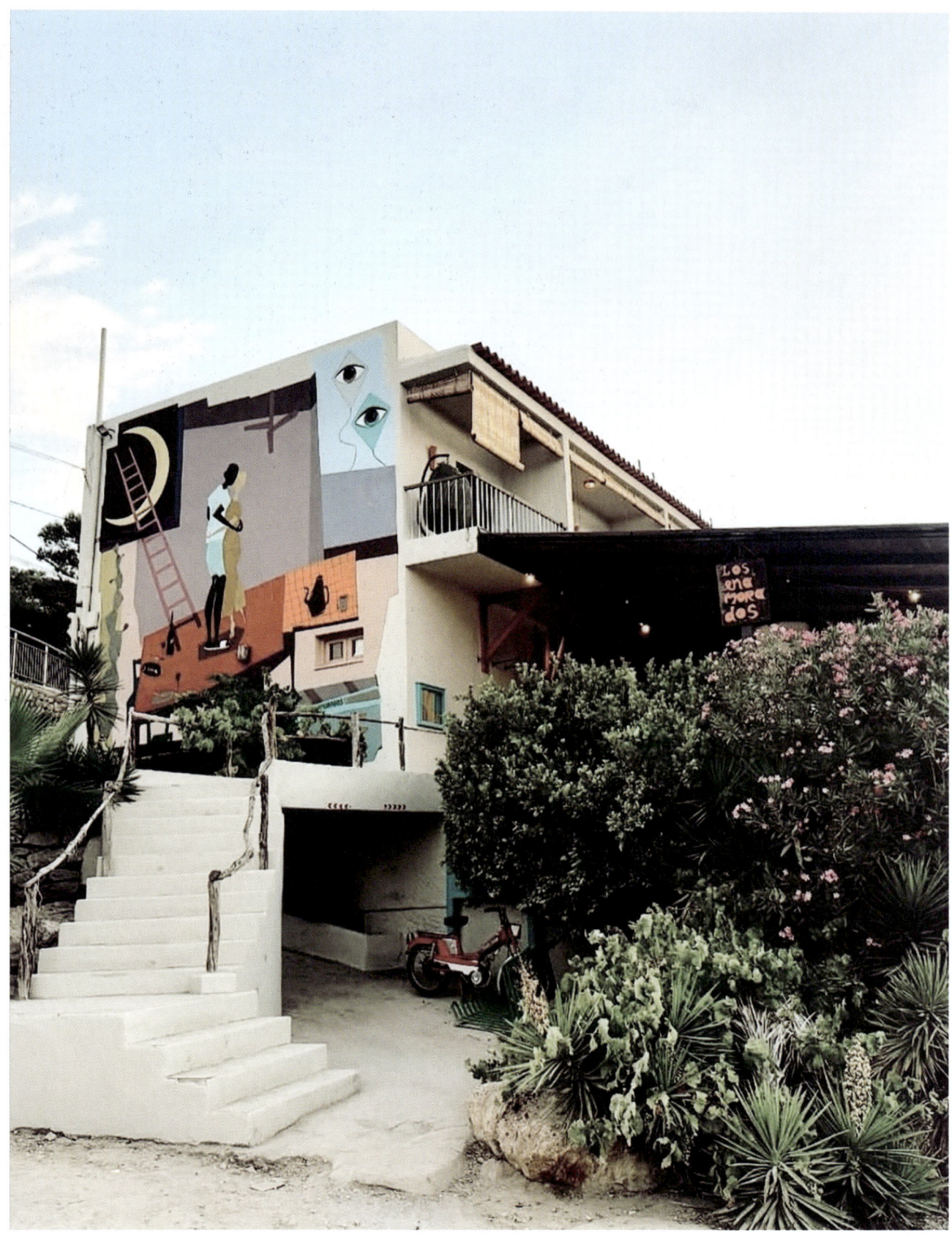

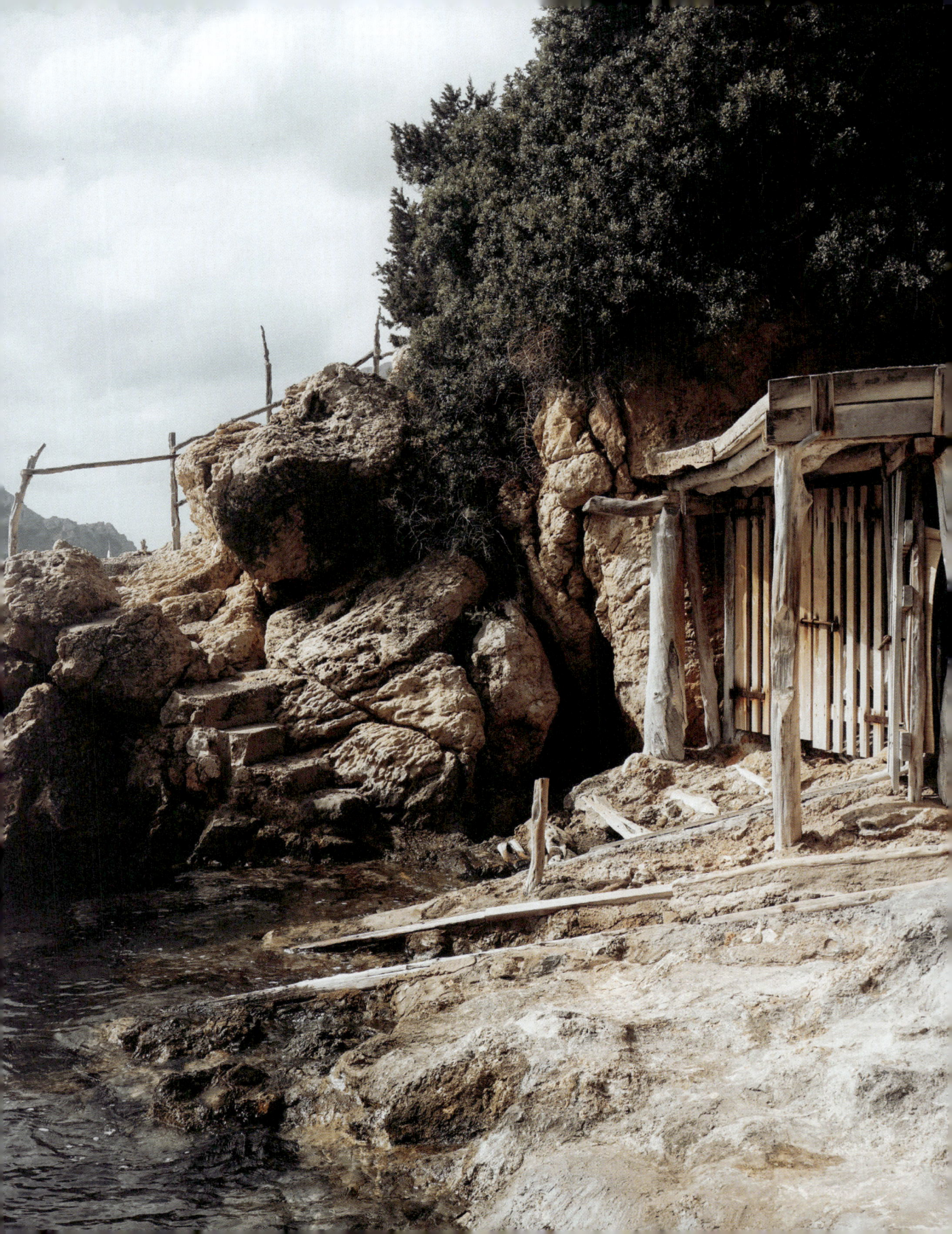

FISHERMEN'S HUTS

HIDDEN STRUCTURES ON THE SHORES OF IBIZA

Ibiza is home to some of the most expensive villas in Europe. For many Ibiçencos, however, a different form of luxury carries more weight: a small fishermen's hut with a boat ramp, known as a *caseta*. They are found on bays across Ibiza, sometimes along the rockiest and most remote sections of shoreline. An extended family might get together for the weekend at one of them and work on a pan of paella. *Casetas* can be bases for kayaking trips and fishing expeditions. People show up to tinker or make some repairs and sometimes surreptitiously spend the night. Ownership of *casetas* is usually passed down through families.

As buildings, *casetas* are distinctive. Many are built of stone, with roofs often reinforced with sabina wood, from a durable variety of Phoenician juniper that grows widely on Ibiza. Access to *casetas* is invariably via some rocky, hard-to-find trail, really more like a goat path. As far as the culture among owners, it's considered generally acceptable to clamber over from one *caseta* to the next or settle in to make yourself comfortable.

The sea views, of course, are spectacular, and ultimately this is a *caseta*'s most indelible feature.

LEFT: *Scattered around the island and tucked away like small pirate hideouts, rustic fishermen's huts are part of Ibiza's character.*

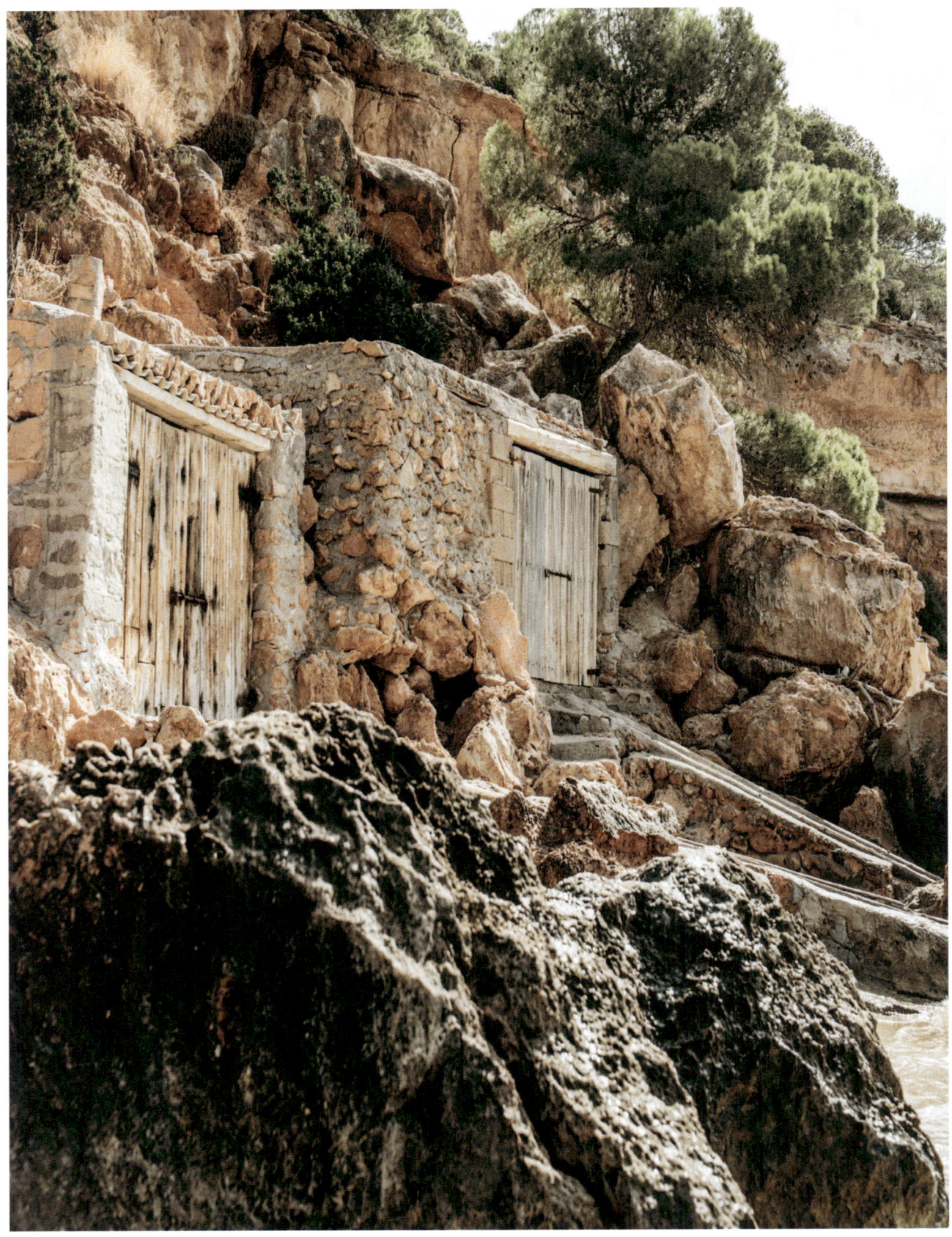

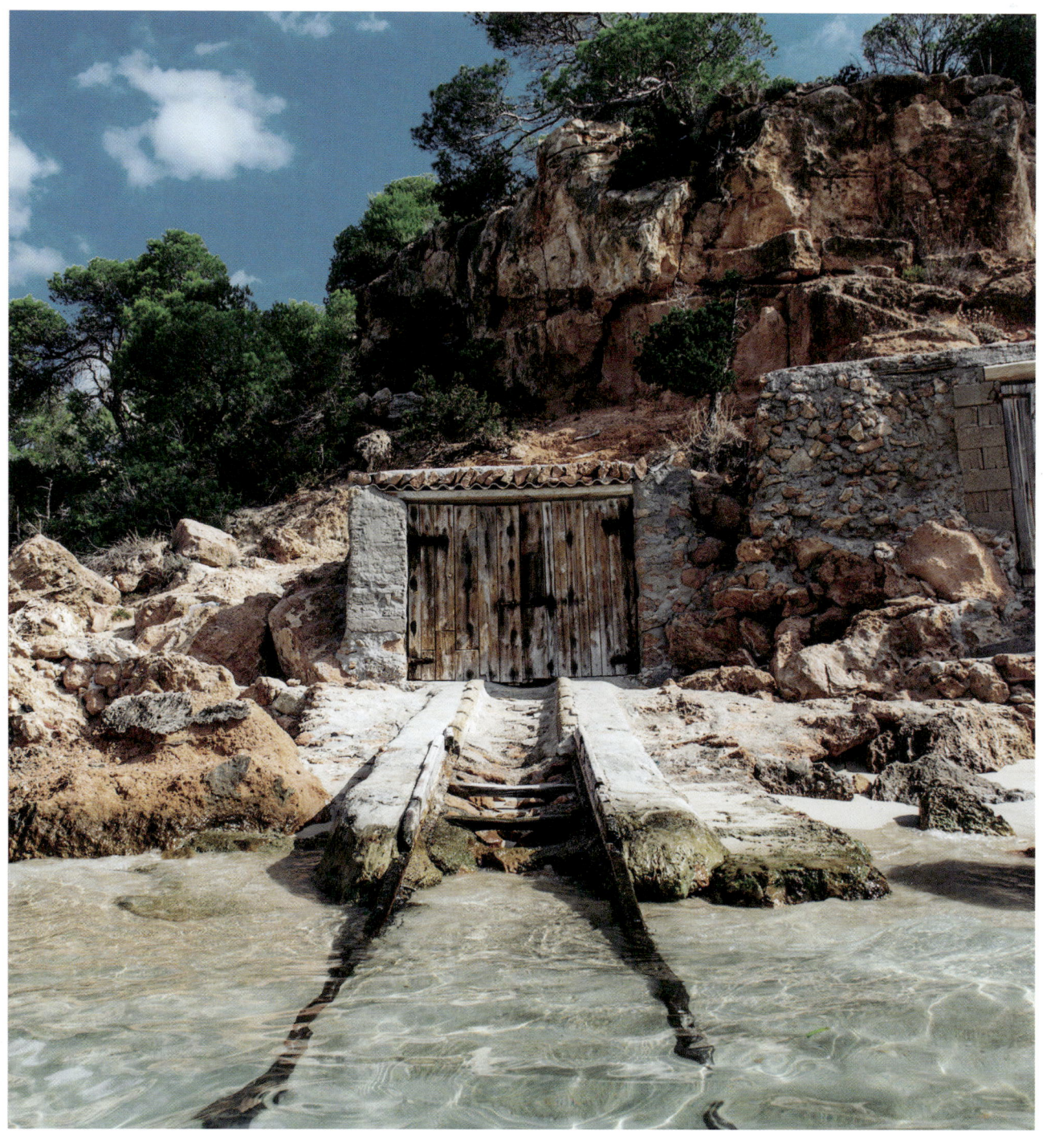

ABOVE AND LEFT: Casetas *hewn directly into the red rocks on the cove of Cala Salada near Sant Antoni, where the swimming is excellent. The picturesque look of a caseta is one thing, but they are still a base of operations for many fishermen.*

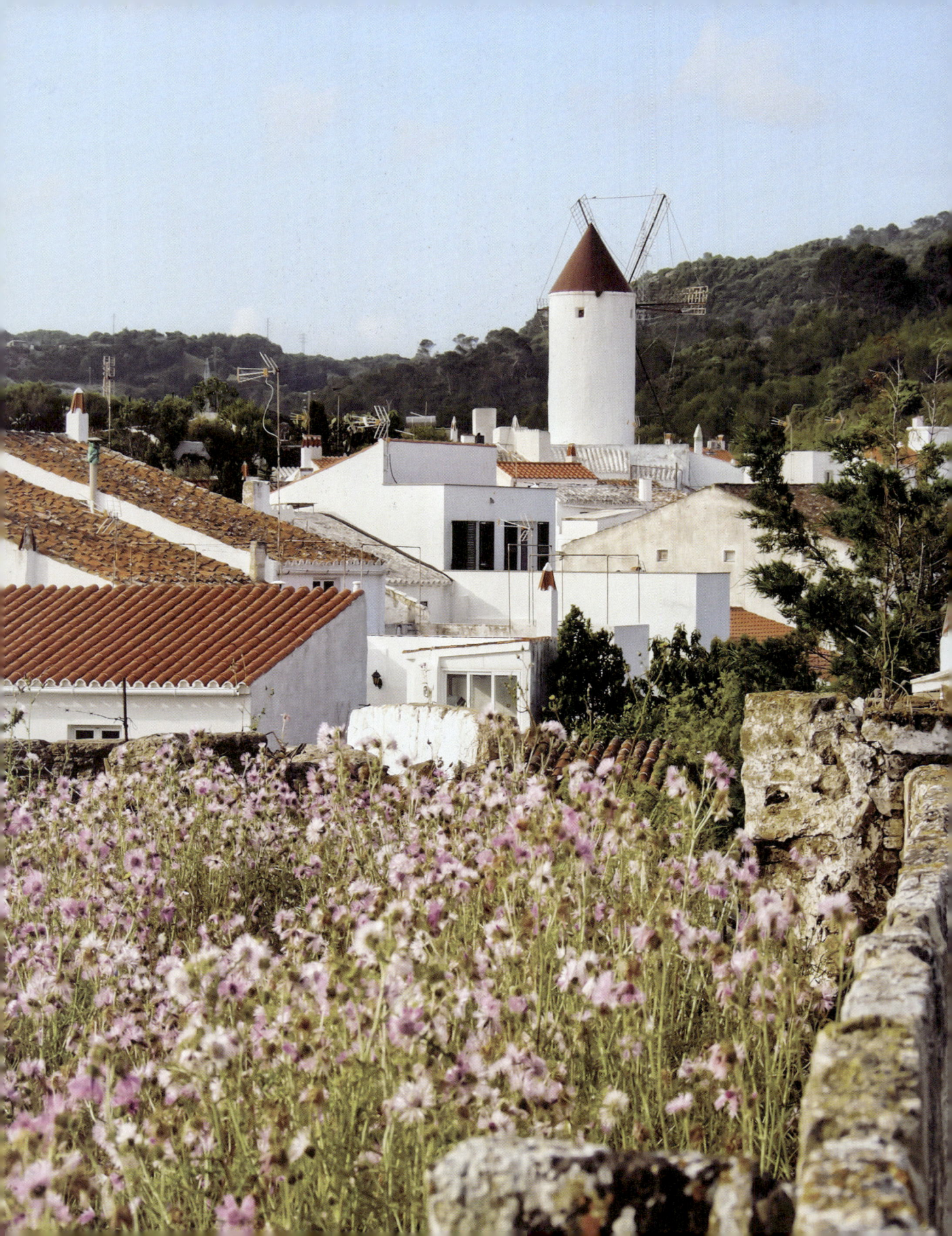

MENORCA

THE QUIET BEAUTY OF THE BALEARICS—A SERENE COUNTERPOINT TO MALLORCA AND IBIZA

Menorca, the easternmost of the Balearic Islands, is all about hiking, cycling, and history. Its landscapes are mostly undisturbed. Tourism here aims to be low-impact and sustainable, and there is little appetite to see that change. And that's fine. Menorca was designated a UNESCO Biosphere Reserve in 1993. The focus is on preservation and values rather than exploitation. Larges areas of the island are undeveloped and not too crowded, and many locals still have a livelihood from agriculture and traditional crafts. There are, of course, plenty of vacationers, lively little towns, and beaches dotted with sunbathers, but noise levels are several decibels quieter, and life is more discreet.

A vacationer's paradise it is nonetheless: coves of clear, turquoise water, perfect for swimming and often only accessible on foot or by boat; long, casual walks around the interior, a landscape full of pine forests, rolling topography, and traditional dry-stone walls. Traces of history abound on Menorca, such as its prehistoric talayot structures. The island has been both a hub and refuge for a procession of cultures, each of which has left visible traces, from the Arabs and Romans of old to the British in the eighteenth century, who ruled Menorca for seventy years. The former British rule still registers in such details as Chippendale furniture, bay windows, and the island's distinctive gin. Along the north shore, Menorca is rocky and exposed, with sparse vegetation, dark red sand beaches, and small offshore islands. The dominant visuals along the south shore are white sandy coves, turquoise water, and steep ravines. The defining feature of the interior is Monte Toro, the island's highest peak. Menorca's two principal towns make for a stark contrast. One is Mahón, or Maó, as it is called locally, the present-day capital; the other is Ciutadella, a majestic beauty whose iconic *marès* stone buildings give the whole place a monumental feel.

LEFT: *Es Mercadal at the foot of Monte Toro, Menorca's highest peak, is known for its weekly and artisan craft markets. It also makes a great home base for walks in the surrounding green hills.*

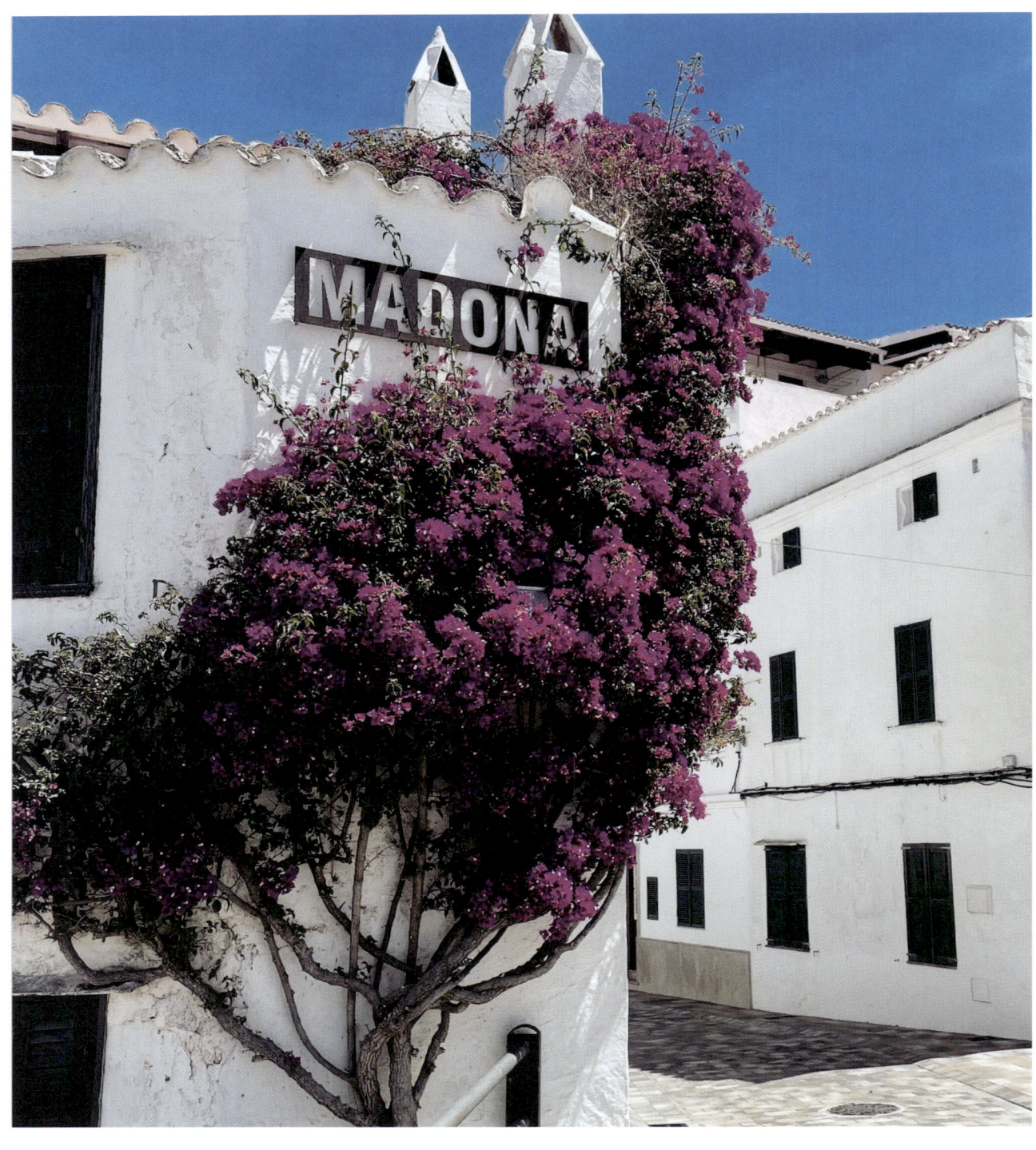

ABOVE AND RIGHT: *Whitewashed houses and narrow streets in the generally quiet village of Es Mercadal, a farming community. Many residents work in agriculture. The grain mill, still in use, now houses the restaurant Es Molí d'es Racó.*

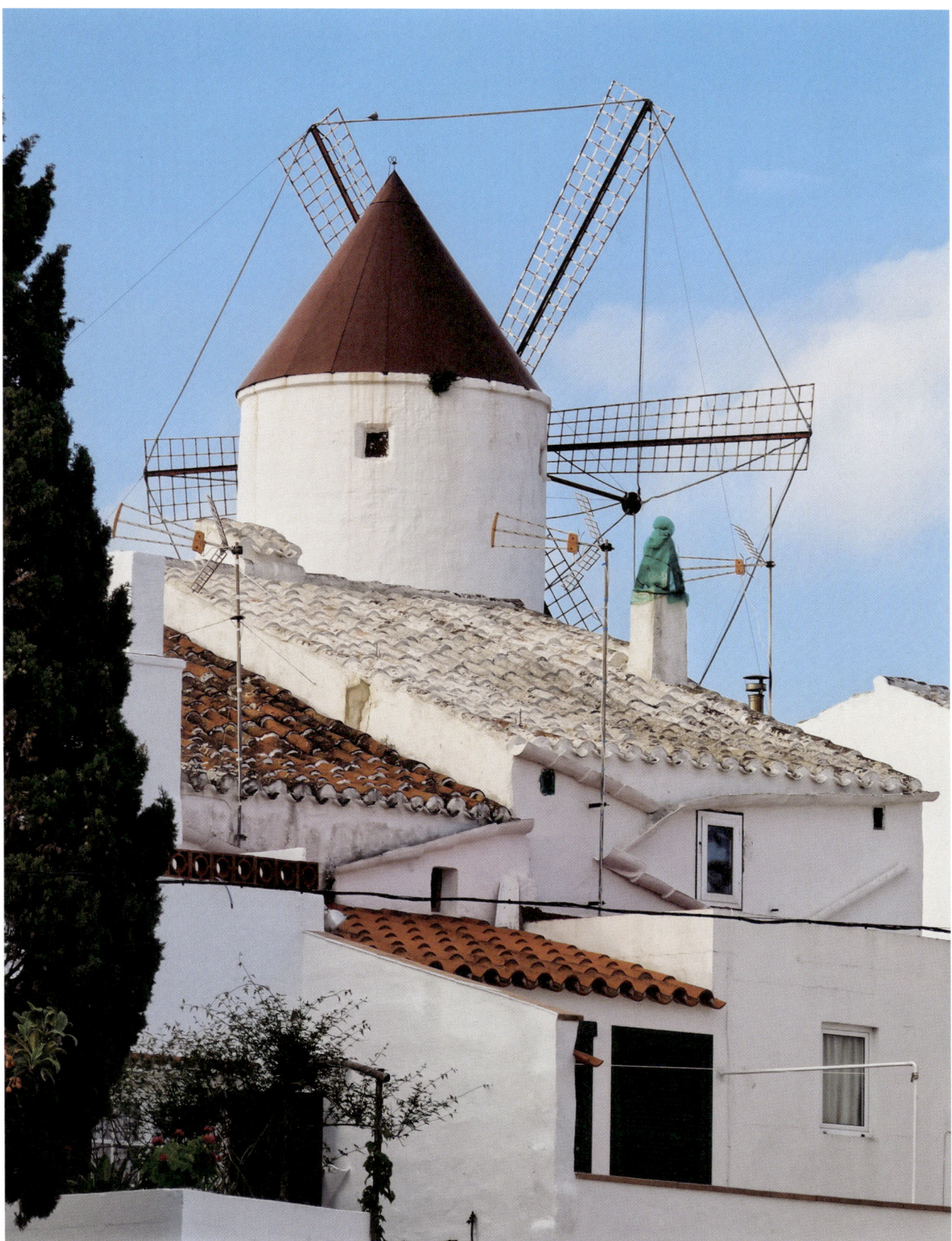

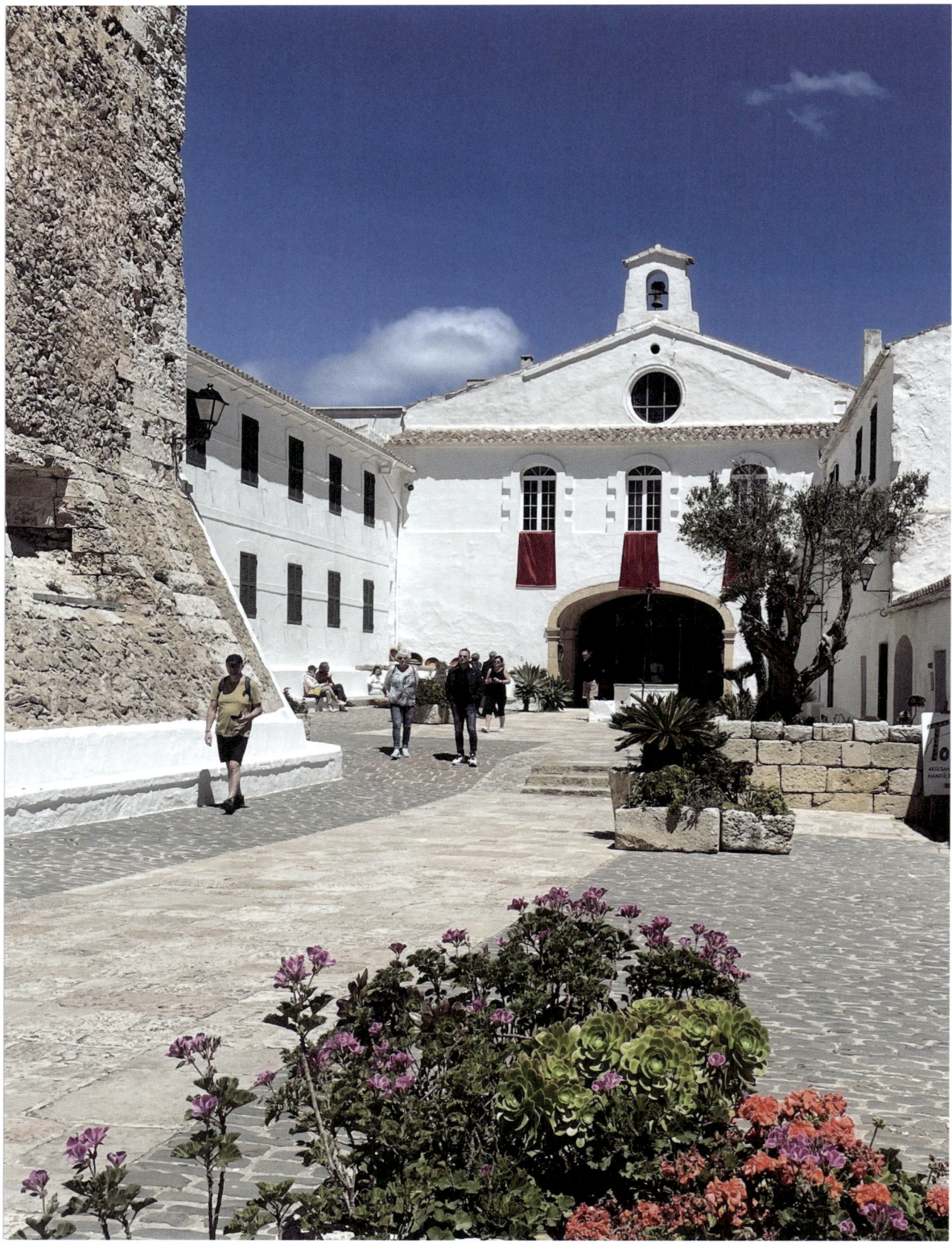

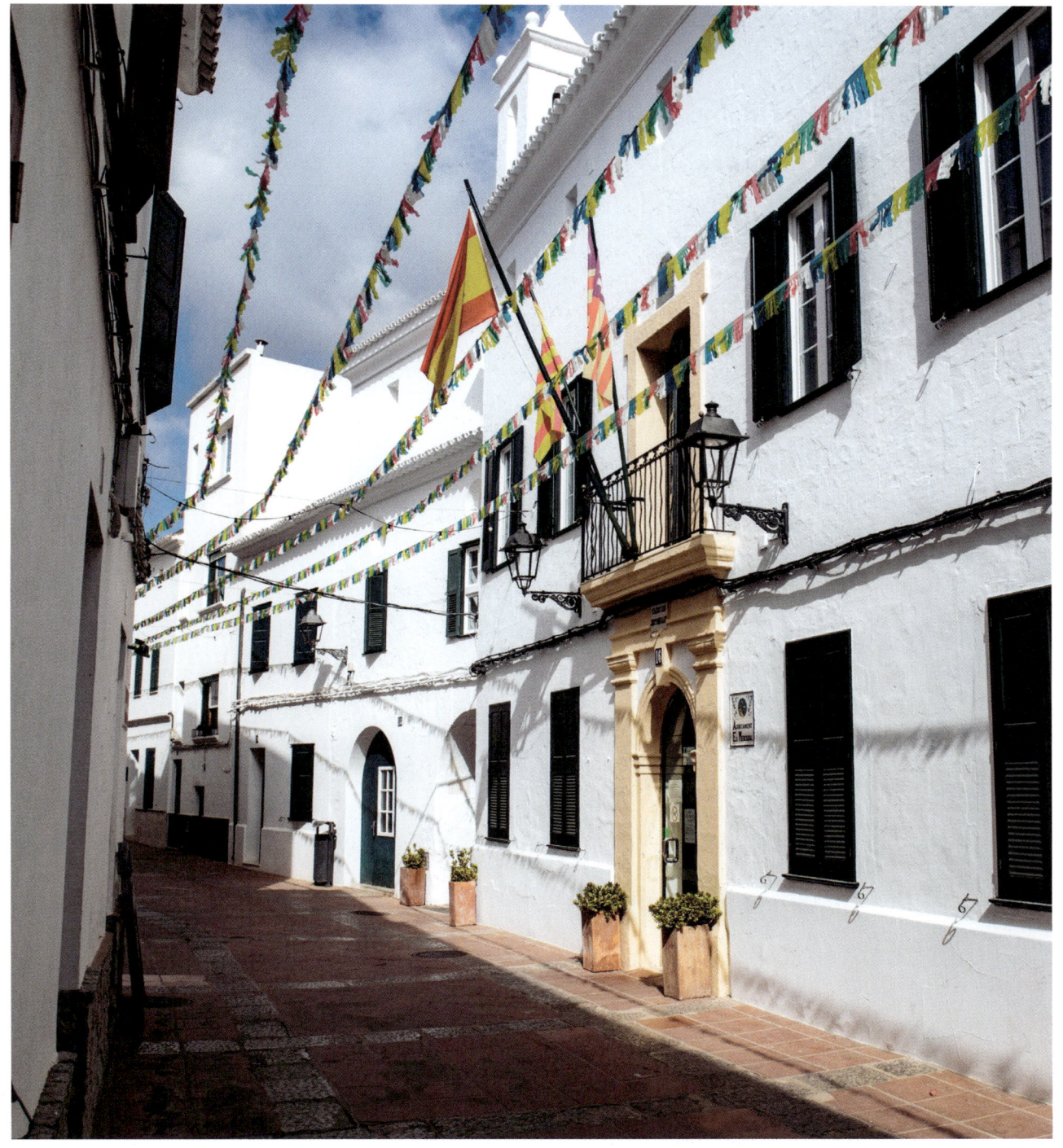

ABOVE: *The town hall of Es Mercadal sits amid a dense warren of streets in the heart of Menorca.*

LEFT: *The inner courtyard of the Franciscan convent Santuari de la Verge del Toro at the summit of Monte Toro, Mencorca's highest point, with spectacular panoramic views of the island. The convent is dedicated to Menorca's patron saint.*

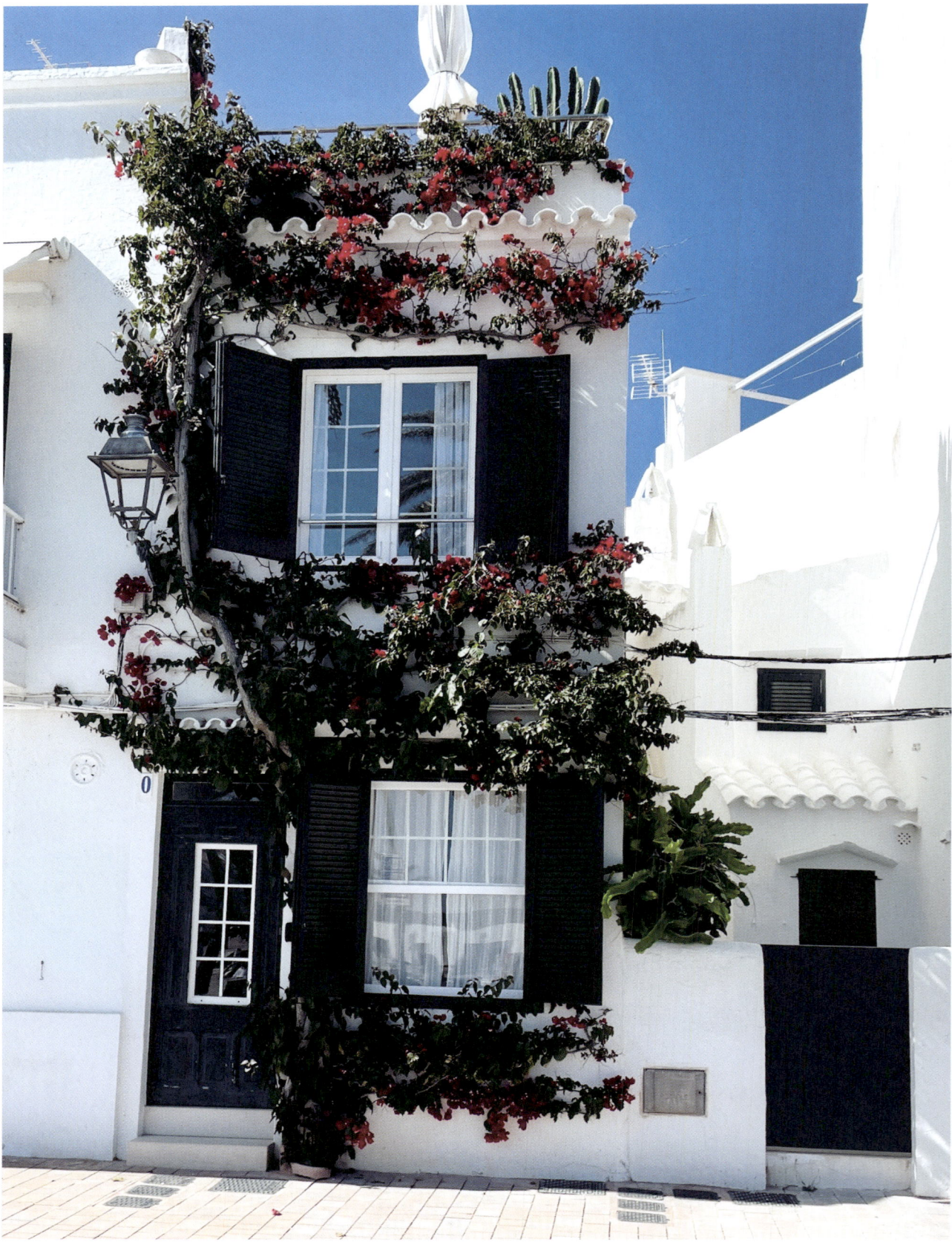

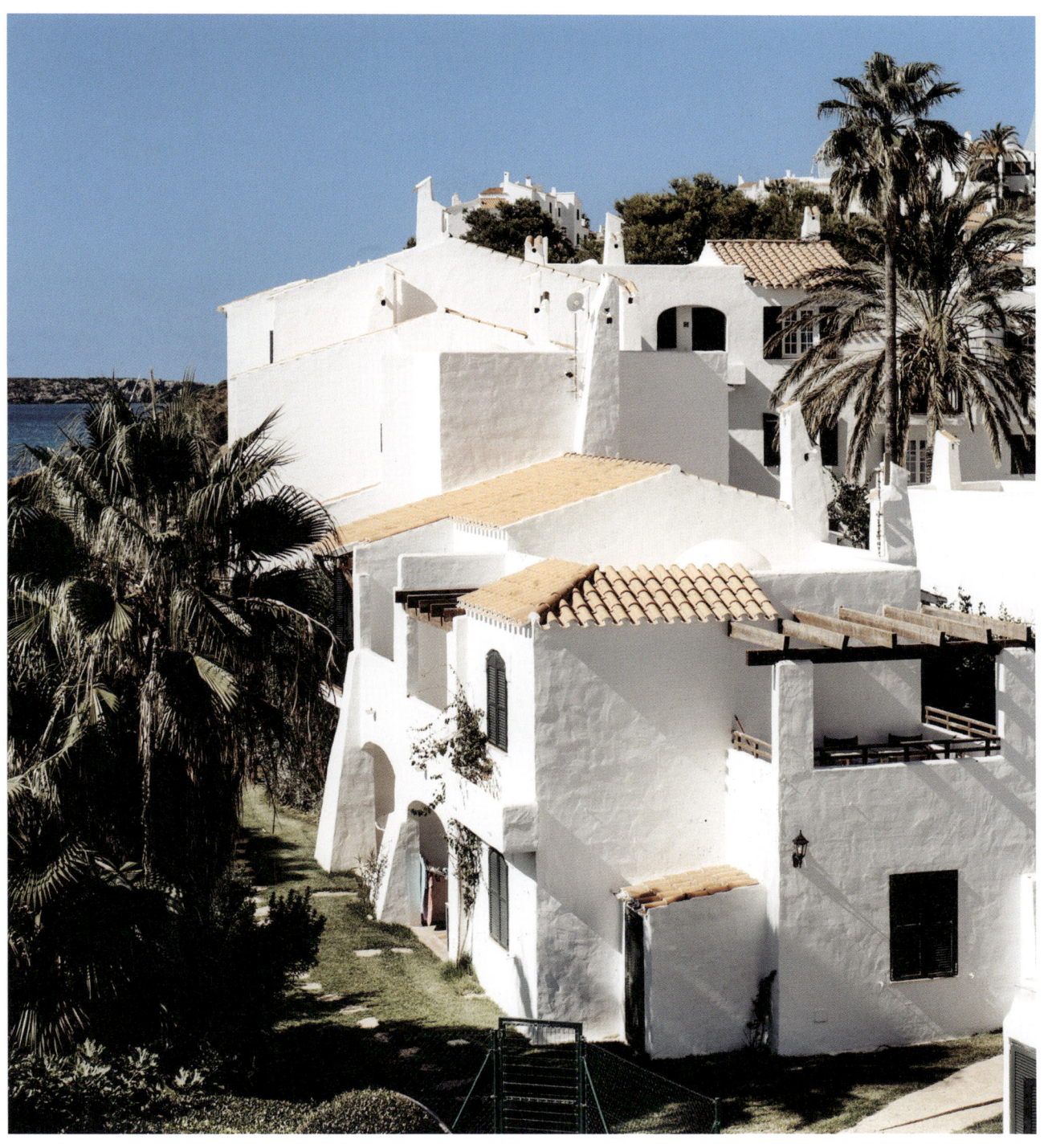

ABOVE AND LEFT: *Small white houses with sea views, inviting passageways, and plenty of peace and quiet are typical of Fornells, a picturesque fishing village on a sheltered, almost lagoon-like bay on Menorca's north shore. Restaurants along the harbor serve regional seafood favorites, particularly the local lobster.*

189

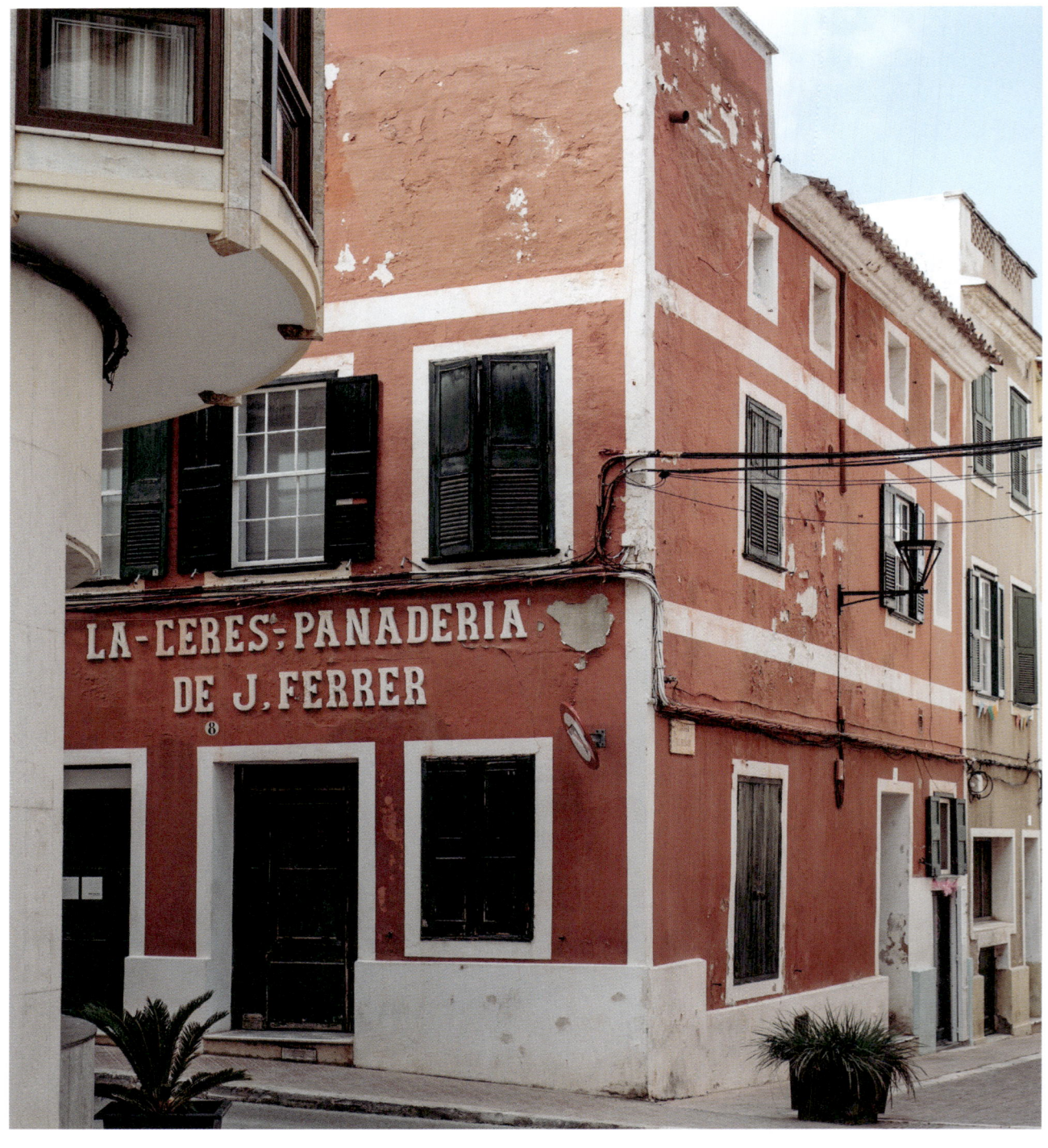

ABOVE: *The small bakery La Ceres in Maó, Menorca's capital, is famous for its traditional bread-making.*

RIGHT: *The bustling town of Maó is as colorful as the facades of its old quarter. Above it, the Església del Carme church, which sits right next to the market in the heart of the town.*

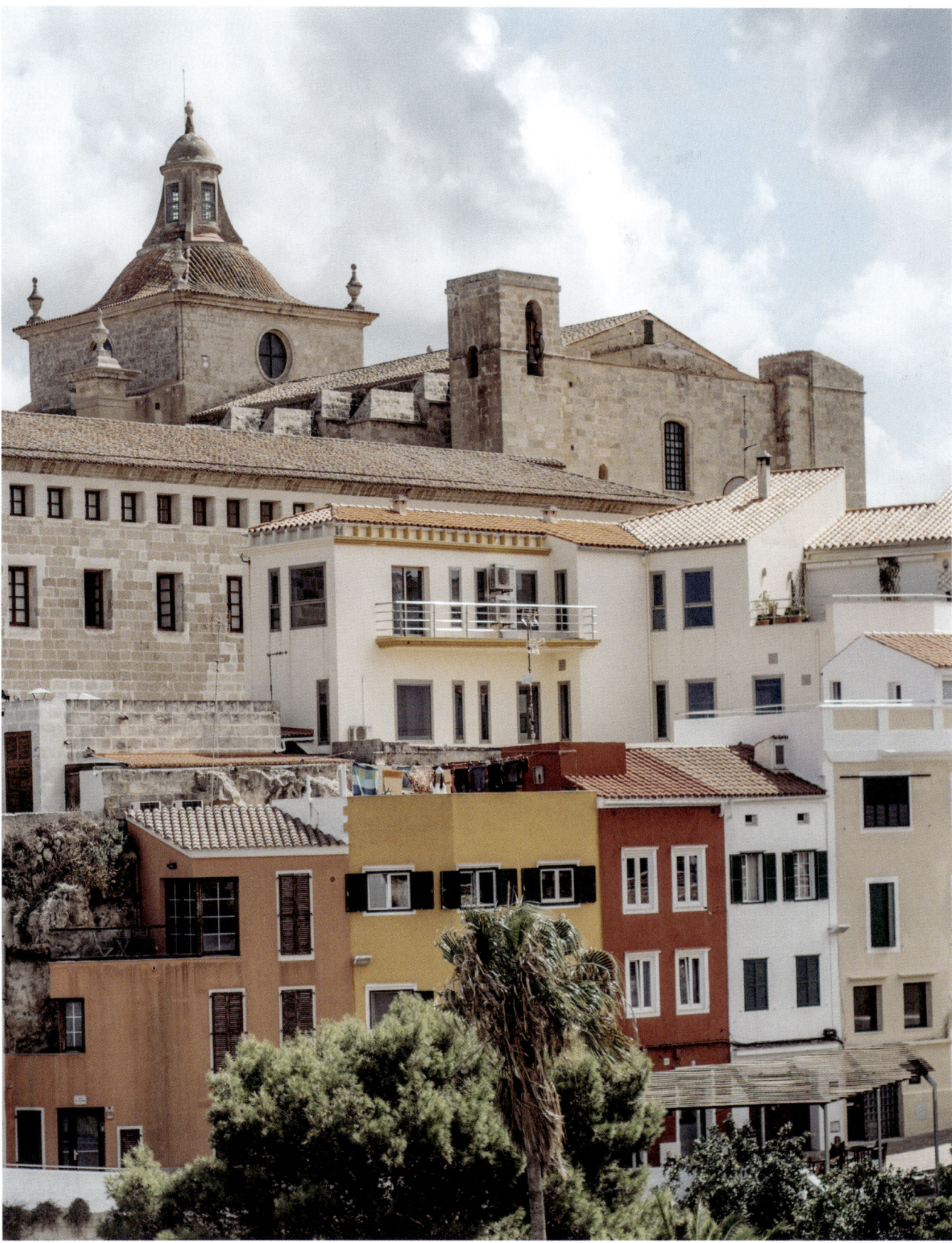

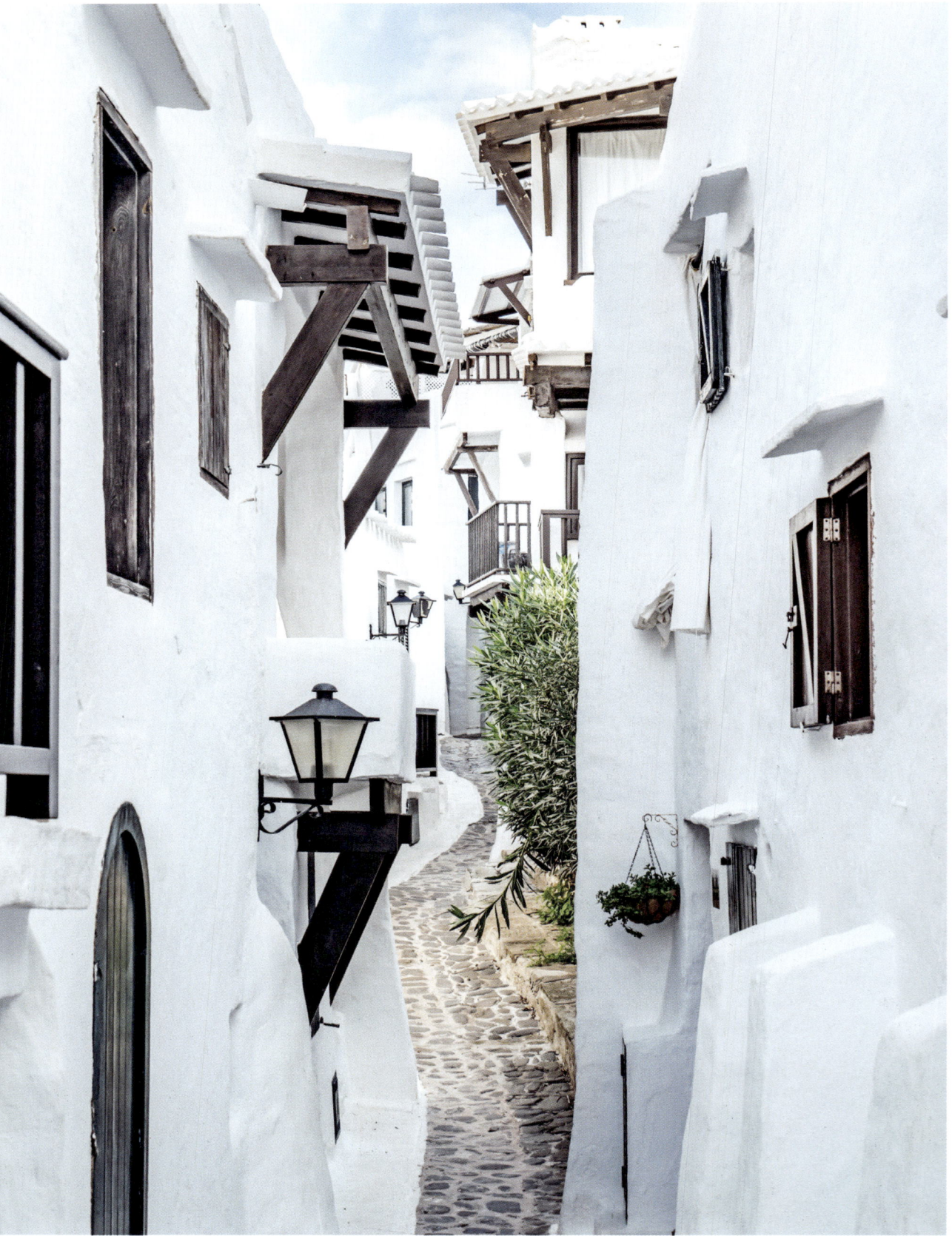

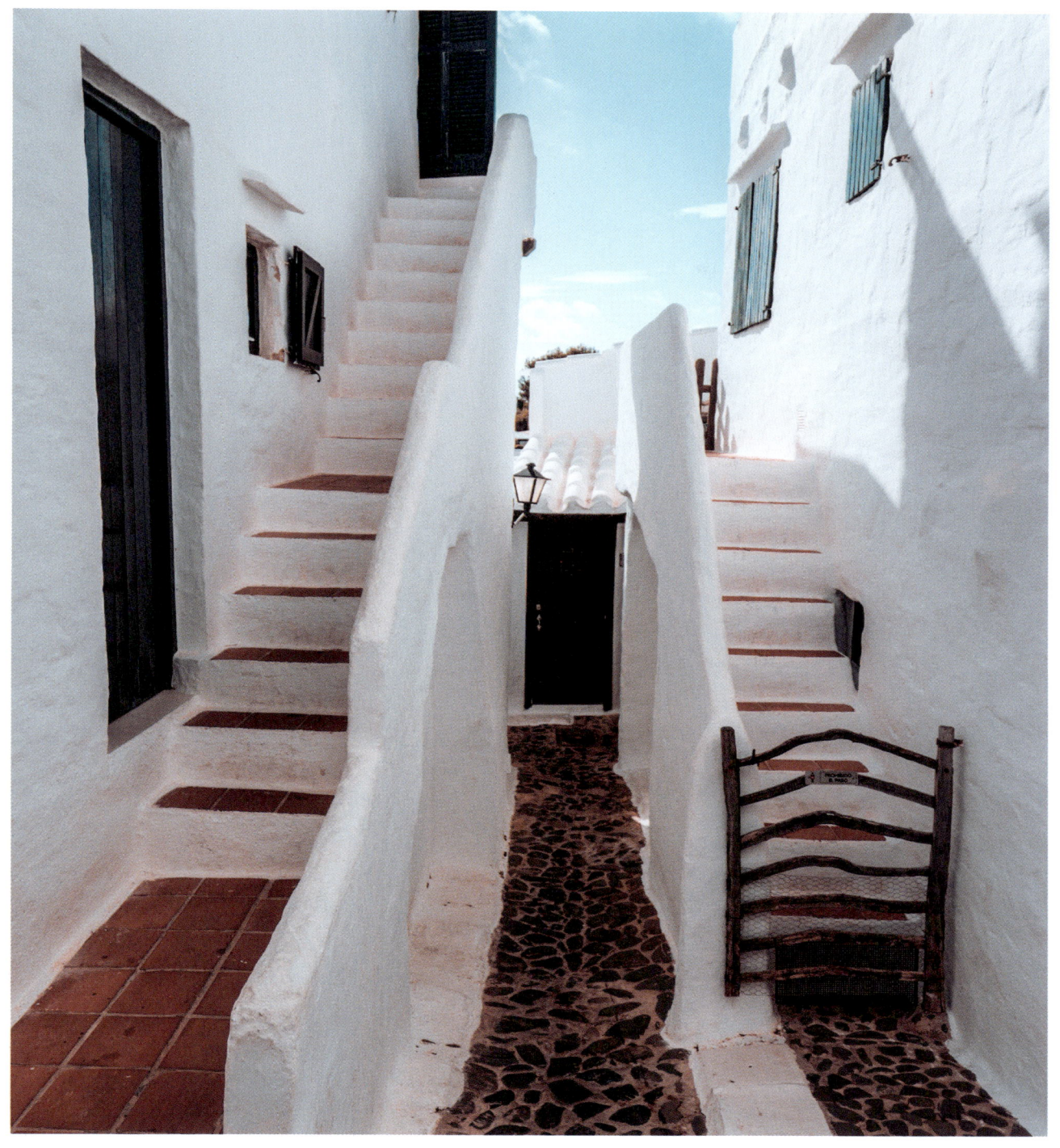

ABOVE AND LEFT: *A labyrinth of narrow passages in the white coastal village of Binibèquer Vell, a tourist destination south of Sant Lluís. Built in the 1970s by the architects Antonio Sintes Mercadal of Sant Lluís and F. J. Barba Corsini, of Barcelona, it is modeled on a typical Mediterranean fishing village.*

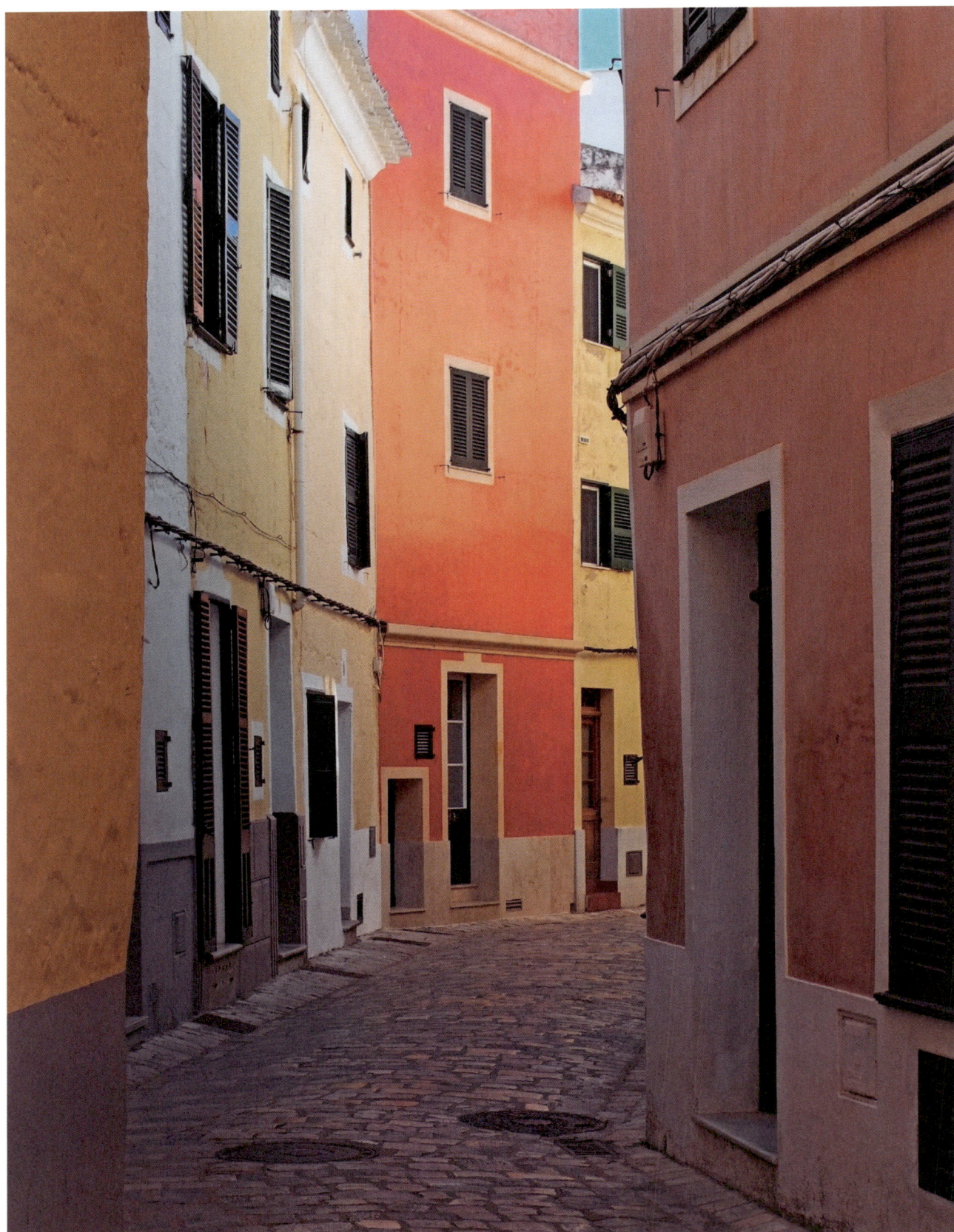

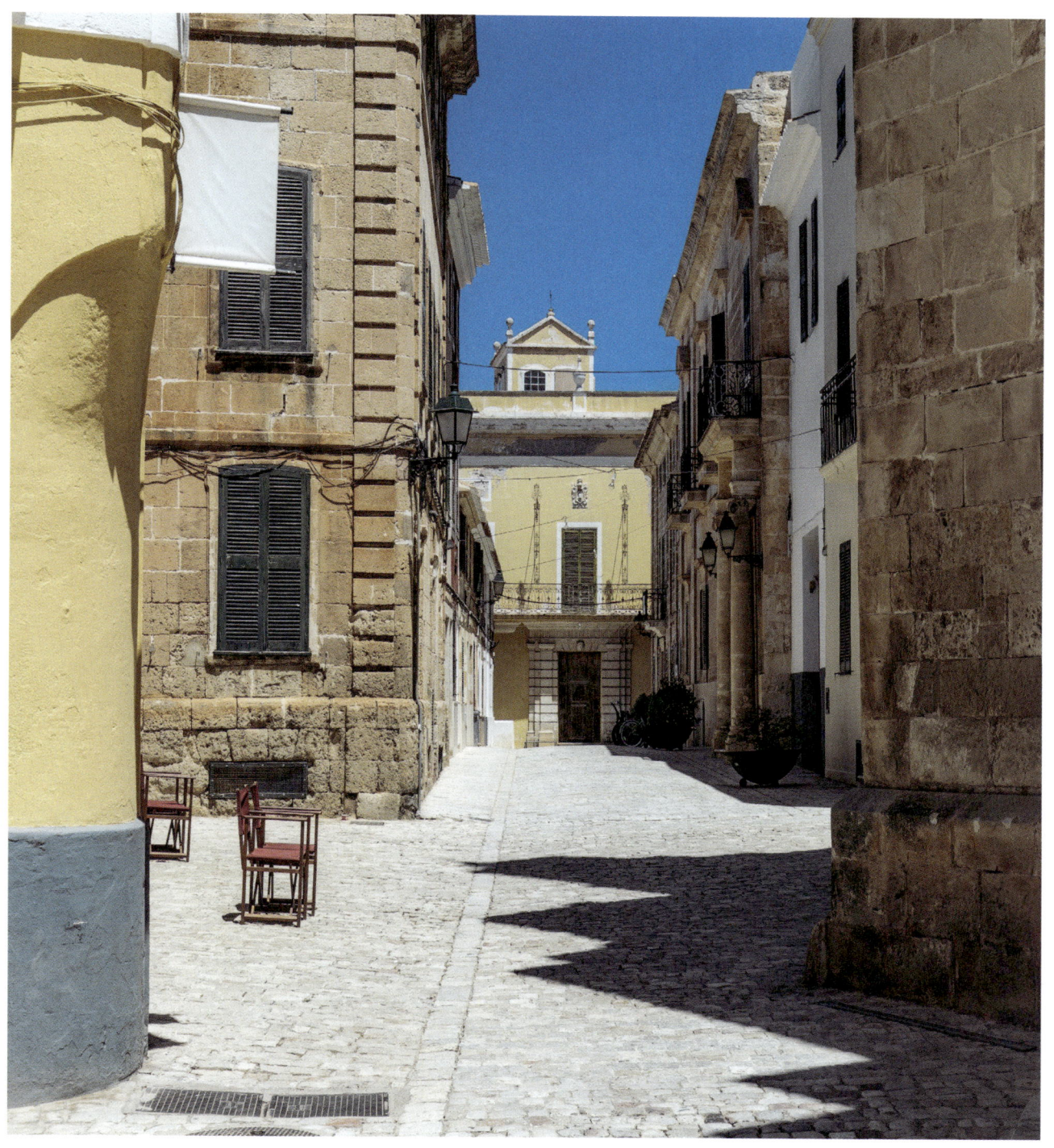

ABOVE AND LEFT: *Surprising spaces open up along narrow streets bordered by brightly painted houses in the old town of Ciutadella, often considered the most beautiful place on Menorca. They lead to a square enclosed by buildings of* marès *stone, typical of the Balearic Islands.*

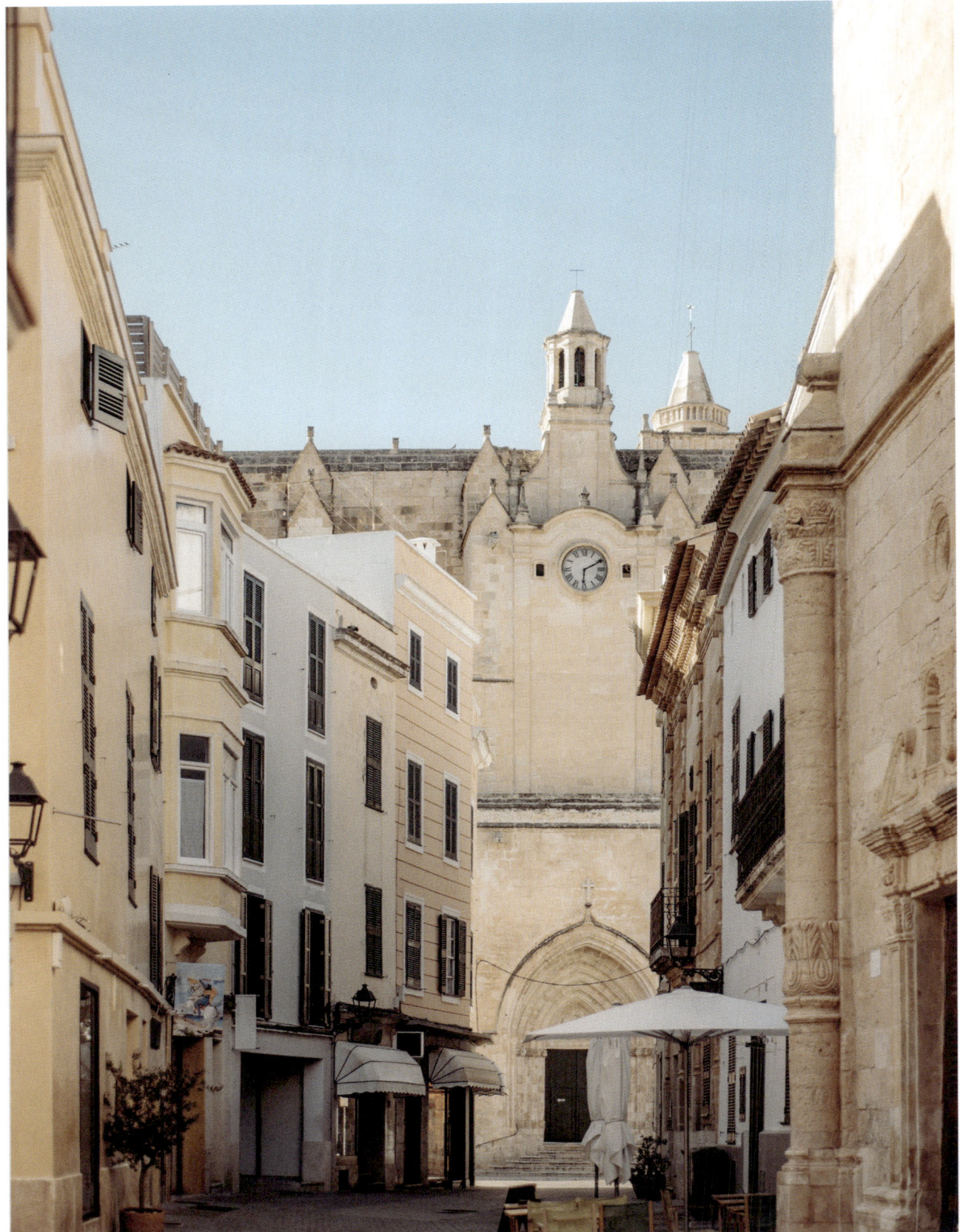

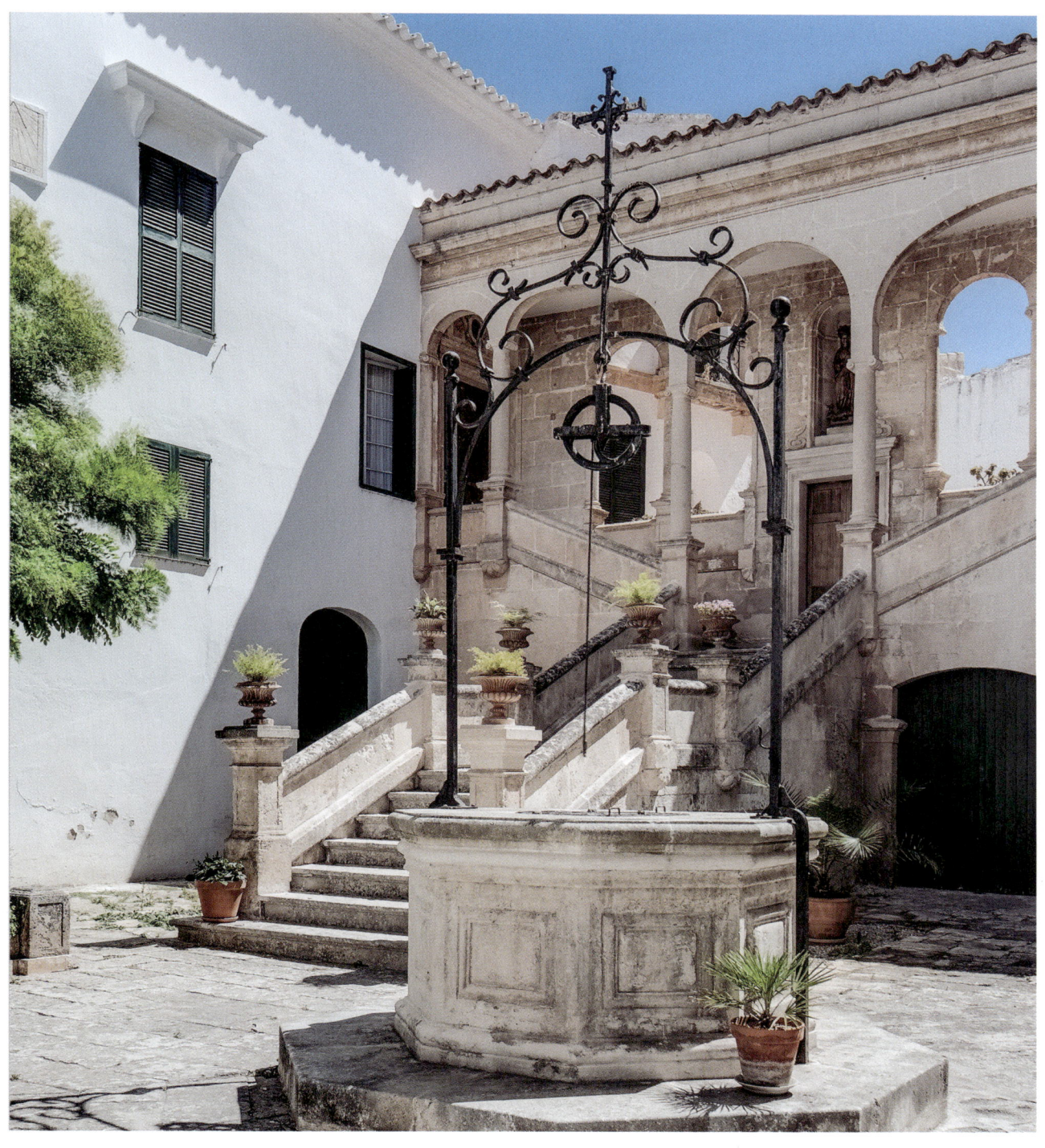

ABOVE AND LEFT: *The beautifully elaborate façade of the Cathedral of Santa Maria stands in the heart of Ciutadella's old town and is one of the highlights of this small harbor town in western Menorca. The fountain is in the courtyard of the Bishop's Palace next to the cathedral.*

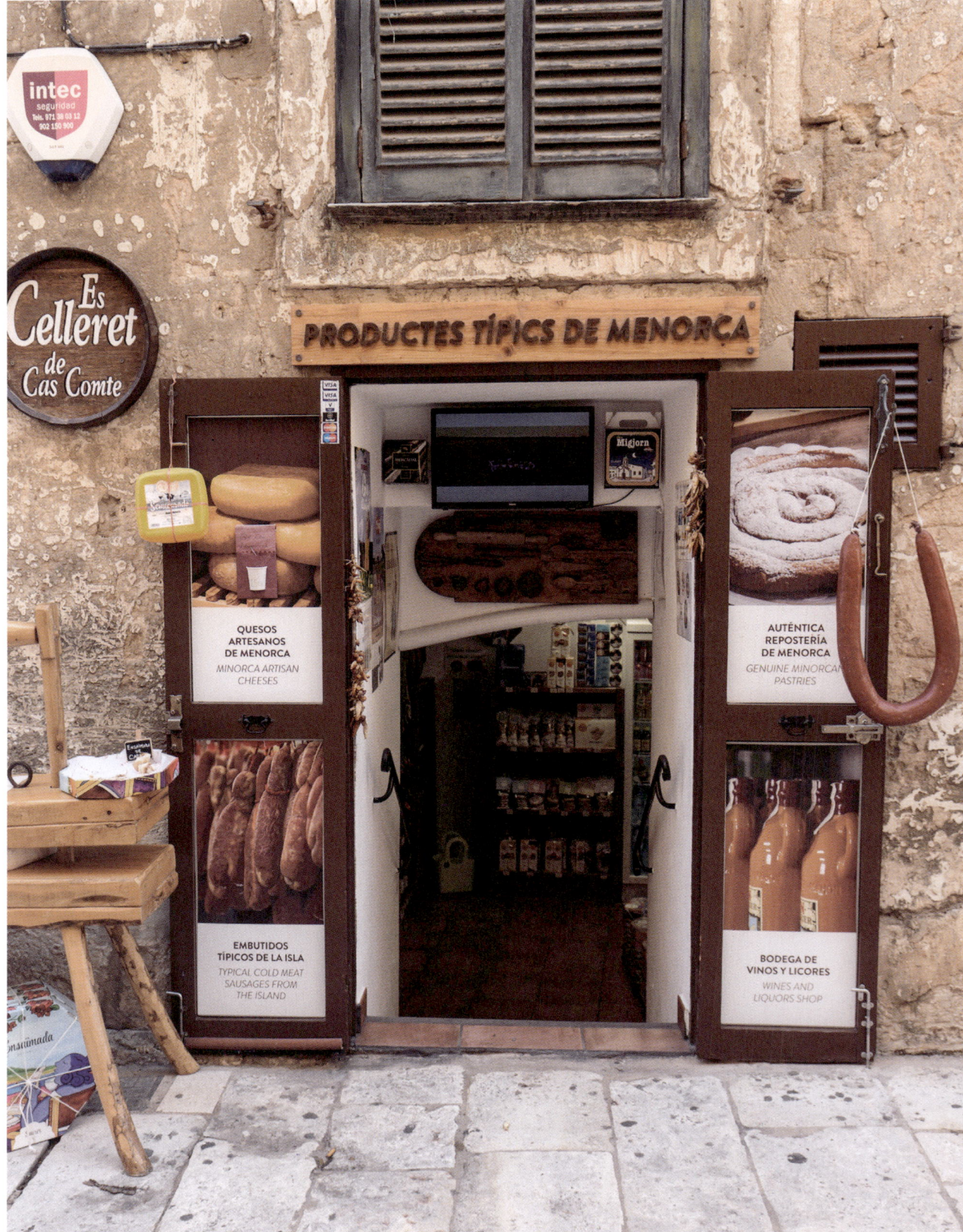

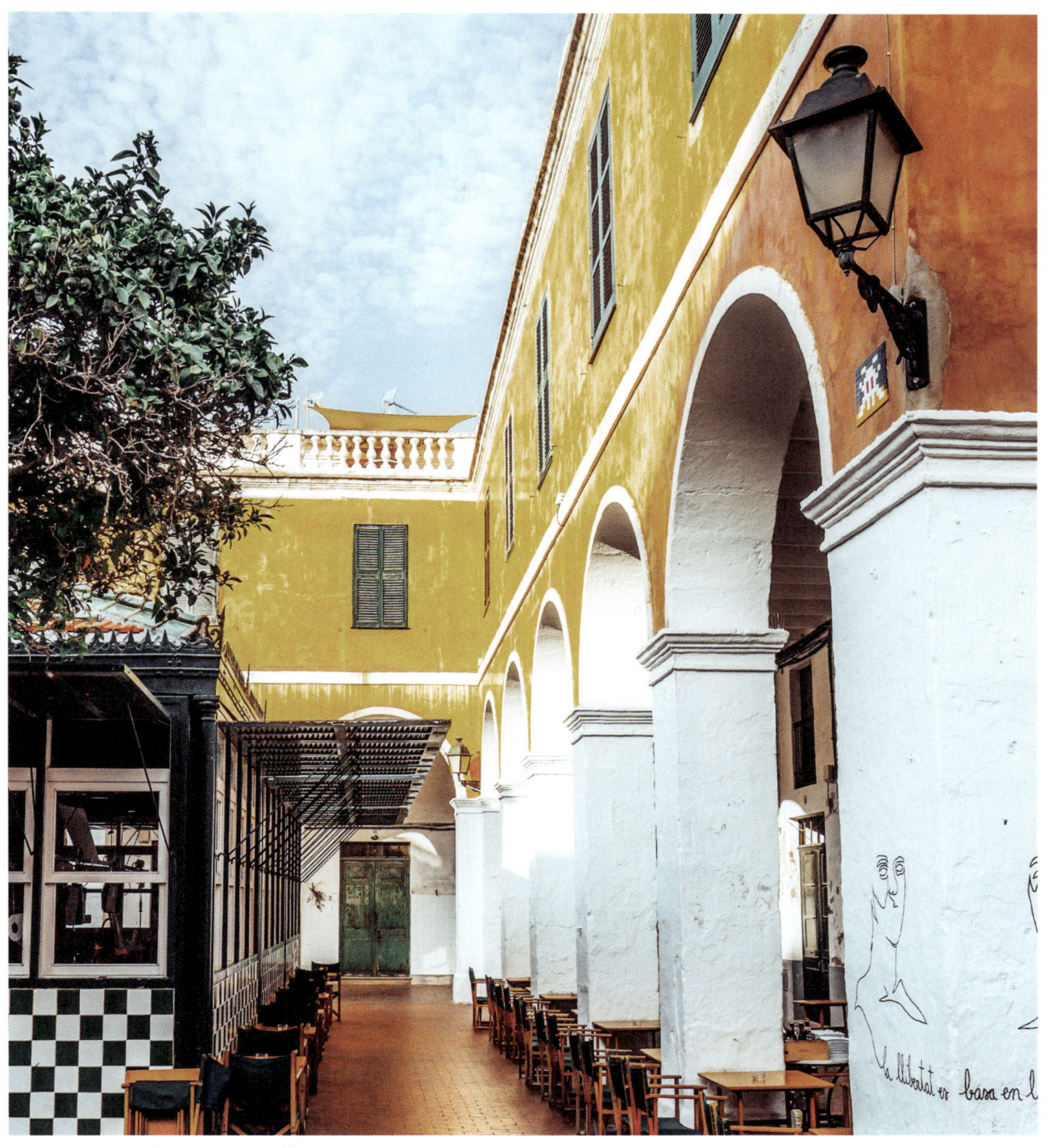

ABOVE AND LEFT: *There is plenty of variety in Ciutadella: bodegas, restaurants, and shops selling local goods in the old town and along the harbor. Not to be missed is a Menorcan hand-made hard cheese, made from cow's milk and aged in a square mold.*

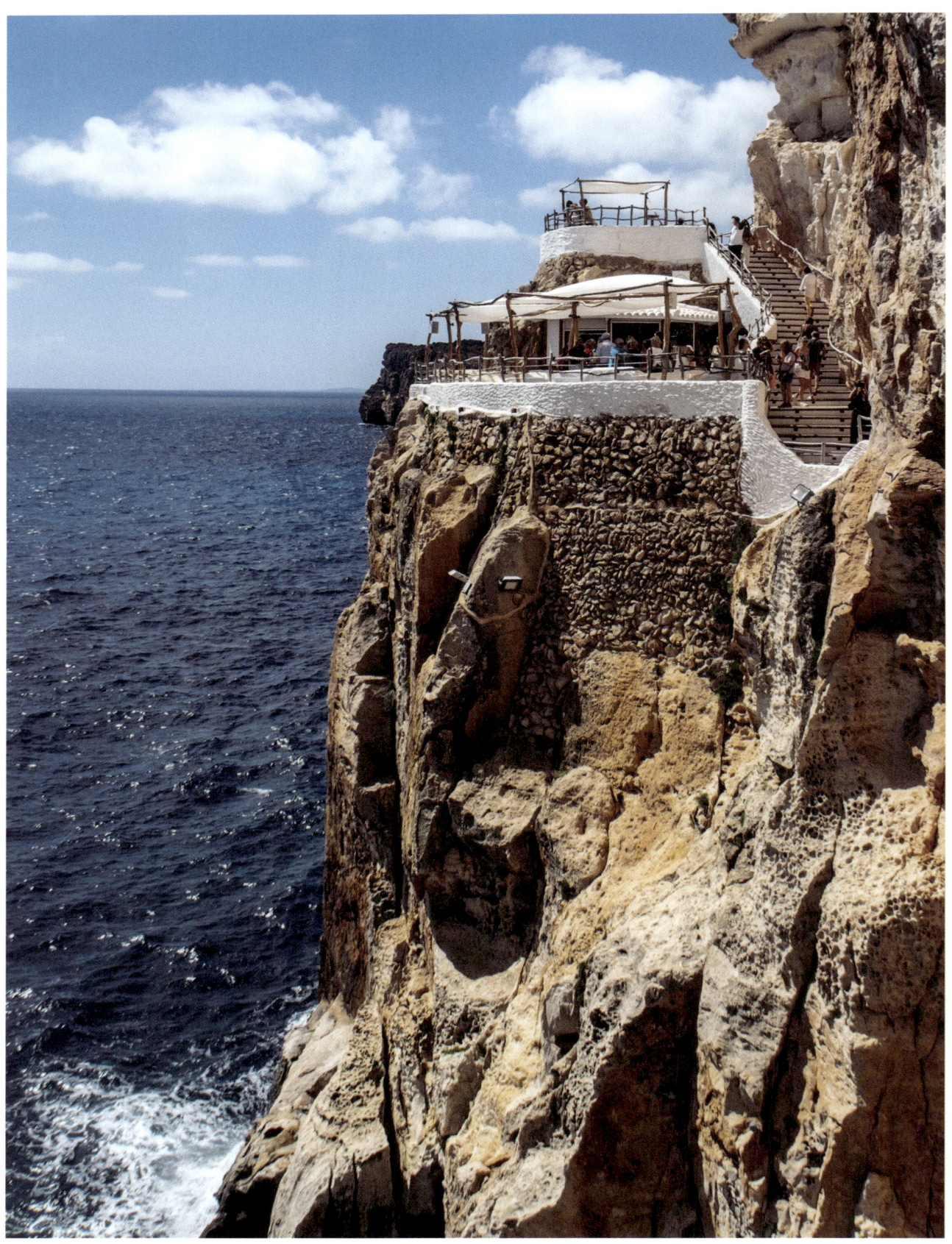

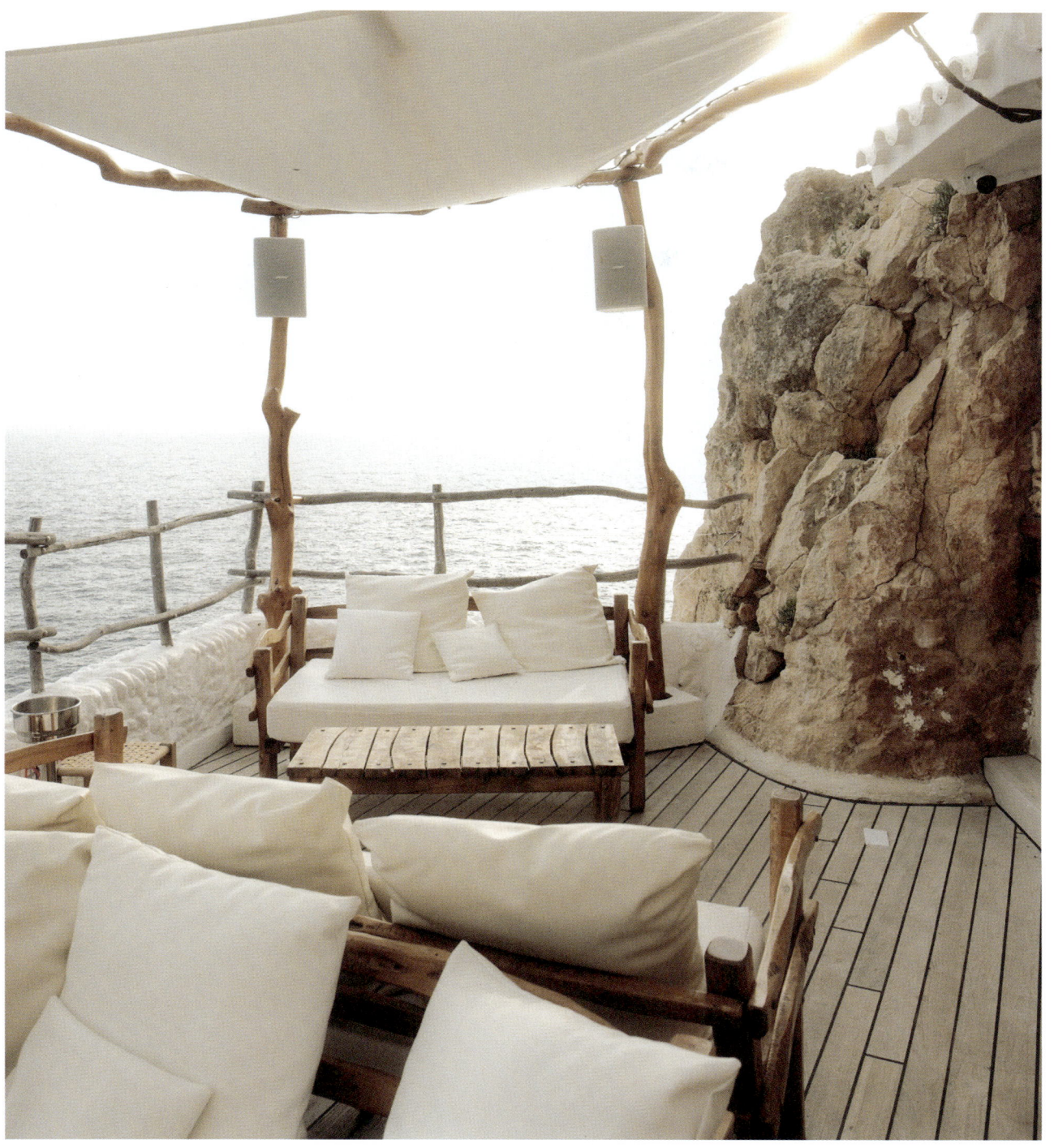

ABOVE AND LEFT: *Perched like an eagle's nest in the cliffs, with terraces and cave passages, you'll find what is perhaps the Mediterranean's most spectacular day and night club. Until sunset, Cova d'en Xoroi is a laid-back bar; afterward, the music turns up for dancing in the moonlight.*

FOLLOWING PAGES: *Tree-shaded paths are common on Menorca; roughly half of the island is forested (p. 202). Faro de Cap Cavalleria (p. 204), a lighthouse at the northern tip of Menorca with a museum and great views.*

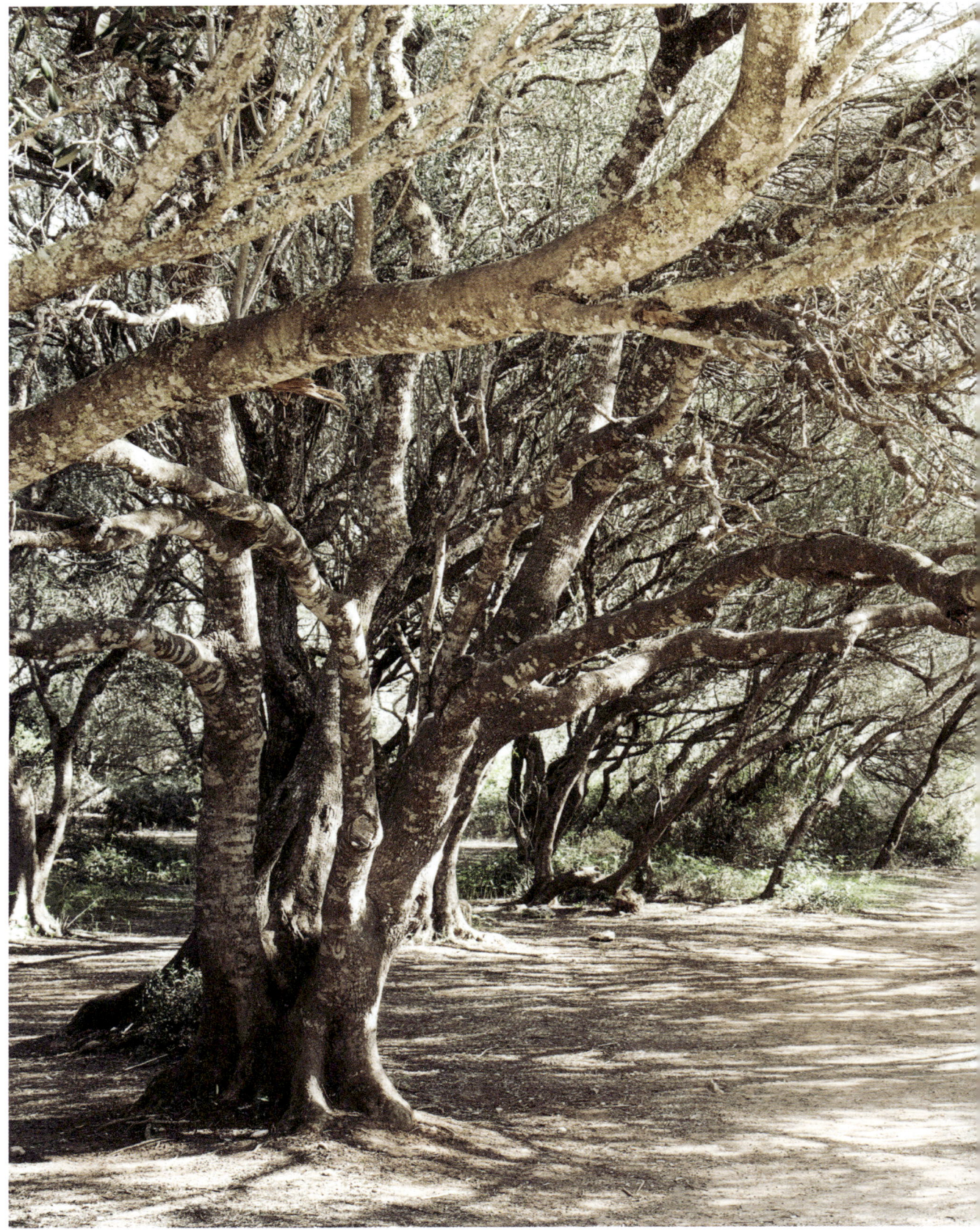

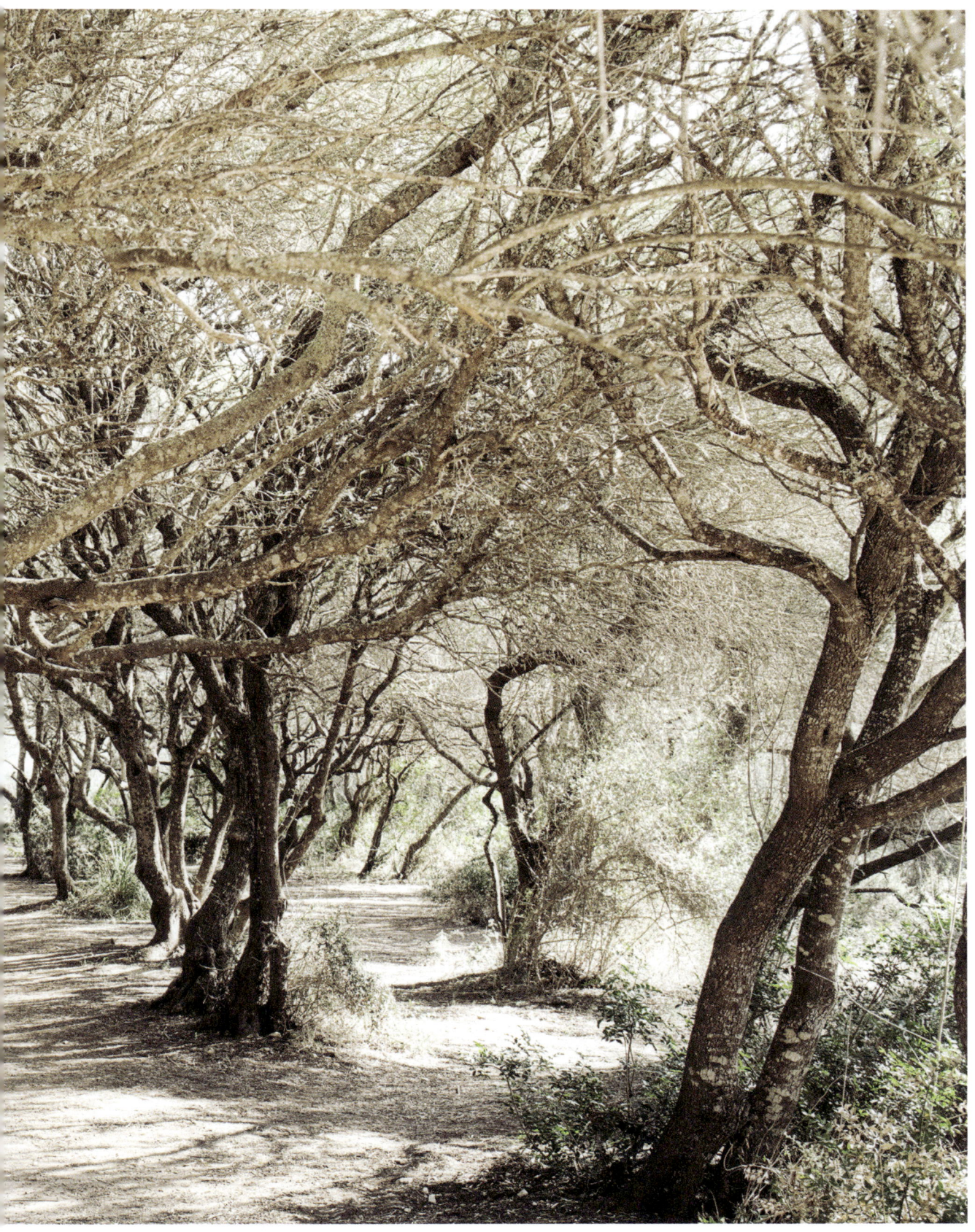

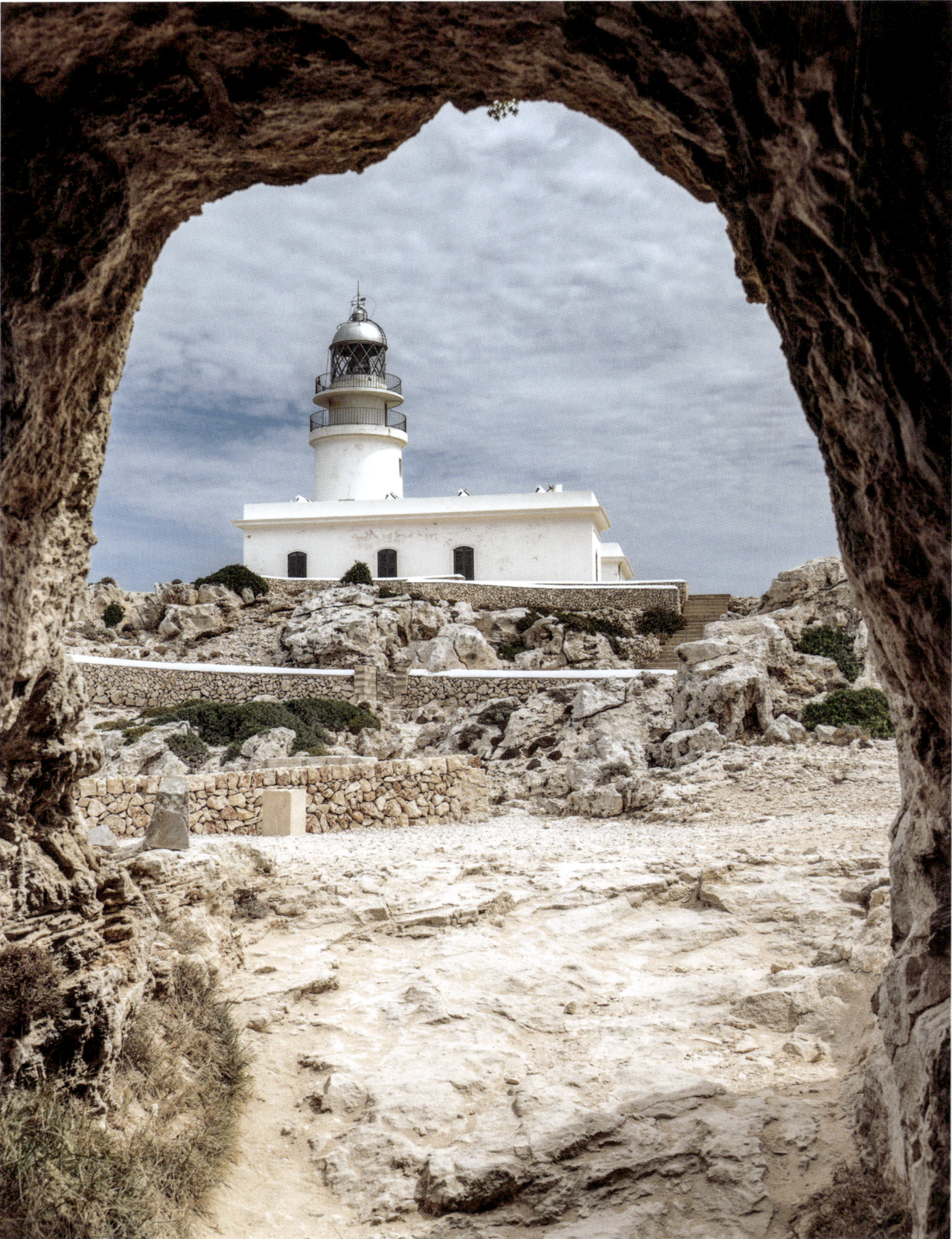

IMAGE CREDITS

ACKNOWLEDGEMENTS

Whether staying with Aunt Rosi or with friends who let me use their *fincas* more than a few times, I experienced constant generosity on Mallorca. Your kindness is what allowed me to truly discover the island. Thank you. Thanks also to Golden Retriever Carlos. There could be no better companion on a long cross-country walk. You helped me discover entirely new sides of the island.

I would also like to thank everyone at the publisher, especially Stephanie Rebel, who gave me the latitude needed to enable a deeply personal book to take shape. *Gràcies* to copywriter Katja Klementz for her perfectly chosen words and zealous advocacy for Ibiza. Thanks as well to Marcus Taeschner for his beautiful graphic design work and for always keeping an eye on the big picture.

And, of course, I am deeply grateful to the many photographers whose work appears in this book. You are the main contributors whose images carry this book all the way. Thank you.

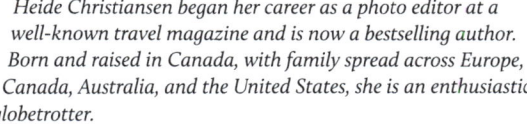

Heide Christiansen began her career as a photo editor at a well-known travel magazine and is now a bestselling author. Born and raised in Canada, with family spread across Europe, Canada, Australia, and the United States, she is an enthusiastic globetrotter.

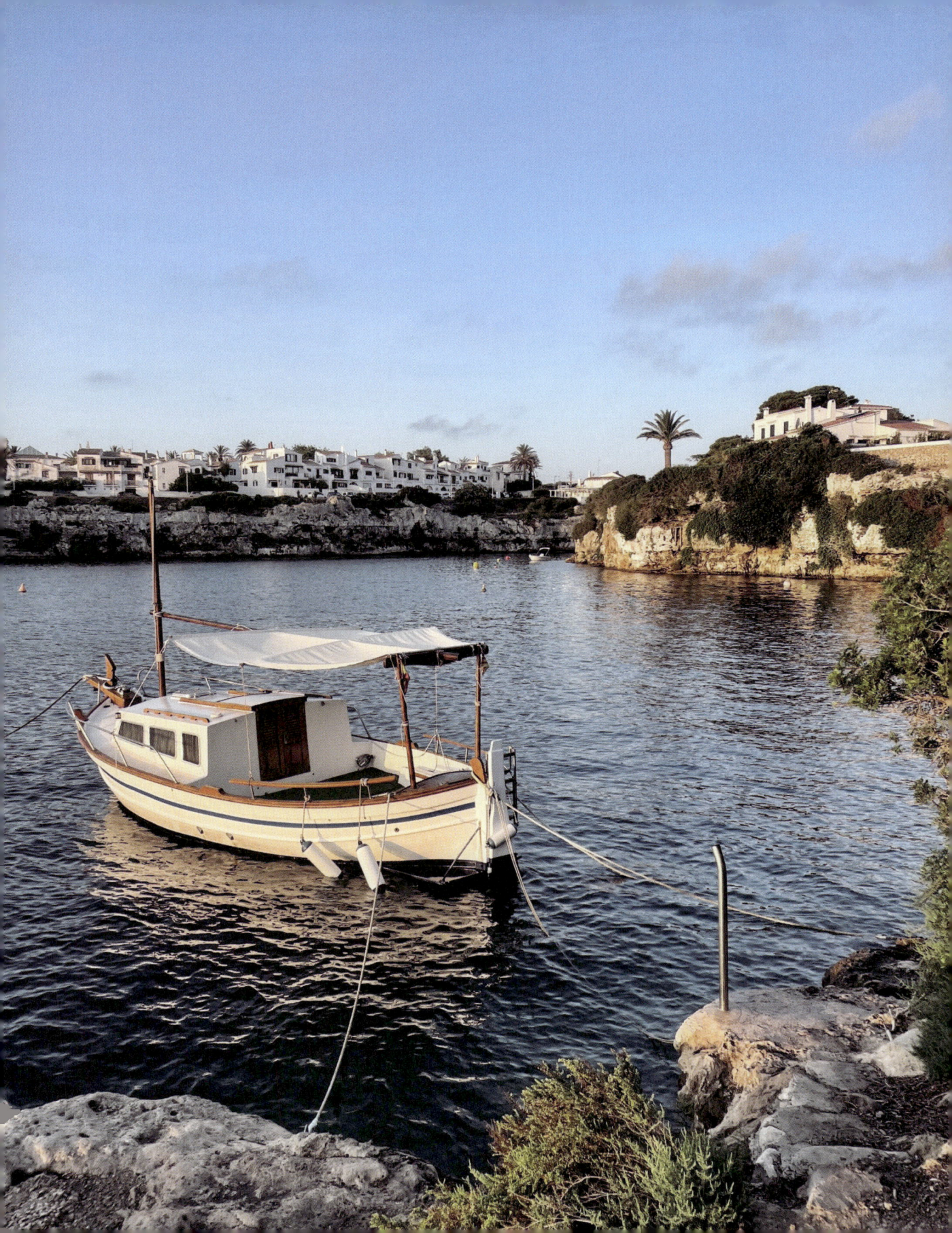

IMPRINT

CHARMING MALLORCA
This book was conceived, edited,
and designed by teNeues.
Edited by Heide Christiansen

Text and preface by Katja Klementz
Translation by John Foulks
Copyediting by Robin Limmeroth
Editorial Management by Stephanie Rebel,
  gestalten Verlag
Design by Marcus Taeschner
Layout by Marcus Taeschner
Photo Editorial by Heide Christiansen
Production by Sandra Jansen-Dorn, gestalten Verlag
Picture editing by Jens Grundei
Map graphic by Thomas Vogelmann
Proofreading by Benine Mayer

Printed in the Czech Republic by Finidr

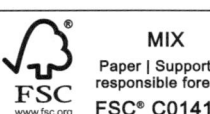

FSC
www.fsc.org

MIX
Paper | Supporting
responsible forestry
FSC® C014138

Published by gestalten, Berlin 2026
ISBN 978-3-96171-752-1
1st printing, 2026

The german edition is available under
ISBN 978-3-96171-754-5

© teNeues, an Imprint of
Die Gestalten Verlag GmbH & Co. KG, Berlin 2026

For more information and to order books, please visit
www.teneues.com and www.gestalten.com

Die Gestalten Verlag GmbH & Co. KG
Mariannenstrasse 9–10
10999 Berlin, Germany
hello@gestalten.com

Krefeld Office
Uerdinger Str. 265/Villa Pattberg
47800 Krefeld, Germany
verlag@teneues.com

teNeues Press Department
press@gestalten.com

Bibliographic information published by the Deutsche
Nationalbibliothek. The Deutsche Nationalbibliothek
lists this publication in the Deutsche
Nationalbibliografie; detailed bibliographic data is
available online at www.dnb.de

https://instagram.com/teneuespublishing

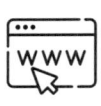

www.teneues.com